THE FLIGHT OF THE ANGELS
Intertextuality in Four Novels by Boris Vian

FAUX TITRE

Etudes
de langue et littérature françaises
publiées

sous la direction de Keith Busby,
M.J. Freeman, Sjef Houppermans,
Paul Pelckmans et Co Vet

No. 167

Amsterdam - Atlanta, GA 1999

THE FLIGHT OF THE ANGELS

Intertextuality in Four Novels by Boris Vian

Alistair Charles Rolls

∞ Le papier sur lequel le présent ouvrage est imprimé remplit les prescriptions de "ISO 9706:1994, Information et documentation - Papier pour documents - Prescriptions pour la permanence".

ISBN: 90-420-0467-3
©Editions Rodopi B.V., Amsterdam - Atlanta, GA 1999
Printed in The Netherlands

TABLE OF CONTENTS

FOREWORD 1

ACKNOWLEDGEMENTS 2

ABBREVIATIONS 3

INTRODUCTION 4
  APPROACHES TO VIAN 6
  INTERTEXTUALITY 10
  INFLUENCE AND THE CRITICS 19
  TOWARDS A TETRALOGY READING 36

CHAPTER ONE *L'ÉCUME DES JOURS:* FROM 'CLINS D'ŒIL' TO INTERTEXTUALITY 40
  THE PARROT AT THE HEART OF *L'ÉCUME* 44
  THE FROTH OF SURREALISM 51
  JAZZ AND THE SYNAESTHETIC NOVEL 62

CHAPTER TWO *L'ÉCUME DES JOURS:* MAC ORLAN, QUENEAU *ET* UN AUTRE 71
  THE ARRANGER OF THE TEXT 71
  VOYAGE AU BOUT DU TEXTE: COLIN AND UNIVERSAL NAUSEA 83
  "LA CHANSON DE LA CLOCHE" AND *LA PETITE SIRÈNE* 99

CHAPTER THREE *L'AUTOMNE À PÉKIN*: ENTRY INTO THE TEXT 103
  AUTUMN IN PARIS 107
  THE ANGEL IS A WHORE 118
  THE FIRST *PASSAGE* INTO THE TEXT: THE DREAM OF AMADIS 126
  THE SECOND *PASSAGE* INTO THE TEXT: THE DREAM OF CLAUDE LÉON .. 133
  THE THIRD *PASSAGE* INTO THE TEXT: THE DREAM OF ANGEL 140

CHAPTER FOUR *L'AUTOMNE À PÉKIN*: AND WHAT THEY FOUND THERE 147
  MURDER IN EXOPOTAMIA 161
  THE FLIGHT OF AN ANGEL 165

CHAPTER FIVE *L'HERBE ROUGE*: THE PROBLEM WITH SCIENCE FICTION 174
Who is Wolf? 191
CHAPTER SIX *L'HERBE ROUGE*: DREAMS OR MEMORIES 201
Wolf as dreamer of the text 201
Memories as the last testament of a dying Wolf 230
CHAPTER SEVEN *L'ARRACHE-CŒUR*: REVENGE 241
CHAPTER EIGHT *L'ARRACHE-CŒUR*:
SACRIFICE AND RETURN 270
Sacrifice 270
Return 291
CONCLUSION 306
BIBLIOGRAPHY 315
Existing bibliographies of Boris Vian 315
WORKS OF BORIS VIAN 315
Novels signed 'Vian' 316
Novels signed 'Sullivan' 316
Plays and operas 316
Poetry: anthologies 317
Nouvelles: collections 317
Screenplays etc. 318
On music 318
Other (Including the articles and letters published by Vian in his lifetime) 318
In translation 319
Articles by Boris Vian (Published posthumously) 320
SECONDARY MATERIAL 321
Books 321
Articles in journals/newspapers 324
Articles/chapters in books 351
INTERTEXTS 359
OTHER MATERIAL CONSULTED 364
INDEX 367

FOREWORD

The following book is an investigation of the textual strategies functioning in four novels by Boris Vian: *L'Écume des jours* (1947), *L'Automne à Pékin* (1947), *L'Herbe rouge* (1950) and *L'Arrache-cœur* (1953). It examines the novels' usage of intertextuality (references, direct and indirect, to other works of literature), and analyses the potentiality for producing meaning that is contained within this usage. By conjoining the four novels in this common textual strategy, it also examines how the novels refer to each other (intratextuality), and how they may, therefore, be considered as a unified and coherent tetralogy. Within this threefold strategy, the book yields a new reading of the four novels: Chapters One and Two deal with caricature and 'clins d'œil' in *L'Écume des jours*, exposing an association with Surrealism and the beginnings of a novelistic mythology; Chapters Three and Four follow the surface structure of *L'Automne à Pékin*, at each stage revealing the veiled intertextual structure, the importance both of Parisian novels and the genre of detective fiction; Chapters Five and Six question the status of *L'Herbe rouge* as a novel of Science Fiction, exposing its oneiric qualities and the role of death; finally, Chapters Seven and Eight show how the tetralogy can be seen to reach its climax in a final novel which closes the circle, bringing the narrative back to the beginning of the first.

This book, therefore, through the use of a critical tool (intertextuality) not before fully exploited in the context of Boris Vian's œuvre, discloses new readings of each of the four 'romans signés Vian', as well as offering a comprehensive view of a tetralogy of texts considered as one self-referential unit.

ACKNOWLEDGEMENTS

I should like to thank the following people without whom this book would not have been possible: Professor Nicholas Hewitt (The University of Nottingham) for his constant guidance and supervision; the staff of The Hallward Library (The University of Notingham); Nicole Bertolt (La Fondation Boris Vïan) for her time and patience in answering my questions and, in particular, for two interviews granted in March 1996 and September 1997; Gilbert Pestureau (Loyola University, Chicago) and Michel Rybalka (Washington University in St. Louis) for their letters of advice and encouragement; The British Academy for financing this project; and finally, Le Département des Langues Pratiques, L'École Normale Supérieure de Cachan, for furnishing me with the facilities which made it possible for me to bring this book to its conclusion.

ABBREVIATIONS

Each chapter is centred upon one novel by Boris Vian. The most recent editions available have been used. Page references occur between brackets in the main body of the text: in Chapter One, *Ej* is used to signify *L'Écume des jours*, texte revu sur manuscrit, Édition critique établie par Gilbert Pestureau et Michel Rybalka (Paris: Bourgois, 1994); in Chapters Two, Three, Four and thereafter, *R* is used to signify *Boris Vian: Romans, nouvelles, oeuvres diverses*, Édition établie, présentée et annotée par Gilbert Pestureau (Paris: Le Livre de Poche/La Pochothèque, 1991).

The intertexts used throughout this book are given equal status to the Vian texts and are, thus, also referenced in abbreviated form, placed between brackets in the text. On the occasion of the first reference to a particular intertext, its full publication details (of the edition quoted), along with the abbreviation by which it will thenceforth be known, are given in a note at the foot of the page.

INTRODUCTION

> "Every writer needs a literature as his frame of reference; a set of models to conform to or to depart from."
> Aldous Huxley, *Island*

The problems associated with producing a book on Vian existed as long ago as 1978, when, by way of a preface to Jean-Jacques Pauvert's anthology of Vian's works, Cavanna vented his frustration in the following terms:

> Parler de Vian en 1978 ressortit du suicide raffiné si l'on tient absolument à trouver à dire quelque chose de relativement neuf et de raisonnablement intelligent, du machinal boulot de recopieur de clichés pour manuel scolaire si le pernicieux prurit d'originalité ne vous dévore pas plus que ça. [...] Oui, mais c'est en 1978 que Pauvert me demande si ça me dirait de faire une préface pour Vian... Oh, mon enthousiasme est là, tout neuf tout piaffant, comprimé recroquevillé qu'il fut si longtemps, ben oui, mais tout ce qu'il a sur la langue, mon enthousiasme, tout ce qu'il a à dire, à crier, à chanter, ça a été dit, et fort bien dit, crié, chanté, vanté, expliqué, commenté, analysé, psychanalysé, prolongé, tamisé, épucé, dépecé, ordinateurisé, séminarisé, colloquisé aux quatre points cardinaux mille et mille et dix mille fois, en français, en iroquois, en auvergnois. [...] L'exégèse n'est pas mon truc, la critique a tout dit. Laissons tomber l'érudition, n'œuvrons point de pertinence.[1]

---

[1] *Boris Vian* (Paris: Pauvert, 1978), p.VII-VIII.

Cavanna's sentiment is understandable. Although spiced with more than a little irony, his outpouring is a typical reaction to this problem: to express one's intimate reactions to a Vian text is to repeat, albeit with slightly different axioms, that which has already been said; whilst to say something new, from an academic perspective, is to depart from the essential 'vianesque' and somehow to do an injustice to the text. The following book represents an attempted reaction to both sides of the coin: it follows a reading of the four novels whilst trying to locate (and, perhaps, to redefine) the vianesque within an academic framework.

The four major novels 'signés Vian', *L'Écume des jours, L'Automne à Pékin, L'Herbe rouge* and *L'Arrache-cœur,* are each considered in turn, both as autonomous, self-justifying works and as a sequence of novels. Indeed, the latter perspective is essential for a thorough understanding of the former: only by seeing that these four novels form a living whole, rather than just a series of four consecutive novels, loosely bound by the common traces of their author's particular weltanshauung, can the reader begin to appreciate Vian's apparent stylistic idiosyncrasies for what they really are. For, beginning in *L'Écume des jours* and reaching into *L'Arrache-cœur,* there is a repetition of 'clins d'œil' the importance of which has been consistently and systematically overlooked by previous criticism. The 'clins d'œil' which are referred to, and upon which the respective analyses of each of the four novels are based, are references to other texts, sources external to the work itself and drawn from sources in both French and anglophone literature and, on occasions, in literature written in neither of these languages.

These references, so easily overlooked or simply disregarded as the quirks of a particular sense of humour, so often dismissed as mere stylistic quirks, are crucial to an understanding of the texts. It is the contention of this study that these references, be they in the form of the name of an author, a title of a work or a fragment of a text transposed from a parent text into the Vian novel, not only imply external influence, but show how other texts provide a framework against which the Vian text can and, indeed, must be read. Meaning is, thus, external as well as internal.

Approaches to Vian

Of those who have written on Boris Vian, few can have failed to notice that his work abounds with these 'clins d'œil'. Gilbert Pestureau, for example, draws heavily upon these for his notes to the texts. And still there is no work which has sought to attempt to raise them to the level of importance which their sheer prevalence in the texts warrants. One reason for this is that criticism of Vian seems to have fallen into a relatively small number of tacitly agreed patterns. In this introduction, those elements of the available secondary material which deal with lines of external influence affecting the Vian text, as well as those which suggest lines of continuity within the texts themselves, will be examined in two sub-sections. A brief exposition of the potentiality and, indeed, suppleness of intertextuality will serve to demonstrate its suitability as a mechanism for exploring new territory within Vian's œuvre. This is territory as yet left unexplored by Vian criticism, but to which the evidence of the Vian texts themselves points.

Noël Arnaud, Gilbert Pestureau and Michel Rybalka are amongst the most prominent figures in the field of Vian criticism. Arnaud's contribution to the available secondary material is massive not only in volume, but in impact; he sets the precedent. His work, *Les Vies parallèles de Boris Vian*,[2] first published in 1970, is a seminal text. It is a step-by-step guide to Vian the man in all his facets. Its thematic layout blends biography and textual criticism, producing chapter titles such as, "Le romancier", "Le musicien" and "Le théâtre". It provides an interesting background to the tastes and habits which go to generate the author's work: it reproduces letters, manuscripts and photographs to enhance the living texts. It covers everything, and, in so doing, sets a pattern for looking at Vian. It is this, then, which becomes the pattern from which Vian criticism becomes disinclined to stray, seeing it as benchmark and role model. As for Pestureau and Rybalka, their work has had a similar impact, its combined influence resulting in the most recent critical edition of *L'Écume des jours*.[3] Rybalka's work, *Boris Vian: Essai*

---

[2] Noël Arnaud, *Les Vies parallèles de Boris Vian* (Paris: Bourgois, 1981).

[3] Boris Vian, *L'Écume des jours*, ed. by Gilbert Pestureau and Michel Rybalka (Paris: Bourgois, 1994).

d'interprétation et de documentation,[4] an adaptation of his doctoral book, will be dealt with in due course, whilst Pestureau's *Boris Vian, les Amerlauds et les Godons*,[5] as the single most important work on external influence, will be closely examined in the relevant sub-section of this introduction. In addition to these contributions, Pestureau is responsible for the most original approach to Vian's work. In his *Dictionnaire Vian*,[6] he draws up an inventory of all the characters of Vian's oeuvre, but in such a way as to elicit the following response from Arnaud himself: "Je n'irai pas par quatre chemins: je tiens ce dictionnaire pour la meilleure étude jamais réalisée de l'œuvre de Vian, de toutes ses œuvres."[7] The remainder of the critical material may be divided into the following basic categories: biography (including bibliography), work-by-work synopses and thematical breakdowns.

It is perhaps unsurprising that such an enigmatic, eclectic figure as Boris Vian should be the attention of so much biographical attention. What is unfortunate is that a critical genre which aims to add useful comment and a decorous backdrop to the work of the man actually has the result of delimiting the ways of viewing the texts. Among the most intelligent biographical analysis, after *Les Vies parallèles*, is Marc Lapprand's *Biographie critique*,[8] which is particularly geared towards the oeuvre in its stylistic dimension. The main problem of the biographical approach is that its analysis of the texts, when textual analysis there is within biography, does not allow the autonomy of the text to be developed. A technique is needed which takes the reality of fiction as its guiding principle. The intertextual technique is appropriate because it is precisely this reality which it takes into account. The binary opposition that contrasts pure textual criticism and biography is paralleled by that which opposes intertextuality and the study of influence: influence seeks to find links between the novel of an author and the works of other novelists;

---

[4] Michel Rybalka, *Boris Vian: Essai d'interprétation et de documentation* (Paris: Minard, 1969).

[5] Gilbert Pestureau, *Boris Vian, les Amerlauds et les Godons* (Paris: U.G.E., 1978).

[6] Gilbert Pestureau, *Dictionnaire des personnages de Boris Vian* (Paris: Bourgois, 1985).

[7] Extract from a letter to Christian Bourgois dated 13 June 1985, reproduced on the cover of *Dictionnaire Vian*.

[8] Marc Lapprand, *Boris Vian: La vie contre* (Ottawa: les Presses de l'Université d'Ottawa, 1993).

intertextuality seeks to develop this link purely at the level of the text, and to discover how, in this case, the Vian text may be (re)read in the light of these textual rapprochements. The most recent biography of Vian, by Philippe Boggio, is a good example of the limitations of the genre when it comes to weighing up the merits of a literary figure.[9] Covering his life and works, this offers a minute examination drawing upon all the primary and secondary sources available. Boggio, as a professional journalist and writer of biographies (he has also written a biography of Coluche), provides an account which is so orientated towards facts and figures that it fails, despite its amassed detail, to find Vian's artistic pulse. The intertextual study which follows will aim to show that the source of life of Vian's novels comes not from his own lived experiences, but from the life of other novels.

The remaining two categories under which criticism has fallen are similar in that they both refer to the works of Vian as texts rather than as extensions of the man, and also in that they both fail to consider the novels on their own terms. The first category is criticism which deals with each individual work in isolation, often with much use of plot synopsis. The most original of these is Freddy de Vree's *Boris Vian: Essai*.[10] Although one of the most persuasive studies of Vian's works, and arguably one of the more useful, it has been denigrated (by Rybalka amongst others) for its unacademic abuse of 'colour': it is a rare example of a critical work which attempts to isolate the Vianesque by adopting, itself, a quasi-Vianesque style. This, then, is at the opposite pole to Boggio's biography. This approach, although useful in its exposition of certain leitmotivs and analytical approaches, fails to respect the liaisons between the novels. To attempt to read between the lines whilst remaining within the scope of a single Vian novel is to miss many of the subtler touches that are so much a part of the Vian's overall writing strategy: to read between the lines of *L'Automne à Pékin* is often to cast oneself back into *L'Écume des jours*.

The other of these approaches is that which deals with individual themes across the boundaries of the novels. This technique is not exploited fully enough. The themes tend to be developed individually with examples taken from different texts; what is not usually considered is the way these themes may be used to unite the novels themselves. There are also attempts,

---

[9] Philippe Boggio, *Boris Vian* (Paris: Flammarion, 1993).

[10] Freddy de Vree, *Boris Vian: Essai* (Paris: Losfeld, 1965).

within this kind of thematic criticism, to classify Vian, to discover whether he sits more comfortably with the Surrealists or with the Existentialists, itself a limiting exercise as far as analysis of the novels is concerned. One of the more thorough works is *'L'Écume des jours'. Boris Vian* by Michel Gauthier.[11] Although it does not target a necessarily highbrow readership, appearing as it does in the 'Profil d'une œuvre' series, it manages to produce both scope of study and depth of criticism. Its themes, which incude 'structures romanesques', 'l'écriture' and 'thèmes et affinités', are intelligent and profound: it is virtually alone in suggesting *Nadja* as a literary predecessor, and is particularly thorough in its coverage of the Surrealist influence in general. The problem, once again, is that such criticism tends to limit the scope of Vian's richest work, his four major novels. The more useful works may be said to be those which limit their own scope to a single theme. Thus, Henri Baudin's *Boris Vian Humoriste*[12] is the most exhaustive study of the ludic dimension of Vian's writing. In fact, it is such a detailed deconstruction of his humour that it removes the sting from the punch-lines: it is a good example of a work which, in attempting to define the Vianesque, succeeds in crushing it beneath its feet. Alain Costes concentrates on a book rather than a theme. The collection of essays, which he assembles under the title *Lecture Plurielle de 'L'Écume des jours'*,[13] forms a serious and informative work including such approaches as the semiotic, the psychoanalytic and the socio-economic. Absent is the intertextual. This study will aim to show that it is precisely this overlooked critical tool which can really open up the potential of the texts, exposing them to manifold readings, not delimiting them within rigid classifications. In the absence of traditional boundaries and taxonomies, it will be interesting to examine to what extent the four novels in question may be shown to be intertextually driven, and consequently linked by this common drive more so than by any other single motif. It is from this perspective that one may begin to consider *L'Écume des jours, L'Automne à Pékin, L'Herbe rouge* and *L'Arrache-cœur* as having a degree of interdependence.

---

[11] Michel Gauthier, *L'Écume des jours. Boris Vian* (Paris: Hatier, 1973).

[12] Henri Baudin, *Boris Vian Humoriste* (Grenoble: Presses Universitaires de Grenoble, 1973).

[13] Alain Costes, ed., *Lecture Plurielle de 'L'Écume des jours'* (Paris: U.G.E., 1979).

Intertextuality

Michael Worton and Judith Still, in *Intertextuality: Theories and Practices*, call for an intertextual view to be considered for all texts, outlining, as follows, the ideas of Julia Kristeva:

> The theory of intertextuality insists that a text (for the moment to be understood in the narrower sense) cannot exist as a hermetic or self-sufficient whole, and so does not function as a closed system. This is for two reasons. Firstly, the writer is a reader of texts (in the broadest sense) before s/he is a creator of texts, and therefore the work of art is inevitably shot through with references, quotations and influences of every kind. [...] Secondly, a text is available only through some process of reading; what is produced at the moment of reading is due to the cross-fertilisation of the packaged textual material (say, a book) by all the texts which the reader brings to it. A delicate allusion to a work unknown to the reader, which therefore goes unnoticed, will have a dormant existence in that reading.[14]

The above theory seems to suggest that all writers and all readers of all texts are playing a part in this thing that is intertextuality. And yet, there are authors who exploit other authors' texts with subtlety and in full consciousness. This book will aim to show that Boris Vian is one of these. A workable theoretical basis for an intertextual study of Boris Vian may be found in the work of Michael Riffaterre. In his article "La Trace de l'intertexte", he provides the following definition:

> L'intertextualité est la perception, par le lecteur, de rapports entre une œuvre et d'autres, qui l'ont précédée ou

---

[14] Michael Worton and Judith Still, eds, *Intertextuality: Theories and Practices* (Manchester: Manchester University Press, 1990), p.1-2.

> suivie. Ces autres œuvres constituent l'intertexte de la première. La perception de ces rapports est donc une des composantes fondamentales de la littérarité d'une œuvre, car cette littérarité tient à la double fonction, cognitive et esthétique, du texte. Or la fonction esthétique dépend, dans une large mesure, de la possibilité d'intégrer l'œuvre à une tradition, ou à un genre, d'y reconnaître des formes déjà vues ailleurs. Quant à la fonction cognitive, elle dépend sans doute d'abord de la référence réelle ou illusoire des mots à une réalité extérieure...[15]

It is the second of these functions which most interests Riffaterre; it is also that which most concerns this study, although the aesthetic dimension is also important and is, often, a necessary step in progressing to the cognitive stage. The problem, as Riffaterre suggests, is that people tend to associate intertextuality with the aesthetic function, and often content themselves with mentioning the names of texts (this is the study of influence rather than the study of intertextuality); discussing the role of *Chanson de Mignon* as an intertext in the work of Nerval, he writes: "La critique n'a vu dans la chanson que la source des détails du décor nervalien, ce qui est une manière d'évacuer les difficultés du texte: on nomme la source, on y refoule le problème, et on l'oublie."[16] In this study the term intertext, whilst generally corresponding to the above definition, will be used to refer to a text in the narrow sense (e.g. a particular novel or poem). Riffaterre, too, has used it in this sense: "An intertext is *one or more* texts which the reader must know in order to understand a work of literature in terms of its overall significance...".[17] (My italics.)

      The key concept, then, is that a work can be understood (differently or more completely) through an understanding of its intertextuality. It is necessary, therefore, if one is to adopt an approach which one calls intertextual

---

[15] Michael Riffaterre, "La Trace de l'intertexte", *Pensée française*, 215 (1980) 4-18 (p.4).

[16] *Ibid.*, p.17.

[17] Michael Riffaterre, "Compulsory Reader Response: The Intertextual Drive", in *Intertextuality: Theories and Practices*, Michael Worton and Judith Still, eds (Manchester: Manchester University Press, 1990), pp.56-78 (p.56).

that meaning be produced. Thus it is that in this study, although some intertexts will merely be mentioned *en passant*, the impetus is towards a reading of the four novels; this will be a reading of the novels as a tetralogy, and a reading which can only be achieved by intertextual means. The meaning of a text lies in the understanding of how it functions vis-à-vis its intertext, how they are linked together:

> La signifiance, c'est-à-dire la littérarité du sens, n'est donc ni dans le texte ni dans l'intertexte, mais à mi-chemin des deux, dans l'interprétant, qui dicte au lecteur la manière de les voir, de les comparer, de les interpréter par conséquent dans leur inséparabilité même.[18]

Not all parts of a text demand an intertext in order to be understood. There are sometimes, however, passages which stand out, due to their difference from the rest of the text, and force the reader to realise that something is missing; this awareness of an absence is what Riffaterre calls 'presuming the intertext':

> [...] Il y a intertextualité obligatoire, lorsque la signification de certains mots du texte n'est ni celle que permet la langue ni celle que demande le contexte, mais le sens qu'ont ces mots dans l'intertexte. C'est l'inacceptabilité de ce sens dans la langue ou dans le contexte qui contraint le lecteur à une présomption, à l'hypothèse d'une solution offerte dans un homologue formel du texte qu'il essaie de déchiffrer. L'intertexte, par conséquent, n'est pas un objet de citation, c'est un objet *présupposé*.[19]

---

[18] "La Trace de l'intertexte", p.14-15.

[19] *Ibid.*, p.9.

In Vian, passages which call for intertextual analysis, like those described above, are referred to here as 'enigmatic'. Elsewhere Riffaterre labels such passages "connectives", as they belong neither to the text itself or to the intertext, but between the two, "signalling in each the presence of their mutually complementary traits".[20] There are times when one can only point to the absence, seeking to enrich the text with a suggestion of potential intertexts for which there seems a deal of evidence. Despite the nature of texts, which define their own 'reality', there are times when one can feel certain as to one disclosure of a particular intertext. For example, when explaining a poem by Mallarmé through another by Baudelaire, Riffaterre exclaims: "Seule lecture acceptable et facile - intertexte obligatoire."[21]

Intertextuality does depend, however, upon the reader's ability to spot the intertexts. A 'well-read' reader will pull more from a text: "Il est évident [par contre] qu'on n'en voit pas la fin. Ces associations sont plus ou moins étendues, plus ou moins riches, selon la culture du lecteur."[22] As this book is dealing with a corpus the size of which depends largely on the capacity of the reader, it would be impossible to claim 'exhaustiveness'. The aim is rather to give an idea of the potential of Vian's novels for proliferating readings (depending on the intertexts used). Thus, the reading presented in this book is but one of many possible readings. Riffaterre suggests a comparable shift away from the need for a definition of limits in criticism:

> Au lieu de reconstituer un corpus, essayer de déterminer la nature des présuppositions, définir les règles par lesquelles un présupposant déclenche chez le lecteur une écriture [...] une activité associative qui lui fait cerner le manque du texte, et compléter un message dont le vide partiel, dont l'incomplétude l'invite à le reconstituer.[23]

---

[20] "Compulsory Reader Response", p.58.

[21] "La Trace de l'intertexte", p.13.

[22] Michael Riffaterre, "L'Intertexte inconnu", *Littérature*, 41 (1981), 4-7 (p.4).

[23] *Ibid.*, p.7.

Of course, there are arguments to be made against intertextuality as a critical tool. To some of these Riffaterre responds in an interview for *Diacritics*. Firstly, the whole process may be seen to be either very subjective on the part of the reader, or rather 'hit or miss' on the part of the author (i.e. if an intertextual link is discovered or set between the host text and an obscure intertext). *Diacritics*, here introducing new terms for intertext and intertextual link, raises the following problem:

> But one of the problems your sympathizers inevitably encounter lies precisely in the phenomenal learning and memory that must underlie your ear for clichés, quotations, cultural or mythological codifications. [...] What seems to be at stake are the procedures for discovering the hypogram. Can they be delineated systematically, or must they be an *ad hoc* function or experience in readings? Do you claim to demonstrate theoretically that accomplished readers *have* to agree on what constitutes the matrix and the hypogram?[24]

Riffaterre's response is that the skill of the analyst lies merely in helping to define the presence behind the absence that all readers should experience in the text. The text functions intertextually whether the intertext is unveiled or not.

> Finding the hypogram is a matter of perception: the reader simply cannot identify it unless it has already become part and parcel of his culture, unless he already knows the other text wherein it is contained. If it *is* part of his heritage, the reader will sooner or later catch the connection. [...] What I must emphasize is that even while the hypogram remains unidentified, the text's troublesomeness keeps pointing to this need: the

---

[24] Michael Riffaterre, "Interview", *Diacritics*, 11 [4] (1981), 12-16 (p.13-14).

> hypogram must be found, a solution outside the text must be found, in the intertext.[25]

In the case of Boris Vian the intertextuality is sometimes apparent; it generates the same feelings in the reader as described above by Riffaterre. In other instances, however, the intertextuality may be so veiled as to arouse only the interest of the reader who is actively looking for hypograms (i.e. solutions can be found inside the text, so the need to look outside fails to trouble the reader).

The other problem faced by Riffaterre is the inevitable charge of reductionism:

> The point would be, not that your approach does not leave the text open to many possibilities for interpretation once the basic form of its unity is perceived, but that for some poems - for example, those which allow for ready comprehension in referential terms, or those to which you attribute a relatively vague or obvious matrix - the determination of matrix and hypogram just yields a structural account that impoverishes the reading experience.[26]

What must be borne in mind is that the readings offered by a practitioner of intertextual criticism are purely examples; no intertextual reading can expect to be hailed as the definitive reading of a text. For some readings there will be the additional weight of proof of readership; for others the weight of their own argument will have to suffice. Whatever the case, a certain amount of common sense is usually required; although no reading can be totally ignored since all readings are, to a certain extent, right, some readings will always be more right than others. Riffaterre offers an outline of his theory of reader response by way of an answer:

---

[25] *Ibid.*, p.14.

[26] *Ibid.*, p.14-15.

As for the charge that determining the matrix of a text is a reductionist strategy, I must insist once again that it is only one of two analytic phases: [...] a primary reading, which deciphers the text at the level of mimesis; and a retroactive reading, which effects the semiotic transformation. The matrix structure sets everything going, triggering as it does the back-and-forth scanning of the textual space. But this *double reading* is the actual literary experience: my analysis explains and preserves its complexity and its richness. For I ascribe two facets to each component, mimetic and semiotic [...]. Every reader's effort to make sure of the semiosis makes him go through a new reading at the mimetic level. This accounts for the continuous re-reading, the inexhaustibility of the experience that is particularly literary.[27]

The intertexts must first be found. And from any given matrix, a given number of critics will produce that number of different interpretations. That is, at least, the theory. In practice, the readings offered in this book are of the less restrictive kind: for example, in Chapter Three it is shown, via intertextuality, not that *L'Herbe rouge* is either a work of Science-Fiction, or of Surrealism, but that it draws on both genres.

The misunderstanding of intertextuality is a problem for many writers. It tends to be mistaken for plagiarism. One case which has come to the attention of the media in recent years is that of Booker prizewinner 1996, Graham Swift. *Last Orders*, the tale of the transporting of a man's ashes from London to Kent for scattering into the sea at Margate, has brought to mind, for many, Faulkner's *As I Lay Dying*. Swift makes his own defence against charges of plagiarism in *The Times*: "The point about the debt to *As I Lay Dying* is not new. [...] I have never pretended the connection is not there."[28] If he denies plagiarism, he does not claim that his work is driven by any

---

[27] *Ibid.*, p.15.

[28] Article headed "I never pretended my novel owed no debt to Faulkner", *The Times*, 10 March 1997, p.3.

conscious use of intertextuality; and if examples of intertextuality there are, then these are, to his mind, of relative unimportance:

> [But] The great number of reviews and commentaries which do not mention Faulkner suggest that the connection is hardly the nub of my book. Indeed, other writers are mentioned: Chaucer, for example, because my novel involves a group of characters journeying from London through Kent; T.S Eliot, because the destination is Margate and Eliot has some lines about Margate. The first echo I was conscious of, the second never occurred to me. [...] It is the nature of literature that books may derive from or be influenced by others. Equally, there are certain things for which there is no literary patent or monopoly. How do you write about a group of travellers on what is effectively a sort of pilgrimage, without evoking Chaucer? How do you write a story in which the living deal intimately with the remains of the dead and not evoke Faulkner's classic?[29]

There is much sense in these lines. There is much also which may be used as an argument against intertextual criticism in general. In Vian, for example, how does one mention a deadly machine without evoking Kafka, or a mirror without evoking Lewis Carroll? The answer, if answer it be, is that Vian's text is deliberately established in such a way as to prompt such response, whereas Swift's novel, if one is to believe the author, is not. The key concept which differentiates intertextuality from influence is one which sails over the debate as to whether or not the author of a text has read somebody else's particular novel: the crucial feature of intertextuality, as far as the scope of this book is concerned, is the relationship between the text and the reader. Riffaterre's definition points in this direction: "L'intertextualité est la perception, *par le lecteur*, de rapports entre une œuvre et d'autres" (my italics). Mary Orr, whose text *Claude Simon: The Intertextual Dimension* provides a useful guide to intertextual analysis, does not believe that absence of authorial intention

---

[29] *Ibid.*

necessarily equals absence of intertextuality. The following passage recalls a famous interview in which Vian claims to have noticed that one of his novels was influenced by Céline, having read the latter only *after* having written his own:

> When I interviewed Simon shortly after the publication of his prose poem *La Chevelure de Bérénice* [...] my question was whether Baudelaire's "La Chevelure" was an intertext within it. Simon's reply was that he was unfamiliar with this poem, but, reaching for a copy of *Les Fleurs du Mal*, he read the poem and grew excited at the similarity of associations and images between it and his own work. This highlights the fact that although parallels may seem obvious between texts, it should not be implied that direct or conscious influence has occurred. This does not detract from the reader's response in equating the two.[30]

She continues:

> Such subjective reading is not a 'wrong' reading: if there are sufficient points of contact between the texts or evidence from other sources (such as interviews) that the original text was familiar to the writer. One must simply be careful not to presume authorial intention or exposure to the precursor.[31]

What is important, therefore, is that one does not mix intertexts proven by textual evidence and influence proven by authorial admission (Alfred Jarry, for example, who is mentioned by Arnaud and Bens, amongst others, as being of great influence for a 'Pataphysician such as Vian, does not leave a

---

[30] Mary Orr, *Claude Simon: The Intertextual Dimension* (Glasgow: University of Glasgow French and German publications, 1993), p.82.

[31] *Ibid.*, p.82-83.

significant intertextual trace in the latter's œuvre; consequently he does not feature in this book).

Influence and the critics

At this stage a brief review of some examples of Vian criticism will be useful, in order to show how the study of intertextuality has been avoided and how it provides a useful supplement to that which has gone before. A more complete listing of the critical material existing on Boris Vian appears as the chapters unfold and, especially, in the bibliography. The debate over 'originality' is a constant factor, appearing throughout the corpus of Vian criticism. The debate which is so central to anyone interested in Vian's use of intertextuality is outlined in clear terms by Noel Simsolo:

> Certains affirment que Boris Vian n'a jamais rien inventé. Il se serait contenté de piller sournoisement Alfred Jarry, Raymond Queneau, Jacques Prévert, Franz Kafka, L.-F. Céline, la comtesse de Ségur, Dario Moreno, la Bible, l'almanach Vermot de 1934, l'annuaire des chemins de fer, les souvenirs d'Eugénie Buffet et un roman pornographique méconnu, écrit par un prêtre défroqué, bègue et arménien, qui se vendait sous le manteau pendant l'occupation allemande et dont le titre indiquait une connaissance vertigineuse de son sujet: «La résistance au priapisme.» [...] Les autres sont d'un extrémisme identique, quoique diamétralement opposé. Ils se mettent en colère pour hurler sur leur lune, en une position assise qui leur colle aux fesses, que Boris Vian a tout inventé.[32]

It soon becomes obvious that it is not so much Vian's originality that is the stumbling block, but the viability of the term itself. Use of intertextuality and

---

[32] Noël Simsolo, "Dé«polar»isation", *Arc*, 90 (1984), 52-55 (p.52).

originality, for the purposes of this study, which is concerned with manipulation of intertexts within a highly creative tetralogy of novels, are not mutually exclusive. Thus, comments such as the following made by Jean-Pierre Enard, in the same journal as those of Simsolo, are the very antibook of what this study is aiming to achieve: "Vian produit un ersatz littéraire, avec un doigt de fantastique, un faux-semblant de polar, un zest d'absurde, un rien de brio emprunté à Queneau, des plaisanteries de potache non distanciées et un formidable apitoiement sur soi-même."[33]

In "L'Univers de *L'Écume des jours*", Marguerite Nicod-Saraiva is aware that this novel can be slotted quite happily into a long-standing tradition of romance fiction:

> On ne peut méditer sur l'histoire de Colin et de Chloé sans que remonte du fond des siècles la voix du conteur:
> «Seigneurs, vous plaît-il d'entendre un beau conte d'amour et de mort? C'est de Tristan et d'Iseut la reine. Ecoutez comment à grand-joie, à grand deuil ils s'aimèrent, puis en moururent un même jour, lui par elle, elle par lui.»[34]

Is it enough, however, to liken Vian to pre-existing texts? Michel Rybalka latches on to certain facile (and naive) uses of allusion in the preliminary novel *Vercoquin et le plancton*:

> Hugo, Signalons [cependant] le rapport étroit qui existe dans *Vercoquin* entre le travesti du langage et le pastiche littéraire; le Major et Vercoquin sont des poètes, mais leurs œuvres sont des pastiches déclarés de Victor Emile Verhaeren et José-Maria de Hérédia. [...] Vian entretient avec la littérature des rapports semblables à ceux qu'il entretient avec le réel; il n'imite pas, il transpose et parodie. Il connaît la tradition littéraire, mais ne se laisse

---

[33] Jean-Pierre Enard, "La Fête à Boris", *Arc*, 90 (1984), 70-72 (p.71).

[34] Marguerite Nicod-Saraiva, "L'Univers de *L'Écume des jours*", in Alain Costes, ed., *Lecture plurielle de 'L'Écume des jours'* (Paris: U.G.E., 1979), p.53.

pas influencer profondément par elle; il s'en tient même résolument à l'écart.[35]

Vercoquin et le plancton is a special case: it is a naive, experimental novel which can be said to 'dabble in' literary allusions. It is precisely in the distance which it puts between itself and *Vercoquin* that *L'Écume des jours* becomes 'le premier roman signé Vian', and, as such, the beginning of a new novelistic strategy. Marc Lapprand, in his critical biography of Vian, remarks upon the stylistic development between the two novels:

> [Enfin] S'agissant de néologismes, procédé déjà employé dans *Vercoquin et le plancton*, ils représentent dans *L'Écume des jours* un projet beaucoup plus ambitieux, car ils créent véritablement ce monde étrange dans lequel évoluent les personnages et dans lequel ils sont tout à fait chez eux. Alors qu'ils étaient relativement gratuits dans *Vercoquin et le plancton*, ils prennent une toute autre dimension dans ce roman, en jouant leur rôle dans la création de ce que Jacques Bens appelle le «langage-univers» de Boris Vian.[36]

The most important work devoted to the influences at work in the novels of Boris Vian is Gilbert Pestureau's *Boris Vian, les Amerlauds et les Godons*. Within this text, Pestureau writes about influence in a way which provides a helpful 'point de départ' for the student of intertextuality. He is in no way perturbed by the arguments outlined above: "[...] Je crois [aussi] que l'étude des influences ou des goûts artistiques d'un auteur éclaire et enrichit la compréhension de l'œuvre."[37] In this respect, Pestureau's ideas concord entirely with those of Michel Gauthier who believes that the way to an author's work is through his literary sources:

---

[35] *Boris Vian: Essai d'interprétation et de documentation*, p.162.

[36] *Boris Vian: La Vie contre*, p.73.

[37] *Boris Vian, les Amerlauds et les Godons*, p.33.

> [...] Toute œuvre est un palimpseste. Elle l'est en un second encore. Car chaque écrivain est l'héritier de la totalité des écrivains qu'il a lus, ou même dont il n'a qu'entendu parler. De cet héritage, il fait ce qu'il veut - peut, et c'est cela qui compte: les «sources» littéraires sont *dans* l'œuvre; elles y sont comme le sont dans le collage cubiste les bouts de papier journal ou de papier faux-marbre: elles y prennent leur sens.[38]

Intertextuality is present therefore; it is simply a question of finding the most effective way of exploiting it.

Pestureau is clear from the outset that his aim is to achieve a deeper understanding of the man behind the mask. If the procedure in this study does at times use similar material to that used by Pestureau, the objective is not to know the man, but to know the texts. The "terrain de fouilles" will be the same (although sources here will be francophone as well as anglophone), as will the spirit of discovery:

> Ce terrain de fouilles [la langue ou les langues anglo-saxonnes, la littérature et la paralittérature - «policier», science-fiction...], limité mais très vaste cependant, j'espère le débroussailler quelque peu, laissant à d'autres le soin d'y creuser plus profondément, s'il le mérite.[39]

The objective of this book is, thus, to discover the intertexts at work in the Vian texts, and to extract from them a meaning in the light of which the novels may be reread.

Any such study is open to the accusation of subjectivity. This is keenly felt by Pestureau. His defence, however, (that the very nature of the

---

[38] *'L'Écume des jours'. Boris Vian*, p.10-11.

[39] *Boris Vian, les Amerlauds et les Godons*, p.34.

text, consciously constructed to that end by Vian, lends itself to this type of analysis) seems justified, especially in the light of Riffaterre's theories of intertextuality:

> Déceler cette «atmosphère américaine» dans l'œuvre de Vian et insister sur elle, est-ce vraiment forcer l'interprétation et tirer le texte à moi? [...] Mon analyse ne cherche qu'à éclairer quelques aspects d'une inspiration consciente ou non, rattacher une œuvre profondément originale à une tradition artistique, à une passion que je sais primordiale chez Boris Vian. Lui-même multiplie les allusions à des écrivains anglo-saxons et me pousse dans la voie que j'explore.[40]

The author to whom Pestureau refers more than any other is Faulkner. He enhances his defence of the rapprochement he makes between his works and those of Vian by adding a little aside called, simply, "Débat":

> - Mais dis-moi, n'es-tu pas en train, pour le simple plaisir de découvrir chez Boris un puritanisme apparemment anglo-saxon et plus précisément faulknérien, de nous offrir une vue sinistre de l'œuvre et une image désespérée de l'auteur?
> - Tu me comprends mal. Relever des jugements pessimistes sur les êtres et leurs rapports mutuels, les relier à des lectures faites à coup sûr à l'époque de la création, est-ce forcer l'interprétation? Mes rapprochements ne te paraissent-ils pas séduisants et convaincants à la fois?
> - Je te l'accorde, quoique tu prennes peut-être pour influence ce qui n'est au fond que hasard.[41]

---

[40] *Ibid.*, p.195.

[41] *Ibid.*, p.238.

If the key word of this study were 'influence' then perhaps the last remark of a hypothetical critic would be worth taking into account. Since, however, the word here is 'intertextuality', the word 'hasard' has little relevance: an intertext is established by weight of textual (and not historical) evidence. These considerations are, of course, of more importance for Pestureau who is trying to establish *who* Vian was. It is worth reiterating that this study is not one of influence; it is an attempt to disclose not only *how* the four Vian novels function intertextually, but *what* such intertextuality produces in terms of meaning. These elements are largely absent from the work of Pestureau who writes the names upon Riffaterre's 'signposts'; it is the intertextual critic who then follows the signs to their full conclusion.

It is clear that Vian was sceptical as to the usefulness of criticism. Pestureau quotes one of his passages from *Jazz-Hot*:

> On peut *apprendre* qui était untel. On peut *étudier* sa vie, son milieu social, son environnement. On peut *rechercher* les influences subies par lui. On peut finalement tenter de *comprendre* pourquoi il a fait telle ou telle œuvre. *Car on ne comprend pas une œuvre* [...] *on comprend l'homme* qui l'a faite, et il faut d'abord, je le crois, aimer l'œuvre, ce qui vous donne le goût de connaître l'homme.[42]

It seems probable that these remarks derive not so much from an over-inflated view of authorial power, as from repeated unhappy experiences of literary criticism in a French classroom. In this study interest does not revolve around the man; neither does it seek out one definitive meaning; rather it strives to work with a method which can unearth a multiplicity of meaning, revering the man only indirectly, in his capacity as author of a text which has been invested with such a wealth of possibilities.

What is being attempted is not, therefore, criticism in the sense of biographical interpretation, or generical classification. The problems facing an

---

[42] *Ibid.*, p.26.

author attempting such criticism are clear to Rybalka, who writes as follows in the introduction to his *Boris Vian: Essai d'interprétation et de documentation*:

> Les renseignements d'ordre biographique font souvent défaut et on ne peut pas toujours tout dire; d'autre part, l'œuvre est assez riche, assez ambiguë pour échapper aux systèmes de valeurs existants et suggérer de nouvelles méthodes et de nouvelles interprétations. [...] Signalons [...] que nous n'avons pas tenté de juger l'œuvre de Boris Vian d'après des critères esthétiques ou purement littéraires et que nous nous sommes contenté, dans la plupart des cas, de porter un jugement de valeur implicite. Nous laissons à d'autres le soin de créer à l'auteur une niche confortable dans le Panthéon des lettres et de l'histoire littéraire, celui de déterminer à l'intérieur de son œuvre une hiérarchie de valeurs et celui de décider s'il a été en fin de compte surréaliste, Existentialiste ou précurseur du Nouveau Roman.[43]

Such a task would clearly be extremely difficult since Vian, whilst fitting into no single category, manages to insert himself partially into all of them. Intertextual criticism has the distinct advantage of highlighting ways in which the four novels can be seen to be working outside themselves *and* inside themselves, to the exclusion of any needless categorisation.

However, the study of influence is itself not favoured by all. Jacques Bens embodies the 'anti-influence' argument, his article "Cinq Livres Pères" representing the strongest single attack on such an approach to the work of Vian. He begins as follows:

> Personne ne se met à écrire sans avoir jamais lu. Mieux: c'est précisément parce qu'on a dévoré certains livres que l'on brûle d'en composer à son tour. [...] Comme généralement, on en a lu pas mal (et parfois énormément),

---

[43] *Boris Vian: Essai d'interprétation et de documentation*, p.11-12.

> il se trouve toujours quelque malin pour découvrir une sorte de relation de similitude entre ce que vous écrivez et ce que vous lûtes. Il désigne cette relation sous le nom d'*influence*, et en tire différentes conséquences, définies, structurées, classées, imperturbables. Et cependant, les choses ne se présentent jamais d'une manière aussi simple.[44]

Once again, it is easy to remove this study from the scope of Bens' attack by merely defining it as one of intertextuality and not of influence. It is worth pursuing his argument, however, since it is not at all clear that it in any way damages the case for influence itself. Thus he continues:

> Vous vous êtes comporté comme le plus innocent et le plus enthousiaste des lecteurs, vous n'avez pas craint d'être bouleversé à la fois par Rabelais et par Flaubert, par Stendhal et par Jarry, par Musset et par Joyce, par Proust et par Céline. Mais quelle que soit l'admiration que vous leur portez [...] vous n'avez pu marcher près d'eux: ni leur pas, ni leur souffle ne s'adaptent aux vôtres. Cela ne vous empêchera pas, bien entendu, de les citer quand on vous demandera vos écrivains favoris [...] Bien malin, alors, qui pourrait décider (sauf cas de trop évidente, et bien rare, similitude) ceux d'entre eux qui auront contribué à mesurer vos marges, à tailler votre plume.[45]

Bens' concern is that a study of (what *he* calls) influence is in some way an attempt to devalue the author by showing that his/her work was created subconsciously with the words of other authors. It is also difficult to imagine how one can read a novel by Boris Vian more than once without noticing the manifold references to other works. And, indeed, Bens himself *has* noticed

---

[44] Jacques Bens, "Cinq Livres Pères", *Obliques*, 8-9, 1976, 143-150 (p.143).

[45] *Ibid.*, p.144.

them; in his attempt to expose various sources of influence as imagination on the part of other critics, he goes on to perform an (for want of a better word) intertextual analysis (albeit extremely cursory) of five texts.

In the course of his discussion of Queneau's *Un rude hiver*, Bens says the following:

> Celui-ci [Vian] aurait certainement aimé écrire les dernières et admirables lignes d'*Un rude hiver*:
>
> "Un pas léger se fit entendre dans l'escalier et Bernard sentit se presser contre lui un petit corps chaud et vibrant, une flamme. «Annette, murmura-t-il, ma vie, ma vie, ma vie.» Dehors il n'avait jamais fait aussi froid."
>
> D'ailleurs, il en a justement écrit de toutes pareilles.[46]

Here he is astute, ironic and apparently oblivious to the import of what he has said. Vian did, indeed, write such lines: in *L'Herbe rouge* there is much play on the hearing of footsteps on stairways, and also on the pressing of small, warm objects against one's chest (in the case of Folavril, a mole). And, in *L'Écume des jours*, Nicolas holds a flame against his heart. Whether these are instances of intentional allusion, or not, the case for intertextuality is strong.

In dealing with Kafka's *In the Penal Colony*, Bens makes the link between Kafka's machine and that of Wolf (a link which is examined in Chapter Three): "On ne peut s'empêcher d'évoquer ici, bien sûr, la machine et la mort de Wolf, dans *L'Herbe rouge*."[47] This, perversely, does seem to be an admission of the possibility of an intertextual reading. He then goes on, however, to defuse this potential flaw in his argument by suggesting that any link with Kafka is only to be expected, to the extent of being irrelevant, due to the general feel of both writers' oeuvre:

---

[46] *Ibid.*, p.147.

[47] *Ibid.*, p.148.

> Mais ne devrait-on pas être également frappé par l'atmosphère et les personnages du conte de Kafka? Le pays étranger que découvre le voyageur a des mœurs juste aussi froidement cruelles que le village de *L'Arrache-cœur*.[48]

This he attenuates by adding: "Le voyageur les désapprouve, il va s'efforcer d'aider à leur disparition: n'est-ce pas Jacquemort?" Despite the obvious similarities between certain texts, Bens believes them to be merely that; subject matter is finite, coincidences are inevitable. One may infer from this that to find influence in a text, all one has to do is pick up the nearest book. In the case of Kafka it is tempting to agree with Bens on this score, as, indeed, does Lionel Richard, who writes in his article "Vian était-il kafkaïen?":

> Que Boris Vian ait baigné dans ce «kafkaïsme» et en ait été impregné plus ou moins voilà qui semble naturel. Mais cette imprégnation est sans doute demeurée superficielle, ne déterminant guère sa vision du monde. [...] Il ne pouvait qu'être sensible à l'intrusion de l'insolite dans cette nouvelle [*La Colonie pénitentiaire*], à la manière dont l'histoire se détraque avec la machine, pour aboutir à l'autodestruction involontaire de l'officier qui en vantait si fort le mécanisme. Au-delà de ces suppositions, il paraît bien risqué de se prononcer sur l'influence que les œuvres de Kafka ont exercé sur lui.[49]

It is true that Vian's writing is not constantly dogged by the shadow of Franz Kafka. It is also true that Vian is *not* 'kafkaïen', just as he is not Sartrean. However, to deny the existence of intertextuality between *L'Herbe rouge* and *In the Penal Colony* is to stretch the logic of one's argument too far. Vian is

---

[48] *Ibid.*

[49] Lionel Richard, "Vian était-il kafkaïen?", *Arc*, 90 (1984), 26-28 (p.27).

not Sartrean, but to deny the importance of *La Nausée* for *L'Écume des jours* is to ignore the weight of textual evidence.

What is important in an intertextual study is not to spot similarity and then to discuss the kinship of the respective authors; rather, the crucial element is the way in which the two texts interrelate and the way in which 'meaning' can be altered in the host text by (analysis of) the intertext. This is where this study diverges from the path followed by Bens and Richard: it is not a study in kinship. It is interesting that, in the special edition of the periodical, *Obliques*, devoted to Vian, Bens' article, in which he goes on to write in reference to Faulkner's *Pylon*, "[...] Le choix de *Pylône* honore donc peut-être davantage l'auteur que le livre",[50] should be juxtaposed with Pestureau's brilliant, and scrupulously thorough, article, "Souvenirs de lectures anglo-saxonnes", in which he devotes much space to the rapprochement of *Pylon* and, especially, *L'Automne à Pékin*.

Much of this fear of intertextuality seems to derive from the belief that such a tool serves to disempower the (host) text, removing from it any vestige of autonomy and, hence, meaning. Jeanne-Marie Baude, in her article "L'Espace vital", writes: "La perturbation du récit ne s'arrête pas là: si elle se réduisait à cette maladie, Chloé risquerait fort d'être «la dame aux camélias» du roman moderne, et le roman ne «tiendrait» pas."[51] It is as if a novel must necessarily have a perfect, innate and wholly necessary meaning from which departure is not possible, and which can only be harmed by the encroachment of alien texts. The meaning of any novel, if not altogether arbitrarily imposed by the reader, is certainly many-layered. A rapprochement of *L'Écume des jours* and Dumas' *La Dame aux Camélias* does not rule out, for example, a socio-economic reading of Vian's first novel.

No matter how much one may try to ignore references to works beyond the bounds of the text, they continue to suggest themselves. In his book, *Boris Vian* Jacques Bens, in apparent contradiction to that which he is trying to establish in his article, produces a whole series of potential sources of influence:

---

[50] "Cinq Livres Pères", p.148.

[51] Jeanne-Marie Baude, "L'Espace vital", in Alain Costes, ed., *Lecture plurielle de 'L'Écume des jours'* (Paris: U.G.E., 1979), pp.70-124 (p.71).

> On pourrait imaginer que ce monde de *L'écume des jours* [*sic*] est d'une essence banalement onirique, qu'on en trouve des modèles chez de nombreux écrivains précédents: Barbey d'Aurevilly, Gérard de Nerval, Edgar Poe, Xavier Forneret, Villiers de l'Isle-Adam - pour ne rien dire des visionnaires scandinaves, ni des impressionnistes allemands. A ce sujet d'ailleurs, on pourrait établir un assez curieux rapprochement avec un texte de Franz Kafka. Dans *Le médecin de campagne*, nouvelle publiée dans le recueil intitulé *La métamorphose*, on trouve ces quelques lignes: "Pauvre garçon, on ne peut plus rien pour toi. J'ai découvert ta grande plaie; tu péris de cette fleur dans ton flanc."[52]

Exponents of the intertextual approach have often sought to ward off arguments such as those outlined above by backing up their readings with 'proof'. Amongst others, Pestureau is happy to cite the famous list of 'my favourite books', as published by Noël Arnaud in his *Les Vies parallèles de Boris Vian*: "En effet, un texte essentiel cité par N. Arnaud signale les préférences marquées et proclamées de notre auteur: avec *Adolphe, le Dr Faustroll, Un rude hiver, la Colonie pénitentiaire*, voici son palmarès anglo-saxon: *Pylône* de Faulkner, *la Merveilleuse visite* de Wells, *la Chasse au Snark*...".[53] If one finds similarity between one of Vian's novels and one of the above, one can at least be confident that Vian had actually read the proposed intertext. This is clearly important, but not a *sine qua non*. Although this work is largely based on the concept of a conscious structuring of the text on the part of the author, it is not the case that he must have read a particular text for intertextuality to exist between it and one of his own. Although proof that an intertext has been read by an author may be desirable, it is not vital: a text, once written, has sufficient autonomy to be able to interrelate with other texts, free from the guidance of its creator.

Rybalka goes to some lengths to establish that Vian's knowledge of Sartre (and his subsequent introduction of a calque of him as Existentialist and

---

[52] *Boris Vian*, p.34.

[53] *Boris Vian, les Amerlauds et les Godons*, p.178.

social icon into *L'Écume des jours*) was born of his reading of *La Nausée*, and not merely through their personal relationship:

> Avant même de faire personnellement la connaissance de Sartre au début de l'année 1946, Vian a été fasciné par son œuvre et intrigué par sa personnalité. Un de ses livres favoris était *La Nausée*, et selon Madame Paul Vian, il y a eu une année (vraisemblablement 1945) où son fils ne jurait que par Sartre. [...] Vian a jugé bon d'introduire, en contrepoint à la fois burlesque et tragique à l'histoire sentimentale de Colin et de Chloé ce qu'il est convenu d'appeler le thème «partrien» du roman. Ce thème se confond avec les malheurs du couple Chick-Alise et il implique à la fois un hommage et une critique de la part de Boris Vian.[54]

The problem with this sort of proof is that one can never be entirely sure that it is reliable, owing much, as it so often does, to the rather distant memories of Vian's entourage at the time when he was working on his own novels. For example, Pestureau, keen to establish whether Vian had read *Ulysses* (a text often mentioned in reference to Vian), turns to the latter's first wife: "J'ai posé la question d'une influence possible de Joyce sur Boris Vian à Michelle Léglise-Vian; sa réponse fut négative: Boris, selon elle, n'a pas lu *Ulysse*, trop savant à ses yeux."[55] Ignoring the point, already so often raised, that such proof is not imperative, can one be sure that such testimony is 'proof' at all? The curator of 'la Fondation Vian', in Cité Véron, Nicole Bertold, replied to similar quesions that one should not be put off by a 'lack of proof' because, in any case: "il avait tout lu".[56] These few words, spoken without a

---

[54] *Boris Vian: Essai d'interprétation et de documentation*, p.84.

[55] *Boris Vian, les Amerlauds et les Godons*, p.155.

[56] Interview conducted with Nicole Bertold at 'la Fondation Vian', 28 March 1996. - On display in Vian's former apartment is a selection of his collection of books. Illuminating as these are, that a book is on a bookshelf is not proof that it has been read, in the same way as the absence of a book from the same shelf does not prove that it has not been read.

hint of irony or hyperbole, serve as a suitable biography of Vian the reader. Furthermore, there lies in his insatiable thirst for literature sufficient grounds for assuming that his own work would seek to reflect that of others: his books are literature (and not the base form which certain critics would have us believe), echo literature and analyse literature. Taking Michelle's testimony into account, Pestureau makes the following remarks:

> [...] Un subtil critique ne pourrait-il rapprocher l'angoisse de Wolf de celle de Léopold Bloom, la promenade de Wolf et Lazuli dans le «quartier des Amoureuses» [...] de celle de Bloom et Stephen Dedalus dans les bouges de Dublin, et le monologue féminin et sensuel qui conclut *Ulysse* du dialogue final de Lil et Folavril?[57]

To all intents and purposes the link with Joyce is self-justifying: it is there because it has been found and it is proved because it is there.

When Pestureau goes on to talk of the scope of Vian's "para-littérature", it is in a positive sense, not in order to classify and catalogue: "[...] des voyages dans les espaces à l'utopie du futur. Poivre et piment du «thriller», sésame-ouvre-toi de la SF, ketchup de la BD, notre Boris ne néglige aucune épice pour relever sa cuisine ou personnaliser sa «salade»".[58] The genres of detective fiction and Science Fiction are broached by Pestureau as examples of anglophone influence. In the study which follows examples from both of these genres will be subjected to intertextual analysis, thereby producing meaning for the overall Vian tetralogy which mere suggestion of influence cannot imply.

Vian's passion for Science Fiction is well documented. Pestureau informs us that it supercedes 'hard-boiled' detective fiction as Vian's bedside reading: "Un autre genre para-littéraire [la SF] prend très tôt le relais de la Série Noire dans la culture vianienne genre venu lui aussi d'Amérique bien qu'inventé par les Européens et fort voisin parfois du précédent...".[59] It is

---

[57] *Boris Vian, les Amerlauds et les Godons*, p.196.

[58] *Ibid.*, p.251.

[59] *Ibid.*, p.281.

interesting to analyse the reflection of this transition of Vian the reader in the work of Vian the writer. The passage can be said to take place somewhere between the second and third novels (i.e. between *L'Automne* and *L'Herbe rouge*). The transition is not as clear cut, however, as some would have us believe: Jacques Duchateau picks up the trace of 'la Série Noire' as late as the final pages of *L'Herbe rouge*: "[Par ailleurs] On verra que ce tailleur noir [as worn by Folavril], dans la bonne tradition du roman policier, se révèle un indice assez fructueux."[60] This is, then, a glimpse of detective fiction in a novel which criticism has up to now considered to be a work of Science Fiction; as such it parallels the intertextual presence of H.G. Wells' *The Wonderful Visit* in *L'Automne à Pékin*, itself a work which may be strongly associated with various works of detective fiction. The novel-by-novel strategy adopted here has the advantage over the genre-by-genre approach of producing a reading which takes changes of genre into account, assessing their importance in terms of the overall novelistic strategy, whilst not getting lost and muddled in a sequence of seemingly haphazard quotations.

In all Pestureau's work on the influence of anglophone texts on the oeuvre of Boris Vian, the author who has pride of place is William Faulkner, both by the sheer weight of the pages devoted to him and by the convincing nature of the 'influential passages' exposed. It will prove useful to give a résumé of Pestureau's work on Faulkner at this point for the following reasons: firstly, as Faulkner's influence recurs over the course of all four novels, it does not fit appositely into a consideration of any one Vian novel; secondly, by the omnipresence of his influence in all four novels, Faulkner can be seen to add support to the concept of the four novels being read as one: the possibility of a 'tetralogy reading' will be broached in this introduction; finally, and not the least important of these points, the body of work devoted to Faulkner is so thorough as to make superfluous any further exploration in that direction. Thus, "Passons donc audacieusement à la parenté des thèmes et des motifs qui laisse largement place au hasard, certes, mais permet des rapprochements suggestifs au comparatiste."[61] Take *Mosquitoes*, for example:

---

[60] *Boris Vian ou les facéties du destin*, p.161.

[61] *Boris Vian, les Amerlauds et les Godons*, p.186.

> Le «large cours d'eau sombre, apparement immobile» [...] est-il la source du ruisseau rouge de *l'Arrache-cœur*? Le «Carré» de *l'Herbe rouge* à la végétation raide et drue évoque-t-il «le vieux carré de la Nouvelle-Orléans», «le square Jackson [où] des cannas et des lantaniers saignaient, saignaient», ou enfin ce décor: «l'herbe croissait raide, dans un carré bordé de plantes rigides»? [...] [Mais] Les bayous de la Nouvelle-Orléans que survolent les *Moustiques* évoquent surtout pour nous le sous-titre de *Chloé - Song of the swamp*, le chant du marécage...[62]

It is perhaps worth speculating here that the references to Duke Ellington may function on one level as indices of 'le roman jazzique', and on another as what Riffaterre might call an ungrammaticality pushing the reader beyond the jazz of New Orleans towards its swamps, and towards the texts of William Faulkner. Pestureau continues to give possibly the most convincing intertextual reading of Chloé's floral intruder:

> Encore plus troublante est la parenté entre le nénuphar qui étouffe peu à peu Chloé et la langueur de Mrs. Maurier, la riche veuve de *Moustiques*, responsable de la croisière dans l'embouchure du Mississippi:
> «à l'intérieur d'elle-même, une chose terrible grossissait, une chose terrible et empoisonnée débordait comme une eau trop longtemps endiguée; on eût dit que s'éveillait, au sein de ce corps si familier, une chose qu'elle y avait abritée à son insu. Cette chose se déployait comme une fleur vénéneuse, un assemblage compliqué de pétales qui poussaient, se fanaient et mouraient, et que remplaçaient aussitôt d'autres pétales plus grands encore et plus implacables. Ses membres tremblaient, et cette fleur

---

[62] *Ibid.*, p.186-187.

secrète, cette fleur sombre, hideuse, grandissait, grandissait, l'étouffant»[63]

It can be seen, therefore, that *Mosquitoes* merits the label intertext. So, too, does one of Vian's 'favourite books':

> [Mais] Surtout *Pylône* est l'évocation d'un monde inhumain, d'un univers de science-fiction, d'un univers de «mutants» [...] Ce sont ces êtres extra-terrestres, aviateurs de course et d'acrobatie [...] volant sur le dos comme le cormoran de *l'Automne à Pékin* [...] - «hommes de fer» tournant follement autour de pylônes qui ne sont pas sans rappeler cette «Echelle» qui, sur le premier manuscrit de *l'Herbe rouge*, annonce «la machine».[64]

And neither does *L'Arrache-cœur* escape the shadow of Faulkner: "Le monde faulknérien de honte, de punition et de rachat se reflète encore dans *l'arrache-cœur*: La Gloïre assumant la honte du village, Culblanc violée par son père, sexualité honteuse, torture des innocents...".[65]

To complete this review of the work carried out by Pestureau in the field of influence, it is worth remarking on the following instances where he finds a particular explanation of the Vian text through anglophone influence and where the same element is given a different interpretation when considered intertextually. For example, where Pestureau sees the demolition of the houses in *L'Automne à Pékin* and *L'Herbe rouge* as echoes of Vian's wartime experiences, and, hence, a biographical, and not intertextual, reference to anglophone conquest ("La maison bombardée du *Brouillard* [a short story by Vian] annonce les édifices coupés en deux de *l'Automne à Pékin*

---

[63] *Ibid.*, p.187-188.

[64] *Ibid.*, p.189-190.

[65] *Ibid.*, p.238.

ou de *l'Herbe rouge*...",[66] here, in a chapter dealing with the Parisian aspects of the text and the continuity of Carrollinian intertextuality, a reading drawing on *L'Hôtel du Nord* and *Alice through the Looking-Glass* respectively is chosen. Likewise, where Pestureau explains the 'ouapiti' of *L'Herbe rouge* through the folklore of the American Indians, here a Carrollinian reading is offered which draws a link between 'ouapiti' and 'Snark'. Pestureau's own work on Lewis Carroll often concentrates on linguistic and semantic rapprochements, such as his suggestion that Vian's La Gloïre is a descendant of Humpty-Dumpty and Alice's argument over the meaning of the word 'glory'.[67] It is true that Folavril's own definition of 'asphodèles', as being called that because that is the name which she is attributing to them, is Carrollinian in origin;[68] however, intertextuality also reveals 'asphodèles' to be the flowers of death and as such loaded with further (intertextual) significance.

Towards a tetralogy reading

It can be seen that, although there has been some useful work performed in the area of manifestations of external influence in the novels of Boris Vian, no real attempts have been made to develop a reading of the novels through investigation (and, to a degree, manipulation) of intertextuality. Thus, a rich source of potential meanings has been long overlooked. For, to recognise that there is intertextuality in a work is not sufficient: such is influence under another name. Studies of this type tend to lead to superficial attempts to posit the author within a particular genre. Intertextuality, by its very definition, entails meaning, a meaning or potential for meaning located half in the text and half beyond, in the intertext.

Consideration of the common intertextual strategy of the four Vian novels leads to a consideration of these novels as a coherent unit. The intertextuality does progress and develop, ceding gradually (in number of intertexts, not in importance) to intratextuality, which will be used here to

---

[66] *Ibid.*, p.45. Note that this book does not try to establish intertextuality within Vian's non-novelistic work - intratextuality is not extended beyond the four novels.

[67] *Ibid.*, p.147.

[68] *Ibid.*, p.148.

signify intertextuality between the four Vian novels. It can be seen that the usage of the intertextuality becomes more tightly bound to a meaning which can only be understood when one appreciates the unified nature of the four novels. Thus, the chapters of this book are structured to reflect the developing nature of the texts: what begins,in *L'Écume des jours*, as a blitz of intertexts, mixing jazz and Surrealism, becomes, by *L'Arrache-cœur*, an organized blend of inter- and intratextuality pointing from the end of the series back to the start.

As the novels are usually read as totally separate texts (although Rybalka juggles examples from all four novels in his "Essai" when dealing with the topic of recurring themes, such as the double and the eternal love triangle, he makes no rapprochement of the novels as whole units), it is interesting to see if a tetralogy reading may be inferred from any of the other existing interpretations of Vian's novels.

Michel Rybalka's thorough review of the notion of the double seems to draw a line of continuity between *L'Automne à Pékin* and *L'Herbe rouge*. His choice of quotation shows that he recognises Anne and Angel as two aspects of a single being (the murder/suicide debate being resolved by the fact that it is both[69]): "Alors ça vous libère de quoi? - De moi [...] Je me réveille."[70] Thus, murder is self-liberation. He then describes Rochelle as the person who says the following: "Il y avait deux hommes amoureux de moi, qui se débattaient pour moi, c'était merveilleux. C'était très romanesque." He is, hereby, placing the stress of his reading on the identity not only of the characters, but of the novel itself. Rochelle's description of her dream reminds the reader of the battle raging within Angel (and not merely against Anne as Other). It also calls into question the status of the novel. Angel and the novel are both aware of the eye of the Other/reader; both are self-consciously fictitious. Though both 'romanesque' and 'romantique' are inherently ambiguous, both adjectives referring to both nouns, the former is the nearer to 'roman', whilst the latter is the nearer to 'romantisme'. From this he passes straight from a comparison of Angel's 'murder' of Anne to Lazuli's killing of his Other, who turns out to be a part of himself: "[...] en tuant le double, ou plutôt les doubles car ceux-ci se multiplient à mesure qu'ils sont poignardés,

---

[69] Many critics are interested in the idea that suicides in Vian are never far from being murderers, Wolf who kills a 'fonctionnaire' just before self-destructing being a case in point.

[70] *Boris Vian: Essai d'interprétation et de documentation*, p.123.

Saphir Lazuli se tue lui-même."[71] Although the ostensible difference is that Angel lives on and Lazuli dies, murder/suicide is effectively for both characters a passage out of one novel (and into the next). Thus, Rybalka draws a line from *L'Automne* to *L'Herbe rouge* which is purely to do with literary similarity.

When Rybalka moves on to discuss Wolf, he does not seem concerned with his possible role as an example of literary continuity, although he does appear to make an allusion to it: "On pourrait voir dans le double que Wolf rejette le passé inconscient. Plusieurs de ses paroles le suggèrent, en particulier: «C'est tuant, de traîner avec soi ce qu'on a été avant»."[72] In terms of our study of the intratextuality in the novels, this "passé inconscient" is a form of Jungian collective sub-conscious (as opposed to something more individual to Wolf), a reflection of Wolf's 'être-en-*L'Automne à Pékin*'.

Despite seeing *L'Automne à Pékin* as a thing apart, a master-piece amongst novels, Freddy de Vree seems to be pointing towards a coherence of vision in Vian's work:

> Entre temps, Boris Vian écrivain allait développer, à partir de *L'écume des jours* et de certaines données du roman, un univers en expansion continuelle: il allait reparler du docteur Mangemanche, de l'arrache-cœur d'Alise, et, enfin, dans le *finale* de l'expansion, faire rétrécir la chambre du Schmürz comme la chambre de Chloé. Entre temps, il écrivait *L'automne à Pékin*.[73]

However, de Vree also places *L'Arrache-cœur* at the top of a hierarchy dependent upon another criterion: "*L'Arrache-cœur* est le roman le plus riche de Boris Vian...".[74] To read the novels as part of a tetralogy dispenses with such obscure divisions.

---

[71] *Ibid.*, p.124.

[72] *Ibid.*, p.125.

[73] *Boris Vian: Essai*, p.48-49.

[74] *Ibid.*, p.103.

De Vree goes on, somewhat incongruously, to pronounce that Vian's novels are born of purest imagination, a stream of consciousness with no premeditation:

> [Ceci dit] placer Vian dans une perspective littéraire, c'est dur. Sur le plan de l'*écriture*, ses livres sont trop hâtivement faits; mais c'est leur grâce; ce ne sont pas des préfabrications mais des improvisations, un cœur mis à nu...[75]

He completes his change of mind with the following bolt from the blue: "Chaque livre est un livre complet, isolé, unique."[76] De Vree, then, encapsulates the divided opinions on the Vian novels.

What follows here is an analysis of the interpenetration of the four novels; the aim will be to show how lines of internal, textual evidence may be traced from Colin's emergence from the shower, through the Exopotamian desert, across the square of red grass and, finally, into the sea at the bottom of the cliffs beyond Clémentine's house. Links of this nature will be examined as part of an intratextual strategy both parallel to and dependent upon the use of intertextuality. For intertextuality will also be shown to be pervasive, and this too will be exposed as progressive, and increasingly methodical in its manner of expression such that it becomes central to and inextricable from the 'meaning' of the texts. Furthermore, it will be shown that, whilst 'meaning' is intertextually produced in each individual novel, the intertextuality also spans the voids between these novels, combining with intratextuality to give coherence to the tetralogy. Thus, efforts will be made to prove intercommunication between groups of intertexts. This book will constitute, therefore, a study of four novels; four novels about love, four novels about other novels and four novels about each other.

---

[75] *Ibid.*, p.172.

[76] *Ibid.*, p.173.

CHAPTER ONE
L'Écume des jours:
From 'clins d'œil' to intertextuality

This study begins with *L'Écume des jours*, the first of Vian's texts to be written with publication in mind, and the text which the author himself considered to be his first novel. It is important to be clear at this stage that the book will consider *L'Écume des jours, L'Automne à Pékin, L'Herbe rouge* and *L'Arrache-cœur* as four novels to be set apart from the rest of his work. They have a quality which demands special treatment; this elitist approach will be offered by this study of one of the defining features of Vian's work: intertextuality.

The cover-page of the manuscript which Vian finally entrusts to his wife's typewriter bears the title "L'ékume des jhours / Poème inédit en / quatorze variantes. / Bisonduravi." (*Ej*, p.215). Thus this original cover-page carries two examples of a style which is already recognisably vianesque: namely the corruption of traditional orthography and the anagrammatism of his own name (here the Bison Ravi, a name with which he often signed his paintings, is further altered). Whether the decision to omit these two traits of his stylistic personality is made independently by the author or following a suggestion on the part of Michelle is, for the purposes of this study, largely irrelevant. What is crucial is that a conscious move is made towards a self-consciously novelistic style. 'L'écume' has a relevance, an importance before which 'l'ékume' must necessarily cede. Thus, the first clue to a potential reading of the novel is laid even before the famous 'avant-propos'.

Of course, it may be argued that *L'Écume des jours* grows naturally out of Vian's earlier work, and that there is no need for such a 'point de départ' to be drawn. Marc Lapprand, for example, sees a progression between *Vercoquin et le plancton* and *L'Écume* such that the latter may almost be read as a sequel to the former. Lapprand's approach, in his article «*Vercoquin et le plancton* comme pré-texte de *L'Écume des jours*: Naissance de l'écrivain Boris Vian», is linguistic, dealing with such stylistic phenomena as 'jeux sur les syntagmes figés', 'prises au pied de la lettre' and so on. His belief is that Vian's texts grow out his use of such recognisable linguistic strategies, and that the essence of a Vian text can, therefore, be reduced to a sequence of sub-headings:

> [On voit donc] en y regardant de près, que cet «Avant-propos» à *L'Écume des jours* pourrait s'appliquer tout autant à *Vercoquin et le plancton*, et soude les deux récits en un même parti pris de réalisation romanesque. Nous allons voir à présent que l'univers romanesque de Vian passe par un abondant travail sur le langage, et qu'il en est en fin de compte entièrement et directement issu.[1]

These two final adverbs make no allowance for the presence of extra-textual phenomena such as intertextuality, although Lapprand himself produces evidence of their existence. There are instances of intertextuality within *Vercoquin*: for example, the creature called Mackintosh, whose presence he describes as being due to «la mystification gratuite», can be seen to have certain intertextual precedents which Lapprand himself cites:

> On sait que Vian avait lu (et apprécié) à cette époque Jarry, et il n'est pas impossible que ce «mackintosh» ait un rapport direct avec le cynocéphale papion «Bosse-de-nage», fidèle compagnon du docteur Faustroll...[2]

It is not the case that intertextuality is of secondary importance compared with instances of plays on words; rather it is the case that such instances of intertextuality in *Vercoquin* reveal the immaturity of Vian as an author at that stage in his development, and thus take on the appearance of casual 'clins d'œil'.[3] In *L'Écume des jours* the examples of intertextuality are

---

[1] Marc Lapprand, "*Vercoquin et le plancton* comme pré-texte de *L'Écume des jours*: Naissance de l'écrivain Boris Vian", *Texte*, 7 (1988), 249-266 (256).

[2] *Ibid.*, p.258.

[3] In this chapter there will be much reference made to these 'clins d'œil': the sense here is of a reference to a work or author so obvious that it should be noticed, appreciated for its comic effect and put aside. The importance of these features here will be seen to be their potential role as intertextual signposts.

much more developed.[4] Thus, Lapprand is right to treat dismissively such instances of what is closer to general influence than intertextuality:

> Les parties I et IV figurent deux énormes surprises-parties, prétextes à de vigoureux déchaînements d'actes de toute nature [...] dont les récits s'inscrivent dans une longue tradition remontant à Rabelais [...] en passant par Jarry [...] et enfin même l'Apollinaire des *Onze Mille Verges*.[5]

In a sense, then, Lapprand is right simply to list these vague instances of influence, since that is what they amount to in *Vercoquin*. By going on to tar *L'Écume* with the same brush, however, his argument being that this novel is an extension of the second, is to do the text, and particularly the intertextuality within it, a great disservice. He discredits intertextuality as a tool across the board:

> L'œuvre de Vian est à tel point unique qu'il paraît stérile de chercher çà et là une parenté avec un texte antérieur d'un autre écrivain, sauf dans les cas précis de pastiche ou d'imitation [...] Mais là encore, et en se mettant momentanément dans le sillage de Genette, on peut toujours considérer *tout* texte comme «hypertexte» d'un «hypotexte» mais cette vision théorique relative à la genèse d'un texte, si séduisant soit-elle, a tendance à réduire l'œuvre d'un auteur à *une imitation à un certain degré* d'autres œuvres qui lui sont antérieures, et diminuer ainsi l'originalité d'un auteur.[6]

---

[4] To mention simply that Mackintosh is like 'Bosse-de-nage' is, however valid and interesting, of limited use to the reader in terms of understanding the text. It is, perhaps, also worth noting that the name Mackintosh may be traced to a short story by P.G. Wodehouse entitled *The Story of the Dog Mackintosh*; such a comment may be considered less random if one considers the Jeeves-like mannerisms of Nicolas in *L'Écume*.

[5] *Ibid.*, p.252.

[6] *Ibid.*, p.263.

In terms of Vian's work, this study will aim to show that the most important cases of intertextuality, both in their interest value per se and in their impact upon potential readings of the text, lie beneath, veiled by what Lapprand labels «les cas précis de pastiche ou d'imitation». It is true that *L'Écume des jours* teems with these; it will also be shown that, whilst the later texts often display a more refined exploitation of intertextuality, this first novel paves the way towards these latter works, allying itself firmly with them, and not with *Vercoquin*. (Although the case for intertextuality is sufficient in itself, there is a whole intratextual argument which will become clear at a later stage and which depends entirely upon a mythological beginning set in *L'Écume des jours*: it will be seen to be important in terms of this book to view *L'Écume* as a clean break from *Vercoquuin*.) The lines of analysis with which this chapter will be dealing, therefore, are lines which lie beneath the surface of the texts, under 'le pied de la lettre'. To remain on the level of the lines on the page is to see the novels as separate, irreconcilable units. It is for this reason (because his study is linguistic) that Lapprand sees *L'Écume* and *Vercoquin* as the only possible pairing:

> [Mais] *L'Écume des jours* marque une nouvelle étape dans le parcours de Vian. Il est devenu écrivain à part entière. Ainsi, ses deux premiers romans sont les seuls à jouir d'une telle cohérence narrative, car les romans postérieurs à *L'Écume des jours* (*L'Automne à Pékin*, *L'Herbe rouge* et *L'Arrache-cœur*) ont chacun leur caractère, et ne s'inscrivent plus dans la trajectoire spécifique définie par ce cheminement (de *VP* à *EJ*), aboutissant à ce que son auteur lui-même considérait comme son premier roman.[7]

The main aim of this chapter will be, then, to work through the various 'clins d'œil' spoken of in the introduction and seen by Lapprand to be the only marks of intertextuality, in order to systematize them and to extract from them some workable meaning: whilst *L'Écume des jours* does represent a significant step forward from *Vercoquin et le plancton*, it is still a tentative beginning, the first in what this book will aim to show to be a sequence of four intercommunicating novels. As the first novel, it can only be coherent with

---

[7] *Ibid.*, p.266.

itself: there is, therefore, no scope for intratextuality as such. Its structure, when compared retrospectively to the novels which follow it, appears relatively haphazard. That said, there is a deceptive code of order within this disorder. The strategy which underlies the novel is exactly the same as that which underlies those which come later: this order is in the form of intertextuality. Vian goes to some lengths to ground his novel in a literary tradition; it is this strategy which will be the central concern of this chapter. The chapter will thus begin by dealing with the remarks made both by Vian and others about this novel, remarks whose flippancy often veils a poignancy which eludes even their utterer, and sometimes this latter is Vian himself. Then will begin follow an examination of the intertextuality existing between *L'Écume des jours* and Flaubert's famous short story, *Un Cœur simple*, examining the rich literary heritage behind Vian's apparent anarchism, and revealing how some of his more 'risqué' portrayals of budding sexuality derive from a subtle manipulation of the pastoral tradition. It will further be shown that Vian's love not only of stories and 'pretty girls', but also his love of jazz do not filter into his novels merely in the form of some kind of vague influence or 'feel'; rather they appear as specific instances, or, in the case of jazz, specific pieces. *L'Écume des jours* will be seen to act, via its 'clins d'œil' as a key to a wider reading, a blue-print for a form of intertextual criticism. This chapter will procede to reveal the importance of the debt to Surrealism, a debt persistently understated, if not overlooked, by criticism and diverted from the attention of the reader by the (feigned) preoccupation with Existentialism; there will also be some consideration of Dumas' *La Dame aux Camélias*, amongst others, as Ur-texts of this tradition. And so, it is neither with Sartre or the Surrealists that this chapter begins, but with a text the importance of which has, until now, remained undisturbed.

The parrot at the heart of *L'Écume*

> C'est une histoire entièrement vraie, car je l'ai imaginée d'un bout à l'autre. merde flaubert l'avait déjà trouvé.
> (*Ej*, p.225)

So reads an "avant-texte" of *L'Écume des jours*. In its initial stages of development, the novel was to be centred around a fairly simple story. A boy and a girl would meet, fall in love and marry. The girl would then turn out to have been fated from the outset: "elle avait un nénuphar dans le poumon droit. Il fleurissait tous les ans" (*Ej*, p.218). Her death would then ensue. The tragedy of her death would be heightened by her innocence and her sweet nature. In as much as the above intentions actually survive, Vian's text may be seen as a parody of *Un cœur simple*, the first of Flaubert's *Trois Contes*.

Although Vian's fleeting and isolated reference to Flaubert is in no way to be seen as proof of intertextuality, it having already been shown that this depends much more on the reader's interpretation of the text itself, it is interesting to see whether or not it does point to something of significance; so often it is in apparently innocuous remarks that one finds the most meaningful comments. However, to assess the actual importance of *Un cœur simple* as a role-model for *L'Écume des jours*, one must return directly to the work itself. In its very inspiration *Un cœur simple* provides a certain sentimentality whose power in *L'Écume* has its poignancy in its very absence. According to Michel Gauthier, Vian had read Flaubert's tale in minute detail. He sees in *L'Écume* not only a kinship with *Un cœur simple* in terms of sentiment and plot, but also in terms of style. He cites a long list of what he calls 'curious imperfect tenses', which seem to derive from Flaubert:

> Or des indices [le curieux usage de l'imparfait], qu'on estimera peut-être ténus, semblent renvoyer à *Un cœur simple* comme à ce que nos illustres prédécesseurs eussent sans hésitation nommé une «source» de *L'Écume* [...] On peut penser à tout le moins que Vian a été un lecteur attentif d'*Un cœur simple*; il faut aussi reconnaître que par cet éclairage a posteriori, c'est le «style» de Flaubert qui apparaît comme extraordinairement neuf, révolutionnaire...[8]

And yet it is not style alone which Vian refers to when he talks of a story that Flaubert had found before him; there is also this play on sentimentality. For, where Vian can rely on his subject matter to arouse the necessary sentimentality in the reader, without having to compromise his own creation Flaubert has a kind of self-generating sentimentality at the core of his intentions. Edouard Maynial notes, in his introduction to *Trois Contes*:

---

[8] Michel Gauthier, *Boris Vian.L'Écume des jours* (Paris: Hatier, 1973), p.103-104.

> Flaubert voulut écrire «un récit où l'on ne pourrait plus l'accuser d'être dur, un récit d'homme sensible, où, sans prêcher la bonté, sans l'annoncer par des phrases d'auteur, il la fît apparaître dans les gestes inconscients de la plus humble et la plus obscure créature.»[9]

According to Maynial, Flaubert was also driven by a desire to undertake an aesthetic project akin to that which will inspire Vian: the creation of reality in (and through) fiction as well as an attempt to locate his story outside the pernicious dominion of everyday life (which, given the importance of the word 'jours', will be henceforth referred to simply as 'days'): "[...] Une même volonté de dominer la réalité pour en faire de l'art, sans consentir à mettre une différence essentielle entre la terne vérité de tous les jours et l'orgueilleuse vérité de l'histoire..." (*Contes*, p.XIV). The text itself provides material for *L'Écume* both in terms of plot and vocabulary. Félicité, the pure-hearted heroine, by virtue of her unflinching altruism and capacity for love (irrespective of whether or not it is requited), reflects both Alise and Chloé respectively.

Grudges are not borne long by any of the three: at one moment "Félicité, bien que nourrie dans la rudesse, fut indignée contre Madame, puis oublia." (*Contes*, p.36) Likewise, Chloé, having reprimanded Colin for his suggestiveness, grants him an almost instantaneous reprieve: "Il avait l'air si désolé qu'elle sourit et le secoua un petit peu pour montrer qu'elle n'était pas fâchée" (*Ej*, p.75). Alise, for her part, has a greater capacity for more complex interaction with her conversationally dominant male counterparts; she can respond with irony, faking annoyance (for example, when her tender years are brought into the conversation: "Je vais ouvrir!... dit Alise. Je suis la plus jeune. C'est vous-mêmes qui me le reprochez..." [*Ej*, p.81]), but she too soon forgives and forgets. Indeed, as one traces her steps, one finds that Félicité reveals numerous links with *L'Écume des jours* that do, in fact, justify the labelling of *Un cœur simple* as 'parent text'. By dealing with some of the textual similarities between the two texts in the approximate order in which they occur in *Un cœur simple*, various patterns will emerge which will enable a more complete analysis of other texts whose intertextual importance will

---

[9] Gustave Flaubert, *Trois Contes* (Paris: Garnier Frères, 1961), p.VI-VII. (Hereafter referred to as *Contes*.)

prove to be more tightly and deliberately constructed by Vian. Thus, via Flaubert, the methodology behind this particular study will be exposed permitting familiarisation with this particular application of intertextuality.

Both texts are rooted in the pastoral tradition, *Un cœur simple* by the description of Félicité's childhood: "[...] Un fermier la recueillit, et l'employa toute petite à garder les vaches dans la campagne" (*Contes*, p.7), and *L'Écume* by the choice of the names Colin and Chloé.[10] The link with the pastoral contributes to the mood of naïve innocence which leaves the principal characters as if in the control of some guiding deity, as well as providing space for the occasional burst of rustic imagery. Longus' and Flaubert's tales, in as much as they are retold through *L'Écume,* become more than simply updated. There is a subversion of the pastoral tradition such that music, love and laughter are transformed, by euphemisms, into dancing and rather heavier petting. For example, Chick selects his words with care, thus carving himself a role suitable for the island of Lesbos: "Alors, mes agneaux, dit-il, ça gaze?..." (*Ej*, p.70) Here, Chick is playing the joint role of shepherd/love god. The sight of himself and Alise performing 'le biglemoi' (a dance which here signifies physical love-making) is supposed to (and, indeed, does) arouse Colin and Chloé. In Longus' tale it is the animals of the herds which provide the necessary stimulus:

> It [the mating of the sheep and goats] was a sight calculated to turn even an old man's thoughts to love; but Daphnis and Chloe, who were young and bursting with health and had long been in search of love, were positively set on fire by what they had heard...[11]

Other examples of behaviour which recall the island of Lesbos are used more or less in the spirit that Longus would have intended (although Vian certainly leaves the onus of Lesbian interpretation firmly on the shoulders of the reader).

---

[10] Vian makes an indirect allusion to the *Daphnis and Chloe* of Longus when he refers to Nijinski, "[...] danseur et chorégraphe russe", as Pestureau notes, "[qui] fit profiter de ses qualités exceptionelles maints ballets - dont *Daphnis et Chloé*" (*Ej*, p.241).

[11] Longus, *Daphnis and Chloe*, trans. by Paul Turner (London: Penguin Classics, 1989), p.77. (Hereafter referred to as *Daphnis*.)

> -Tu me chatouilles! dit Alise qui commençait à rire. Chloé la caressait exprès à l'endroit où ça chatouille, sur les côtés et jusqu'aux hanches. La peau d'Alise était chaude et vivante. [...]
> - Embrasse-moi, dit Chloé. Je suis si contente! Alise l'expulsa de la salle de bains et Chloé s'assit sur son lit.
> (*Ej*, p.88)

This scene, usually interpreted as frolicsome behaviour deriving from a need to express happiness amongst good friends, does, however, exhibit an example of 'homosexual fore-play'. More importantly, this brief exchange witnesses Alise's denial of Chloé's advances. This interpretation, although more hazardous, is potentially more fruitful: a sexually ambivalent Chloé is more likely to represent love itself than a precise love of Colin; this is the Chloé seen by Marie Redonnet: "[...] C'est une femme-fée à la sexualité sublimée... «la sensualité à l'état pur, dégagée du corps»"[12]. This would have an effect on the reading of *L'Écume* as a love-story (which it most certainly is), but cannot be overlooked. Indeed, Daphnis himself, the purity of whose love is never in question, does not share his first sexual experience with Chloe, but allows himself to be tempted by another. Colin also finds himself in the position of almost having to spurn a partially veiled offer of homosexual love: "- Tu es un chic type! dit Chick. Je ne sais pas comment te remercier, d'ailleurs tu sais très bien que je ne peux pas te remercier comme je le voudrais... Colin se sentait un peu réconforté. Et Alise était vraiment en beauté ce soir." (*Ej*, p.79)

This dual refusal (reinforced by the juxtaposition, in the latter instance, with the sentence "Et Alise était vraiment en beauté ce soir") has the force of joining Alise and Colin in a certain solidarity, their kindred spirits running a parallel course which will not allow their hearts to converge. Finally, the pastoral also brings together love and music, a union so essential to Vian's novel. In Longus the Pan-pipe is a symbol/conjuror of beauty: "While he was piping he again seemed to her beautiful, and this time she thought that the beauty was caused by the music" (*Daphnis*, p.27), and: "This Pan-pipe of ours was originally not a musical instrument but a beautiful girl who had a lovely voice..." (*Daphnis*, p.65). This nymph by whom Pan was so enamoured will reappear as the notes of *Chloe*.

---

[12] Marie Redonnet, "Une Petite arche miraculeuse", *Infini*, 38 (1992), 80-87 (p.83).

In *Un cœur simple*, the love of beauty (in the form of a beautiful maiden) is no less lethal than it is in *L'Écume des jours*. Félicité, just as does Colin, falls in love with a girl who is doomed by fate, and, by the same token, seems to weave her own web (it is worth noting that Félicité's love for the coughing Virginie is sexual to the same extent that Colin's love for the coughing Chloé is paternal). Félicité's young charge - and recipient of her love - is also tightly entwined with a murderous plant: "Virginie... tressait des joncs..." (*Contes*, p.21). According to *Le Petit Robert*, 'un jonc' is: "(Une) Plante herbacée, à hautes tiges droites et flexibles, qui croît dans l'eau, les marécages...". The 'jonc' plays here a role comparable to that played by Vian's 'nénuphar'. This is the plant growing as part of a girl who dies; this is Chloé whose killer Colin seeks beneath the surface of the water; this is a plant which so resembles its victim that the two become indistinguishable: "[...] Au fond (de la rivière), de grandes herbes s'y penchaient, comme des chevelures de cadavres flottant dans l'eau." (*Contes*, p.39) The rapprochement of water and death can already be seen to be present in the 'joncs' of *Un cœur simple*. But, as also in *L'Écume*, water is equally the place of birth; whilst Colin is born in the shower, youth is portrayed running along the water's edge:

> [...] Et les enfants couraient, pour saisir des flocons d'écume que le vent emportait. Les flots, endormis en tombant sur le sable, se déroulaient le long de la grève; elle s'étendait à perte de vue, mais du côté de la terre avait pour limite les dunes la séparant du marais... (*Contes*, p.22)

Here, children run side by side with death, their lives traced (from the shore of birth to the swamp of death) by bubbles of froth floating on the breeze. (The 'children of the froth' are personified in the young cabin-boy, 'mousse' in French; here he is referred to, more specifically, as "un petit mousse" [*Contes*, p.24].) Chloé, too, lives her life endowed with the beauty of the piece of jazz, *Chloe*, apparently temporarily made oblivious to her sub-title, *The song of the Swamp*. Pestureau reminds us of the full significance of this wholly appropriate alternative title:

> [...] Elle est sous-titrée «Song of the Swamp» ou «chanson du marécage», ce qui offre maintes connotations avec les bayous du Mississippi, les plantes aquatiques tel le

nénuphar, l'univers louisianais du roman de William Faulkner, *Mosquitoes* (*Ej*,p.250).[13]

The items of the lexical group of which 'écume' is a part proliferate throughout *Un cœur simple*, providing a stock of vocabulary on which Vian will be able to draw for the title of his novel and the most poignant passages therein. It is this froth which ends Félicité's life: "Son agonie commença. Un râle, de plus en plus précipité, lui soulevait les côtes. Des bouillons d'écume venaient aux coins de sa bouche et tout son corps tremblait." (*Contes*, p.71)

Flaubert's short story appears also, and perhaps more surprisingly, to be at the origin of the comical representations of the members of the Church. (Michel Gauthier remarks: «[...] Il y a enfin une certaine similitude profonde entre le conte de Flaubert et celui de Vian dans la présentation en quelque sorte existentielle de l'illusion chrétienne.»[14]) The deformation of the titles of Vian's clergymen have been well documented, but the fact that his 'clin d'œil' to Flaubert ("merde flaubert l'avait déjà trouvé") is a clue as to the origin of three of his most colourful characters seems to have been overlooked. In a religious procession in *Un cœur simple* we find: "[...] Le suisse armé de sa hallebarde, le bedeau avec une grande croix... [et] la religieuse inquiète de ses petites filles." (*Contes*, p.70) In *L'Écume* 'le Chuiche' is not merely 'armé de sa hallebarde'; rather, he receives, on its account, what Queneau might call 'des conseils vestimentaires'. When he suggests that he should carry his red halberd on the occasion of Colin and Chloé's wedding, he is quickly brought in line with the more suitable colour scheme: "Non, dit le Religieux, il faut la hallebarde jaune et la canne violette, ça sera plus distingué." (*Ej*, p.85)[15] Although Vian's Bedon does not carry 'une grande croix', le Religieux does have 'la grosse caisse' (le Bedon is left playing the fife). As the final touch, and that most characteristic of Vian's sense of humour, it is not the job of le

---

[13] Faulkner's work clearly has a wide and deep influence in terms of Vian's novels (both those 'signés Vian' and those of the Sullivan series). However, to highlight instances of intertextuality here would be simply to repeat work already covered in the introduction. For a complete review of Faulkner's influence, therefore, the reader should consult the following studies by Gilbert Pestureau: "Souvenirs de lectures anglo-saxonnes," *Obliques*, 8-9 (1976), 165-180; "L'influence anglo-saxonne dans l'œuvre de Boris Vian," in *Boris Vian: Colloque de Cerisy/2* (Paris: U.G.E., 1977), pp.285-308; *Boris Vian, les Amerlauds et les Godons* (Paris: U.G.E., 1978).

[14] Boris Vian. *L'Écume des jours*, p.104.

[15] There is a more serious motive behind the admonition of le Religieux which will be discussed later.

Religieux to look after the little girls; in *L'Écume* the attention paid to the 'Enfants de Foi' takes on a more dubious aspect: "Le Bedon et le Chuiche déshabillaient les Enfants de Foi pour remettre leurs costumes en place, et le Chuiche se chargeait spécialement des petites filles." (*Ej*, p.96) All this, in addition to the constant references in both texts to the brilliance of sunlight streaming through blinds (and, more especially, the gradual attenuation of this brilliance in *L'Écume des jours*), serves to show that what may have been regarded as merely the object of an off-the-cuff remark is, in fact, a generating text of Vian's first novel, and, as such, a work of some import. But the disclosure of the relevance of Flaubert's short story is just the beginning; it is now necessary to explore how Vian then proceeds to develop his own personal literary stance, his own intertextual project. For this, we must return to the original manuscript.

The completion of the first 'dactylogramme' in the April of 1946 represents the birth of Vian the novelist. The question of the extent to which Michelle Léglise contributes to the evolution of the final version of the text is raised by consideration of the 1994 version of *L'Écume des jours*, but, although a point of interest in its own right, this does not concern this study. What we are interested in is the evolution of a tentative and naïve draft, reminiscent of the earlier *Vercoquin et le plancton*, into the wholly professional finished product which appears on sale, proudly bearing the title *L'Écume des jours*, on 30 April 1947.

The froth of Surrealism

As well as providing an initial insight into the seriousness of the novelistic project which Vian is seeking to undertake in the writing *L'Écume des jours*, the use of the word *écume* provides a key to the web of intertextuality through which the writing functions. *Écume,* firstly through its appearance in the title, heralds a proliferation of paradigms, and, indeed, a vocabulary rich in its frothiness (it is worth noting that the importance of froth is deemed crucial by Stanley Chapman who was responsible for the English translation of the text in 1967.[16]) The most important function of this

---

[16] Boris Vian, *Froth on the Daydream*, trans. by Stanley Chapman (London: Rapp and Carroll, 1967).

recurrence is not merely to set a mood whose importance lies in its obscurity (here, there is no facile use of obscurity for obscurity's sake), but, rather, it serves to focus the reader's attention towards certain privileged (to use a word whose own intertextual relevance will become clear in due course) passages which receive 'meaning' via consideration of a network of key feeder texts. The reader of *L'Écume* will, to some extent, be sent on a voyage of discovery which recalls the practice laid out by Breton in his first manifesto of Surrealism:

> [...] Rappelons que l'idée de surréalisme tend simplement à la récupération totale de notre force psychique par un moyen qui n'est autre que la descente vertigineuse en nous, *l'illumination systématique des lieux cachés et l'obscurcissement progressif des autres lieux*, la promenade perpétuelle en pleine zone interdite... (My italics.)[17]

The idea Breton presents here is calling for a new vision of the material world; in terms of the Vian novel it suggests a method of reading and/or interpretation. The italicised portion of the above text makes its way into *L'Écume* in the following, initially obscure, statement made by Colin whilst applying for his first job : "Le plus clair de mon temps, [...] je le passe à l'obscurcir." (*Ej*, p.155)

Indeed, the passage to which the reader is led in the pursuit of 'words of frothiness' is profoundly obscure. Standing as it does in the middle of a dialogue, this the most enigmatic paragraph of the novel becomes the single most important key to any understanding of Vian's literary project:

> A l'endroit où les fleuves se jettent dans la mer, il se forme une barre difficile à franchir, et de grands remous écumeux où dansent les épaves. Entre la nuit du dehors et la lumière de la lampe, les souvenirs refluaient de l'obscurité, se heurtaient à la clarté et, tantôt immergés, tantôt apparents, montraient leur ventre blanc et leur dos argenté. (*Ej*, p.122)

---

[17] André Breton, *Manifestes du Surréalisme* (Paris: Gallimard, 1972), p.92.

This 'endroit' is the location of the novel. As do the rivers, all potential lines of criticism come together to fuse. It is within this fusion that lies all meaning. Thus, to some extent, all readings contain validity, their combined total producing a richness which then mirrors/creates the richness of the text itself.

What Vian is actually doing here is not, however, constructing a work whose vagueness alone will provide its meaning through a complex of posthumous criticism. He quite deliberately sets out to ground his novel within the framework of pre-existing texts which themselves adhere to their own respective schools of analysis and meaning. There is one artistic movement whose weltanschauung is grounded precisely in this kind of fusion: the eddies of 'la barre difficile à franchir' are in the middle of two contrary currents: they mark the impossibility of going one way or the other. This ground which is neither one thing or the other finds resonance in the school of Surrealism. Again it is Michel Gauthier who draws attention to the importance of Surrealism upon Boris Vian's work:

> On a indiqué [déjà] la probabilité que les surréalistes, et en particulier Breton, ont joué, comme ils l'ont fait pour la plupart des gens de sa génération, le rôle d'intercesseurs entre Vian et certaines références d'importance majeure.[18]

Moments of 'surreality' are precisely moments of coincidence of two worlds, those of the conscious and the subconscious, which normally run parallel. One of the most famous depictions of this simultaneous movement and non-movement, this meeting of contrary and incompatible forces, is given by André Breton. The following lines are taken from *Nadja*:

> Elle [la beauté] est comme un train qui bondit sans cesse dans la gare de Lyon et dont je sais qu'il ne va jamais partir, qu'il n'est pas parti. Elle est faite de saccades, dont beaucoup n'ont guère d'importance, mais que nous savons destinées à amener une *Saccade*, qui en a.[19]

---

[18] *Boris Vian. L'Écume des jours*, p.104.

[19] André Breton, *Nadja* (Paris, Gallimard, 1945), p.214. (Hereafter referred to as *Nadja*.)

According to the vision of the world developed in *Nadja*, this interstitial region is the meeting place of the individual sub-conscious and a consciousness of the material world: the resultant plane of existence is another reality, or surreality. Surreality becomes the truth within which beauty can attain its essential reality: "La beauté sera CONVULSIVE ou ne sera pas." (*Nadja*, p.215) It is thus the quest for this beauty which becomes the stuff of life, not only for Breton, but also for Vian who, in his 'avant-propos', stresses the primacy of love and beauty: "Il y a seulement deux choses: c'est l'amour, de toutes les façons, avec des jolies filles, et la musique de la Nouvelle-Orléans ou de Duke Ellington, c'est la même." (*Ej*, p.40) Gauthier explicitly mentions *Nadja* when discussing the influence of the Surrealists (he also mentions other texts which will serve as intertexts at some stage in this book):

> La *Chasse au Snark* était en 43 ou 44 un texte rare, et sans doute l'a-t-il connue dans la traduction d'Aragon, et peut-être le chat du dernier chapitre de *L'Écume* doit-il aussi quelque chose à *Alice*; le pianocktail, c'est l'idée de l'orgue à liqueurs reprise et élaborée par un ingénieur-pour-de-bon pour réaliser l'essence inspirée de Colin; mais n'a-t-il pas fait la rencontre de Huysmans d'abord chez Breton qui dans *Nadja* lui voue une révérence elle aussi à première vue surprenante?[20]

At this stage it is clearly not enough to say that Vian is simply making allusions to various literary genres; he is not merely playing at Surrealism. By interpreting the textual messages left in the text, the reader can employ various different reading strategies in order to isolate the relevant meanings. Despite Jean Clouzet's claim that Vian's project was quite other than that carried out by the Surrealist group[21], the textual keys that have been exposed thus far do offer

---

[20] *Boris Vian. L'Écume des jours*, p.105.

[21] "Il n'existe aucune affinité profonde entre Boris Vian et la famille des surréalistes. Certes, plusieurs de ses œuvres, sinon toutes, font intervenir des procédés qui rappellent souvent la manière surréaliste. Nombre de ses actions paraissent même avoir été mises en scène par le Buñuel du *Chien andalou*, tandis que nombre de ses créatures paraissent avoir été rechampies par Salvador Dali. [...] Mais, à y regarder de plus près, on s'aperçoit qu'il ne s'agit là que de co-incidences dans la recherche de l'inouï et dans le refus des conformismes. En réalité, les analogies prennent fin avec cette constatation. Si les effets obtenus sont parfois comparables, les moyens d'y parvenir et, plus encore, les intentions sont radicalement opposés. En schématisant à

the reader particular reading strategies that cannot be explained by analysis of the Vian text alone. The interstitial area where rivers meet the sea is home not only to the characters of *L'Écume des jours*, but to all characters born in the fusion of dream and objective reality: this is the realm of 'le hasard objectif'. For the Surrealists objective chance was the imposition of the subjective world of the individual's dream onto that of objective 'reality', thereby the very centre of surreality. The centre of the surreality inherent in *L'Écume* is to be found in Chloé.

When Colin meets Chloé it becomes instantly apparent that she encapsulates the two virtues extolled by Vian in his 'avant-propos'. Firstly, she is clearly 'une jolie fille'; Colin's libidinal compass has already directed him towards her, at a party where: " La moyenne des filles était présentable." Secondly, she is the music of Duke Ellington: "[...] Etes-vous arrangée par Duke Ellington ?" (*Ej*, p.67) Thus, Chloé is the product of a dual projection of Colin's subconscious desire onto external reality. The nature of this reality is unique, and, as such, not to be confused with any reality experienced by the reader. This is an instance of Surrealist reality; Michel Gauthier believes Colin's attraction to Chloé to be an example of 'l'amour fou':

> [...] Breton et Vian sont hommes d'une énorme culture tous azimuts [...] notamment picturale [...] L'amour fou: il lui suffit d'une rencontre, il est donné tout entier, et pour toujours, coup de foudre sublimé par la si longue tradition courtoise que Colin et Chloé n'ont plus guère besoin, pour philtre, que d'un cocktail.[22]

---

l'extrême, on peut dire que le surréalisme fait un usage intensif du 'hasard objectif', ce qui n'est pas, *nous l'avons vu* [my italics], le projet de Vian. A moins qu'on ne commette l'erreur de confondre la liberté totale dont jouissent les protagonistes de ses œuvres - liberté totale mais *après* 'programmation' - avec le hasard, 'objectif' ou non." (Jean Clouzet, *Boris Vian*, p.60-61.)

This adamant denial of any rapprochement of Vian's writing with that of the Surrealist groups seems to take precious little account of *L'Écume des jours*, and seems to arise from a belief that 'effects', 'methods' and 'intentions' are each independent, autonomous beings; this study considers that the opposite is the case: it is, thus, precisely the literary procedures which Vian employs that help create effect, and therein lie his intentions...

[22] Boris Vian. *L'Écume des jours*, p.110.

The creation of Chloé is the goal both of author and 'main protagonist' (the inverted commas express certain doubts as to the actual value of the respective characters since Colin is not necessarily at the top of every hierarchy):

> Sa réalisation matérielle proprement dite consiste essentiellement en la projection de la réalité en atmosphère biaise et chauffée, sur un plan de référence irrégulièrement ondulé et présentant de la distorsion. (*Ej*, p.40)

The reality into which Colin is transported is one in which he and Chloé become the sole purpose for each other's existence, a reality in which "la majeure partie du monde se mit à compter pour du beurre." (*Ej*, p.68) It is the very concept of reality which is challenged here. Vian quite deliberately exploits the notion that objectivity equals truth. In the following passage 'la vraie réalité' is more blatantly oneiric than the (dream)world to which Colin is transported by the playing of the record (the encounter between the physical manifestation of Chloé and the Platonic essence of *Chloe*, the arrangement by Duke Ellington providing the port-hole into another world):

> Mais comme il fallait s'y attendre, le disque s'arrêta. Alors, seulement, Colin revint à la vraie réalité et s'aperçut que le plafond était à claire-voie, au travers de laquelle regardaient les locataires d'en dessus, qu'une épaisse frange d'iris d'eau cachait le bas des murs... (*Ej*, p.68)

The existence of an alternative to the material world is postulated here, and attempts to sustain the personal world (that sought by the individual's subconscious desires) provide the driving force of the narrative. Crucial is the issue of the possibility of investing the characters of a self-consciously fictitious work of literature with a 'real' psychological profile, including subconscious desires. At times the brief exchanges of dialogue between characters seem to be reminiscent of the enunciations of theatrical creations such as 'les Smith', the two-dimensional mouth-pieces for Ionesco's theatricality in *La Cantatrice chauve* (one of the works which can be most usefully used when searching for influences on Vian's later theatre). In Ionesco's work the only 'real' character could be said to be language itself which seeks existence via the puppet-like Smith family. In *L'Écume des jours* (which appeared three years before *La Cantatrice chauve*) there is an intricate balance between instances of puppet-like behaviour and insight into glimpses of actual psychological identity. It would seem to be the case that Colin, Chloé and Alise are the first tentative expressions of Vian's novelistic reality, the materialisations of his creative desires. Roger Shattuck, in his introduction to Richard Howard's translation of *Histoire du Surréalisme* by Maurice Nadeau, speaks of the objectives of the Surrealists in terms which are more than appropriate to Colin's enterprise with regard to Chloé: "Driven by extreme inquisitiveness and self-imposed daring, they dropped everything else and affirmed these moments (of 'objective chance') as the only true reality, as expressive of both the randomness and the hidden order that surrounds us."[23] These words capture another possibilty of understanding the fusion of the waters of the rivers and the sea: the meeting of chance (the justification of free will) and fate (the order of determinism). Clearly the two binaries, free will and determinism and psychological and two-dimensional, run parallel. Before the effects of these binaries can be assessed, a closer look at how Colin's meeting with Chloé functions as an example of objective chance is needed.

Objective chance is based on the premise expounded by Freud in *The Psychopathology of Everyday Life* that one is made prone to certain occurrences due to one's subconscious wishes. Colin's wishes are made explicit both to himself and to the reader (it will be argued later that Colin's desire to be in love is not necessarily the full expression of his subconscious wishes): "Je voudrais être amoureux, dit Colin." (*Ej*, p.62) The proof that the encounter with Chloé is an example of objective chance does not rely solely, however, on the conjugating, in a sort of summoning ritual, of the verb 'vouloir être amoureux'. Chloé's status as the descendant of pre-existing literary figures provides more useful evidence. It is precisely the example of an encounter with an enigmatic woman that Breton uses to develop his theory of objective chance. In *Nadja* Breton is similarly drawn to the object of his desires: "Tout à coup, alors qu'elle est peut-être encore à dix pas de moi, venant en sens inverse, je vois une jeune femme, très pauvrement vêtue, qui, elle aussi, me voit ou m'a vu." (*Nadja*, p.78) Although Breton's desire for Nadja remains more firmly in the subconscious than does Colin's, there are too many

---

[23] Roger Shattuck, "Love and Laughter: Surrealism Reappraised", in Maurice Nadeau, *The History of Surrealism*, trans. by Richard Howard (New York, The Macmillan Company, 1965), pp.11-34 (p.21).

similarities for the intertextual link to be ignored. For example, the fortuitous nature of further meetings:

> [Breton] Contrairement à l'ordinaire, je choisis de suivre le trottoir droit de la rue de la chaussée-d'Antin. Une des premières personnes que je m'apprête à y croiser est Nadja, sous son aspect du premier jour. (*Nadja*, p.98)

> [Colin] Et, dans le gâteau, il y avait un nouvel article de Partre pour Chick et un rendez-vous avec Chloé, pour Colin. (*Ej*, p.73)

In *The Psychopathology of Everyday Life*, Freud reveals how the wishes of the subconscious become apparent to consciousness via slips of the tongue, bungled actions and so on. Given the importance of this book (as well as that of Freud's work on the interpretation of dreams), it is clear that Breton was keen to reveal the strength of his own subconscious, to show how the dreamworld, running parallel to the world of waking thought, can direct actions. This he did by his exploitation of the theme of the dream-woman. So it is that when we look at Nadja, we see not an ordinary woman, but an example of a woman who is as she is named: "Elle me dit son nom, celui qu'elle s'est choisi: «Nadja, parce qu'en russe c'est le commencement du mot espérance, et parce que ce n'en est que le commencement.»" (*Nadja*, p.84) Thus, Nadja is not love itself; she is but the beginning, the beacon heralding the woman who will let Breton feel 'l'amour fou'. Nadja is the pathway to X, the woman who will be moulded by the true intensity of objective chance, by whom he will be inspired to conclude in the necessarily convulsive nature of love. By the same token, it is not the case that Chloé is merely playing the role of indicator of Colin's subconscious; it is in Chloé that Colin has his fictional identity, his psychological depth. For, Chloé too is codeword. As so often in Freud's examples, a word's real meaning lies in its sound. The phonetic transcription of her name permits an analysis of Chloé's textual significance:

$$\text{CHLOÉ} \quad > \quad /\text{klo}/ \quad + \quad /\text{e}/$$

The first word contained within Chloé is 'clos' (/klo/). This means 'closed', 'finished'. Whereas Nadja is pure beginning, Chloé is the beginning of the end: her beginning is an end. And just as Nadja is the beginning of love, so Chloé is its end. We find the repetition of the phoneme /e/ in the word 'aimer' (/eme/). Indeed, what else does the Surrealist object represent if not love? Roger

Shattuck is categorical about the importance of the woman/love-object for the Surrealists:

> Much more than in any 'mental vantage point', they found in passionate devotion to a single woman over a long period of time the surest means of liberating desire. [...] Amazingly enough, that kind of imagination, kindled in the house of love, brought back to poetry the long lost figure of woman as embodiment of magic powers, creature of grace and promise, always close in her sensibility and behaviour to the two sacred worlds of childhood and madness. The cult of the mythical woman, foreign as it may be to some contemporary readers, lies at the heart of the Surrealist credo.[24]

Nadja and Chloé are therefore Surrealist objects, each "without any other purpose than the satisfaction of its maker" a "created object that realizes the desires of the unconscious, of the dream."[25] Their artificiality is crucial to an end made explicit in *Nadja*, and left repressed (at least for the reader) in *L'Écume des jours*. Nadja is the oneiric expression of Blanche Derval, the actress by whom Breton was bewitched. With the paints and brushes of his mind he created his own ersatz Blanche (much as le Maréchal-ferrant seems to do with the robotic Clémentine in *L'Arrache-Cœur*):

> Curieusement fardée, comme quelqu'un qui, ayant commencé par les yeux, n'a pas eu le temps de finir, mais le bord des yeux si noir pour une blonde. [...] Il est intéressant de noter, à ce propos, que Solange, même vue de très près, ne paraissait en rien maquillée. (*Nadja*, p.78)

Even the heavy theatrical make-up, with which we can assume Blanche to have been covered, cannot dim her radiance as a 'mythical woman'. The

---

[24] *The History of Surrealism*, p.25.

[25] *Ibid.*, p.185.

implication has already been made that, in as much as it expresses a wish known to his conscious mind, Colin's desire to be in love is insufficient. It is a real love which satiates this desire, a love which has its object in Chloé. But where is the fruit-bowl behind the still-life? By clever Freudian analysis of a parapraxis, Alain Costes provides the clue[26]. Colin, struck by the radiance of Alise and knowing her to be Chick's by right, makes a conscious effort to keep her out of his mind: "C'était une pensée à éviter. Alise appartenait à Chick de plein droit." (*Ej*, p.56) He then tries to force himself to fall in love, as has Chick, to be happy through the completion of a process of 'meet > fall in love with > love' (/klo/ /e/). The result is the following slip of the tongue: "[...] Elle s'appellerait Al... elle s'appellerait Onésime." (*Ej*, p.63) Costes reconstructs the fragmentary name and the (innocent) replacement:

   al/oné/zi/me

which he then rewrites:

   oné/me/al/iz

or :

   on aime Alise

Whether it is to this, or to the following hypobook ("[...] Pour peu, il est vrai, que l'on inverse le son <zi> en <iz>. Justement, les deux lettres <i> et <z> suffisent à elles seules à reconstituer le nom d'Isis. [...] on aime Isis."[27]), which Pestureau objects[28], it is possible that even Costes does not grasp the full implications of his analysis.

It is not the case, then, that the feelings which Colin has towards Alise only become love when he meets Chloé. Chloé actually is the expression of Colin's love for Alise. The same division exists between these two 'jolies filles', as did between Nadja and Blanche. The love object is once again an artificial representation of her (mythical) original:

[...] Alise était vraiment en beauté ce soir.

---

[26] The following analysis of Colin's slip of the tongue appears in Alain Costes' paper "Le Désir de Colin" which can be found in *Boris Vian: Colloque de Cerisy/1* (Paris, U.G.E., 1977), pp.169-177 (esp. p.173).

[27] *Boris Vian: Colloque de Cerisy/1*, p.173.

[28] "Alain Costes a offert une (psych)analyse intéressante - peut-être trop subtile? - de la substitution de Colin." (*Ej*, p.254)

> - Quel parfum avez-vous? dit-il. Chloé se parfume à l'essence d'orchidée bidistillée.
> - Je n'ai pas de parfum!... dit Alise.
> - C'est naturel! dit Chick. (*Ej*, p.79)

This short burst of dialogue, at first glance so innocuous, is saturated with textual keys. It is not only the act of wearing perfume which is important here; why is it 'd'orchidée bidistillée'? After Colin's first encounter with Alise he picks two orchids, which just happen to appear before him. The first, 'une orchidée bleue et rose', recalls the perfume of Alise's hair. The second, 'une orchidée orange et grise', resembles the mouse with the black whiskers. The essence of both these orchids goes into the distillation of Chloé's perfume: Colin, thus, gives her her fragrance. The act of picking the orchids is also important because their very existence is derived from Colin's walk in the street. Colin becomes the urban 'flâneur'. With the streets of Paris, emanating from his flat, as the place of his 'flânerie', Colin is more tightly bound to his literary past. It is essential that Breton be walking in Paris for his dreams to become reality (even when he tries not to summon his dreams, his location can prove too propicious: "De manière à n'avoir pas trop à flâner..." [*Nadja*, p.97]). The combination of the flowers and the 'flânerie' summons another literary predecessor of vital importance to the understanding of *L'Écume des jours*. Marguerite, the heroine of *La Dame aux Camélias*, is both named after the flowers she wears and summoned from the Parisian streets by her lover, Armand. Chloé, who, like Marguerite, has an infection of the lungs, could easily bear the title 'la Dame aux Orchidées'. This would, of course be to draw too heavily on just one feature of rich cultural heritage. For, although Chloé does bring about the beginning of the end, she cannot be pinned down to one single literary origin; as has been seen, Jeanne-Marie Baude points out in her article "L'Espace vital": "La perturbation du récit ne s'arrête pas là: si elle se réduisait à cette maladie, Chloé risquerait fort d'être «la dame aux camélias» du roman moderne, et le roman ne «tiendrait» pas."[29] It is precisely because Chloé has such a diverse background that she controls such a plurality of 'meaning' within the text, and, therefore, that the novel does 'hold up'. Chloé is daughter both to Nadja and to Marguerite, but her role here is to represent the

---

[29] Jeanne-Marie Baude, "L'Espace vital", in *Lecture plurielle de 'L'Ecume des jours'*, ed. by Alain Costes (Paris: U.G.E., 1979), pp.70-124, (p.71).

materialisation of Colin's love for Alise. To this end, it must not be overlooked that the principal utensil with which Colin fashions her is the music of Duke Ellington.

Jazz and the synaesthetic novel

This composer, pianist, band leader and, importantly, arranger of music is not only much appreciated by Colin, but by the inhabitants of Vian's world in general. So great is the desire to absorb this music that the auditory senses alone are insufficient. Those seeking an orgy of synaesthetic pleasure have only to fall back on their literary predecessors. Thus, when Colin creates a piano which can blend a cocktail to match the melody he plays, which, in turn, corresponds to his mood, he (just as his author) is not creating in a void:

> C'est l'un des objets fétiches du roman: il matérialise des synesthésies privilégiées, il renouvelle, perfectionne et modernise le «clavecin pour les yeux» du Père Castel qui voulait rendre visible le son [...], ainsi que l'«orgue à bouche» de Des Esseintes, héros raffiné de Joris-Karl Huysmans... (*Ej*, p.243-4)

Pestureau is right to refer the reader to *A Rebours*, where des Esseintes, possibly the greatest aesthete of them all, creates his 'orgue à bouche' as just part of a comprehensive aesthetic project: "Des Esseintes buvait une goutte, ici, là, se jouait des symphonies intérieures, arrivait à se procurer, dans le gosier, des sensations analogues à celles que la musique verse à l'oreille."[30] This experience is particularly savoured by Vian's 'antiquitaire', who, at his first attempt, remains incredulous: "C'est exactement le goût du blues, dit-il. De ce blues-là même."(*Ej*, p.159)

Those who sit at the 'pianocktail' to create cocktails to assuage their particular thirst (the connoisseur being able to express the current state of his desire with perfect exactitude thanks to this fantastic machine) draw almost

---

[30] J.-K. Huysmans, *A Rebours* (Paris, Garnier-Flammarion, 1978), p.99. (Hereafter referred to as *A Rebours*.)

exclusively on the 'airs' of the Duke. But as with all cases of intertextuality, and indeed 'intermusicality', it is the exceptions which provide the most interesting examples (for, otherwise, it would indeed be sufficient to say that Vian has used his own musical tastes as a means of 'colouring' his text). Chick's first mood is best rendered drinkable by *Loveless Love*. Pestureau points out in his notes that this title refers to "l'un des nombreux blues recueillis dans la tradition ou composés par W.C. Handy" (*Ej*, p.244), a piece of music which Ellington had arranged, but not written. For Pestureau, the importance of this reference lies in the deliberate transposition of the original title, *Careless Love*, which defines his subsequent treatment of his own love ("les deux titres - amour sans amour ou amour négligent - annoncent la conduite future de Chick avec Alise"). The transposition can be seen to be yet more revealing when one discovers that Handy did actually write a piece entitled *Loveless Love*. Whether the similarity of the two titles contributes to a parapraxis on Chick's part (his subconscious thinking of his 'careless' treatment of Alise), or whether he correctly selects this piece, with the full agreement of his subconscious, remains nicely unclear. The lyrics of *Loveless Love* convey the sentiments of the whole story, and not merely Chick's perspective:

> Love is like a goldbrick in a bunco game, like a bank-note with a bogus name. Both have caused many downfalls, Love has done the same. [...]
> Love has for its emblem Cupid with his bow. Loveless love has lots and lots of dough. So carry lots of Jack and pick'em as you go. [...]
> For Love, oh love, oh loveless love has set our hearts on goalless goals. From milkless milk, and silkless silk, we are growing used to soulless souls. Such grafting times we never saw [...] In eveything we find a flaw. Even love, oh love, oh loveless love.
> You set our hearts on goalless goals, with dreamless dreams and schemeless schemes, we wreck our love boats on the shoals.[31]

---

[31] For the complete scripts of *Loveless Love* and *Careless Love*, see *A Treasury of the Blues*, ed. by W.C. Handy (New York: Charles Boni, 1925), p.129 and 46 respectively.

These words convey a real feeling of melancholy, a disillusionment with love itself; they also reflect upon the nature of *L'Écume*, at once real and oneiric (what could be more apt than 'dreamless dream'?). A further look at *Nadja* reveals the same idea of a being/non-being : "[...] Elle [the star which Nadja can see and to which Breton cannot aspire] est comme le cœur d'une fleur sans cœur." (*Nadja*, p.91) The heart of which heartless flower? It is tempting to suggest the artichoke, since in French 'avoir un cœur d'artichaut' means 'to wear one's heart on one's sleeve', and it is precisely this tendency which *Careless Love* warns against: "If I were a little bird, I'd fly from tree to tree, I'd build my nest way up in the air where the bad boys could not bother me." The song also recognises the difficulty of putting such wise counsel into practice: "Now I wear my apron high, and he never, never passes by." Certainly, for the cast of *L'Écume des jours*, to remain aloof where love is concerned is an impossibility (note that for Chick, 'l'amour fou' comes in the form of Jean-Sol Partre, and that all his 'jack' departs in the same direction[32]); the literary tradition of fatal love is too strong. When one has for a predecessor a woman named Marguerite, known as 'la Dame aux Camélias', one's heart becomes inextricable from one's sleeve.

The other piece of Blues which derives from an arrangement by, and not a composition of, Duke Ellington is *Chloe*. Thus, her father is not the Duke (although it has been commented upon that the 'le chef d'orchestre' plummets to his death, in a final fit of paternal jealousy, just before Chloé's act of marriage[33]); he is responsible for her arrangement. Colin is not actually her father (although the closeness of the couples in the text, at times, suggests a family rather than pairs of lovers); he is her interpreter[34]. She is born of the Blues, and is thus summoned into the text by virtue of her 'moody' qualities (note that W.C. Handy may well, as 'Father of the Blues', be attributed the title of Chloé's grandfather...). For, Blues is music which, more than any other,

---

[32] As Pestureau points out, "la variante première" of Chick is «Jacques Chicago». As before, it is crucial that Jacques (Jack and Jacques Loustalot/Le Major) and Chicago ("l'une des grandes villes de jazz) cede before the pleasingly English/American-sounding version.

[33] As Alain Costes notes in "Le désir de Colin": "Et si l'on peut trouver dans la chute du chef d'orchestre, lors de la cérémonie de mariage, une représentation de la «chute» du père - après tout Chloé n'est-elle pas «arrangée» par un chef d'orchestre de haute renommée? - on voit du même coup que c'est un père qui choit de lui-même." (*Boris Vian: Colloque de Cerisy/1*, p.175)

[34] Vian talks himself of the respective importance of composers, interpreters and arrangers in *En Avant La Zizique* (Paris: U.G.E., 1993).

relies on mood; it *is* mood. Just as Chloé is Blues, so is *L'Écume des jours* (in *The Concise Oxford Dictionary of Music*, Blues is defined as follows: "**BLUES**. Slow jazz song of lamentation, generally for an unhappy love affair."). And, as those who drink their moods via the wonders of the 'pianocktail', Colin creates a girl to meet his desire. Abbe Niles writes: "Typically it [a Blues] originated as an expression of the singer's feeling, complete in a single verse."[35] Whereas Stanley Chapman's version picks up the aspect of the dream in its title, other translations of *L'Écume des jours* have singled out the importance of the Blues, and indeed Chloé as the Blues (for example, John Sturrock's American translation has an Ellington piece as its title, *Mood Indigo*[36]).

Are we, then, to suppose that were *Chloe* to be played on the 'pianocktail' a deep, ink-blue coloured cocktail would be created? This is not impossible; and yet, such a cocktail would only capture the 'blue' mood which Colin feels when she is gone. Chloé combines the dark moodiness of the Blues with a golden warmth (which is what Colin feels at the birth of their love). It seems tempting to suggest, therefore, that the cocktail of the song would be similar to a Tequila Sunrise, combining both a dark and a golden layer; more precisely, a 'Chloé Sunrise' would be, in harmony with the predominant colour scheme of the novel as a whole, a blend of violet and yellow.

This is the colour scheme to which all the characters of *L'Écume* adhere. Clearly, such a deliberate and persistent use of these two colours implies that these colours have a real significance for Vian, and that he is tempting the reader to delve further. Pestureau suggests a direction for such a search:

> Y aurait-il une relation entre ces couleurs et la musique? Il est précisé dans l'article «Clavecin» de l'*Encyclopédie* que le jaune correspond à mi et le violet à la. (*Ej*,p.246.)

The idea of an example of one of the senses corresponding to one from another sense, this concept of synaesthesia, is part of a larger French literary tradition. The word correspondence itself recalls a poem by Baudelaire on

---

[35] Abbe Niles, "The Story of the Blues", in *A Treasury of the Blues*, pp.9-32 (p.9).

[36] Boris Vian, *Mood Indigo*, trans. by John Sturrock (New York, Grove Press, 1968).

exactly this idea of the fusing of the senses. The following line, from the second stanza of "Correspondances", describes nature's own 'pianocktail' according to which: "Les parfums, les couleurs et les sons se répondent." Rimbaud, too, constructs a keyboard upon which vowel sounds correspond to colours, colours to smells and, ultimately, to a woman; the last line of "Voyelles" reads: "- O l'Oméga, rayon violet de ses yeux!".

And yet, Colin's most 'colour-conscious' literary predecessor is he to whom Pestureau has already referred in relation to the 'pianocktail': des Esseintes. To discover if and when des Esseintes uses yellow and violet would be to gain an understanding of Vian's palette. And use these two colours he does; in fact, they expose the very heart of his aesthetic project:

> Regardant, un jour, un tapis d'Orient, à reflets, et, suivant les lueurs argentées qui couraient sur la trame de la laine, jaune aladin et violet prune, il s'était dit: il serait bon de placer sur ce tapis quelque chose qui remuât et dont le ton foncé aiguisât la vivacité de ces teintes. (*A Rebours*, p.95)

It becomes apparent that des Esseintes and Colin are joined in the pursuit of a common aim. They are both (being at the mercy of authors whose aims are to blend intimately, and to the point of indistinguishability, fiction and reality) so concerned with their own manipulation of reality that all else fades by the wayside. Vian's stated intent, which defines Colin's actions, ("[...] Sa réalisation matérielle proprement dite consiste essentiellement en la projection de la réalité en atmosphère biaise et chauffée, sur un plan de référence irrégulièrement ondulé et présentant de la distorsion." [*Ej*, p.40]) can be seen to coincide with des Esseintes' own theory:

> A son avis, il était possible de contenter les désirs réputés les plus difficiles à satisfaire dans la vie normale, et cela par un léger subterfuge, par une approximative sophistication de l'objet poursuivi par ces désirs même. (*A Rebours*, p.79)

What is more, neither of them realises that he already has achieved more than he ought really to expect from life (is this the moral of the tale?). Des Esseintes has already selected his yellow and violet carpet because of its beauty; Colin is already surrounded by beauty, wrapped, more often than not, in the same colours (when he goes ice-skating, he dons "une paire de chaussettes de laine à larges bandes jaunes et violettes alternées" [*Ej*, p.51] only to meet two pretty girls identically dressed in outfits which complement his own); but they both feel the need to enhance that which is already perfect.

Des Esseintes takes a tortoise (whose shell endows it with a striking natural beauty, to the qualities of which one would expect this aesthete to be sensible), which he then has gilded. Still not satisfied, he further adorns the shell, this time with precious gems. He does not, however, select any ordinary jewels; rather, he searches for shades of colour, and then for nuances of those shades:

> Il se décida enfin pour des minéraux dont les reflets devaient s'alterner: pour l'hyacinthe de Compostelle, rouge acajou; l'aigue marine, vert glauque; rubis-balais, rose vinaigre; le rubis de Sudermanie, ardoise pâle. (*A Rebours*, p.98)

Huysmans quotes Verlaine to reveal the purity of des Esseintes' treatment of the artificial:

> Car nous voulons la nuance encore,
> Pas la couleur, rien que la nuance
> ....
> Et tout le reste est littérature. (*A Rebours*, p.212)

Reasons for pedantry of this kind can be traced in another story concerned with the quest for ultimate beauty, Balzac's *Le Chef-d'œuvre inconnu*, where beauty does not just happen, but where, instead, it must be pinned down and conquered:

> La beauté est une chose sévère et difficile qui ne se laisse point atteindre ainsi; il faut attendre ses heures, l'épier, la presser et l'enlacer étroitement pour la forcer à se rendre.[37]

---

[37] Honoré de Balzac, *Le Chef-d'œuvre inconnu* (Paris: Gallimard, 1994), p.44.

Balzac's story is the tale of a painter, Frenhofer, who leads the world in the rendering of life to paintings, a master of form. It is his desire to create the most beautiful form ever witnessed by the human eye. He only fully realises the futility of his quest when he is confronted by the naturally, and outstandingly, beautiful Gillette. The relationship between Gillette and the painting (a poetic representation of an idealized Gillette, whom Frenhofer had previously only imagined) is akin to that which will exist between Blanche Derval and Breton's Nadja. Artificial beauty appears to be ephemeral, and cannot endure in the face of its model. The love of the artificial thus becomes inevitably linked with madness.

Although des Esseintes' project is primarily concerned with the purest aesthetics, the reader is permitted a brief glimpse of the aesthete confronted by the sheer sexuality of the female form. Here, Salomé brings together devastating beauty, the perfection of a painter's art and the power of death. The combination enthrals des Esseintes; it also forms a model for Chloé which Colin will have little choice but to follow:

> Le peintre semblait avoir voulu affirmer sa volonté de rester hors des siècles, de ne point préciser d'origine, de pays, d'époque, en mettant sa Salomé au milieu de cet extraordiaire palais, d'un style confus et grandiose, en la vêtant de somptueuses et chimériques robes, en la mitrant d'un incertain diadème en forme de tour phénicienne tel qu'en porte la Salammbô, en lui plaçant dans la main *le sceptre d'Isis*, la fleur sacrée de l'Egypte et de l'Inde, *le grand lotus*. (My italics.) (*A Rebours*, p.107)

Thus, spurning that which surrounds him (despite knowing, in his heart of hearts, that he has already experienced love), he will accept 'le sceptre d'Isis' (it is at a party that Isis introduces Colin to Chloé, and where he perhaps prefers to ignore her true identity as the great water flower) in order to create a different order of beauty. For colour he selects a mood (the Blues), for shade of that mood he chooses *Chloe*, in the arrangement of Duke Ellington. For his basic object, he does not choose a tortoise (not even Colin has sunk as far as des Esseintes), but colours his other favourite creature, 'la jolie fille'. Colin thus arranges Chloé the girl in the same way as Ellington arranged the piece of music.

Unsurprisingly, crushed by the weight of its own beauty, or, rather, by the facticity of its own beauty, des Esseintes' tortoise dies. Colin is not deterred by this failure. He decides that he must build a safety measure into his creation. Where des Esseintes mixed colours and then perfumes, Colin (as we have already seen) combines the two arts. Unfortunately, Colin's desire to create conjures up the essence of death, in the form of the orchid. And yet, Chloé is not killed by an orchid, but by a 'nénuphar'. This twist is actually predictable if one takes the time to examine des Esseintes' methods more closely:

> Presque jamais, en effet, les parfums ne sont issus des fleurs dont ils portent le nom; l'artiste qui oserait emprunter à la seule nature ses éléments, ne produirait qu'une œuvre bâtarde, sans vérité, sans style, attendu que l'essence obtenue par la distillation des fleurs ne saurait offrir qu'une très lointaine et très vulgaire analogie avec l'arôme même de la fleur vivante, épandant ses effluves, en pleine terre. (*A Rebours*, p.153)

So, although as toxic as 'Essence of Orchids', Chloé actually receives 'Essence of Water Lily'. Whatever the similarities and differences between the aesthetic projects of Colin and des Esseintes, their final desolation is the same. Colin, in the misty swamp where his beloved Chloé is thrown into her watery grave, hears the other side of *Chloe*; he walks away with *la Chanson du marécage* for his sole accompaniment. Des Esseintes, too, has heard this funereal song:

> Jamais, sans que de nerveuses larmes lui montassent aux yeux, il n'avait pu se répéter «les Plaintes de la jeune fille», car il y avait dans ce lamento, quelque chose de plus que de navré, quelque chose d'arraché qui lui fouillait les entrailles, quelque chose comme une fin d'amour dans un paysage triste. (*A Rebours*, p.228)

Thus, *L'Écume*, which has an aesthetic project at its core, is itself part of a similar project. By this careful arrangement of his own work of art, Vian, too, puts himself on the side of the 'arrangers'; Colin is to Chloé precisely what Vian is to *L'Écume des jours*. Vian then, by his careful use of intertextuality, creates what could be called an artificial text. It is safe to assume that *L'Écume des jours* would have found a place on the book-shelves of des Esseintes ("En raison de son maquillage et de son air factice, ce paysage ne déplaisait pas à des Esseintes" [*A Rebours*, p.82]). The concept of bibliophilia is important in *L'Écume*, not only in as much as it forms the character of Chick, but since it underpins much of the structure of the novel itself. It seems clear that book-shelves and their contents are quite likely to have played an important role in the life of an avid reader such as Boris Vian.

CHAPTER TWO
L'Écume des jours:
Mac Orlan, Queneau *et* un autre

The arranger of the text

Much of the thrust of this study hinges upon Vian's literary intake (without which his output would not have been possible). When looking to create Chick, it is to his book-shelves that he turns for inspiration. Pestureau draws our attention to this early indecision: "Introduire l'histoire du type qui collectionne Mac Orlan ou Queneau ou un autre." (*Ej*, p.219) This chapter will deal with the importance of Queneau, Mac Orlan and Sartre, showing how their importance as cultural figures (especially in the case of Sartre whose role as contemporary icon clearly *is* satirised in the entrance of Partre) is secondary within *L'Écume des jours* to the intertextual importance of their respective novels, *Le Chiendent, Le Quai des brumes* and *La Nausée*. Just as the importance of Surrealism lies partially veiled beneath the superficial layers of Existentialism, so too Sartre's seminal pre-War text, and its own Surrealist elements, become obscured beneath his immediate post-War status. These three texts will each be shown to have an independent bearing upon *L'Écume*; and also, through their common features (including a debt to Céline's *Voyage au bout de la nuit*) they will be shown to have a certain degree of interdependence within a larger literary tradition. And finally, through these examinations of the complexity of Vian's plays on words, there will be shown to be the beginning of a mythology: the chapter will end with the disclosure of a tale for which the whole text becomes an allegory; and this tale can be seen to light the way forward into the second novel. There is, therefore, if not intratextuality itself, then, at least, a glimpse of what is to come.

Vian was a great reader, undervalued writer, but also a frenetic socialite. As a personal friend, Queneau's relationship with Vian is a matter of clear importance. It is, indeed, through Queneau that Vian meets the man whose work will finally consume Chick: Sartre is the 'autre', a man whose importance for Vian will gradually elevate him to the rank of 'Autre'. The links between Vian and both Queneau and Sartre are, then, clear: he was a friend of one and well-known, at least, to the other. All three belonged to the same extensive group of socialites. But what of Mac Orlan? Here the link is more exclusively literary. Vian was certainly as familiar with his works as he was with those of Queneau. The title of Mac Orlan's novel of 1927, *Le Quai des brumes*, and that of Vian's own are strikingly similar, both grammatically and phonetically:

        Le Quai des brumes > /lke/ /de/ /bRym/
        L'Écume des jours > /lekym/ /de/ /zur/

By the time of the composition of *L'Écume des jours*, the sea whence these titles arise had long since left its tide-mark in a cabaret well known to the inhabitants of Montmartre. A visitor's book in 'Le Lapin Agile' (whose proprietor, Frédé, is a character in Mac Orlan's novel) bears the following lines:

> Paris, la mer qui passe apporte
> Ce soir au coin de ta porte
> O tavernier du quai des Brumes
> Sa gerbe d'écume.

Max Jacob, in leaving mist and froth entwined in these enigmatic lines, bound together two novels, one of which would have to wait several years to be written.
      What is more, within the two books (which, for all that, are not strongly linked in terms of structure, being conjoined, rather, by a certain oneiric feel) the respective roles of 'mist' and 'froth' are highly comparable. Both are substances made of water, and yet which are sufficiently unlike water to warrant a different name. They float off the sea, bringing life and death in the same gust. Des Esseintes himself, with whose project Colin's own has been closely compared, retreated further into aesthetics when encircled by mist:

> [...] Des Esseintes qui, par les jours de brume, par les jours de pluie, [...] se grisait les yeux avec les chatoiements de ses étoffes, avec les incandescences de ses pierres... (*A Rebours*, p.213)

Colin can produce the same effects by raising coloured screens to filter the sunlight streaming through the windows of the white car. Why Chloé actually says to Colin, "Mets quelques couleurs" (*Ej*, p.99) is unclear. The reader is led to believe that the light is less good than on the usual road, which has become worn out since: "Tout le monde a voulu y rouler parce qu'il faisait beau tout le temps..." (*Ej*, p.99). The changes being forced upon Colin (whose love of light caused the presence in the novel of two suns) since his marriage to Chloé are already manifesting themselves. It is possible that Chloé is exhibiting a negative phototropism (actually shrinking away from the light) because there are already, in her lung, the beginnings of a 'nénuphar' which is straining to feed itself on every drop of available nourishment. Whatever the reasons for the adoption of des Esseintes' aversion to light (it will be seen later to what extent Chloé is a projection of Colin's heightening sense of nausea), the effects are the same:

> Colin pressa des boutons verts, bleus, jaunes, rouges, et les glaces correspondantes remplacèrent celles de la voiture. On se serait cru dans un arc-en-ciel, et sur la fourrure blanche, des ombres bariolées dansaient au passage de chaque poteau télégraphique. Chloé se sentit mieux. (*Ej*, p.99)

In Mac Orlan's novel, 'Le Quai des brumes' is the interstitial area which generates the characters; this is the "endroit où" of Vian's own novel. The 'épaves' which dance in Vian's frothy eddies, here, take the form of ladies of the night: "Le long de la Seine, des filles couperosées, quelquefois jeunes, guettaient dans l'ombre du quai."[38] And like 'souvenirs' which "refluaient de l'obscurité, se heurtaient à la clarté", they exist in the half light: "Le peuple de la nuit disparaissait, d'ailleurs, avec les premières lueurs du jour." (*Quai*, p.100)

Of all the characters it is Ernst who is drawn most strongly to 'le quai'. Dependent on the lifeblood of 'le peuple de la nuit', his existence becomes that of the vampire. This translation of the obsession with the created object from

---

[38] Pierre Mac Orlan, *Le Quai des brumes* (Paris: Gallimard, 1972), p.99. (Hereafter referred to as *Quai*.)

the standard *objet d'art* into the female form stands as an intermediary between the respective attitudes of des Esseintes and Colin:

> Ernst attendait le soir avec impatience, car il pouvait vivre sans vergogne. Il connaissait une fille toute jeune, blonde et gracieuse. Elle était rongée par la vermine, et si stupide qu'on ne savait en quelle langue lui adresser la parole. (*Quai*, p.100)

Although Chloé is not to be described as stupid, she is certainly depicted with an excessive childishness.

As is that of Colin and Chloé, the love that is between Ernst and the girl is the corporeal expression of a piece of music: "Ils ne se parlaient pas et marchaient côte à côte de même que les éléments simples d'une chanson populaire." (*Quai*, p.101) Like des Esseintes before him and Roquentin some years later, the artist of the story, Michel Kraus, seeks, in his art, escape from the nausea of existence. The peace that he finds he describes in terms of a record: "Une grande paix mécanique tournait en lui comme un disque de phonographe d'une musique particulièrement fluide." (*Quai*, p.108) (This is not the escape from existence which Roquentin seeks from the same source; it is precisely the pre-ordained rigidity of the sequence of notes that he cherishes in a record.) To become one, to fuse with his creations (in this case, his puppets) is what Michel hopes will remove him from the pain of living:

> Ah! si je n'étais pas plus haut que cet artilleur, pensait Michel Kraus, je pourrais vivre encore sans faire intervenir cet abominable dégoût de tout ce qui resurgira quand j'aurai décidé d'ouvrir les yeux. (*Quai*, p.109)

Colin is driven by the same desire, which Alain Costes, in his paper, "Le désir de Colin", calls, appropriately, "un besoin d'objet".[39] In response to Costes' paper, André Jarry underlines the attempt to fuse with the object which fuels this desire:

---

[39] *Boris Vian: Colloque de Cerisy*, p.172.

> "[...] Alors il fourra sa figure dans les cheveux de Chloé."
> Ce: *fourra sa figure dans les cheveux* décrit quelque chose de très fusionnel. C'est toute une coloration de leur relation qui est impliquée ici.[40]

Significantly, in *Le Quai des brumes*, the artist finds himself no more equipped to escape life than Ernst. It is precisely when his puppets appear to be acting in the same vampire-like fashion as Ernst that Michel's defence breaks down:

> Le gros pantin mordit l'autre au cou, derrière la nuque, et il resta longtemps accroché à sa victime, sans desserrer les dents et en fermant à demi ses gros yeux en os gratté.
> (*Quai*, p.110)

The kiss of Michel's puppet when compared to that of Colin reveals a certain similarity: "Il inclina légèrement sa tête et l'embrassa entre l'oreille et l'épaule. Elle frémit, mais ne retira pas sa tête."(*Ej*, p.69)[41]

As both fail, both Colin and Michel choose to die with, and in the manner of, their projects.[42] The death of Michel shares many elements with *L'Écume des jours*, particularly with the death of the mouse; both Michel and the mouse die with a feeling of remorse at leaving their fellow characters:

> Je ne regrette qu'une chose, pensa Michel Kraus, c'est de ne pas savoir de quelle manière mes compagnons de la dernière nuit vont liquider leurs petites affaires sérieuses.
> (*Quai*, p.113)

---

[40] *Ibid.*, p.182.

[41] This kiss will be discussed again later from Chloé's point of view. The two analyses together have the advantage of revealing how Chloé, as object, functions as Sartrean Other; both kiss, the active and passive roles being shared, depending on the perspective taken.

[42] Colin may or may not actually die. What is clear is that he gives up on life/living.

If her regrets can be said to resemble closely those of Michel Kraus, the manner of the mouse's death, at the end of *L'Écume*, is ordered by the fate of another mouse, this time from the works of Franz Kafka. In Kafka's short story, *A Little Fable* (which I shall quote in its entirety), the reader finds in condensed form all the crushing weight of life's attempts to overwhelm the individual (which pervades the oeuvre of both Kafka and Vian). The cat's words suggest that the mouse did have an alternative path (although this is probably a closed choice made apparent only in hindsight). Colin, too, has the possibility of acting otherwise, but the froth of days again takes over. Thus, both mice die (one directly, the other indirectly) as a result of a whole way of life (an apartment in *L'Écume*) being crushed to nothing:

> "Alas," said the mouse, "the world is growing smaller every day. At the beginning it was so big that I was afraid, I kept running and running, and I was glad when at last I saw walls far away to the right and left, but these long walls have narrowed so quickly that I am in the last chamber already, and there in the corner stands the trap that I must run into." "You only need to change your direction," said the cat, and ate it up.[43]

Although, in *Le Quai des brumes*, Juni does not decapitate him, Michel, like the mouse, commits suicide before a cat. He also, this time like Colin, decides to die with the music of his failure ringing in his ears (instead of a musical recording, Colin will take to his grave a photographic recording of his lost world: "il revient sur le bord et il regarde la photo." [*Ej*, p.207]):

> Soudain Michel Kraus sentit que les larmes lui montaient
> aux yeux. Il prit alors son phonographe, le remonta, choisit

---

[43] *The Short Stories of Franz Kafka*, ed. by Nahum N. Glatzer (London: Minerva, 1995), p.445. (Hereafter referred to as *Kafka*.)

un disque, le mit sur le plateau de l'appareil à portée de sa main sur le haut de l'armoire, à côté de Juni. (*Quai*, p.113)

Like Roquentin, in Sartre's *La Nausée*, it is as the record plays for the last time that Michel faces the after-life:

> D'une main, il poussa le déclic du phonographe et le disque se mit à tourner. Michel Krauss entendit le grincement caractéristique de l'aiguille sur le plateau de cire. Alors il donna un grand coup de pied dans la chaise et se pendit. (*Quai*, p.114)

Even that most obscure of lines which is the last one of Vian's novel finds a precursor in *Le Quai des brumes*. The suicide of the mouse is to be accomplished by means of a feline reflex, the trigger for which being the approach of: "onze petites filles aveugles de l'orphelinat de Jules l'Apostolique." (*Ej*, p.208) The little orphan girls are singing, what we are not told. Perhaps theirs is the same song which accompanies the suicide of Michel Krauss, who also performed before an audience: "Devant la fenêtre, une douzaine d'enfants qui se regardaient d'un air ravi, écoutaient le phonographe qui, consciencieusement, débitait une marche tzigane..." (*Quai*, p.114).

Intertextuality can be seen to provide a strong link between Mac Orlan's text and *L'Écume des jours*; and this link would appear to be a consciously worked one on the part of Vian. Apart from a single line of a manuscript documenting his indecision as to which author should so inspire this 'type' (Chick), Vian also uses the figure of Chick himself to symbolise his own authorial attitude. Chick is, like Vian, a collector of books. He is no more than that; this we have from his own testimony: "Je suis un salaud" (*Ej*, p.79). This is an admission that he has become one with his obsession, that he can only act according to his title (here, 'collectionneur'): he is guilty of 'mauvaise foi'. (Sartre's famous example, from *L'Être et le Néant*, of the waiter, whose bad faith is revealed by his justification of his existence in terms of his occupation, is calqué beautifully in *L'Écume* when a locker-attendant's bad faith is signalled by his anticipated use of the 'pourboire' to buy food: "Un homme à chandail blanc lui ouvrit une cabine, encaissa le pourboire qui lui servirait pour manger, car il avait l'air d'un menteur."[*Ej*, p.50-51])

Chick shows, in regard to Jean-Sol Partre, what can best be described as 'l'amour fou'. And, it is his own desperate need to possess which condemns Colin to undertake his parallel project; his envy of Chick's removal from reality is not even dulled by his disapproval, in his moments of mundane reflection, of his off-hand treatment of Alise (his careless/loveless love).

Firstly, he falls totally (and quite genuinely) in love with Chick's girl-friend. Secondly, he proclaims that, if he cannot vie with Chick in his love for Alise, he will collect the works of an author who may be seen, in some ways, as in rivalry with Partre:

> [...] Si ce soir je ne suis pas amoureux pour de vrai, je... je collectionnerai les œuvres de la Duchesse de Bovouard, pour faire pièce à mon ami Chick. (*Ej*,p.62)

Both are seeking to be 'real collectors', as described by Walter Benjamin:

> Of no one has less been expected, and no one has had a greater sense of well-being than the man who has been able to carry on his disreputable existence in the mask of Spitzweg's "Bookworm". For inside him there are spirits, or at least little genii, which have seen to it that for a collector - and I mean a real collector, a collector as he ought to be - ownership is the most intimate relationship that one can have to objects. Not that they come alive in him; it is he who comes alive in them.[44]

This rivalry, which holds as sacred the above tenet that ownership is sacred (Colin tries to ignore his love on the basis that "Alise appartenait à Chick de plein droit" [*Ej*, p.56]), turns out to be fatal for both of them. Not only does Chick's uncontrollable need to buy Partre lead to his 'disappearance' by the state police, it is he who makes sure that, what Cocteau would call 'la machine infernale' runs according to plan. Although Colin must create Chloé

---

[44] Walter Benjamin, *Illuminations* (London: Fontana, 1973), p.67.

because of his literary heredity, and although she must die because of hers, it is still Chick's hand which sets the machine in motion:

> Chick écouta. C'était *Chloé*, dans l'arrangement de Duke Ellington. Chick regarda Colin. Il était tout pâle.
> - Je... n'ose pas le couper... dit Colin.
> Chick lui prit le couteau des mains et le planta d'un geste ferme dans le gâteau. (*Ej*, p.73)

It is not just as a collector that Chick 'stands for' Vian inside the novel. What he does with his collection is equally vital: he is also an 'arranger'. His technique for extracting new ideas from Partre's speeches is like Vian's own treatment of his own literary material. But, whereas Vian's blending of philosophies and novelistic techniques is done with meticulous care such that the product is as original as each of its constituent influences, Chick's juxtaposition of Partre recordings relies on random collision:

> Chick souleva le couvercle de son pick-up à deux plateaux et mit deux disques différents de Jean-Sol partre. Il voulait les écouter tous les deux en même temps pour faire jaillir des idées nouvelles du choc de deux idées anciennes. (*Ej*, p.186)

It is by drawing a parallel between the birth of Chick's ideas and the birth of Chloé that Vian distances Colin from the music that is *Chloe*. For, the blues is a kind of primal scream, giving direct vent to the composer's emotions. This is a story about the manipulation of material. Vian's eulogy to Duke Ellington is very real, and much more poignant than initial recognition of the various jazz references would have us believe. He is doing precisely with literature what Ellington does with pieces of jazz music. Talking of jazz in *En avant la zizique*, Vian divides its history into three general categories: "Elles correspondent aux deux guerres mondiales... La période du «ragtime» date d'avant la première.'"[45] It is to a piece of Ragtime music which we shall now return, more precisely to 'un vieux ragtime'.

The single most persistent and thorough caricature made throughout *L'Écume* is that of Jean-Paul Sartre. So dominant is this, that it cannot be overlooked, nor, in terms of this study, treated too lightly. Traditionally, there seem to have been two major reactions to Vian's treatment of Partre. In the light of the careful redrafting to which the initial manuscript of *'L'ékume des jhours'* was submitted, however, to dismiss Partre as either a light-hearted joke, or as the barely-veiled manifestation of a vehement antipathy would be to do a great disservice to both work and author. *L'Écume des jours* is neither a puerile send-up, nor is it a 'Chronique du Menteur'. Jean-Sol Partre is a son of Sartre, but not of direct descent. By 1946 Sartre had already been satirised by Robert Scipion in his pastiche, *Prête-moi ta plume*.[46] This caricatural overview of France's social icons of the immediate post-war period receives 45 lines in Vian's own book of 1950, *Manuel de Saint-Germain-des-Prés*.[47] If one accepts that Vian is not the first author to play with the name Sartre or to satirise the Existentialist band, then Partre can already be seen to be a work of intertextuality. His birth-place is 'la place municipale de Flaure', his family 'les Genpolçarthres':

> Fumeurs de pipe (une pipe finie en rallumant une autre, faute de quoi l'on est menacé de tomber dans le néant) et suceurs de nausées, voilà les Genpolçarthres.[48]

It is precisely in the *Manuel* that Vian offers a cursory description of Sartre himself. Compared with the 45 lines that Scipion receives, and the 35 lines devoted to Simone de Beauvoir, the 5 lines on Sartre become even more significant:

---

[45] *En avant la zizique*, p.168.

[46] Robert Scipion, *Prête-moi ta plume* (Paris: Gallimard, 1946).

[47] Boris Vian, *Manuel de Saint-Germain-des-Prés* (Paris: Le Chêne, 1974).

[48] *Prête-moi ta plume*, p.211.

> Écrivain, dramaturge et philosophe dont l'activité n'a rigoureusement aucun rapport avec les cheveux longs, et qui mériterait bien qu'on lui foute un peu la paix, parce que c'est un chic type.[49]

That a jocular reference ('clin d'œil') to the great philosopher does exist, but comes some four years after the writing of *L'Écume*, helps to alleviate the burden which Partre has had to shoulder, and allows him to function in the same manner as the other characters. As has been seen, Pestureau also draws our attention to Vian's early indecision, when searching for the inspiration for his author within the novel: "Introduire l'histoire du type qui collectionne Mac Orlan ou Queneau ou un autre." (*Ej*, p.219) Here, then, Partre reflects not just Sartre the man, but also Sartre the producer of writing, and of *La Nausée* in particular. That is not to say that Queneau is left out. Indeed, as "Don Evany Marqué, le joueur de baise-bol célèbre", he is inserted into the novel in a similar fashion.[50] It would be easy to suggest that these anagrammatical references to Vian's acquaintances are merely innocuous 'clins d'œil'; for the purposes of an intertextual study, however, such textual indicators take on a far more important role: they point not to the men behind the anagrams, but rather they point, via an accumulation of further references in a similar vein, to the novels behind the men. In this case, it will be seen that *La Nausée* and *Le Chiendent* are the novels in question. Similarly, the justification for treating Sartre's novel as an influence of primordial importance does not depend solely upon an accumulation of transparent puns on the word 'nausée'; far more enlightening is the revelation that one of the early titles Vian considered for his work was *Le jour en loques*.[51] And what

---

[49] *Manuel de Saint-Germain-des-Prés*, p.244.

[50] The inclusion of this anagram of Raymond Queneau highlights the importance that this novelist played in Vian's life, both as a friend with whom he could 'talk books', and also as a prominent presence "in book form" upon Vian's book-shelves. Pestureau refers the reader to "les Ziaux" (in *Œuvres complètes, I* (Paris, La Pléiade, Gallimard, 1989), a poem by Queneau in which "celui-ci avait tenté de faire le bilan de toutes les combinaisons anagrammatiques prononçables de ses nom et prénom, sauf celle-là..." (*Ej*,p.292).

[51] D (verso)
    La lumière déchirée
    les loques [le jour en loques] (*Ej*, p.223)

else is 'le jour en loques', if not a translation of the English 'ragtime'? This is, however, not a random synbook of a style of music and a pun on its literal English meaning. Rather, it can be seen as a desire to create a discreet union between the 'air' that is *Chloe* and the tune that is a constant and emblematic reminder, in *La Nausée*, of Roquentin's lost love, i.e. 'un vieux ragtime'.[52] Vian's novel, thus, follows a progression along a line from ragtime to boogie-woogie, but also, it moves forwards whilst remaining fully conscious of its musico-literary roots.

La Nausée, if one chooses to follow, or simply to enumerate, these intertextual signposts, can be seen to be the most explicitly influential text 'behind' *L'Écume des jours*. One might say that *La Nausée* is influence par excellence. Despite being the most blatant literary caricature to be found in *L'Écume des jours*, and therefore a veil beneath which the deeper lines of intertextuality (those of Surrealism, for example) are hidden, Sartre's text is still of great intertextual importance in its own right. Michel Gauthier notes:

> Une «situation» de Vian par rapport à Sartre et à l'Existentialisme apparaît d'emblée comme plus malaisée à établir, comme plus complexe et intimement contradictoire, que par rapport à Breton et au surréalisme. [...] Mais Vian avait sans aucun doute lu *La nausée*, et il me paraît probable qu'il avait lu aussi *L'Etre et le néant* et qu'il avait appris quel usage philosophique on peut faire de l'écriture des choses.[53]

Thus, as has already been hinted, this is not an example of facile word-play; rather, Vian, whose own use of humour is so often viewed as blatant caricature very much in the style of Robert Scipion, is concerned here with a careful manipulation of certain well-known texts. In as much as his 'avant-propos' sets out his project (indeed, his very projection of the novel "en atmosphère biaise et chauffée, sur un plan de référence irrégulièrement ondulé et présentant de la distorsion" [*Ej*, p.40]), he is conscious of presenting his own text against the

---

[52] "C'est un vieux *rag-time* avec refrain chanté."
    Jean-Paul Sartre, *La Nausée* (Paris: Gallimard, 1988), p.40. (Hereafter referred to as *Nausée*.)

[53] *Boris Vian. L'Écume des jours*, p.122.

backdrop of another famous 'avant-propos', this time not Sartrean, but Célinian.

Voyage au bout du texte: Colin and universal nausea

It is in his famous opening of *Voyage au bout de la nuit*, that Céline sets out a literary project so similar in design to that proposed by Boris Vian as to make of his seminal pre-war text an important role-model for *L'Écume des jours*:

> Voyager, c'est bien utile, ça fait travailler l'imagination. Tout le reste n'est que déceptions et fatigues. Notre voyage à nous est entièrement imaginaire. Voilà sa force.[54]

In the light of these words, Vian's text represents a voyage, not only into the imagination of the reader (although the reader is an assumed, and integral part of any intertextual project), but into other works of imagination. Perhaps it is these works which are represented by the suns which illuminate Colin's corridor (and whose gradual death could, perhaps, symbolise the autonomy of *L'Écume*, an autonomy which a work based on satire alone could scarcely hope to achieve), and which inspire Colin to seek a mooring, and, tragically, to bring his own voyage to an end.[55] For Colin's is a voyage, with all that this represents for Céline. That which Céline captures in voyage, Vian captures in pretty girls and jazz; similarly, Vian cannot tolerate the existence of 'le reste' which, in his opinion, "devrait disparaître, car le reste est laid." (*Ej*, p.40)

Any intertextuality that exists with Céline has the inevitable effect of establishing *L'Écume des jours* within a history of texts whose major feature

---

[54] Louis-Ferdinand, *Voyage au bout de la nuit* (Paris: Gallimard, 1992), p.11. (Hereafter referred to as *Voyage*.)

[55] Colin's voyage is not undertaken in darkness, as is that of "Les Gardes suisses" whose anthem precedes Céline's "avant-propos": "Notre vie est un voyage / Dans l'hiver et dans la Nuit / Nous cherchons notre passage / Dans le Ciel où rien ne luit." (*Voyage*, p.9)

has arguably been their very fictitiousness. "C'est un roman, rien qu'une histoire fictive", announces Céline (*Voyage*, p.11). Vian's response, although weighted slightly differently (where Céline plays the fictitiousness of his text off against the disappointments of reality, Vian claims that the 'real reality' of his text lies precisely in its fictitiousness...), carries the same sentiment:

> [...] Les quelques pages de démonstration qui suivent tirent toute leur force du fait que l'histoire est entièrement vraie, puisque je l'ai imaginée d'un bout à l'autre. (*Ej*, p.40)

So close is this to the opening of *Voyage* that one might even be tempted to read the last part of this sentence as 'd'un bout de la nuit à l'autre'.

Sartre's own concerns, from the outset of *La Nausée*, are not far removed; the proximity of his textual strategy and that of Céline are indicated by a similar tension between reality and fiction. Therein lies the importance of the 'mise en abyme' of the diary within a novel and the established technique, rarely used since the eighteenth century, of 'l'avertissement des éditeurs'), concerns which he signals by the inclusion of the epigraph, which he takes from Céline's own *L'Église*: "C'est un garçon sans importance collective, c'est tout juste un individu." (*Nausée*, p.9) The potential impact of this epigraph is a tightening, via a common interest in the work of Céline, of the link between *La Nausée* and *L'Écume des jours*: for, what else is Colin, if not a champion of the individual?

In her article "Une petite arche miraculeuse" Marie Redonnet considers the importance of *L'Écume* in terms of its historical context. In seeing the novel as "l'anticipation de ce que la modernité de l'après-nouveau roman allait avoir à réinventer, un univers de langue, de fiction et d'imaginaire, une pensée critique du monde et de l'Histoire", she sees the debt owed to the writing of Céline, and uses Vian's own elusiveness to support her belief, suggesting that 'he doth protest too much':

> «C'est comme ça qu'on doit écrire», dit Vian de Céline, tout en reconnaissant, «c'est drôle, je ne me sens pas influencé par Céline, et pourtant ça me rappelle Céline».[56]

---

[56] "Une Petite arche miraculeuse", p.81.

By portraying Vian as a saviour, giving second birth to the pre-war novel, Redonnet also isolates *La Nausée* from Sartre's later work and implies a rapprochement with *L'Écume*: "Camus et Sartre ont tous les deux très opportunément refoulé leurs écrits d'avant-guerre, *L'Etranger* et *La Nausée*, pour s'engager."[57] Michel Gauthier, too, sees a Surrealist side to *La Nausée*, a side which Vian's intertextual juxtaposition with *Nadja*, amongst others, helps to highlight:

> [D'autre part] malgré un écart de quinze ans, et des modes très différents de formation, il paraît assez que Sartre et Vian ont fait dans certains secteurs au moins de la culture contemporaine des choix analogues. Il y a eu tout un «surréalisme» de Sartre que l'œuvre d'après la guerre nous a fait oublier…[58]

Pestureau is keen to stress the notion of the reality of fiction and refers to Queneau amongst others when he notes: "Mais maints auteurs, de Flaubert à Queneau en passant par Cocteau [...] et Faulkner ont affirmé que la fiction est précisément le vrai." (*Ej*, p.233) Indeed, Queneau, the third of the original candidates for the object of Chick's obsession, seems to attempt a similar project in the form of his novel *Le Chiendent*. It is a novel which continually challenges the identity of its characters; rather than striving to make them appear real, it forces the reader to come to terms with their status as works of fiction. So closely can the pattern followed by *Le Chiendent* be compared to that followed by *L'Écume des jours* and *La Nausée* that the three texts become inextricably linked. It could be said that all the action of *Le Chiendent* is entirely true because Pierre Le Grand imagines/dreams it. This is at once reminiscent of Carroll's *Alice in Wonderland* in which both the sleeping of Alice and the Dormouse are responsible for the very sustenance of the narrative, and of Céline's *Voyage au bout de la nuit* where "Il suffit de fermer les yeux." (*Voyage*, p.11) And yet Pierre, in his café outside la gare du Nord, is not an exact replica of Bardamu drifting into reverie on a terrace of the place

---

[57] *Ibid.*

[58] *Boris Vian. L'Écume des jours*, p.122.

de Clichy since it often seems that the characters he dreams into existence have the power to then 'dream' him. Neither does *Le Chiendent* conclude with a line aware of its position as last line of a story:

> Un masque traversa l'air, escamotant des personnages aux vies multiples et complexes, et prit forme humaine à la terrasse d'un café. La silhouette d'un homme se profila; simultanément, des milliers. Il y en avait bien des milliers.[59]

'Le chiendent' appears to be that, after some 400 pages, the reader's faith in the story is destroyed. The text is *a story*, not the story, and its 'masks' will be donned by all such characters as follow (including, and these two in full knowledge of their status, Roquentin and Colin).

In all three texts, *Voyage au bout de la nuit* acts as framing device. *L'Écume* begins with the Célinian 'avant-propos' and ends with Colin looking into water, just as Bardamu is left listening to boats sailing out to sea. *La Nausée* begins with the epigraph and ends with Roquentin trying to leave the watery grave that is Bouville, but it is not certain that he succeeds in continuing where Bardamu and Colin finish: "Je n'ose pas prendre de décision. Si j'étais sûr d'avoir du talent..." (*Nausée*, p.250). And, as we have seen, *Le Chiendent* opens with a dozing client on a café terrace and ends in purest fiction. But it is most particularly in *La Nausée* that we find the fictional truth which Vian expounds in the 'avant-propos':

> J'ai l'impression de faire un travail de pure imagination. Encore suis-je bien sûr que des personnages de roman auraient l'air plus vrais, seraient, en tout cas, plus plaisants. (*Nausée*, p.30)

---

[59] Raymond Queneau, *Le Chiendent* (Paris: Gallimard, 1993), p.432. (Hereafter referred to as *Chiendent*.)

The above quotation shows Roquentin at an early stage in his development of a theory of 'aventure'. The development of this parallels Colin's use of 'le hasard objectif'. To have an adventure one must be in a privileged position where one knows instinctively how to act, as if all is pre-ordained, scripted: "[...] Pour que l'événement le plus banal devienne une aventure, il faut et il suffit qu'on se mette à le *raconter*." (*Nausée*, p.64) This theory of adventure gives rise in Roquentin to the desire to live his life as a character in book, or, indeed, diary (it is only when he realises the futility of his attempt to 'fictionalise' himself, an attempt aided, perversely enough, by the 'real' looking 'avertissement des éditeurs', that he decides to write novels). What is crucial, when looking at the similarity of Roquentin's and Colin's projects, is the following question: why does Roquentin develop his theory of adventure?

The answer, reduced to its simplest terms, is: because he loves Anny.[60] It is she who, during the period of their romance, first theorizes adventure in terms of 'moments parfaits'. For Anny, a perfect moment could abide no pain. When she was in love with Roquentin, her love filled her senses (this is the synaesthesia which 'le pianocktail' is striving to achieve). But when Roquentin finally meets Anny in the text, it becomes clear that these moments of absolute love were contrived: "Il ne suffisait pas de ne pas marquer ma souffrance: il fallait ne pas souffrir." (*Nausée*, p.211) Love in itself was not enough to guide Anny; her consciousness was still solely responsible for her actions. This insufficient love could therefore be no more. However, death of love does not equal Death; this Roquentin finds hard to accept:

> [...] Je suis surpris! Je croyais que cela faisait partie de toi-même, que si on t'avait ôté cela, ç'aurait été comme si on t'avait arraché le cœur. (*Nausée*, p.203)

If love's demise does not kill (unlike the tearing out of a heart, which Alise finds to be adequately lethal), then its pursuit is an impure project, condemning the hapless lover to a fate worse than death.[61]

---

[60] For a more complete reading of Anny's importance as Roquentin's motivation, see Nicholas Hewitt, "'Looking for Annie': Sartre's *La Nausée* and the Inter-War Years", *Journal of European Studies*, 12 (1982), 96-112.

[61] A fate which will not reach its paroxysm until the final novel the title of which, *L'Arrache-cœur*, is emblematic of the failure of Colin's love.

Nausea itself can be understood in similar terms: "J'ai même retrouvé cette petite fièvre qui m'agitait toujours en sa présence et ce goût amer au fond de ma bouche." (*Nausée*, p.204) This is a vestigial love, the distorted memory of a former passion. And so it is that when Colin first meets/summons Chloé, he experiences the reality of 'la nausée': "Colin avala sa salive. Sa bouche lui faisait comme du gratouillis de beignets brûlés." (*Ej*, p.67) This reaction is not so much a response to the outstanding beauty which he has created, as to the realisation of its imperfection when compared to its model. And just as Roquentin's nausea never entirely subsides with regard to Anny ("Anny ne change guère d'expression; elle change de visage; comme les acteurs antiques changeaient de masque: d'un coup." [*Nausée*, p.204]), Colin's love for Alise is never satiated ("[Mais si, dit Colin.] Les gens ne changent pas. Ce sont les choses qui changent." [*Ej*, p.183])

Colin and Roquentin are not the first literary creatures to be ravaged by nausea. It is nothing other than nausea which lies behind des Esseintes' project: "rongé d'ennui, il se détermina, pour occuper sa vie devenue oisive, à réaliser un projet..." (*A Rebours*, p.131). No sudden aberration this; his current *état d'âme* is the maturation of an inherent weakness:

> Depuis son extrême jeunesse, il avait été torturé par d'inexplicables répulsions...par exemple, quand il voyait du linge mouillé qu'une bonne était en train de tordre... (*A Rebours*, p.130)

Is this not precisely the phenomenon which Sartre elevates to the status of a philosophical malaise (and that only after having developed it with all its novelistic connotations)? The climax of des Esseintes' nausea gives rise to an hallucination which generates, in *La Nausée*, Roquentin's worst attack, and, in *L'Écume*, the complete destruction of Colin's world.

It is at the end of chapter VII of *A Rebours* that it becomes clear that des Esseintes has nausea. Chapter VIII opens with the following words: "Il avait toujours raffolé des fleurs...". And not merely flowers, but: "les fleurs de haute lignée telles que les orchidées." (*A Rebours*, p.132) As in Colin's case, orchids are symptomatic of decay. Colin's nausea has generated Chloé; she becomes the centre-piece of the floral stage of the disease. Whereas des Esseintes covers himself with flowers, Colin covers Chloé. This is why Colin can never steal ("Les boutiques des fleuristes n'ont jamais de rideau de fer.

Personne ne cherche à voler des fleurs."[*Ej*, p.56]) He must pay an artificial price to cure an artificial disease (which is consuming an artificial woman who is but the epicentre of his artifice). When the flowers have encircled him, des Esseintes becomes delirious; in a moment of lucidity that only intoxication can stimulate, all becomes explainable: "Tout n'est que syphilis..." (*A Rebours*, p.137) In a dream, syphilis becomes a woman (just as Chloé and the nénuphar become indistinguishable):

> Une soudaine intuition lui vint: c'est la Fleur, se dit-il; et la manie raisonnante persista dans le cauchemar, dériva de même que pendant la journée de la végétation sur le Virus. (*A Rebours*, p.140)

As surely as Chloé's nénuphar is taken from a cutting grown by des Esseintes, Roquentin's 'marronnier' has its roots in the same soil:

> Il les avait écartés, repoussés, éprouvant un dégoût sans bornes à voir grouiller entre ses doigts ces tiges tièdes et fermes; puis subitement, les odieuses plantes avaient disparu et deux bras cherchaient à l'enlacer... (*A Rebours*, p.141)

These words, which describe the pull of 'la Syphilis' in *A Rebours*, could so easily describe Roquentin's roots ("Et cette racine? Il aurait fallu que je me la représente comme une griffe vorace, déchirant la terre, lui arrachant sa nourriture?" [*Nausée*, p.190]). Are these roots the imploring arms of Anny, the Anny whose absence has left Roquentin so empty?

Nausea seems to centre itself inevitably around women. For des Esseintes, who declares that "ce n'est, Dieu merci, qu'un rêve" (*A Rebours*, p.141), Syphilis is nonetheless a woman as real as Chloé. The cures that he and Colin seek are both water treatments; whilst des Esseintes tries to soak away his anguish ("[...] Malheureusement les moyens de dompter l'inexorable maladie manquèrent. Il avait sans succès tenté d'installer des appareils hydrothérapiques" [*A Rebours*, p.142]), Chloé is starved of water, allowed no more than "deux cuillerées par jour." (*Ej*, p.143) All attempts are useless.

Why must love fail between these characters? Simply, because they are the way they are. A man born in the froth of the waves must, at the end, return to water. In Colin's case bending the rules provides only ephemeral relief, and actually seems to hasten the inevitable. As for Roquentin, whether or not he will realise his project remains shrouded in doubt. What is certain is that, confronted with the same problem, they respond in the same way.

In both cases they follow the pattern established in *Nadja* where the 'real' Blanche Derval becomes translated into the 'artificial' Nadja. This results in an interesting inclusion of techniques of Surrealism in this the first novel by the man who would become the most famous of all the Existentialists. Thus, as if to confirm the importance of Breton's text, Roquentin catches his last glimpse of Anny in a railway station, the ultimate breeding-ground of 'le hasard objectif':

> Ils [Anny et 'L'Etranger'] sont montés dans le train sans me voir. [...] Anny a baissé la glace de son compartiment; elle m'a vu. Elle m'a longtemps regardé, sans colère, avec des yeux inexpressifs. Puis le type est remonté dans le wagon et le train est parti. (*Nausée*, p.219)

Having left behind his love, once before, to seek solace in Bouville, it is now as his love leaves him that his despair moulds his project. Project becomes the search for completeness. In *L'Écume*, this brings death (Alise, whose decision to undertake a project follows her last, departing view of Colin, dies having killed the man whose works put the name to 'engagement'). Although, for Roquentin and Colin, projects remain only provisional and potential (respectively), both eventually yield themselves to water (symbol of death): Roquentin's (pronounced in terms reminiscent of the purest romance fiction) last words are "[...] Demain il pleuvra sur Bouville." (*Nausée*, p.250)

It is death's attraction (which once enticed Bardamu onto the field of battle) which actually inspires the project, the search for an ending (this is signified in the subconscious desire /klo/ + /e/, in which very formula both birth and death certificate are signed for Chloé): "Tout s'est arrêté [...] cet air lourd, bleu comme de l'eau, et moi-même, nous formons un tout immobile et plein: je suis heureux." (*Nausée*, p.86)

In what exactly does death's enticement consist? What are these characters of fiction actually seeking in her cold embrace? The answer is completion. In this contingent world of existents, there can be no essential life without the intervention of death. *La Nausée*, in its search for essentiality, provides an allegorical reading for Chloé's creation and her subsequent (auto)destruction.

As has been seen, the Blues *Chloe* encapsulates Colin's subconscious desires; in the same way, in *La Nausée*, Roquentin's desire for Anny to come back to him, to resume a love which he still feels, and the loss of which has contributed to his strange sensory experiences, is coded in the words of his favourite song (*Some of these days*, 'le vieux ragtime'):

> Some of these days
> You'll miss me honey. (*Nausée*, p.41 & 249)

The words are those of a composer, whom Roquentin imagines immortalised, 'essentialised'; the voice is that of 'la Négresse', similarly made essence; but the sentiments are those of Roquentin. The bewitching apparition that is the union of voice and music (recorded, and thus put into a parallel universe out of time's dominion) does not *exist*:

> *Elle* [cette petite douleur de diamant] n'existe pas. [...] Elle n'existe pas, puisqu'elle n'a rien de trop: c'est tout le reste qui est de trop par rapport à elle. Elle *est*. (*Nausée*, p.245-246)

The weight of grammatical importance put upon 'cette petite douleur de diamant' is too great, the sequence of dependent 'elle's too long for 'elle' not to begin to represent Anny. Anny, removed from Roquentin's life in any real sense, now becomes a kind of Surrealist love-object. The debt to Surrealism (and to *Nadja* especially) is categorical: the importance of the train sequence, the 'clin d'œil' to the leitmotiv of people falling from windows[62] and, as if that

---

[62] "J'essaie de retrouver cette belle fureur qui me précipita du troisième étage, quand j'avais douze ans, un jour que ma mère m'avait fouettée." (*Nausée*, p.205)

were not sufficient, the outlining in Roquentin's imagination of a Surrealist painting.[63] (There is an ineluctable rapprochement of 'le hasard objectif' and Sartre's 'aventure' - just before the 'autodidacte' arrives, for perhaps the last time, at the library, Roquentin notes: "Je sentis juste à temps que j'allais me laisser reprendre au mirage de l'aventure."[*Nausée*, p.228]) Like Nadja who 'n'est que le commencement', the record (progressing via a pre-established sequence of notes) presents a potential infinity of beginnings: "Elle tourne la manivelle et voilà que ça recommence." (*Nausée*, p.248)

It is from this understanding of the nature of things that Roquentin proceeds; instead of viewing Rollebon as an historical figure (as would a 'salaud), he determines to 'record' him. Thus, by deciding to write a novel, Roquentin hopes to access the plane of essential being. In *L'Écume*, there is, in the ineluctable absence of Alise, no third party. With no Rollebon to fictionalise, with no X to receive his love, Colin fuses Anny and record: the synbook, as we know, is Chloé.

As a record, Chloé must die ("Mais comme il fallait s'y attendre, le disque s'arrêta." [*Ej*, p.68]) She is not one of these existents "las et vieux [...] *parce que la mort ne pouvait leur venir que de l'extérieur*", but rather she announces her own fate: "[..] *Il n'y a que les airs de musique pour porter fièrement leur propre mort en soi comme une nécessité interne.*" (*Nausée*, p.190) She has a certain allocation of playing-time, each note of which brings her nearer her conclusion. And, being a Blues, she offers no hope for future resurrection (contrast this with the ever optimistic "Some of these days/ You'll miss me honey."). She is the recording of the loves of her literary predecessors, and when the needle reaches her final groove she will die their deaths. For, as a descendant of Marguerite, 'la Dame aux Camélias', she is composed of the flowers of death. When Chloé is confined to her bed, she is only following the path that the death of Dumas' leading lady has predestined:

- Qu'a-t-elle donc?

---

[63] "Et celui... se réveillera tout nu sur un sol bleuâtre, dans une forêt de verges bruissantes..." (*Nausée*, p.224).

> - Elle a qu'elle est poitrinaire, et que, comme elle a fait une vie qui n'est pas destinée à la guérir, elle est dans son lit et qu'elle se meurt.[64]

As Marguerite, the flower-lady par excellence, dies of an infection of the chest, Chloé languishes in her own bed, then, by virtue of her literary constitution; Colin kills her by summoning her and not merely by marrying her (as he presumes), although, once she is created, death must come via marriage. André Jarry finds this fatality in the fusion of the 'enigmatic paragraph' (i.e. "A l'endroit où les fleuves se jettent dans la mer..."). In what he calls the "point focal du récit", Jarry stresses "la difficulté, précisément, de la barre à franchir": "Toute communication entre Conscient et Inconscient à jamais impossible, sinon sous le signe de la mort.[65]"

Chloé's status as record is further reinforced by the association with *Le Chiendent*. It is precisely a record that one cleans with a "brosse en chiendent"[66]. Queneau also uses an image taken from daily life to introduce this philosophical problem of repeated beginnings. Instead of using a record, however, he suggests that life is like a bowl of soup. Life as something, here, which must be drained and begun again is akin to love in *L'Écume*, love which is deprived of immortality and which, since the marriage of Colin and Chloé, has left the realm of the 'froth' to dwell under the governance of 'days'. The image of a group of people (wedding guests in this instance) ingesting their soup in the same way forms a microcosm of society in general:

> On lappe et l'on clapote. [...] De cette musique, naît peu à peu une harmonie élémentaire; bientôt de bouche en oreilles, les paroles vont voler et, passant de l'animal au social et de la gloutonnerie au bavardage, chacune des

---

[64] Alexandre Dumas, *La Dame aux Camélias* (Paris: Gallimard, 1994), p.71. (Hereafter referred to as *Dumas*.)

[65] André Jarry, "L'Écume des mots: un Janus *Uni-frons*", in *Boris Vian: Colloque de Cerisy*, pp.149-58 (p.157).

[66] "L'homme des disques était en train d'en passer un à la brosse en chiendent pour enlever les aspérités nées de l'usure." (*Ej*, p.119)

> quinze personnes énumérées plus haut commence à s'apercevoir de nouveau de la présence de quatorze autres. Car à gamelle vide, nez qui se lève. (*Chiendent*, p.266-267)

Life can thus function happily ('normally') so long as there is soup in the bowl (i.e., to enclose Roquentin and Colin within the analogy, when one is in love). If only love could last a life-time... "Fantaisie que tout cela!... Les assiettes ont un fond, et dans ce fond, le potachistagneu." (*Chiendent*, p.268) And so it is that all the characters in *Le Chiendent* are gradually plunged deeper into an ironisation of what will be expressed tentatively five years later in *La Nausée* and subsequently, and more systematically, in *L'Être et le Néant*. Life in Queneau's world also gives rise to feelings of nausea: "[...] Narcense eut comme une nausée et laissa tomber sur le plancher le coupe-œufs-durs-en-tranches-minces" (*Chiendent*, p.123), and more significantly (where Étienne's boredom = Colin's despair = Roquentin's nausea): "Il se formula son état *en termes vulgaires*: «C'que j'm'emmerde aujourd'hui»" (*Chiendent*, p.207, my italics.[67])

However, the most fundamental (intertextual) importance of *Le Chiendent*, as far as *L'Écume des jours* is concerned, is best revealed by careful analysis of one particular passage, in this case the marriage of Ernestine. Even when le père Taupe is but an ardent admirer of Ernestine, his song of love recalls the Blues *Chloe*, a song at once of love and of death:

> Mais le plus joli rêve, c'est le rêve de l'amour,
> Que l'on fait sur la grève
> A l'heure où meurt le jour. (*Chiendent*, p.89)

---

[67] In terms of the triad of texts, *Le Chiendent* (meant as a vulgarisation of Cartesian philosophy), further narrows the gap between Surrealism and Existentialism, especially by the coded (i.e. trains etc.) use of 'hasard objectif' to conjure the Other. Thus 'l'être-pour-autrui' becomes the dependence upon a dreamer/voyeur. It is noteworthy that Queneau's text, which turns out to be, in fact, a near perfect vulgarisation of Sartre's philosophy of the various 'être's, should predate even *La Nausée*.

And, as is meet and right, the song of le père Taupe is toasted by a suitably frothy drink ("Ernestine rentre avec le mousseux ..." [*Chiendent*, p.89]). And if the destinies of Ernestine and Chloé are not bound tightly enough by song, then the nightmarish appearance, just before the wedding feast, of their ghostly predecessor seals their fate. The removal of the commas from the following sentence reveals the face of death: "La nouvelle, Camélia, essuie les verres en reniflant: c'est un tic." (*Chiendent*, p.247)

Whereas Marguerite, the original incarnation of 'la Dame aux Camélias' (who, since her exhumation at the hands of Armand, has become a prophet of doom: "Les yeux ne faisaient plus que deux trous, les lèvres avaient disparu, et les dents blanches étaient serrées les unes contre les autres" [*Dumas*, p.56]) coughed, and where Chloé will cough again, Camélia sniffs. Add to this the arrival of a magician who specialises in the conjuring up of flowers and things could not look worse.

The picture painted by the guests, on their return, of the day out in the country draws heavily upon scenes from *Voyage au bout de la nuit*, where the hours spent on the barge represent a few fleeting hours of happiness. Here too, adulation mingles with events of bad-omen: "Mme Cloche faillit faire chavirer une barque et Florette faillit se faire mordre par un chien." (*Chiendent*, p.259) Within the text the ubiquitous reference to dog-bites ('chien' + 'dent') is more than a simple leitmotiv; rather, the bite of the dog is used as an indicator of evil tidings. In Céline's novel of 1936, *Mort à Crédit*, it is a postman who brings disaster, in the form of letters; and it is indeed the role of harbinger of 'bad news' which will become the lot of Colin in *L'Écume*: "Mme Saturnin... raconte que ses parents restèrent six mois sans nouvelles de leur fils, parce que leur chien ne pouvait souffrir les facteurs." (*Chiendent*, p.272) Furthermore: "Dans le régiment de Thémistocle, dit ce dernier, on a supprimé les sonneries de clairon parce qu'elles tapaient sur les nerfs du lévrier du colonel." (*Chiendent*, p.272)

Had such rallying bugle calls been banned by the regiment which passed La Place Clichy, would not Bardamu have been spared his journey? The moments of rapprochement with Céline's text serve to damn the union of Taupe and Ernestine, just as Robinson died as the result of his union with Madelon. Madelon is, of course, another example of a woman who is a song, *La Madelon* (a song which is also mentioned in *Le Chiendent*). Indeed, by virtue of her being a song, she, like Chloé, lures her helpless victim with the beauty of her serenade, and weaves her web of doom with the power of her kiss. The similarity in the way which Chloé and Madelon entice their respective partners, allowing the man to assume what he takes to be control (this is the strategy of the woman, 'sticky' in her treacherousness, on whom Sartre theorizes in *L'Être et le Néant*) can be revealed by a comparison of the following two quotations (the kiss of *La Madelon*, although here directed at Bardamu (apparently through his instigation), will have a more direct effect on the life, or rather the death, of Robinson (her fiancé); however, the patriotism of which the song is symbolic can also be seen to have enticed, and similarly doomed Bardamu): "[...] Je l'embrassai un petit peu autour du cou. Elle a protesté d'abord, mais pas trop." (*Voyage*, p.486) Thus, as has been seen, Colin is similarly lured to Chloé: "Il inclina légèrement la tête et l'embrassa entre l'oreille et l'épaule. Elle frémit mais ne retira pas sa tête." (*Ej*, p.69) (This is the same kiss which sends Michel to his doom in *Le Quai des brumes*.)

To return to Ernestine, the joys of the whole day provide her with the few moments of happiness to which she has no right ("Camélia... renifle plus fort que jamais" [*Chiendent*, p.260]), the happiness for/by which she must die. The Hobson's choice is as follows: choose happiness and die (the symbolic representative of which is Chloé), or choose to act/live and know no happiness (this would seem to be the lot of Alise - although Alise's death is a kind of heroic suicide by action)[68]. Curiously, Ernestine seems to stand both for Chloé's happiness and for the purity of the golden-haired Alise ("Ernestine rayonne. Ernestine resplendit. Ernestine scintille." [*Chiendent*, p.260]). The bitter-sweet irony of the association between flowers and death (marked by the oxymoronic 'immense petite') reaches an apotheosis with the climax of Ernestine's contentment:

> Ernestine sent croître dans son cœur une immense petite fleur bleue qu'elle arrose d'un pernod fils dont les soixante degrés d'alcool sont légèrement éteints par l'adjonction de quelques centimètres cubes d'eau pure, mais non distillée.
> (*Chiendent*, p.261)

Even the gaiety of alcohol on which Colin's 'pianocktail' thrives, cannot dilute the toxicity of water, and, even when 'bidistillé', the flower is equally lethal.

---

[68] This choice is one which is effectively closed for Chloé, since she is a literary puppet, and is scarcely more open to Alise whose fate lies in the hands (or, more precisely, in the love) of Colin; it is nonetheless there, and is the same choice which must be made by Andersen's *Little Mermaid*.

In *L'Écume des jours*, Alise is an exemplary figure in as much as she wishes her beloved Colin happiness on the day of his wedding. In *Le Chiendent*, the cries of "Vive la mariée! Vive Taupe!" lack the sincerity of the 'injures' which rain upon Colin and Chloé. When pronounced by mouths incapable of the slightest altruism, these toasts sound like the last orders of an execution squad. Indeed, so venimous are the lips of Madame Pic that they become one with the mark of death:

> [...] Et son cœur saigne pendant que ses lèvres, conservant précieusement un sourire crispé, trempent dans un verre de grenadine, sur les bords duquel sont profondément gravées les empreintes digitales de Camélia. (*Chiendent*, p.263)

As before, it is a song which prompts the shift from catching the disease to actually suffering the symptoms. Like an evil fairy called upon to bless a child, Mme Cloche is called upon to sing:

> Mme Cloche, priée de montrer ses talents, mugit une lugubre histoire. [...] Cette lugubre aventure suscite une impression considérable.
> - T'aurais pu nous chanter quelque chose de plus drôle, lui dit
> Dominique.
> - J'sais qu'deux chansons; celle-là et puis celle de la guillotine tragique. J'ai choisi la moins triste. (*Chiendent*, p.286-287)

Her name, whose primary importance lies in fact in its proximity to 'clochard', also means 'bell'; it does not, however, render her singing voice a succession of sweet chimes. In fact, as she tolls, Ernestine's life ebbs steadily away.

Whilst Ernestine lies in the throes of agony, the images of death (and particularly of the death of love) proliferate. Light is shed upon the rose which Colin causes to grow from the end of a rifle when one considers the following motif: "une large arête de poisson transperçait un pétale de fleur." And finally, when satisfied with the outcome of her work, the Angel of death departs:

"Camélia vint renifler jusqu'à la porte, regarda l'assemblée muette, puis retourna dans les ténèbres." (*Chiendent*, p.292)

Yet Ernestine does not receive her full, literary funeral until the curse of this ill-starred marriage has run its course:

> Mme Cloche et Dominique Belhôtel marchaient donc à travers la nuit le long de la rivière goudronneuse [...]
> - R'garde c't'eau, elle est sûre, elle est tranquille, c'est une eau qui ne parle plus (- "*qu'on n'en parle plus*" -). Quand le vieux sera au fond, i n'remontera jamais. I s'aura suicidé par désespoir d'amour. (*Chiendent*, p.306)

The aftermath of Ernestine's death is represented in terms which only serve to reinforce the union between the texts discussed thus far. *Voyage au bout de la nuit* ends in such a way as to recall the fictitious project expounded in the 'avant-propos': it is a tug which drags all the characters out of the narrator's ear-shot, and out of the story itself: "Il appelait vers lui toutes les péniches du fleuve toutes, et la ville entière, et le ciel et la campagne et nous, tout qu'il emmenait, la Seine aussi, tout, qu'on n'en parle plus." (*Voyage*, p.636)

It is not merely *Voyage au bout de la nuit* that is recalled by Queneau; it is significant that it is *the end of the story*. In Ernestine dies also the love of Taupe. It is an end to his love story, a story carved on the back of a door, a story which therefore provides the impetus for the novel itself (the intrigue gradually focuses upon the enigma of 'what lies behind the door'...). The end of this love-story seems to point forward into another great romance turned sour (which, with words now made so famous as to be almost clichéd, Queneau himself was to describe, in his 'avant-propos' to *L'Arrache-cœur*, as "le plus poignant des romans d'amour contemporains"): that of Colin and Chloé. The last line of the above quotation ("I s'aura suicidé par désespoir d'amour.") refers to (and, indeed, causes, since words have the same effect as the teeth of the dog) the death of Taupe, and seals Colin's fate in the same breath.

"La chanson de la Cloche" and *La Petite Sirène*

Colin is clearly not the only one to die of a broken heart. Alise, too, is condemned by her heart. When Alise looks into Colin's eyes for the last time she realises that it is too late for their love; despite their silent vows (Alise, on whose arm Colin entered the church on that fateful day, is the only girl wearing his ring: "une grosse bague d'or en forme de nausée" [*Ej*, p.79]) they must part company. She is driven by this rejection of her love, in the same way as is Roquentin, to undertake her existential project. Alise's influence does not, however, end with her death. In fact, there is reason to believe that she does not die at all.

The song of Mme Cloche points in this direction:

> Mme Cloche [...] mugit une lugubre histoire de marin estropié dont la fiancée préfère épouser un jeune homme très bien au premier abord mais qui, par la suite, devient alcoolique et fou; alors la fiancée recherche le marin estropié, mais ses camarades l'ont consommé un jour de vent d'ouest et il n'en reste plus qu'un petit morceau de mollet conservé dans la saumure. [...]
> la fiancée prend le petit morceau de mollet, et elle le mange et elle se jette ensuite du haut d'un phare dans l'Océan homicide, en chantant: Il était un p'tit marin...
> (*Chiendent*, p.286-287)

The tragedy of death and lost love, at the centre of both *L'Écume* and *Le Chiendent*, has an entire fairy tale devoted to it. In as much as she is a creature born of the froth whose death results from the spurning of her love, Alise is Hans Christian Andersen's *La Petite Sirène*[69].

---

[69] The shelves of the apartment which is now home to 'La Fondation Vian' at Cité Véron attest to Vian's passion for fairy tales, and for *La Petite Sirène* in particular. Also, in 1949, he translated several 'contes d'Andersen' for 'La Bibliothèque Rouge et Or'; in 1957 Philips published various 'contes d'Andersen' and 'contes de Grimm', translated by Vian for the series 'Livres-Disques'.

La Petite Sirène is a classic tale both of love and love lost. The little mermaid falls in love with a prince from the other side of the sea; she rescues him from a shipwreck and begins to question the status of her kind who live long lives but have no soul, simply returning to the froth at the instant of their demise. She, too, begins to desire her part in the kingdom of heaven. Thus, she decides to make a pact with a sea-witch who grants her human form in exchange for her beautiful voice. Her life as a woman will be one of constant pain and sacrifice; for, in addition to being dumb, her newly formed legs will forever make her feel as if she were walking on needles. And neither will she be able to revert to her mermaid form, or ever see her family again. And still this sacrifice is not in itself sufficient to gain her entrance into the kingdom of heaven; that is dependent upon her finding a man who truly loves her. It is, indeed, for the love of this particular man that her decision has arisen, her desire for love and immortality blending into the same human face. Thus, she becomes a woman. The prince, however, can never really love her because, unknown to the little mermaid, his near-drowned body had been found, shortly after she had left it, by a village girl in whom he now sees the reason for his salvation.

There is much similarity already between Andersen's tale and *L'Écume des jours*: Alise is mute, in as much as she cannot speak of her love for Colin and appears compelled to leave the initiation of their togetherness in the hands of Colin; and Colin himself, is, like the prince, bound by a misplaced sense of loyalty. In both instances Love (with a capital L) is lost for the sake of 'love'. Both the prince and Colin choose the accessible and deny their dreams; they choose days and reject froth.

When finally the prince finds his beloved village girl, they are instantly engaged. The mermaid's fate is sealed; the price of her failure is that she must return to the froth: "Le lendemain matin du jour où il en épouserait une autre, ton cœur se briserait et tu ne serais plus qu'écume sur la mer."[70] The result of her sacrifice is that her prince gives himself to another, rejecting the woman he really loves. The mermaid's fate, as is Alise's, is sealed by a wedding, not yellow and violet this time, but gold and purple: "Au milieu du pont, une tente d'or et de pourpre avait été dressée, garnie de coussins moelleux où les époux reposaient dans le calme et la fraîcheur de la nuit." (*Andersen*, p.49)

---

[70] Hans Andersen, *La Petite Sirène*, in, *Andersen: Contes* (Paris: Librairie Gründ, 1995), pp.26-51 (p.40). (Hereafter referred to as *Andersen*.)

Even at the very last, the little mermaid is given a chance to return with her family; her sisters have made a pact for her right to live out her days in the sea:

> Soudain elle vit ses sœurs apparaître au-dessus de la mer. Elles étaient pâles comme elle-même, leurs longs cheveux ne flottaient plus au vent, on les avait coupés. (*Andersen*, p.49)

For her part, she must kill the prince. However, her love for him is such that, despite his betrayal, she cannot bring herself to harm him. Such, too, is the power of Alise's love: she shows her true self to Colin, then leaves. As he walks away, determined to devote his life to a lost love, or, indeed, to the loss of his love, there is regret in her eyes; the pain of this farewell is, as is typical of Vian's truest show of feelings, tragically understated: "Colin la prit par la main et ils descendirent l'escalier. Ils glissaient, de temps à autre, sur les marches humides. En bas, Colin lui dit au revoir, elle resta debout et le regarda s'en aller." (*Ej*, p.184) As with Andersen's little mermaid who cries out with muted words, this is the pathos of silence. Alise's vengeance is turned against Partre and then against the tide of days. In the light of the above quotation, Alise's golden hair points, intertextually, to the survival of her immortal soul; for the mermaid does not die in the froth. As she is on the very point of reverting to the foam of the sea, she is transformed into a daughter of the air, who, as a spirit, will continue to exert her influence:

> Elle voyait le clair soleil et au-dessus d'elle, planaient des centaines de charmants êtres transparents. [...] Sans ailes, elles flottaient par leur seule légèreté à travers l'espace. La petite sirène sentit qu'elle avait un corps comme le leur, qui s'élevait de plus en plus haut au-dessus de l'écume. (*Andersen*, p.50)

And neither will Alise die in *L'Écume*. Instead, her ultimate choice of froth (in the sense of the true course of love, be it unilaterally assumed) and her rejection of days (the tendency to allow life to make choices in the place of the individual) similarly secure her salvation from the apocalyptic finale of

L'Écume. Her phoenix-like ascension out of the pages of *L'Écume*, the result of her magical status as mermaid-cum-angel, will, to some extent, hold the key to *L'Automne à Pékin*.

> Il [Nicolas] pensait qu'Alise ne serait pas restée dans le feu, mais il ne voyait pas la porte par où elle aurait pu s'en aller [...] Il restait au milieu des cendres sales une brillante lueur, plus brillante que les flammes. [...] Sous une poutre de fer tordue, il aperçut l'éblouissante toison blonde; les flammes n'avaient pu la dévorer car elle était plus éclatante qu'elles... (*Ej*, p.196-197)

For it is in this act that Alise leaves the novel. As the chapters which follow, and the intratextuality which they expose, will reveal, she returns temporarily to the froth, that area which is at once part of the novel and exterior to it; it is the watery zone from which Colin emerges in his bath-tub, and into which he gazes at the end of the story. It is framing device for the novel and emblem for the failure of love. It is, thus, an area into which Alise, as daughter of the air (and sea: froth), must return and from which she must re-emerge continually until love conquers days. *L'Écume des jours*, therefore, establishes the beginnings of an Alisian mythology which will exert its influence over the reading of the subsequent novels. It also sets a pattern for analysing the novels: the intertextuality within this opening novel is complex and intertwined; although it will remain complex, it will become progressively ordered, becoming a structuring tool for the texts. The method of using 'clins d'œil', whilst remaining the same in terms of the reader response elicited, will become more subtle. Thus, when Alise flies from Colin, she takes with her a whole textual approach which is set to improve with maturity.

    This flight of an angel that Alise takes is emblematic of the concerns of the principal character of *L'Automne à Pékin*, Angel. Already, by merely suggesting a link between Alise and Angel, the ambiguity of the relationship which exists between their respective novels becomes manifest. On the one hand, there is an apparent diaspora; the inhabitants of the city of the froth are thrown out onto the hot desert sands where they are free to live (and love) as they choose. On the other hand, this land may be cast in the same froth as the first (the wings of our itinerant angel beating over the heads of a new cast of characters), any differences in surroundings being mere mirages.

CHAPTER THREE
L'Automne à Pékin:
Entry into the text

In Vian's second major novel, as in *L'Écume des jours*, there is a proliferation of intertextuality. One of the objectives of this chapter will be to investigate to what extent the various lines of intertextuality can be seen to work in a more complex and systematic manner than was the case in the first text. The text of *L'Automne à Pékin* is itself carefully structured, and this in a way which has tended to place the various 'movements' and 'passages' at the centre of much of the critical discourse surrounding the novel. Analyses of *L'Automne à Pékin* have often centred upon the significance of the concept of the archeological dig: Freddy de Vree (in his *Essai*) and Noël Arnaud (in *Obliques* 8-9) in particular concentrate their readings on the alchemical/mystical quest beneath the earth. The quest here will be to find the intertexts beneath the lines of the text. The study of lines of intertextuality will involve the concept of genre and, particularly, of manipulation of genre. Bruno Maillé, in his article entitled "*L'Automne à Pékin*: Un roman surréaliste?" in which he aims to place the novel within this particular genre, is keen to distance himself from the 'alchemical school':

> On a prétendu que son roman décrivait une quête mystique, alchimique, souterraine: Athanagore, son archéologue, ne trouve en vérité que «l'odeur sèche du vide pur» et quelques momies...[1]

His article aims to posit *L'Automne* as an example of the Surrealist novel (the possibility of which was ardently denied by the Surrealists themselves): "Vian, le plus surréaliste des romanciers, reste avant tout romancier."[2] And this, he argues, may be shown by an examination of various techniques; firstly, there is the manipulation of the concept of dreams:

---

[1] Bruno Maillé, "*L'Automne à Pékin*: Un roman surréaliste?", *L'Atelier du Roman*, 9 (1996), 115-122 (122).
[2] *Ibid.*

> *L'Automne à Pékin* est le roman du rêve - mais aussi le roman du réveil... Imitant les sentences du sévère Breton, nous dirons: «Vian est Surrealiste dans le rêve et le réveil».[3]

The concept of dreams, and of dream journeys, has already been broached in reference to *L'Écume des jours*, a text which seems to evoke the waking dream (*Froth on the Daydream*). *L'Écume* and *L'Automne* may, it appears, also be considered as Surrealist texts in respect to their treatment of youth:

> «Le surréalisme est né d'une affirmation de foi sans limite dans le génie de la jeunesse.» Cette foi porte le début de *L'Automne à Pékin*, splendide d'énergie et d'enthousiasme. Mais tout au long du roman, elle va peu à peu s'éteindre, à l'épreuve du réel.[4]

This loss of enthusiasm has already been seen in *L'Écume des jours*, depicted as a loss of light; the above quotation seems to pierce both Vian texts, evoking the ascension of the dominion of days over that of froth, a concept to which this study will frequently return. This particular chapter will seek to examine the concept of light, its loss and its tendency to change, thereby placing *L'Automne* into a context from within which its Surrealist elements may be highlighted.

Despite seeing *L'Automne* as *the* Surrealist novel, Maillé considers the text against a background of Surrealist ideology which was not based upon the novelistic genre:

> Le roman entier est une immense rencontre *fortuite* dans un désert. Sa composition semble suivre le modèle de la phrase de Lautréamont chère aux surréalistes: «Beau comme la rencontre fortuite sur une table de dissection d'une machine à coudre et d'un parapluie.»[5]

Rather than being considered as random events, it is possible to consider the

---
[3] *Ibid.*, p.117.
[4] *Ibid.*
[5] *Ibid.*, p.116.

sections A-D as lines of intertextuality, a carefully constructed series of entries into the text: Vian may, thus, be shown to be manipulating Surrealist concepts of objective chance in such a way as to create a work which, as Maillé himself hinted earlier, has more to do with novels than with Surrealism itself. (Nadja herself may now be considered as a character in a novel, Breton's text functioning, despite the quasi random dispersal of photographs throughout, according to various novelistic strategies.) Maillé points to the dream element of the text which draws Amadis Dudu into the story; Dudu, thus, can be seen as carrying out to the letter Paul Éluard's Surrealist prophecies:

> Dans la conférence qu'il prononce le 24 juin 1936 à Londres, Paul Éluard parle du monde idéal libéré par la poésie: «L'homme, s'étant enfin accordé à la réalité, qui est sienne, n'aura plus qu'à fermer les yeux pour que s'ouvrent les portes du merveilleux.»[6]

As will the mechanisms which Vian employs for introducing his characters into the story, this quotation recalls the famous "Il suffit de fermer les yeux" of *Voyage au bout de la nuit*. Maillé then cites Dudu's entry into the text. Once Dudu's entry into the text is complete, Maillé's contention is that the rest of the story may be read as a dream: «Tout le reste du roman peut être compris comme un rêve.»[7] This is perfectly feasible; Dudu, after all, is not far removed from 'dodo'. Dudu thus becomes a kind of Alice figure, dreaming the text. An intertextual analysis of the lines of entry into the text, however, does not give such pride of place to Dudu. It will, on the contrary, be shown that each of the sections A-D represents an individual line of intertextuality, and as such an entry for its respective characters into the text proper; in intertextual terms, all those who go to Exopotamia experience a common dream. Thus, the famous dream/waking moment binary, so central to the school of Surrealism, can be seen to be at the heart of *L'Automne*. Maillé writes: "Dans le navire de rêve sur lequel ils sont embarqués, les personnages font ce que recommande Breton: «Maintenir à l'état anarchique la bande chaque jour plus redoutable de ses désirs.»"[8] It is therefore a set of principles akin to those of the Surrealist school which bring the principal characters onto the stage. Once there, however, the lines of intertextuality at work are multiple. For example, the deterioration of the state of desire within

---

[6] *Ibid.*, p.117.
[7] *Ibid.*, p.118.
[8] *Ibid.*, p.121.

Angel can be seen to reflect patterns laid out in Constant's *Adolphe* and Miller's *Tropic of Cancer*. Thus, there will be a movement between states of consciousness, but there will also be a movement between lines of intertextuality.

This chapter will, therefore, take as a premise the concept that, in much the same way as
L'Écume des jours, the second novel of the tetralogy functions according to a Célinian concept of voyage. Thus the ambiguity which will be seen to be at the heart of *L'Automne à Pékin* is one with which the reader of *Voyage au bout de la nuit* will be familiar: as Bardamu has his dream in 'la place Clichy', his subsequent voyages being ones of the imagination, so, too, the characters of Vian's text will dream themselves away. This story of exotic adventure will, then, (ironically) find it hard ever to leave Paris.

Here the quest will, thus, be to see in what ways *L'Automne* does, in fact, move on from *L'Écume*. How will the tension that is the similarity/difference existing between the two texts manifest itself in terms of intertextuality (will, for example, the desert sands prove as suitable a location for encounters with the Surrealist love object as the eddies of froth)? The answer, as will be seen, is that whilst retaining (and exploiting to its own ends) some of the intertexts so vital to *L'Écume*, *L'Automne* also carves out a certain autonomy in the shape of new intertexts. Thus, there will also be a parallel intertextual tension, and the movement from one genre into another will prove as complex as the apparent changes in location undergone by the characters.

For location, as regards any Vian text, one would do better to read 'dislocation'. Thus, the reader who picks up *L'Automne à Pékin* ought not to be surprised to see proclaimed on the back cover: "Inutile d'ajouter que rien dans cette histoire ne concerne l'automne, ni Pékin."[9] True enough. But not the whole truth. In his postface, "Avant de relire *L'Automne à Pékin*", François Caradec goes further: "*L'Automne à Pékin* n'est pas un roman à clefs."[10] If he is implying that the novel can only be understood in a void, then it will be shown that this view, although perfectly tenable within the context of Caradec's classic essay, is quite inappropriate in a context such as that given

---

[9] Boris Vian, *L'Automne à Pékin* (Paris: Minuit, 1991)

[10] François Caradec, "Avant de relire *L'Automne à Pékin*", in *L'Automne à Pékin* (Éditions de Minuit), p.288.

by intertextuality. There are, perhaps, no keys for the door which he is content to see remain closed; but it is possible to try another door. If, however, he is implying simply that the characters, such as Claude Léon, whose names coincide with those of real people have no dependence upon their extra-textual, living counterparts, then he has a point. And yet, if Claude Léon is not the living friend of Boris Vian, he is a fictional character and as such has a relationship with other fictional characters. Similarly, if Pékin is not Peking, neither is it without relationships to other fictional towns; and of these, one more than any other.

Autumn in Paris

The starting point of this examination of *L'Automne à Pékin* is a remark (which he modestly calls "une remarque très plate") made by Gilbert Pestureau during the colloquium held at Cerisy-la-Salle between July 23 and August 2 1976:

> Alors il a écrit *L'Automne à Pékin* en automne, à Paris, ça commence à Paris, avec les problèmes de bus qu'il y avait à l'époque, et je me demande s'il n'y a pas simplement une sorte de plaisanterie de centralien; *L'Automne à Pékin*, c'est l'automne à Paris, et puis ensuite ça démarre.[11]

Thus, if one considers that Pékin is used here as a slang term for Paris, what appears to be a change of location seems, rather, to be a change within the location. It is worth noting that in 1947 a book was published which described the implications of centralisation and the relative importance within France of Paris. Although this text describes the rest of France, and not Paris, as a desert, the title, *Paris et le désert français*, may well have seemed particularly attractive to a writer looking to write a sequel to a Parisian novel.[12] The new novel, completed in the same year as *L'Écume des jours*, is the second of a

---

[11] *Boris Vian: Colloque de Cerisy/1*, p.262.

[12] J.-F. Gravier, *Paris et le désert français* (Paris: Portulan, 1947).

sequence, and its changes are progressions. Bearing this in mind, the search for the intertextual references, which will show that the novelistic strategy has not altered, will begin in a classically Parisian text.

> La lumière ne se comprend que par l'ombre, et la vérité suppose l'erreur. [...] Nous n'existons qu'en fonction de ce conflit dans la zone où se heurtent le blanc et le noir. Et que m'importent le blanc ou le noir? Ils sont du domaine de la mort.[13]

These words, coming as they do from a Surrealist text such as Bruno Maillé considers *L'Automne* to be, strike the very essence of Vian's novel: with its baleful expanses of blackness carved out against the dazzling light of the desert sky, is Vian's desert not the very 'domaine de la mort'? It is apt that, where the core of Colin's love for Chloé could be found in Breton's *Nadja*, the spirit of the 'Exopotamian' desert lies in Aragon's *Le Paysan de Paris*. Before one can attempt to ascertain exactly what this side-step, in terms of the pattern of intertextuality, means vis-à-vis Vian's overall strategy, it is necessary first to establish its significance for *L'Automne* itself.

Aragon's Paris stands on the brink of change. The streets once so propitious for idle daydreaming are now under the threat of 'la pioche'. The developers are coming. What exactly is it that will be lost? The answer is: 'les passages'. It is these glass-covered precincts whose imminent loss is mourned by Aragon in this their eulogy. They focussed the light, the source of reverie for the urban 'flâneur':

> Elle [la lumière moderne de l'insolite] règne bizarrement dans ces sortes de galeries couvertes qui sont nombreuses à Paris aux alentours des grands boulevards et que l'on nomme d'une façon troublante des *passages*... (*Aragon*, p.20-21)

---

[13] Louis Aragon, *Le Paysan de Paris* (Paris: Gallimard, 1994), p.15. (Hereafter referred to as *Aragon*.)

This chapter will focus on the mourning of the passages as an allegory for the loss of a fundamental part of Parisian culture; moreover, it will centre upon Vian's stylistic use of small passages of italicized text, which he boldly labels 'Passages' and which lead from one part of the story to the next as the passages of which Aragon writes led from one Parisian street scene to another. In this way, Vian assimilates into his text a variety of Surrealist texts, and, in particular, those which reminisce about the good old days when Paris bathed in a different light. This light was already the source of life in *L'Écume des jours*. Colin's 'flânerie' begins in his own private passage: "Le couloir de la cuisine était clair, vitré des deux côtés, et un soleil brillait de chaque côté car Colin aimait la lumière." (*Ej*, p.42-43) The gradual loss of this light (itself an allegory for the disappearance of the passages) accompanies Chloé's decline. The streets which were to give Chloé to Colin did also warn of potential disaster in the form of a woman who looms up in front of him just before Isis's party:

> Elle allait dans la même direction. On voyait ses jolies jambes dans ses bottillons de mouton blanc, son manteau de peau de pandour décatie et sa toque assortie. Des cheveux roux sous sa toque. [...] Il la dépassa et se mit à pleurer. Elle comptait au moins cinquante-neuf ans. (*Ej*, p.64-65)

And yet, in *L'Écume* there is, at least at the start, some hope. Although the light will fade, Colin does find love. With the weight of her literary heritage hanging over her like a veil of death, it is not sure whether the darkness kills Chloé, or if her marriage kills the light. (To continue the idea of Alise as angel, it seems possible that the ultimate failure of the love which she shares with Colin may play some part in the morbid dénouement.) In *L'Automne* there can be no doubt; in the absence of light the streets can only bring unmitigated disaster. With this in mind, Vian's periodic use of stylistic 'passages' can be seen to be more than a device whereby the authorial voice can gain direct entry into the text. Understanding Vian's use of these passages has always been considered difficult; Pia Birgander, in her study *Boris Vian romancier: Étude des techniques narratives*, writes:

> Le choix d'un terme passe-partout comme Passage convient tout à fait aux fonctions multiples qu'il remplit

> dans *L'Automne à Pékin*; c'est un terme qui semble volontairement ambigu et qui échappe à l'interprétation incontestable et définitive.[14]

However, when placed into the context of *Le Paysan de Paris*, it seems no coincidence that these inserts are given the same name as those Parisian arcades of which the 'flâneurs' were so fond; rather, Vian seems to be giving voice to the streets themselves.

Whereas in *Le Paysan de Paris* the passages are a starting point from which departs a long piece of Surrealist writing (morbid this time in regret for that which will be no more), in *L'Automne* it is a sequence of disasters, originating on the Parisian streets, which bring the novel before the judgement of the passages. Vian gives voice to these monuments; they, as sources of light (and so, of love, purity and the dream of the vianesque), can destroy as well as nurture.

> [...] Il y a déjà une fille, une jolie fille. Il en viendra d'autres, et rien ne peut durer dans ces conditions-là. [...] Avec les filles il faut du triste; ce n'est pas qu'elles aiment le triste - elles le disent, du moins, - mais il vient avec elles. (*R*, p.257)

Thus speaks the first passage. The myth of the pretty girl is shattered. Once basking in the light, shedding love as flowers shed their pollen, they are now reminders of the reign of the 'nénuphar'. The tone of the passage, as voice of the omniscient narrator, then becomes bitter. The second tightens its grip on the hapless protagonists: "[...] Mais il est trop tard maintenant. Cruc, son bateau fera naufrage, et tout sera terminé lorsqu'il arrivera. Alors j'en reparlerai seulement dans le passage suivant, ou même pas." (*R*, p.315)

Walter Benjamin, in his study of Baudelaire, lays the demise of the 'flâneur' at the door of standardisation (in Paris this produced, for example, a new system of house numbering). Thus, with his anonymity shattered, Baudelaire can only regret his lost Paris:

---

[14] Pia Birgander, *Boris Vian romancier: Étude des techniques narratives* (De Lund: Gleerup, 1981), p.190.

> So he roved about in the city which had long since ceased to be home for the 'flâneur'. Every bed in which he lay down had become a 'lit "hasardeux" for him.[15]

The precariousness of illumination, which entailed the loss of the passages, heightened the feeling that the Parisians were living their lives on borrowed time.

> Later, when the disappearance of the arcades made strolling go out of style and gaslight was no longer considered fashionable, it seemed to a last 'flâneur' who sadly strolled through the empty Colbert Arcade that the flickering of the gas-lamps indicated only the fear of the flame that it would not be paid at the end of the month.[16]

Is it this strange quality of basic lighting which is the cause of the 'black and white' of which Aragon spoke in terms of death, and to which Vian is referring in one of his passages: "[...] Car le désert constitue un décor sur lequel tout ressort bien, surtout si le soleil est doué, par hypothèse, de propriétés spéciales"? (*R*, p.257)

It is certainly the case that Vian's characters have but a tenuous hold over the paths of their own lives; Mangemanche, for example, runs out of credit and, as a consequence of his irregularities, which are instantly discovered by the authorities in this 'standardised Paris', is forced to flee from the police. Indeed, the flight of Doctor Mangemanche relies itself on imagery already established in earlier works also concerned with the development of a new Paris far removed from that of the Parisians' memories. As he pulls away in his car he passes the officer charged with his arrest:

---

[15] Walter Benjamin, *Charles Baudelaire: A Lyric Poet in the Era of High Capitalism* (London: Verso, 1992), p.47.

[16] *Ibid.*, p.50-51.

> En haut de la dune, il évita de justesse un cycliste suant, vêtu d'une saharienne de toile cachou du modèle réglementaire et de forts souliers à clous... Une casquette complétait la tenue de vélocipédiste. (*R*, p.370)

That a policeman should venture into the desert sands on such inappropriate transport is not merely an example of Vian's taste for the unusual. He is, in fact, adhering to the standard description of the Parisian policeman: "Des agents cyclistes arrivaient par pelotons. Pluche brailla: - Voilà les vaches à roulettes!"[17] Thus arrive 'les flics' in Dabit's *L'Hôtel du Nord*. A similar description can be seen in Mac Orlan's *Quartier Réservé* (although, it must be noted, this particular novel is set not in Paris, but in the south of France):

> [...] Je surveillais la rue dans la direction de la Maison Rouge. Une avant-garde d'agents cyclistes ne tarda pas à s'abattre comme un vol de rapaces sur le trottoir surchauffé.[18]

The point may be raised that at a time when policemen rode bicycles, a description in a novel of a policeman in such garb is only to be expected. However, a caricatural image of a policeman dressed, 'à une saharienne près', for French city streets pedalling his way across a desert not only says 'policeman', but also 'city'. And when a text which is intertextually motivated to this degree says 'city', it also says 'urban novel'. Such 'cyclistes', then, ride from the streets of Paris (i.e. from the pages of Dabit and Mac Orlan which pave Vian's Paris), via Amadis Dudu's 'raccourci', straight into the shadowlands of Exopotamia. They are summoned not so much by the termination of Mangemanche's credit, as by the sound of 'la pioche'. And this is what the passages have come to represent: the destruction of light and the introduction of darkness ("Et que m'importent le blanc ou le noir? Ils sont du domaine de la mort"). They have become hallowed ground, and a sequence of

---

[17] Eugène Dabit, *L'Hôtel du Nord* (Paris: Denoël, 1990), p.178. (Hereafter referred to as *Dabit*.)

[18] Pierre Mac Orlan, *Quartier Réservé* (Paris: Gallimard, 1994), p.99-100. (Hereafter referred to as *Quartier*.)

novels are their church. And this, perhaps contrary to the expectations of Louis Aragon:

> [...] Car c'est aujourd'hui seulement que la pioche les menace, qu'ils sont effectivement devenus les sanctuaires d'un culte fantomatique des plaisirs et des professions maudites, incompréhensibles hier et que demain ne connaîtra jamais. (*Aragon*, p.21)

In *L'Automne à Pékin*, it is the hotel run by Joseph Barrizone (whose name is a neat combination of 'barre', or 'barricade', and 'zone') which is under direct threat. Joseph, alias Pippo or 'la Pipe', expresses his anxiety in his idiosyncratic dialect:

> C'est des histoires diplomatiques à Amapolis, dit Pippo. Il veut m'extérioriser... Putain, il a que des mots comme ça dans la gueule, ce pourrrque! Il dit qu'il envisageait ça. (*R*, p.329)

However, despite the particularity of Pippo's language, Athanagore has no trouble in interpreting its meaning:

> T'exproprier? dit Atha.
> - C'est ça, dit Pippo. C'est le mot terrestre. (*R*, p.329)

And this facility of comprehension despite Cuivre's earlier difficulties: "C'est des pourrrques!... - Des quoi? demanda Cuivre" (*R*,p.328). The fact is that these characters know the script beforehand. Already theorized in Benjamin's study of Baudelaire, mourned in *Le Paysan de Paris*, the most poignant expression of Pippo's fear has, in fact, already been rendered in the form of the novel. *L'Hôtel du Nord* faces the same fate as 'Chez Pippo': "Dame! Depuis sept ans que j'habite l'hôtel! T'y resteras pas si longtemps. On parle d'exproprier la maison." (*Dabit*, p.166) Not only are both hotels bound to the same fate, but they also share a common adversary:

> Lecouvreur était tout oreilles. Une pensée subite lui traversa l'esprit: l'expropriation! A force d'entendre rabâcher là-dessus, il était devenu sceptique. Et pourtant... depuis que les lignes du chemin de fer de l'Est aboutissaient au canal, on construisait beaucoup dans son voisinage... (*Dabit*, p.210)

> - C'est le chemin de fer qui est gêné par l'hôtel? demanda Cuivre.
> - Oui, dit Pippo. C'est leur putain de chemin de fer... (*R*, p.329)

It must, however, be borne in mind that the fears of these hoteliers are not the expression of general public opinion. 'Les industriels', in whose best interests the picks and shovels make their inexorable progress, are, on the contrary, backed by this powerful voice, as Mac Orlan describes: "On demandait sérieusement aux édiles de donner le signal du premier coup de pioche dans nos maisons moisies. On, c'était l'opinion publique." (*Quartier*, p.91)

For, *Quartier Réservé* is not the story of a poet gracefully strolling along elegant boulevards. 'Et pour cause'. It is precisely in the less salubrious alleyways that the artists have always looked for their illumination. Indeed, Aragon's hotel, the blueprint for those of Dabit and Vian, is not the height of luxury:

> Je me souviens que pour la première fois mon attention fut attirée sur lui par la contre-réclame... qui affirme fièrement qu'il n'a rien à voir avec le meublé du Passage. Ce meublé, au premier étage, est une maison de passe... (*Aragon*, p.23)

In Vian's work the gap between hotel/house and brothel, and, indeed, between whore and angel is often imperceptible. As was seen, in the context of *L'Écume des jours*, the face of woman doubles as that of death. Thus it is that the gradual degradation of women (reified, in *L'Automne à Pékin*, through the tangible decomposition of Rochelle) comes to reflect changes occurring in the streets of Paris. The light in which we gaze upon the girls wandering through these streets, and the pages which constitute their homage, dims, leaving our perception impaired. The change from the 'jolies filles' of *L'Écume* to the brazen girls of *L'Automne* parallels that of the movement from playful innuendo to the less delicate proposition; it is the direct result of the loss of the 'passage'.

It is no coincidence that the girls who bask in the light of *L'Automne à Pékin* (or, rather, its areas of light and dark) are so strangely coloured. Vian's creative use of light achieves an effect similar to that produced by a photographer such as Man Ray. In a foreword to a compilation of Man Ray's photographs, L. Fritz Gruber writes:

> He was an experimenter, who deliberately used «fault» techniques for aesthetic purposes. The technical terms are familiar to every student of photography: solarization (exposing the captured image to flash of light during development to produce a strikingly dark contour), granulation (emphasizing the silver grains of the light-sensitive medium to give the picture an irregular texture), negative printing (reversing the black and white elements of a picture to alienate and enhance the impact of the image), distorsion (angling the enlarger to produce an oblique image of reality), relief processing (placing a transparency over a slightly displaced negative to create a three-dimensional effect on the ultimate print).[19]

Such a description would be fitting for the novelistic techniques used by Vian. In particular, the technique known as 'distorsion' recalls the 'avant-propos' of *L'Écume des jours*:

> Sa réalisation matérielle proprement dite consiste essentiellement en la projection de la réalité en atmosphère biaise et chauffée, sur un plan de référence irrégulièrement ondulé et présentant de la distorsion. (*Ej*, p.40)

---

[19] *Man Ray 1890-1976*, (Köln: Benedikt Taschen, 1992), p.8-9.

There is, however, more than just a general comparison to be made between their respective techniques: *L'Automne à Pékin* provides a clear example of 'negative printing'. Lavande is a negative image of Cuivre: "Sa peau avait exactement la couleur des cheveux de Cuivre, et vice versa." (*R*, p.313) A good example of this from the work of Man Ray is provided by a photograph entitled "Woman with Flowing Hair". This piece shows a woman with a dark face (with bright eyes and lips) and a flowing mane of light-coloured hair. What is even more interesting is that another piece, entitled "Woman with Long Hair", reveals Man Ray's model to be a blonde. This then raises the possibility that, in addition to being negative images of one another, both Cuivre and Lavande are negative images (or, perhaps, distorsions) of Rochelle. Thus, there, is more at work here than simple 'tricks of the light'.

To look back, in the light of this, is to discover the power of the passage in *L'Écume des jours*. The light streaming through the 'plafond à clairevoie', bathing the apartment of Isis Ponteauzanne in 'la vraie réalité', is at the heart of the surreality which generates Colin's encounter with Chloé. It also serves, however, to cast into shadow the seedier side of 'chez Isis'. For, whilst it only heightens the romantic aspect of *L'Écume* to see in her the following aspect of her namesake in Egyptian mythology who "represented the female productive force of nature", it is, perhaps, less tempting to reveal the duality of her heritage ("She was also, with Osiris, thought of as ruler of the Underworld"[20]): could it be that Isis' principal role is that of the madam of a brothel? The loss of the 'passages' is mourned not as a loss of one particular aspect of Parisian architecture; the loss is of an entire subculture. Approximately contemporaneous with the writing of *L'Écume* and *L'Automne* (1946) was the 'Loi Marthe Richard', a law disbanding the brothels. It is certainly interesting to consider Chloé as one of Isis' girls: her name (clos + é) could, thus, signify the termination of a certain kind of 'love', and the subsequent contraction of Colin's apartment 'la fermeture des maisons closes'.

The brothels of *L'Automne* are, like their occupants, scarcely veiled. The extent to which the girls do, or do not lose their innocence reveals both the complexity of both Vian novels and, more importantly, the links between them. The ascent into the heavenly clouds of *L'Écume* is mirrored by the descent into the infernal heat of *L'Automne*; both are depicted by a winding stairwell:

---

[20] *The Concise Oxford Companion to Classical Literature*, ed. by M.C. Howatson & Ian Chilvers (Oxford: Oxford University Press, 1993).

> L'escalier tournait trois fois sur lui-même et amplifiait les sons dans la cage... Colin montait, le nez sur les talons des deux filles. (*Ej*, p.65)

> Cela se passait au sous-sol. Un petit escalier y menait en se tortillant... C'était aussi, par endroits, garni de cuivre rouge et de hublots. (*R*, p.238)

The first stairs lead to the dancing of 'le biglemoi'; the second set expose "le vague brouhaha de pieds remués, de torses pelotés, de rires confidentiels et d'autres moins discrets..." (*R*, p.239): these passages conjure the musicality of the universal brothel.

Aragon, too, sensed the double-edged sword that is the love of the woman of the night, exposed, as it is, by the light of the passage:

> J'oubliais donc de dire que le passage de l'Opéra est un grand cercueil de verre et, comme la même blancheur déifiée depuis les temps qu'on l'adorait dans les suburbes romaines préside toujours au double jeu de l'amour et de la mort [...] On voit dans les galeries à leurs changeantes lueurs qui vont de la clarté du sépulcre à l'ombre de la volupté de délicieuses filles servant l'un et l'autre culte avec de provocants mouvements des hanches et le retroussis aigu du sourire. En scène, Mesdemoiselles, en scène, et déshabillez-vous un peu... (*Aragon*, p.44)

The scene is indeed set, but not merely for the works of Boris Vian. Once again, just as with the threat of expropriation, this call for the undressing of young beauties arrives on the pages of Vian's novels only after passing through the filter formed by the work of his contemporaries. And, again as before, at the forefront of the latter is Raymond Queneau who had himself been part of the Surrealist movement in France, and who seems to share Aragon's grief at the loss of the passages. Thus, in Queneau too, there is a reflection (and this as oblique as in Vian) of the concept of this change in the Parisian cityscape.

The angel is a whore

In Queneau's novel, *Pierrot mon ami*, there is a move from the glass-covered arcades into a glorified peep-show. Instead, as is the case of a crowded street, of the crowd being in the foreground whilst the voyeur gazes furtively on, here the voyeurs themselves become a crowd before which phalanxes of people are put on display. For the pleasure of the so-called philosophers, a trio of fairground workers help reveal more fully the pretty female elements of the elaborate sideshow that is 'le Palace de la Rigolade':

> Petit-Pouce la saisit alors par les bras et, la portant à demi, la fit traverser sans encombre l'appareil; mais, au sortir, la déposa sur une bouche d'air qui, soufflant dans la robe, découvrit deux jambes et des dessous: les philosophes ravis applaudirent, tandis que des personnes à l'esprit innocent se contentaient de rire de la mésaventure arrivée à la dame.[21]

This benevolent view of what may be seen as the seedier side of Parisian pleasures is all part of a wistful look back to a time gone by. As in *Le Paysan de Paris*, this is not idle recollection of a time of 'flânerie' which time and tide have forced into decline, so much as the mourning of a deliberate 'cleansing' of Paris which has left, at least temporarily, a cultural void. The destruction of 'l'Uni-Park' (representative of the pleasures of Mac Orlan's *Quartier Réservé*), which is burned down in a mysterious fire, leaves Pierrot disconsolately wandering the boulevards. Cultural loss is reflected, too, in the loss of friends (through their loss of memory) and more poignantly in the loss, for Pierrot, of love. Life in the good old days had, as integral part, the brothel and the peep-show; for the philosophers had to pay for their pleasure (thus lowering/raising Pierrot to the rank of 'maquereau'): "Une queue se forma, composée de grouillots, de commis et de potaches prêts à lâcher vingt ronds pour voir de la cuisse." (*Pierrot*, p.11)

---

[21] Raymond Queneau, *Pierrot mon ami* (Paris: Gallimard, 1992), p.14. (Hereafter referred to as *Pierrot*.)

The mystery of the destruction of 'l'Uni-Park' (as is the ultimate disaster for all concerned in the journey to Exopotamia) is clearly announced by Aragon:

> Lueur glauque [the light of the passage], en quelque manière abyssale, qui tient de la clarté soudaine sous une jupe qu'on relève d'une jambe qui se découvre. Le grand instinct américain... qui tend à recouper au cordeau le plan de Paris, va bientôt rendre impossible le maintien de ces aquariums humains déjà morts à leur vie primitive, et qui méritent pourtant d'être regardés comme les recéleurs de plusieurs mythes modernes... (*Aragon*, p.21)

And so, it is not only through the exploitation of the term 'passage' that Vian constructs his Parisian texts: the allure and sexual precocity of 'la jolie fille', which began in *L'Écume* and continued in *L'Automne*, is an extension of this intertextual pathway. Hence Colin's ascent to Isis' boudoir is assured by the essential accompaniment of a hint of thigh:

> Colin montait, le nez sur les talons des deux filles. De jolis talons renforcés, en nylon chair, des souliers hauts de cuir fin et des chevilles délicates. [...] Maintenant, il voyait le haut des bas de celle de gauche, la double épaisseur des mailles et la blancheur ombrée de la cuisse. (*Ej*, p.65)

Rochelle, in *L'Automne*, is a direct descendant of these 'filles'. So strong is her literary/socio-cultural heredity that she is unable to remove her uniform, no matter how impractical:

> Ce n'est pas commode, dans ces dunes, dit Angel.
> - Non, avec des souliers à hauts talons, surtout.
> - Vous en mettez toujours pour sortir?
> - Oh, je ne sors pas souvent. Je reste plutôt avec Anne à l'hôtel. (*R*, p.345)

Whereas the girls whom Colin follows up the stairs are given a certain style (they conform to the concept of 'jolies filles' as described in the 'avant-propos'), the Rochelle of the above passage is already wilting, the paraphernalia that was once source of her charms now seeming little short of ridiculous. Other parallel passages reveal a similar trend. On board the ship bound for Exopotamia, for example, the young girl Olive is subjected to the lewd manhandling of the captain. The pathos of this situation, which takes place ironically in one of the most touching scenes in any of Vian's novels, is such that the reader's anger is aroused against the paedophilia of the old man:

> Didiche n'aimait pas que le capitaine devienne rouge comme ça et que ses veines sortent sur son front. [...] Et puis Didiche entendit qu'Olive se mettait à pleurer qu'il la pinçait, et elle se débattit et il vit que le capitaine la tenait en lui faisant mal. (*R*, p.282)

This loss of control on the part of the captain recalls the avuncular caresses of Nicolas of which Alise is the recipient: "Comment ça va, ma nièce? Toujours belle [...] Il lui caressa la poitrine et les hanches." (*Ej*, p.81) However, this isolated incident attracts no complaints of incest or paedophilia (it is true that Alise is not as young as Olive); read, as it is, under a 'purer light', it is dismissed as playful frolicking. It is only when all such incidents are considered together that the exiguity of the gap between the two novels becomes apparent. *L'Automne à Pékin* is simply set in the era of bad light; everything is situated one remove nearer to oblivion. The attitudes of the two girls with regards to their own sexuality are identical: only Olive's age is the difference between precosity and depravity:

> A quoi vois-tu que c'est une fille? dit le capitaine. C'est à cause de ces deux petits machins-là?
> [...]
> - C'est pas si petit que ça, dit Olive.
> Pour faire voir, elle bomba le torse... (*R*, p.282)

> Je ne suis pas si jeune! dit Alise en se redressant sur la banquette capitonnée, pour mettre en valeur sa poitrine provocante. (*Ej*, p.80)

Le Paysan de Paris does not only provide Vian's novels (particularly *L'Automne à Pékin*, without which the more subtle aspects of *L'Écume* as a Parisian text would be incomprehensible) with context and mood, it also has a contribution to make in terms of plot. One particularly surreal occurrence which Aragon recounts seems to have particular relevance to both *L'Automne* and *L'Écume*. It begins as he is looking into the window of a walking stick shop.

> [...] Je m'aperçus que celle-ci baignait dans une lumière verdâtre, en quelque manière sous-marine, dont la source restait invisible. [...] Je ne revenais pas encore de cet enchantement quand je m'aperçus qu'une forme nageuse se glissait entre les divers étages de la devanture. Elle était un peu au-dessous de la taille normale d'une femme, mais ne donnait en rien l'impression d'une naine. Sa petitesse semblait plutôt ressortir de l'éloignement, et cependant l'apparition se mouvait tout juste derrière la vitre. [...] J'aurais cru avoir affaire à une sirène au sens le plus conventionnel de ce mot, car il me semblait bien que ce charmant spectre nu jusqu'à la ceinture qu'elle portait fort basse se terminait par une robe d'acier ou d'écaille, ou peut-être de pétales de roses, mais en concentrant mon attention sur le balancement qui le portait dans les zébrures de l'atmosphère, je reconnus soudain cette personne... C'est dans l'équivoque de l'occupation insultante des provinces rhénanes et de l'ivresse de la prostitution que j'avais rencontré au bord de la Sarre la Lisel... (*Aragon*, p.31)

Entranced by this apparition, he can only stare in her direction and call out: "L'idéal!" Upon the utterance of these words, Aragon's view of the shop becomes distorted ("Alors l'étalage fut pris d'une convulsion générale"). And then the vision is gone: "La clarté mourut avec le bruit de la mer." (*Aragon*, p.32)

Alise, too, dies in a shop. It is in her love for Colin that she generates the froth behind the daydream. This passage may be read as a foretelling of 'the myth of Alise'; it establishes both her death, and the subsequent banishment of the light, and of her potential coming again. She is Alise the martyr, the angel and the frothy revenant. She is the mermaid of folklore, whose power of seduction is matched only by the purity of her heart. But here she is also recognized in her earthly incarnation: she is prostitute, a woman whose destiny it is to live for love and to die by it.

What would the consequences be should Alise the revenant decide to rebel against the injustice of the forsaking of her love? The above passage continues, tracing the path (of Alise's influence) into *L'Automne à Pékin*.

> Il faut dire que le marchand de cannes possède à la vérité deux vitrines et que c'est dans la plus voisine des boulevards que s'était produit le sortilège dont j'eus l'esprit occupé toute la nuit. [...] des pipes font un grave cercle de muettes à la partie moyenne, où la lumière, en jouant, vient caresser leurs têtes hétéroclites. Or, quand je revins au matin, tout avait repris son aspect normal, sauf dans la seconde vitrine, une pipe d'écume qui figurait une sirène, et qui, au râtelier, sans qu'on s'en aperçût, s'était brisée comme dans un vulgaire tir forain, et qui tendait encore au bout de son tuyau d'illusion la double courbe d'une gorge charmante: un peu de poussière blanche tombée sur la silésienne d'un parapluie attestait l'existence passée d'une tête et d'une chevelure. (*Aragon*, p.32-33)

Was the visitation, then, nothing more than the play of light on a rack of pipes? The result of this 'trick of the light' seems nonetheless to be the decapitation of one of the pipes. This need not, however, worry the characters of *L'Automne*, unless they set great store by the breaking of earthenware. But what if the curse of Alise should be carried to a place where the breaking of earthenware is of prime concern?

> Lorsque le nettoyage [du pot] fut chose faite, [Athanagore] remplit le pot de sable, pour ne plus voir l'oeil, le retourna sens dessus dessous et le brisa de plusieurs coups de marteau, puis il ramassa les fragments épars. (*R*,p.262)

And, of course, the article in question is a meerschaum pipe, a pipe cast in 'écume'. When we look more carefully at *L'Automne*, the decapitation of a pipe finally becomes significant:

> Il vit, dans la paroi vitrée, un trou de forme précise. Des éclats de vitre jonchaient le sol. Des gens s'agitaient dans la salle. Angel poussa la porte et entra. Il y avait Amadis, l'interne, Anne et le docteur Mangemanche. Devant le comptoir reposait le corps de Joseph Barrizone. La moitié supérieure de sa tête manquait.
> Angel leva les yeux et vit, fiché dans le mur opposé à la façade vitrée, le Ping 903, engagé jusqu'au train d'atterrisage dans la maçonnerie. Sur le plan supérieur gauche, il y avait le reste du crâne de la Pipe qui glissa doucement jusqu'à l'extrémité effilée de l'aile et s'abattit sur le sol avec un choc mat, amorti par les cheveux noirs frisés de la Pipe. (*R*, p.347)

This death is just the beginning. The death of 'l'interne' is supposedly caused by a mysterious infection of the bite he had received from 'le Ping'. Anne, too, is to die. There is a possibility that their deaths, although apparently unrelated, share a common cause: Exopotamia is ravaged by a strange epidemic. This epidemic is literary by nature. There is a moment when Anne and 'l'interne' act together; a moment when they are both exposed to the same infection:

> [Anne] prit le cadavre sous les aisselles et l'interne saisit les pieds. A reculons, Anne se dirigea vers l'escalier. Il monta lentement; il maintenait loin de lui la tête saignante de Pippo et le corps s'incurvait entre leurs bras pour traîner presque sur les marches, inerte et inconsistant. L'interne souffrait beaucoup à cause de sa main. (*R*, p.347-348)

It is the death of 'la Pipe' which infects Anne and l'interne (the final perfunctory sentence of the above quotation is particularly typical of Vian, that is of Vian leaving one of his clues). Before we can move on, there is one more text, whose part in the death of 'la Pipe' (and thus in the role of death itself) is vitally important, and which must therefore be considered. Aragon provides motive and scenario, but it is Céline who unleashes the mechanism.

Although, as in *L'Écume des jours*, there are glimpses of *Voyage au bout de la nuit*, it is Céline's *Mort à crédit* which best captures the spirit of *L'Automne*. As the railway line approaches, the characters may all be said to be 'living on borrowed time'. In *Mort à crédit* there is a constant feeling that life is moving too fast, and that to reach out for the old times is to admit defeat, effectively to kill oneself. Therein, perhaps, lies the significance of the desert: as the future sweeps away one's past in such a way that the present leaves time only for a fleeting sensation of regret, then there is a need to regress to a kind of primitive state, to escape to the wilderness. Walter Benjamin, in his work on Baudelaire, wrote in connection with the changing of Paris:

> These tendencies [i.e. to break with what is out-dated] turn the fantasy, which gains its initial stimulus from the new, back upon the primal past. In the dream in which every epoch sees in images the epoch which is to succeed it, the latter appears coupled with elements of pre-history - that is to say of a classless society. The experiences of this society, which have their store-place in the collective unconscious, interact with the new to give birth to the utopias which leave their traces in a thousand configurations of life, from permanent buildings to ephemeral fashions.[22]

These utopias are clearly avoided in *L'Automne*; the captain expressly steers away from the island of La Toupie (TOUPIE = UTOPIE). What remains is the regret that is epitomised, in *Mort à crédit*, by the failure of Courtial des Pereires. In particular, the failure of the hot air balloon, 'le Zélé'. In *L'Automne à Pékin*, the failure of 'le Zélé' is reflected in the uncontrollable flight of 'le Ping 903'.

The episode of the launching of the Ping establishes, in a sort of intertextual paroxysm, all the elements of a rapport between *L'Automne* and *Mort à crédit*, especially that of the father/son relationship which exists

---

[22] *Charles Baudelaire: A Lyric Poet in the Era of High Capitalism*, p.159.

between Mangemanche and 'l'interne'. With the disappearance of the Ping are lost all the dreams of professor Mangemanche for whom it represented the pinnacle of his scientific eclecticism. It will reap a rich harvest of death, without bringing the professor very much credit; indeed, his preoccupations with model aircraft (which were common knowledge as far back as the time of his treatment of Chloé) do little to reestablish his 'credit' with the agency in charge of regulating patient recovery/fatality ratios. Mangemanche could no more surely have killed Pippo had he fired on him with a gun: "Le Ping partit comme une balle et s'évanouit en quelques secondes." (*R*, p.344)

Despite the quasi-sadistic attitude which Mangemanche adopts vis-à-vis 'l'interne', there is a certain tenderness between them (they stay together rather like Salamano and his dog in Camus's *L'Etranger*). In fact, Mangemanche fills both the role of Auguste (in his constant criticism which leaves 'l'interne' desperate to be left alone) and that of Courtial (ideal/ersatz father who commands true respect). Even the loud yellow shirts bring to mind the sartorial particularity of Céline's eccentric inventor: "Pour mieux dominer l'assistance, il se juchait en équilibre sur le bord de la nacelle, extraordinairement décoré, redingote, panama, manchettes..."[23] It seems likely that it was purely with this allusion to Courtial in mind that Vian suddenly, as if from nowhere, has Mangemanche (chasing the Ping) dressed in a 'redingote': "Son col vif luisait au-dessus de sa redingote démodée."[24] (*R*, p.344)

Good intentions negated by bad luck, as well as a profusion of mucus, confirm 'l'interne' in his role as Ferdinand.

> - Passez-moi votre mouchoir, dit Mangemanche.
> L'interne lui tendit son dégoûtant chiffon, et Mangemanche tant bien que mal lui banda la main en donnant tous les signes d'une répulsion prononcée.
> - Ça va?
> - Ça va... dit l'interne. (*R*, p.343)

---

[23] Louis-Ferdinand Céline, *Mort à crédit* (Paris: Gallimard, 1992), p.397. (Hereafter referred to as *Mort à Crédit*.)

[24] For the importance of 'la redingote', see Chris Bongie, "Fathers and Sons - The Self-Revelation of Flaubert and Céline", *Romanic Review*, 77 (1986), pp.428-47.

The young assistant's bad luck, which results in a (mortal) bite, is symbolic of Ferdinand's doubts as to the flight of 'le Zélé': "Moi je rigolais beaucoup moins!... Je le prévoyais l'horrible accroc, le décisif! Le funeste! La carambouille terminale..." (*Mort à Crédit*, p.398) Disaster clearly does ensue; in *L'Automne*, however, it is the young assistant 'qui canera' (although the father figure does disappear in strange circumstances).

Disasters happen because Paris, as Baudelaire had known it, underwent change; by the same token, these disasters *are* the changes: thus, Paris is at once location, represented symbolically, and generator of narrative. Similarly, the 'passages' are not only geographical landmarks, separating out the different 'quartiers' of the text, but rites of passage providing entrance into the text for the principal characters. Adrian Rifkin, in his *Street Noises*, writes:

> It seems reasonable that the Passage, with its function of linking of streets and often sharply contrasting social spaces, its reputation as a place of overlapping leisures, should have slipped into becoming a metaphor for passage, should have become so fascinating, whether as a way into the past or as a route between levels of experience.
>
> So too the movement from the edges of Paris to the centre, and from the centre outwards, is a passage and sometimes a rite.25

The first *passage* into the text: the dream of Amadis

The beginning of *L'Automne* is consciously different from the beginning of *L'Écume*. Whereas Colin walks happily from his bathroom, in a direct line towards the kitchen, basking in the sun as it streams through his own glass-covered arcade, Amadis Dudu "suivait sans conviction la ruelle étroite qui constituait le plus long des raccourcis permettant d'atteindre l'arrêt de l'autobus 975" . The pavements, too, are those of Paris in the post-Chloé era: "Il y avait du soleil, pas beaucoup, mais juste devant lui, et le bout de la ruelle luisait doucement, car le pavé était gras" (*R*, p.213). These are quite

---

[25] Adrian Rifkin, *Street Noises: Parisian Pleasure 1900-40* (Manchester: Manchester University Press, 1993), p.50.

clearly the soft pavements which (as well as being flaccid in the sense of which Sartre would have greatly disapproved) hinder Colin's progress in all senses, signifying, as they do, Chloé's demise. They are, then, not pavements propitious for the chance meeting with a love object. Ill-augured pavements bring forth similarly flaccid women: "Des femmes aux gros désirs mous... leur peignoir ouvert sur un grand manque de vertu...".

It is ironic, then, that in such perverse circumstances, Amadis should have any sort of surreal experience. And yet, as he makes his way to the bus stop, policemen and prostitutes begin to merge strangely before his eyes:

> D'après l'ombre de la lanterne rouge du grand six, où vivaient des agents de police camouflés (c'était en réalité un commissariat; et, pour dérouter les soupçons, le bordel voisin portait une lanterne bleue)... (*R*, p.214)

This rapprochement of a police station with a brothel is similar to one taken from the pages of Breton's *Nadja*, source par excellence of the Surrealist love object:

> Il n'y a que quelques jours, Louis Aragon me faisait observer que l'enseigne d'un hôtel de Pourville, qui porte en caractères rouges les mots: MAISON ROUGE, était composée en tels caractères et disposée de telle façon que, sous une certaine obliquité, de la route, «MAISON» s'effaçait et «ROUGE» se lisait «POLICE». (*Nadja*, p.67)

Perhaps this 'clin d'œil', though insufficient to prolong the life of the 'flâneur' in the absence of the arcades, represents the final vestiges of the former power of the streets. This final adieu made, Amadis can expect no deliverance.

This use of *Nadja* as an intertext becomes more significant because of its place of insertion in *L'Automne*. The lettered sections, A to D, represent rupture, the departure from one place to another (here the change is one of geographical location, used to signify a chronological passage in Parisian history), and so, from one text (or set of texts) to another. We find ourselves, once more, "à l'endroit où les fleuves se jettent dans la mer" (*Ej*, p.122). Thus, as the novel leaves behind *Nadja*, so too it leaves behind *La Nausée*.

The mode of transport by which Amadis leaves the city for Exopotamia is the bus. The route taken by this bus is the first 'line' along which the novel is constructed (the second, if the complex division into sections is to be considered as a kind of topographical plan of the action); it is also a framing device (Angel leaves by the same bus at the end). It is, thus, interesting that as important a text as *La Nausée* should provide the model for this passage:

> Les boutiques se succédaient dans un chatoiement de couleurs brillantes; il se plaisait à entrevoir son reflet dans les grandes glaces des devantures, mais rougit quand il le vit profiter de sa position commode pour dérober des choses qui étaient en vitrine, et se tourna de l'autre côté. (*R*, p.218)

And in the scene set on 'le tramway de Saint-Elémir' in *La Nausée*:

> Derrière les vitres, des objets bleuâtres défilent, tout roides et cassants, par saccades. Des gens, des murs; par ses fenêtres ouvertes une maison m'offre son coeur noir, bleuissant ce grand logement de briques jaunes qui s'avance en hésitant, en frissonnant, et qui s'arrête tout d'un coup en piquant du nez. Un monsieur monte et s'assied en face de moi. [...] Toute la droite de son corps s'est affaissée, le bras droit est collé au corps... (*Nausée*, p.178-180)

Both scenes offer an encounter with the Other, each typical of the respective author: Vian's suggests the Other through a reflection of self, a self beyond one's control; Sartre's, on the other hand, conveys discomfort caused by the realisation that one is fundamentally like the Other, and that he is mere object. The problem of the Other, so prominent in the work of Vian, is in a transitional phase in *L'Automne*. The extreme similarity of certain characters in *L'Écume* is never fully developed; *L'Automne* introduces the idea that Angel and Anne may be two sides of the same coin[26]; it is finally in *L'Herbe rouge* that Vian really focuses on the existential crisis and the reality/lethality of the Other. In terms of a progressive development of this kind, it is interesting to speculate that the final lines of *L'Automne* are a continuation of Sartre's early contemplation of the reality of his fellow man:

> Et puis la main s'est mise aussi à trembler et, quand elle est arrivée à la hauteur du crâne, un doigt s'est tendu et s'est mis à gratter le cuir chevelu, de l'ongle. [...] Les vitres tremblent, le bras tremble, l'ongle gratte, gratte, la bouche sourit sous les yeux fixes et l'homme supporte sans s'en apercevoir cette petite existence qui gonfle son côté droit, qui a emprunté son bras droit et sa joue droite pour se réaliser. Le receveur me barre le chemin.
> - Attendez l'arrêt.
> Mais je le repousse et je saute hors du tramway.
> (*Nausée*, p.180)

A comparison of the above monstrous description of the corporeal nature of man with the final lines of *L'Automne* shows this disturbing animality translated into the simian behaviour of 'le receveur':

> Le receveur s'approcha de lui.
> - Terminus!... dit Angel.
> - Vole!... répondit le receveur en levant le doigt vers le ciel. (*R*, p.420)

---

[26] Raymond Radiguet's novel, *Le Bal du Comte d'Orgel*, has as main protagonist a man named Anne. His full name, Anne d'Orgel, can be seen to contain both of Vian's principal male characters. A rearrangement of the constituent letters could be said to reveal an interesting insight into Angel's heritage:

Anne d'Orgel > An (ne d'Or) gel > Angel né d'or

It has already been shown how Alise's golden fleece survives her bodily death, giving life, as it were, to the second novel. (However, despite these features which make Radiguet's novel of illusion and the complications of a ménage à trois a possible source of influence, the problems of Vian's triad have a closer affinity with those of Constant's in his *Adolphe*.)

The situation is clearly reversed here: whereas Roquentin flees the confirmation of his own reality, Angel, seeking to 'go all the way', is warned (seemingly) of his difference. However, the importance of any intertextuality existing between *La Nausée* and *L'Automne à Pékin* should not be exaggerated: it is, rather, part of a cumulative process. Vian's final lines act as a node (as does the hotel) where several intertexts meet to contribute to a final definition. Indeed, in a text which is constructed around the conjunction of a system of 'lines', the simple coming together of the various intertexts is definition enough. Thus, Angel's 'terminus' is intertextual, and must be reached outside the mother-text; hence the command to fly.

Amadis' actual entrance into the story proper is made on the back of a fairy tale. In classic style he falls asleep:

> Le receveur s'endormit et glissa sur la plate-forme où il chercha, dans son sommeil, une position plus commode. Amadis se sentait gagné par une espèce de somnolence hardie qui s'infiltrait en lui un poisson ravageur. (*R*, p.218)

Prior to his getting on the bus, Amadis' preoccupations had been with the time, and particularly the consequences of each of his actions vis-à-vis the time of his arrival at work. Alice herself entered Wonderland thanks to the 'possibility of being late':

> [...] But when the Rabbit actually *took a watch out of its waistcoat-pocket*, and looked at it, and then hurried on, Alice started to her feet... and burning with curiosity, she ran across the field after it...[27]

As in Alice's case, for Amadis: "It *was* a curious dream" (*Alice*, p.125). It is a dream in which others will take part, rather like "the experiences of this society, which have their storeplace in the collective unconscious" of which Benjamin wrote. If we consider Amadis as principal dreamer, given his

---

[27] Lewis Carroll, *Alice's Adventures in Wonderland & Through the Looking-Glass* (New York: Airmont, 1965), p.16. (Hereafter referred to as *Alice*.)

privileged position as first character to be introduced, then the scenes entitled "RÉUNION" become the fulfilment of his wishes. What could be more desirable for a humble office clerk, constantly under the yoke of the 'l'horloge pointeuse', than to be the much eulogized director of a successful foreign enterprise? The unlikeliness of this eventuality (and, thus, the oneiric nature of the story) is suggested by Athanagore who, along with l'abbé Petitjean, is an omniscient figure, overseeing and guiding events with a paternal benevolence: "N'empêche que vous faisiez moins votre directeur en attendant le 975..." (*R*, p.289)

Yet such is his dream. It is also a dream which fulfils, by virtue of its repetition and its cast of characters, a literary prophesy. By passing back from Benjamin and his work on Baudelaire to Baudelaire himself, one can find the future of Paris foretold, as if in hieroglyphics, in the lines of *Les Fleurs du Mal*. For example, "Les sept vieillards" recalls a vision of death, the death of a "fourmillante cité, cité pleine de rêves"; the grotesque nature of this vision is powerful enough to leave the poet "malade et morfondu, l'esprit fiévreux et trouble"[28]. What is this vision that it has such an effect?

> Tout à coup, un vieillard dont les guenilles jaunes
> Imitaient la couleur de ce ciel pluvieux,
> Et dont l'aspect aurait fait pleuvoir les aumônes,
> Sans la méchanceté qui luisait dans ses yeux,
>
> M'apparut. [...]
>
> A quel complot infâme étais-je donc en butte,
> Ou quel méchant hasard ainsi m'humiliait?
> Car je comptais sept fois, de minute en minute,
> Ce sinistre vieillard qui se multipliait!

This evil septet becomes a powerful part of a modern Parisian mythology. Thus, in *Le Paysan de Paris*, seven is again the number, this time of barbers:

> Au lieu de porter comme la précédente un aventureux nom
> d'Opéra, *Norma*, qui est comme un balcon sur des vignes,

---

[28] Charles Baudelaire, "Les sept vieillards", in *Les Fleurs du Mal*.

> la maison se recommande des patronymes de sept coiffeurs:
> VINCENT
> PIERRE
> HAMEL
> ERNEST
> ADRIEN
> AMÉDÉE
> CHARLES (*Aragon*, p.55-56)

It is unsurprising to learn, therefore, that the total number of people present at the meetings of the board is none other than seven, a fact which Vian is at pains to indicate:

> Le dernier était en retard et la séance commença sans lui.
> Ce qui fait cinq personnes et un huissier, et une personne en retard, qui compte tout de même, soit sept en tout... (*R*, p.269)

Even the 'guenilles jaunes' and the 'méchanceté qui luisait dans ses yeux' recur in the pages of *L'Automne*: in the shirts of Mangemanche and in the eyes of 'l'huissier' ("[...] Une vilaine lumière grise clignotait dans ses yeux ternis" [*R*, p.267]) respectively.

Finally, the poem also contributes to the means of transportation of the sleeping Amadis into the dream-world (where he will have his dream in a dream...). As town cedes to desert, bus becomes boat:

> Les arbres brillaient au soleil, comme les boutiques; leurs feuilles fraîches frottaient le toit de l'autobus, et faisaient le même bruit que les plantes marines sur la coque d'un petit bateau. Le roulis de l'autobus berçait Amadis... (*R*, p.219)

The changing of a bus into a boat is not without significance. Sea journeys which are, in fact, symbolic representations of dreams recall Céline's *Voyage au bout de la nuit*. Here, and later when it is the turn of Angel to voyage into the desert, the intertextual references to Céline, as well as to other texts, are such that the reader can only be inclined to view Exopotamie as a dream kingdom, and more precisely an oneiric representation of Paris. The journey of Amadis has taken the reader through a significant mutation: Paris has become desert, a bus a boat and waking moment has turned into dream. The effect is double: the text is leaving behind former intertexts in search of new inspiration; this is representative not only of the development of the novel, but of the continuing development of Vian the author. By leaving behind the intertexts of *L'Écume des jours*, Vian is demanding acceptance as a writer of mature fiction. Secondly, the reader becomes gradually conditioned to the usage of sending the characters to sleep in order to place them into the text proper: this at once places the text in the oneiric tradition of Carroll (and Queneau who was influenced by him) and Céline, and allows a retrospective understanding of Colin and Alise's place in *L'Écume*.

The second *passage* into the text: the dream of Claude Léon

It is on just such a boat that begins the journey of the second character, Claude Léon: "Claude Léon entendit à bâbord la sonnerie de trompette du réveille-matin..." (*R*, p.224). This can be read as another instance of a character from Vian's 'real' life (Claude Léon was a work colleague of Vian) entering the realm of his fiction. But, just as in the case of Pippo, Vian adds to this character of *L'Automne à Pékin* extra 'fictional' weight; in this way, he seems to be attempting (with a minimal amount of success) to dispel the increasingly dominant myth that his work exists "pour amuser les copains"[29]. Thus, Claude Léon, from the moment that he wakens on the frothing sea of the Vian novel, becomes literary figure extraordinaire.

His first task, as one of the assembling departees for Exopotamia, is to have an experience of the Other. In Léon's case, the Other comes from within; it is himself ("Il avait éteint brusquement la veille, juste en faisant une grimace devant la glace, et voulait la revoir avant d'aller à son bureau. Il alluma d'un

---

[29] Perhaps one might add to the comment made by Pestureau regarding Exopotamia ("Exopotamie: Pays imaginaire à partir de «exo»: en dehors, hors de et «potamos»: fleuve." [*R*, p.1308]) by suggesting that this desert constitutes an 'Ex aux potes [et aux] amis'... (My thanks here to Anne Frémiot.)

seul coup. Sa figure d'hier était encore là." [*R*, p.224]) In terms of the four novels, this 'insight' is a glimpse forwards. For it is Wolf of *L'Herbe rouge* who will begin his solipsistic voyage of discovery in a mirror. Wolf's use of the mirror is, of course, (amongst other things) a reference to the voyage made by Carroll's Alice through the looking-glass; here, too, the world of Carroll is but the thickness of a paperback away: "Le sommeil ne s'échappait qu'à regret de tous ses pores dilatés, en faisant un bruit très doux, comme une souris qui rêve." (*R*, p.224) Without the steady build-up of references to sleep, mice and adventure, this strange adjectival phrase would elude the reader. This mouse has an alias. He has already appeared before Amadis, just as he sleep-fell into his bus/rabbit hole: "Le receveur s'endormit et glissa sur la plate-forme où il chercha, dans son sommeil, une position plus commode"(*R*, p.218). In *Alice's Adventures in Wonderland*, the Dormouse strives to continue his sleep:

> The Dormouse had closed its eyes by this time, and was going off into a doze; but, on being pinched by the Hatter, it woke up again with a little shriek... (*Alice*, p.77)

The insistence shown by his companions on keeping the little Dormouse awake is almost pathological. On his conscious existence rests the concrete reality of Wonderland, which is being dreamt by Alice. As the dream of the Dormouse is a dream within a dream, so, by association with it, the dreams of *L'Automne* come to represent different levels of consciousness; and each level of consciousness is reflected in a different literary source. So where exactly does Claude Léon come from? His Sartrean nature is such that he will be defined in his actions.

The catalyst for Léon's departure is his boss, M. Saknussem[30]. With his desire to take arms, he is quick to reestablish the links between *L'Automne* and the decay of Paris. He is ready to man the barricades which Paris has seen before on numerous occasions. It would seem that Saknussem is ready for revolution. Benjamin sees this instinct for revolution and building barricades at the heart of Baudelaire's poetry; he writes:

---

[30] Pestureau notes the literary heritage of Saknussem: "[...] Chez Verne, Arne Saknussemm est un «hardi et fantastique voyageur» relatant son exploration inouïe sur un manuscrit runique qui guidera le professeur Libenbrock et le jeune Axel (*Le Voyage au centre de la Terre*)." (*R*, p.1308)

> As a recent historian of the Commune writes, these workers 'preferred battle in their own quarters to an encounter in the open field... and if it had to be, they preferred to die behind a barricade built of cobblestones from a Paris street'.[31]

In this light one of Nicolas' more peculiar utterances can be understood: "Je trouve qu'une certaine familiarité n'est admissible que lorsque l'on a gardé les barrières ensemble, et ce n'est point le cas" (*Ej*, p.57). Whether Nicolas has manned a barricade with Saknussem remains unknown.[32]

It is Saknussem's desire that Léon provide him with a revolver that combines the anger at the loss of Paris as an urban ideal and the fear of the Other. In his acquisition of the revolver, Léon becomes Sartre's Érostrate. The character of the short story bearing his (chosen) name is not a run of the mill misanthropist; he is literally petrified by other people (and, indeed, by the idea that there should be Others), and his answer is to kill. Vian describes the sensation of carrying the revolver in the streets in terms very similar to those used by Sartre:

> Il le sentait le long de sa cuisse, lourd et glacé comme une bête morte. Le poids tirait sa poche et sa ceinture, sa chemise bouffait à droite sur son pantalon. Son imperméable empêchait que l'on voie, mais, à chaque avancée de la cuisse, il se dessinait un grand pli sur l'étoffe et tout le monde allait le remarquer. (*R*, p.228)

> Je le prenais le dimanche, je le mettais tout simplement dans la poche de mon pantalon et puis j'allais me promener - en général sur les boulevards. Je le sentais qui tirait sur mon pantalon comme un crabe, je le sentais contre ma cuisse tout froid.[33]

---

[31] *Charles Baudelaire: A Lyric Poet in the Era of High Capitalism*, p.16.

[32] This talk of manning barricades together may be more than a simple 'turn of phrase'; barricades were put up in Paris as recently as during the liberation of Paris in the closing stages of the Second World War.

[33] Jean-Paul Sartre, "Érostrate", in *Le Mur* (Paris: Gallimard, 1992), pp.79-99 (p.81).

Vian's Érostrate, however, is a condensation of the original. On carrying the gun, Léon is instantly struck down with the paranoia which is later to consume Érostrate; he is terrified that he should be 'seen'. For Sartre's character the purchase of the revolver provides temporary relief from the fear of the Other: "De ce point de vue, tout est allé beaucoup mieux à dater du jour où je me suis acheté un revolver". In fact, the early behaviour of Sartre's Érostrate is a distorted form of 'flânerie': the revolver (so loaded with Freudian significance as to be clichéd) is like an erect penis, actively thrusting his identity against the clammy suffocation of the Other:

> Mais peu à peu, il se réchauffait au contact de mon corps. Je marchais avec une certaine raideur, j'avais l'allure d'un type qui est en train de bander et que sa verge freine à chaque pas. (*Mur*, p.81)

This exhibitionistic side of Érostrate is captured neatly by Vian, however, in a passing image:

> L'égalisateur noir et froid n'avait encore rien dit; il reposait lourdement près du fromage qui, effrayé, s'éloignait de toute sa vitesse, sans oser toutefois quitter son assiette nourricière." (*R*, p.228)

This desire to remain beyond the gaze of the outside world, within a protective womb, the fear of becoming a living penis is the quintessence of 'mauvaise foi'. And it is panic caused by the tauntingly hostile faces of the crowd which forces both Sartre's and Vian's Érostrate to fire:

> A ce moment je *sus* que j'allais me mettre à hurler. Je ne voulais pas: je lui lâchai trois balles dans le ventre. Il tomba d'un air idiot, sur les genoux, et sa tête roula sur son épaule gauche.

(Hereafter referred to as *Mur*.)

> - Salaud, lui dis-je, sacré salaud! (*Mur*, p.97)

> [...] La colère commençait à saisir Claude [...] Il plongea la main dans sa poche et tira l'égalisateur, et il se mit à rire parce que le cycliste bafouillait et reculait, puis il sentit un choc terrible sur sa main, et le bâton du flique retomba. (*R*, p.229)

It is the 'bâton du flique' which suddenly sends Léon from one nightmare to another. More precisely, Léon is sent tumbling from "Érostrate" into *L'Etranger*. The story does not end with the standard intervention of the strong arm of the law. Léon finds himself, once more, with the gun in his hand:

> [...] Et puis il le déchargea avec soin sur le cycliste qui porta les deux mains à sa ceinture et s'assit tout doucement en faisant âââh... du fond de la gorge. (*R*, p.229)

The motives for this crime are confused; the only discernible evidence is intertextual. Talking of Léon, Petitjean later exclames: "Vous comprenez, dit-il, que ce garçon ne méritait pas de rester en prison. [...] Il méritait d'être guillotiné." (*R*, p.310) The facts are indisputable, and there is, after all, a precedent against which he may be judged: Meursault. The events which condemn Meursault (other than that of not having cried at his mother's funeral) are common to those in the case of Claude Léon: he fired first, for reasons unknown (even to himself), and then he fired again:

> Alors, j'ai tiré encore quatre fois sur un corps inerte où les balles s'enfonçaient sans qu'il y parût. Et c'était comme quatre coups brefs que je frappais sur la porte du malheur.[34]

---

[34] Albert Camus, *L'Etranger* (Paris: Gallimard, 1990), p.95. (Hereafter referred to as *Camus*.)

For Léon, too, these shots buy his ticket into another world (another part of the story), a world which, for want of a better name, could be called 'le malheur'.

In typical style, Vian then enhances his own text by drawing a thin veil over the link with *L'Etranger*, which he wishes to remain free to develop more fully in the following passage. Thus, immediately the fatal act is committed, Léon, whose weapon has already been referred to in typically 'hard boiled' style as an 'égalisateur' (*R*, p.228), is turned into a cross between Philip Marlowe and John Wayne: "La fumée des cartouches sentait bon et Claude souffla dans le canon, comme il l'avait vu faire au cinéma" (*R*, p.230). The influence of 'La Série Noire' throughout the text, if relatively minor in comparison with certain other genres, is continuous. Despite the comical edge (or, perhaps, because of it), the contribution of so-called 'hardboiled' detective fiction is a real one.

As in the story of Meursault, the events culminating in the murder take up only half the story. Both Léon and Meursault stick to the only version of events that they are able to recount: the truth. Their respective lawyers are not enraptured by this lack of inventiveness:

> Je vous laisse, dit-il [l'avocat]. Il n'y a plus qu'à attendre. Je tâcherai de faire de mon mieux; vous ne m'y aidez guère! [...] De nouveau, il [Léon] avait chaud dans les mains et les jambes." (*R*, p.230)
>
> Mon avocat n'avait pas l'air content. Il m'a dit: «Ceci n'est pas assez.»
> [...] Il faisait très chaud. (*Camus*, p.102-103)

The links between the two texts become tighter still when a guard, whom Léon admonishes for the poor quality of the string he has provided that Léon might hang himself, replies: "Ça m'est égal..." (*R*, p.232). After this occurrence, this phrase, which has become synonymous with Meursault, becomes as ubiquitous in *L'Automne* as in *L'Etranger*. It is at this point that Léon goes through another 'passage'; he had already passed from the pages of Sartre to those of Camus in the same way as Amadis does, by falling asleep ("[...] Il remit l'égalisateur dans sa poche, et il s'affala sur le flique, il voulait dormir." [*R*, p.230]). He now passes away à la Meursault. On trying to hang himself from braces attached to the bars of his cell window...

> Il se lança une seconde fois; les bretelles s'allongèrent à fond, et il atterrit mollement sous la fenêtre. Alors le barreau se descella et lui arriva sur la tête comme la foudre. (*R*, p.232)

The powerful blow to the back of the head which is dealt by the falling bar is not unlike that which Meursault is destined to receive from Madame la Guillotine. Given that L'abbé Petitjean, who makes his appearance the following day, is able to inform Léon as to the good health of his mother ("Ma mère va bien? demanda Claude Léon. - Mais certainement, dit Petitjean." [*R*, p.233]), and then announces that he will come to pick him up in "la voiture des morts", one may be tempted to suggest that Léon's rite of passage is death itself (*L'Etranger* does, after all, begin: "Aujourd'hui, maman est morte" [*Camus*, p.9]).

The implications of the death of Claude Léon are far-reaching. To cast Petitjean in the role of 'Grim Reaper' (and himself and Athanagore as a pair of overseeing deities) is to speculate that all the characters who travel from the city to the desert do, in fact, die. In one sense all are perfectly eligible for the role; all experience the presence of the Other. In his play of 1944, *Huis clos*, Sartre makes the claim that "l'enfer, c'est les autres"[35]. In this case, all the characters are dead, a hotel room their place of eternal torment. What could be more pertinent? Is this incarceration in the Exopotamian desert a test to see how they will react when isolated from the Parisian crowds? If it is rather the case that the characters of the novel are the only gods, it is perhaps possible to consider Atha and Petitjean as more than simple masters of ceremonies. It may be, in continuation of the theme of the loss of the 'arcades', that the novel can be read as a satire of social codification, raising these two characters to the level of ministers in charge of a standardizing 'clean-up' operation. To take all the homosexuals, psychopaths and general deviants and let them fight it out is certainly a radical solution to the problems of the modern city. *L'Automne à Pékin* as satire of social codification? If Petitjean is in charge of collecting samples, it is in the pages of Benjamin that Atha's role as resident rock-collector is justified: "Delvau... claimed that he could easily divide the Parisian

---

[35] Jean-Paul Sartre, *Huis Clos* (Paris: Gallimard, 1989), p.93.

public according to its various strata as easily as a geologist distinguishes the layers in rocks."[36]

The departure of Claude Léon is parallel to that of Amadis, both manifestly (all the sections A-D being feeders into the main text) and in terms of the textual strategy. Once more, there is a Carrollinian entry into the dream which is also an entry into new literary ground for Vian. The significance of Claude Léon lies not in the fact that it is a 'clin d'œil' to an actual friend of the author, but that this character is effectively lost to the text: his dream is the most intimately linked with death both textually and intertextually (through the execution of Meursault). This is memorial to the ploy of using real people as characters. The Vian novel is beginning to come of age. But what does all this mean for Angel? The possibilities are at least twofold. Supposing, for example, that Atha and Petitjean rule their desert province like Pontius Pilate: one of the convicts may be granted his freedom ("Vole!"). Apropos of Anne's death, Atha asks: "Pourquoi fallait-il choisir?" (*R*,p.401). (In *La Nausée*, Sartre writes: "Mais il faut choisir: vivre ou raconter." [*Nausée*, p.64]) Thus it is that Angel flies (is made angel); Anne dies that he may live on. Alternatively, perhaps Angel's very difference lies in the fact that he is, from the outset, an angel, and, thus, the only one who is really alive.

The third *passage* into the text: the dream of Angel

Angel's entrance into the text is interesting in that it is intratextual in nature rather than intertextual. Angel comes from the pages of *L'Écume des jours*. The pigeons which once (as "les Pigeons-de-Rechange pour les Squares et les Monuments" [*Ej*, p.77]) gave character to the strolls of Colin and Chloé are now being shaved: "[...] Il regardait les techniciens procéder à la tonte annuelle des pigeons du square." (*R*, p.234-235)

Against this familiar background of strangely suited workers and flying feathers, Angel waits. Small wonder (especially since the pigeons are 'aquatiques'), then, that: "Cela faisait penser à la mousse de la mer quand le

---

[36] *Charles Baudelaire: A Lyric Poet in the Era of High Capitalism*, p.39.

vent souffle..." (*R*, p.235). The down of the pigeons helps form the transition from froth to sand, from *L'Écume* to *L'Automne*:

> [...] On la voit [la mousse] sur le sable en gros paquets blancs qui vibrent sous le vent, et si l'on pose le pied dessus, elle vous ressort entre les doigts de pieds. C'est doux et ça a l'air de se feutrer un peu à mesure que ça sèche. Anne et Rochelle n'arrivaient pas. (*R*, p.235)

Although he is born of the froth, he cannot become whole before the arrival of the others (the Others before whom he will have his 'être-pour-autrui'), those of the sand. Like the froth, he must dry and set. For, as much as Rochelle can be said to be the perfect love object generated by the combined passions of Angel and Anne (she, as 'roc' or 'roche', is a raw material for their social production: they make pebbles for railways and glass for lightbulbs respectively), she also helps to generate Angel:

$$AN (ne) + (roch) EL (le) = AN (g) EL$$

It is impossible to be sure of the exact relationship that exists between this triad of characters; this is, clearly, a deliberate ploy on Vian's part. What we can be sure of is that Angel is empty before their arrival, and that he is less empty (ready to fly) when he has, to a certain extent, consumed them. The Sartrean elements of the triad ('être-pour-soi', 'être-en-soi' and 'être-pour-autrui') are there, the concentration of Sartrean intertexts and of experiences of Otherness prove as much.

When Angel first meets Rochelle, he tries to place her in terms of intratextuality. Since she is beautiful, he wonders if she may be the original beauty: "Il trouvait difficile de la regarder en face. Elle brillait trop. Pourtant, ses yeux [...] Il fallait voir la couleur..." (*R*, p.237). He is blinded by her resemblance to a figment of a literary past; in Rochelle's eyes there is the briefest flash of the brilliance of Alise.

> Oh! dit Rochelle. Vous ne devez pas dire des choses comme ça! [...] Rochelle avait un peu rougi, et Angel regrettait ce commentaire perfide. (*R*, p.237)

Unfortunately, she is more Chloé (whose name is contained within Rochelle) than Alise. Angel's love for her will be that of Colin for Chloé (unshakeable despite everything), except that its emptiness will be more obvious; once more man will love Alise in absentia. The love which Angel will desire from her will come closer to breaking *Le Tabou de l'inceste* (the text made famous by its place of honour as first epigraph in *L'Automne*) than did the various near incestuous loves of *L'Écume*. Rochelle's interest (which is, even at the start, so close to being sexual) in Angel is that of a sibling: "Vous êtes le type dont on a envie d'être la soeur" (*R*, p.240). The confusion into which Angel is thrown is increased by Rochelle's sadistic impersonations of Alise: "[...] Et Rochelle riait, agitant ses cheveux éclatants sur le col de son tailleur vert vif..." (*R*, p.241). Indeed, the Œdipal nature of the passions which torment this curious ménage à trois will finally lead to murder.

So, Angel, too, has an experience of Otherness; it is more like that of Claude Léon than that of Amadis, since it is a vision of himself and not of another. Whether he sees himself in Anne (where Anne is an embodiment of his desire for Rochelle), or whether he sees himself in Rochelle (where Rochelle is an embodiment of his desire for Anne) is not at all sure: it may be that they are both reflections of his distant love for Alise. Or none of the above. However, experience of the Other there is.

The method of travel of Angel, Anne, Rochelle and the remaining characters is also typical: they fall asleep: "L'interne dormait comme un bienheureux, Anne aussi et Cornélius aussi. Mangemanche bâilla." (*R*, p.255) The final White Rabbit is a nurse who "entra avec tout ce qu'il fallait pour les piqûres" (*R*, p.256).

Before battle can be joined in the desert, there remains one final passage which must be looked at in order to combine all the different forms of entry into the story in some kind of theoretical unity. This passage is the final in the series of 'sea journeys', the voyage which will transport Angel and the others to the desert. As has already been mentioned, the maritime theme of this and the previous journeys serves to unite *L'Automne* with the great text of a voyage which crosses miles of sea without ever leaving Paris: *Voyage au bout de la nuit*.

On board the ship two new characters appear: Olive and Didiche. The two children, whose own intertextual sources are diverse but traceable (to such texts as Richard Hughes' *A High Wind in Jamaica*, where children and their various adventures with pirates and the like make up the story), are, here, more important as intratextual signposts, pointing forward to a time when they will take to the skies (in *L'Arrache-cœur*). The two children are also born of intertextuality in the sense that their parents are imbued with a literary heritage in line with trends already manifest in the novel (and they look forward, therefore, as the new generation). They are "la fille de Marin et... le fils de Carlo, les deux agents d'exécution embauchés par la compagnie" (*R*, p.279). As 'agents d'exécution', Carlo et Marin reinforce links with *L'Etranger* (the execution of Meursault) and with *L'Écume*, where even the execution of a prescription was carried out with a little guillotine.

It is the events which come to pass between the two children and the old captain of the vessel which are of significant intertextual importance. The episode begins with a less than skilful exhibition of 'vol sur le dos' by a passing cormorant. This recalls the poem "L'Albatros", in which Baudelaire likens the poet's life to that of a grounded albatross. Vian turns the poem around, his 'cormoran' displaying an evident lack of grace on the wing as well as on the deck. The idea of a poet lacking the social skills necessary for the 'real world' is expanded by Vian who shows this world for what it is: a cruel and twisted menagerie. Thus, Baudelaire's lines apply to Man, and especially to the captain here present:

> Ce voyageur ailé, comme il est gauche et veule!
> Lui, naguère si beau, qu'il est comique et laid![37]

'Naguère' because once there was the filter of the arcades to show everything in a different light. Vian's attack on men is subtly strengthened by his parody of the humiliation meted out by Sartre to his famous humanist, 'l'Autodidacte'. In *La Nausée* the humanism of 'l'Autodidacte' is tainted by his paedophilia. (In *L'Automne*, the optimism of the humanist is rejected in a double-edged assault incriminating the paedophile and the homosexual both of whom can be labelled by the French term 'pédéraste': "Est-ce qu'on ne peut pas aimer les hommes sans être pédéraste?" asks Amadis [*R*, p.291].) The scene in which l'Autodidacte cannot restrain himself from touching two boys is set in a library, a place for silent study away from the hubbub of conversations, a library run by an authoritative Corsican. The setting for the captain's indiscretion is not dissimilar: "Le capitaine aimait bien qu'on vînt le déranger sur sa passerelle, car il avait horreur du gendarme et c'était formellement interdit de lui parler." (*R*, p.279)

The method of acquiring knowledge which 'l'Autodidacte' has chosen is to read every book in the library in alphabetical order. This behaviour,

---

[37] Charles Baudelaire, "L'Albatros", in *Les Fleurs du Mal*.

although idiosyncratic, is not unique: the ornithological knowledge of Vian's captain is also the result of a curiously random learning technique. To Didiche, who wishes to know the name of the bird which they have befriended, he replies:

> Je ne sais pas... et ça prouve bien que ce n'est pas un oiseau ordinaire, parce que les oiseaux ordinaires, je les connais: il y a la pie, le fanfremouche et l'écubier [...]
> - Mince!... murmura Didiche. Vous en savez des choses, capitaine.
> - C'est que j'ai appris, dit le capitaine. (*R*, p.281)[38]

For their offences the two paedophiles receive the same punishment:

> [...] Le Corse émit un petit gémissement voluptueux et soudain il écrasa son poing sur le nez de l'Autodidacte. (*Nausée*, p.235)

> [...] Il [Didiche] vit que le capitaine la tenait en lui faisant mal. Il prit le pavillon et en donna, de toutes ses forces, un coup sur la figure du capitaine... (*R*, p.282)

---

[38] The actions of the captain are not necessarily ordered by one intertext alone, Vian's reading being as eclectic as that of 'l'Autodidacte'. Another possible text, describing a sea voyage of a group of small children and their capture by pirates, and which provides an example of a friendship between a man and a girl *almost* lapsing into paedophilia, is Richard Hughes' *A High Wind in Jamaica*:

> At that moment Jonsen had staggered up to Emily, and putting one hand under her chin, had begun to stroke her hair with the other. A sort of blind vertigo seized her: she caught his thumb and bit as hard as she could [...] And yet Jonsen, in avoiding her, had himself more the air of being ashamed than angry... which was unaccountable. (*A High Wind in Jamaica* [London: Harvill, 1994], p.142-144) (Hereafter referred to as *Hughes*.)

Whereas in *La Nausée* sympathy is aroused for 'l'Autodidacte', as he is actually driven on by the joint desire of the 'salauds' who wish to empower themselves in their joint condemnation of a disgusting act, in Vian's version there is little compassion for the ugly fumblings of the captain; Didiche's action is noble by virtue of the purity of his intentions: this is purity as only a child (or an Angel) can show it.

As with the other examples of parody and intertextual association which have preceded this scene, its importance lies in its contribution to an overall strategy. To some extent these uses of parody function themselves as a parody of the same techniques as used in *L'Écume des jours*. The combined effect is a progression from the first novel. At first glance, the text deals with a movement away from the city; as we have seen, this is not quite so, Paris being equally represented in the city streets as in the desert dunes. In the same way, any movement away from *L'Écume*, in terms of genre (there is a real movement towards the more modern genres of 'le Roman Policier' and 'la Série Noire') and narrative technique, is tempered by a comparable use of intertextuality both in the method and in the identity of the intertexts. *L'Écume des jours* set a precedent, it established 'une barre difficile à franchir'. Thus, when Angel sets out on the journey into his story, he finds that history will not let him go easily: "Le bateau longeait le môle pour prendre son élan et franchir la barre." (*R*, p.278)

The very structure of the text (and it is, by far, the most complicated novel in terms of structure) indicates the arduous nature of the struggle: both the prolonged entry into the story (expanding over four sections, fourty-four pages in length) and the 'passages' force introspection. It is as if the text itself has its own existential crisis. Once more, therefore, the contents of the novel reflect the strategies which drive it.

The identity-crisis experienced by the novel, as it passes from froth to the desert is reflected in the passage from one set of intertexts to another. For example, two of the text's important influences are texts which strive to reject the influence of heredity: Camus' *L'Etranger* opens, as has been seen, with the famous words "Aujourd'hui, maman est morte", whilst the entire length of *Mort à crédit* may be read as an appeal for the silence of the father ("Je voulais qu'il se taise"). And yet, perversely, *L'Etranger* and *Mort à crédit* both announce the intertextual threads of *L'Écume*: *L'Etranger* reflects *La Nausée*, in as much as both are texts 'dits Existentialistes'; similarly *Mort à crédit* corresponds to the intertextual presence of *Voyage au bout de la nuit* in Vian's first text, and thereby takes up a preexistent set of Célinian references.

Despite the conflicting tides, the boat moves on. Progression is made. The use of a sea voyage as entrance into the text proper, the epicentre of the novelistic/artistic action, is clearly not an original one; its use here, thus, takes the reader into not only Vian's story (of desire, otherness and of death), but into a new set of intertexts.

CHAPTER FOUR
L'Automne à Pékin:
And what they found there

This chapter will deal with the dénouement of the Exopotamian action. This section, be it considered as the dream or the novel proper, takes the reader into new ground: in terms of intertextuality, this section will begin by exploring the role of Miller, an author whose influence upon the Sullivan texts has already been documented by Pestureau, and of Constant, whose *Adolphe* is one of the famous 'favourite books'.

The image of the sea crossing is ubiquitous, not merely in the domain of literature, but equally in painting. Henry Miller, in *Tropic of Cancer*, describes the poetic artistry of Matisse in the following terms:

> By whatever vision one passes there is the odour and the sound of voyage. It is impossible to gaze at even a corner of his dreams without feeling the lift of a wave and the cool of flying spray.[39]

The importance of this notorious text is pointed out by Pestureau who cleverly deciphers the following line, one of the most elaborately concealed clues left by Vian as to the identity of possible intertexts: "Voyons si ce Cointreau pique dès qu'on sert" (*R*, p.306). He notes:

> Cointreau pique dès qu'on sert: à-peu-près burlesque sur le titre de Henry Miller, *Tropique du cancer*, traduit chez Denoël en 1945 et objet de poursuites en même temps que *J'irai cracher sur vos tombes*. (*R*, p.1311)

---

[39] Henry Miller, *Tropic of Cancer* (London: Flamingo, 1993), p.168. (Hereafter referred to as *Miller*.)

The influence of Henry Miller upon Boris Vian is well documented. However, despite his discovery of the title *Tropic of Cancer* encoded within the text of *L'Automne à Pékin*, Pestureau does not attempt to assess Miller's text as a potential intertext of this particular Vian novel. To suggest that *L'Automne à Pékin* functions according to several codes present in *Tropic of Cancer* is to open up an old polemic: should one hold the Sullivan texts as 'Vian novels' in the same light as those signed in his own name? In *Boris Vian, les Amerlauds et les Godons*, Pestureau is quick to spot, and thorough in his treatment of, the link between Miller and the Sullivan texts: "Évidemment, certaines précisions sexuelles de Sullivan - sécrétions ou combinaisons du couple variant de l'éternel et trop commun «missionnaire» - ne seraient pas déplacées chez Miller."[40] And although he concedes that there is similarity between *Tropic of Cancer* and the work 'signé Vian', he does not pass *L'Automne à Pékin* through the filter of Miller's writing; he notes: "Je pense donc au total, que le rapport avec l'œuvre de Henry Miller se borne à quelques ressemblances de détail."[41] The contention of this book is that four Vian novels, owing to the superior craftsmanship and 'loving care' which went into their construction, should be viewed independently of *all* his other work; if there is a link with Miller, it is, if limited to similar stylistic elements in the Sullivan texts, more detailed when it comes to *L'Automne*. Nevertheless, in this instance, it is to the credit of *L'Automne* that it should be seen to share the source of an influence so keenly felt in his most famous 'Sullivan', *J'irai cracher sur vos tombes*. And to delve below the surface of the Miller text is to find a novelist whose literary, not to mention intertextual, strategies are very much those of the 'real' Boris Vian. Consider, for example, two of the riddle-like commands which stand as mirages in Vian's desert. Firstly, in response to a simile, in which Angel likens Rochelle to 'un fruit un peu pourri', Petitjean, adopting the voice of Verlaine, reprimands him with the following stern advice: "Ne faites pas de littérature" (*R*, p.362) Is this an outcry against literature in general, against that kind of literature which abounds with ornate similes, or is it a warning that what the reader has before him is not literature? The following passage from *Tropic of Cancer* can enlighten us:

---

[40] *Boris Vian, les Amerlauds et les Godons*, p.231.

[41] *Ibid.*, p.233.

> That guy never says a thing that's original, I found that out. You have to get a clue like... find out whom he's been reading lately... and it's hard to do that because he's so damned secretive. (*Miller*, p.124)

This appears to be an indictment of Vian's work in the sense that originality equals literature. But this is to scratch the surface. The second command(ment) is this: (Petitjean to Claude Léon) "Méfiez-vous de l'originalité, mon fils" (*R*, p.314)

Vian reveals his whole strategy in this one line. This is a warning that all is never as it first appears. And yet, the implications of this are *not* that the reader has been duped, but, on the contrary, that the mirage is of greater importance than the dunes (which are, after all, only sand). Miller, too, reveals that a burning desire to be different is misguided, and that so-called authenticity can only hold back literature:

> The book [Van Norden's] must be absolutely original, absolutely perfect. That is why, amongst other things, it is impossible for him to get started on it. [...] And so, instead of tackling his book, he reads one author after another in order to make absolutely certain that he is not going to tread on their private property. And the more he reads the more disdainful he becomes. (*Miller*, 137)

Thus, with the tacit consent of Henry Miller, Vian not only ignores Van Norden's example, but actually turns it on its head.

All the elements which have been described thus far reveal themselves across a complex network of plot lines. These lines do converge, however, into two principal themes: 'l'usure' and desire. The metaphorical interpretations of these themes, as they occur in their various manifestations, are manifold. However, it should not be forgotten that their textual relevance in *L'Automne à Pékin* is as *real* fictional occurrences: Rochelle's decay is actual and Angel's desire to fuck is very physical. The potentiality for interpretation makes any definitive pronouncements about 'meaning' hazardous. The best way to analyse these themes is, therefore, to seek their possible literary sources, and thence to speculate as to what may be happening beneath the surface. For, as Vian himself concludes, "[...] On peut concevoir n'importe quelle solution" (*R*, p.421).

As the 'lignes' of the story seek out the hotel, they also find Angel; he is the master of the lines. As such he can but bear the burden of both his intertextual and his intratextual heredity: "Il hocha la tête et reposa son tire-lignes" (*R*, p.317). It is he who senses the convergence of all lines; it is a task for which he, as Colin before him (who pronounced: "le plus clair de mon temps, je le passe à l'obscurcir" [*Ej*, p.155]), has no relish: "Je ne cherche pas à être clair..." (*R*, p.352). Atha, whose surname, Porphyrogénète, reflects the domination of heredity in the text[42], feels Angel's catalytic power: "Tout ce que disait Angel remuait de très vieilles choses au fond d'Athanagore." (*R*, p.296) Angel is he who desires. And it is Rochelle who is object of his desire.

If Alise was an angel trussed in the clothes of a seductress, then Rochelle is a whore in the same garb. But, as Miller points out, whore and angel are so far apart that they almost touch: "Germaine had the right idea: she was ignorant and lusty, she put her heart and soul into the work. She was a whore all the way through - and that was her virtue!" (*Miller*, p.54)

By his own admission, it was Anne who has taught her to "un peu mieux se débrouiller dans un lit", and yet she is decaying by herself: "Elle s'abîme elle-même." (*R*, p.322) There is, as in the case of Colin and Chloé (who are representatives of the most important line running through the text - that of death), a feeling that Rochelle is playing out a part in a tragedy. She cannot tear herself from the destruction administered by Anne's body. As Miller suggests: "There's something perverse about women... they're all masochists at heart." (*Miller*, p.135) And so, Angel's desire (and its progressive corruption), although real, is also preordained. At first, his love for Rochelle is akin to that which Colin feels for Chloé: "Je ne l'abîmerais pas, dit Angel. Je ne la toucherais pas. Juste l'embrasser et la mettre toute nue dans une étoffe blanche." (*R*, p.321)

He wants to wrap her in a white sheet. Thus, too, was Colin's desire: it is a shroud, no more no less. Unfortunately, Angel will not have the same short script which left Colin no time to have his naïve vision of love tainted by life (Colin lives until the curtains fall on his life of light, Angel must live on afterwards). Anne also has Colin's view of life and love:

---

[42] "**PORPHYROGÉNÈTE** Se disait des enfants des empereurs d'Orient nés pendant le règne de leur père." *Le Petit Robert*, 1990. Atha's name also signifies his profession, drawing on the meaning of "Porphyre": for a more complete onomastic study of *L'Automne à Pékin*, see Jean-Pierre Vidal, "La déviance générale", in *Boris Vian: Colloque de Cerisy/1*, pp.263-296.

> Il y a tant de choses. Rien que cette herbe verte et pointue. Rien que toucher cette herbe et craquer entre ses doigts une coquille d'escargot jaune, sur ce sable sec et chaud, et regarder les petits grains luisants et bruns qu'il y a dans ce sable sec, et le sentir dans ses doigts. (*R*, p.321)

> Je voudrais... être couché dans de l'herbe un peu rôtie, avec la terre sèche et du soleil, tu sais de l'herbe jaune comme de la paille, et cassante, avec des tas de petites bêtes et de la mousse sèche aussi. (*Ej*, p.71)[43]

Colin's desires, his taste for the same sensual pleasures, result in an analagous choice of partner. Anne is merely honest about his physical need for Rochelle; sex in *L'Automne* stands for the thoughts which Colin tries to avoid. The corruption of Rochelle parallels the corruption of an ideal, an ideal in the absence of which Chloé herself is but a diversion. Only on Chick's prompting ("Et Chloé") does Chloé fit into the frame ("Chloé dans l'idée"). Thus, if Colin is not a paragon of virtue, then Anne is not depravity incarnate. Angel and Anne can be seen to personify the ambivalence of Colin's nature, an ambivalence which will never have the time to mature.

Angel's desire to protect Rochelle progresses to its adult human form by becoming the desire to have her for himself. The attraction of purity cedes naturally to the temptation of the flesh, the need to violate:

> Elle doit sentir l'algue qui a mijoté au soleil dans l'eau de mer... Quand ça commence à se décomposer... Je voudrais qu'elle ne se lave pas pendant un mois, et qu'elle couche avec Anne tous les jours une fois par jour pour qu'il en soit

---

[43] Desire is being gradually degraded: love had a freshness at the beginning of *L'Écume des jours*; Alise, who had 'green pastures' to offer, was replaced by an ersatz who was 'coloured' by tinted windows. Desire, as it moves from love towards lust, is now directly pointed towards 'yellow grass'. In the next novel, which will be seen to be rife with sexual inhibitions and onanism, the grass will be distinctly 'red'. This traffic light progression will only come to an end when Clémentine forces the issue in the last novel of the sequence.

> dégoûté, et puis la prendre juste à la sortie. Encore pleine.
> (*R*, p.362)

This is the desire which drives *Tropic of Cancer*, in which can be found the following outburst:

> You think, you poor, withered bastard, that I'm no good for her, that I might pollute her, desecrate her. You don't know how palatable is a polluted woman, how a change of semen can make a woman bloom. (*Miller*, p.66)

Petitjean, however, reads in Angel's desire not Miller, but Sartre: "Ça suffit, à la fin... Vous êtes un salaud." To slip into Rochelle's hole, to assume Anne's place, will not be to become full of her or him, but to lose oneself. In Sartrean terms Rochelle provides an illusory answer to the problem of Otherness: Angel cannot fuck her better or make her bloom; he can but lose himself in her. Dudu expresses his disgust for the female body in such terms: "C'est inconcevable! Ces choses molles qu'elles ont partout. Ces espèces de replis humides..." (*R*, p.337). It seems that, if an attempt to become whole by gluing himself to both Anne and Rochelle within her body is bound to fail, Angel must be free of their presence altogether. Thus, the project changes from one of desiring to be made whole by unification to one of freedom by dissolution. The paroxysms of death and orgasm are, like the angel and the whore, two of a kind. Miller felt this too:

> I even count sometimes, or I begin to think of a problem in philosophy, but it doesn't work. It's like I'm two people, and one of them is watching me all the time. I get so goddamned mad at myself that I could kill myself...and in a way, that's what I do every time I have an orgasm. For one second like I obliterate myself.(*Miller*, p.135)[44]

---

[44] The death by orgasm described here by Miller is similar to the death by 'coitus interruptus' which Lazuli experiences in *L'Herbe rouge*.

It is precisely hot from an orgasm ("tout chaud du corps de Cuivre" [*R*, p.399]) that Angel approaches the mine shaft into which Anne will 'fall'. To follow Miller's description, Angel 'kills himself' in Cuivre. As he is, to a certain extent, what he does, he is his desire for Rochelle. His orgasm inside Cuivre is, therefore, onanistic and suicidal. "Car Angel savait ce qu'était Cuivre et il perdait d'un coup tout ce qu'Anne avait eu de Rochelle." (*R*, p.399) As his desire dies, Anne, to the extent that he personifies that desire, becomes redundant. Angel (the man, the animal that desires) dies in Cuivre's hole, and Anne, too, will fall to his death. Murder and suicide mix as Anne takes his leave: "Il faut y aller, dit Anne. Allons, tu as peur?" (*R*, p.400) In *Tropic of Cancer* a hole also claims a victim, this time a man who has the same occupation as Miller (just as Anne and Angel perform the same task): "One of the proof-readers fell down the elevator shaft. Not expected to live." (*Miller*, p.141)

With desire comes decay. The decay which eats away at Rochelle already existed in *L'Écume* and will continue through the tetralogy. For its particular manifestation in *L'Automne* a look at another classic French text proves useful. Noël Arnaud, in his *Les Vies parallèles de Boris Vian*, reproduces an interesting league table of Boris' favourite books:

> Zut, ça ressemble de moins en moins à *Adolphe*. Mais c'est une rage, *Adolphe* on va me dire. Ce n'est pas une rage, c'est un des seuls livres classiques que j'ai eu la veine de lire tard.[45]

Benjamin Constant's *Adolphe* expounds a young man's fear of dying and ageing which is exemplified in his relationship with a woman. As Colin, prior to his meeting with Chloé, has a premonition of the monstrosity that is ageing, Adolphe is scarred at an early age: "J'avais à l'âge de dix-sept ans vu mourir une femme âgée..."[46]. (The influence which *Adolphe* exerts on

---

[45] This famous quotation, which usefully provides an insight into Vian's preferred reading, continues: "...*Adolphe, le Docteur Faustroll, Un rude Hiver* et *la Colonie pénétentiaire*. Et *Pylône*. C'est mes cinq grands." (*Les Vies parallèles de Boris Vian*, p.220)

[46] Benjamin Constant, *Adolphe* (Paris: Le Livre de Poche, 1964), p.23. (Hereafter referred to as *Adolphe*.)

L'Automne parallels that exerted on *L'Écume* by *Un cœur simple*, in which the conclusion focuses precisely upon the death of an old woman.)

Also in *L'Écume* one finds a dislike of empty clichés on the subject of which Constant is quite adamant:

> Lors donc que j'entendais la médiocrité disserter avec complaisance sur des principes bien établies, bien incontestables, en fait de morale, de convenances ou de religion, choses qu'elle met assez volontiers sur la même ligne, je me sentais poussé à la contredire, non que j'eusse adopté des opinions opposées, mais parce que j'étais impatienté... (*Adolphe*, p.25)

Should this induce in Vian's works a reflex which forbids that axioms be bandied about unpunished, it would certainly account for such obscure responses as the following from Colin: "C'est la vie, dit Chick. - Non, dit Colin." (*Ej*, p.133) This becomes quite a philosophy in *L'Automne*, where Anne can be found refusing to let Amadis hide behind the barricades of (in this instance, homosexual) dogma:

- Je pense plutôt que c'est une preuve d'originalité que d'être pédéraste.
- Non, dit Anne. C'est idiot. Ça vous limite énormément."
(*R*, p.382)

However, in Constant as in Vian, it proves difficult to apply such clear-headed reasoning to affairs of the heart. Love of a woman is held up in *L'Écume* as the ultimate beauty, it is especially in the field of love that one must refuse to yield to the stranglehold of the adult world (a world where one becomes immunized against those childish impulses which make life worth living). It is also, however, love which becomes the target par excellence of life's attack.

So it is that Adolphe sets out to conquer the heart of Ellénore, who is, furthermore, another man's woman. Where Colin forced himself to avert his gaze from the girl he loved because she 'belonged' to Chick, Angel cannot abandon Rochelle. She is the forbidden fruit (a fact underlined by allusions to their near sibling relationship), a challenge. Adolphe feels compelled to steal Ellénore from the arms of le Comte du P: "[...] Je n'avais point eu jusqu'alors de liaison de femme qui pût flatter mon amour-propre..." (*Adolphe*, p.28). This self-esteem is always there, looking over his shoulder; it is a bogeyman like Colin's 'nénuphar', Angel's Anne and Lazuli's 'homme sombre': "Cet amour-propre était en tiers entre Ellénore et moi." (*Adolphe*, p.33)

The conquest of Ellénore in *Adolphe* is at the heart of the dissatisfaction from which Colin is spared through Chloé's premature death (or, rather, he feels the pain of death instead of that of dissatisfaction that the acquisition of the love-object brings), which Angel learns of (and tries to eradicate at its source) from the philosophical Anne and which will reach its climax in the quest for the 'ouapiti' in *L'Herbe rouge*. As Rochelle can only please Anne for a limited time, until the novelty wears off, Ellénore is only desirable whilst unattainable: "Ellénore était sans doute un vif plaisir dans mon existence, mais elle n'était plus un but, elle était devenue un lien." (*Adolphe*, p.49)

In Anne's opinion, a man must have a plan to shake off the love of a woman for whom one no longer feels any desire: "[...] Si elle t'aimait encore de la même façon à ce moment-là, c'est toi qui arrangerais pour changer." (*R*, p.320) Otherwise dissatisfaction will lead to despair. And this despair is keener than the initial desire (the capture of a 'ouapiti' is fatal):

> C'est un affreux malheur de n'être pas aimé avec passion quand on aime; mais c'en est un bien grand d'être aimé avec passion quand on n'aime plus. Cette vie que je venais d'exposer pour Ellénore, je l'aurais mille fois donnée pour qu'elle fût heureuse sans moi. (*Adolphe*, p.61)

Adolphe provides the blueprint of 'love turned sour', every stage being catalogued before Constant arrives at the inevitable conclusion, from which he does not flinch. With love dies also the light: "Le jour s'affaiblissait: le ciel était serein; la campagne devenait déserte; les travaux des hommes avaient cessé, ils abandonnaient la nature à elle-même." (*Adolphe*, p.82)

'L'usure' is strong; it is strong enough to bring a halt to the railway; it is even strong enough to wear away the stone of Sisyphus which was being rolled on and on by Carlo and Marin ("Quand on aura fini... - On n'aura pas fini [...] Peut-être que le désert dure jusqu'au bout" [*R*, p.333]). Although the myth of Sisyphus, maintained throughout the text by the constant occurrence of both "ça m'est égal" and "c'est ce sable" which pertain to *L'Etranger*, plays its part in the circularity of the text, the idea of toiling at clearing a path through harsh terrain, a path which will be reclaimed by the land and need to be recleared, is one which comes more directly from Céline:

> Sa fonction consistait à diriger la construction de routes en pleines forêts. [...] Mais comme aucun blanc ne passait jamais sur les nouvelles routes que créait Tandernot... et comme au fond elles ne menaient nulle part les routes de l'Administration à Tandernot, alors elles disparaissait sous la végétation fort rapidement, en vérité d'un mois à l'autre, pour tout dire. (*Voyage*, p.176)

In both novels about voyages which are not voyages and pathways which are not pathways, everything must be being done for reasons which are not those given. All is pretext, but pretext for what? Aragon, whose work *Le Paysan de Paris* is in so many ways a blueprint for *L'Automne*, adds the idea of pretext to his list of characters (which Vian will then adopt):

> [...] Les naufrages dans la poche (-"Il y a un naufragé sur la Toupie"[*R*, p.280]-) [...] Tiens une scène de commandement de navire, l'officier porte, l'imbécile, à sa bouche un porte-voix de carton (-"Dans l'entrepont, le capitaine courait de long en large, cherchant son pavillon à donner des ordres"[*R*, p.278]-) [...] Plus loin ce sont des casseurs de pierres à un croisement de chemins dans la montagne (-"le désert"-) [...] Une lettre d'affaires, qui n'est pas précisément une lettre d'affaires, mais un prétexte, allons tranchons le mot une lettre d'amour, s'envole, vole, vole. (-"Vole!... répondit le receveur"[*R*, p.420]-) (*Aragon*, p.211)

In the heat of the desert all seems to be a pretext for seduction. Amadis' pile of business letters cannot hide his principal aims which are to do with sexual conquest. Not satisfied with his attempts to seduce Martin and eventually Dupont, Amadis, alone, having sent Rochelle (on the pretext of having) to post his letters ("Je l'ai envoyée à l'arrêt du 975 porter le courrier" [*R*, p.338]), does not squander an opportunity to try his luck with the handsome Angel ("Parce que je suis séduisant?" [*R*, p.337]). Such use of letters as pretext for getting rid of women occurs also in Mac Orlan's *Le Quai des brumes*. In this case, Rabe, desirous of having his warm bed all to himself, gets rid of Nelly (a small-time whore who will grow into an angel amongst her colleagues) by sending her to post a letter. On one level, then, the letter is a pretext (for sensual pleasure); it also contains a pretext (for it is an attempt to extort money): "Il fallait trouver un prétexte." (*Quai*, p.117) The pretext within the pretext is "l'amour de la famille".

The concept of love in *L'Automne*, however, has been worn away with 'usure'. Desire has developed from its foetal state (in *L'Écume*) into something far more adult and sordid. We are now in Miller's Paris where survival admits little place for love: "One can live in Paris - I discovered that! - on just grief and anguish." (*Miller*, p.184) The role of the woman is precisely to be used, to wear herself out in the ephemeral assuagement of men's desire:

> Everywhere a man, and then she has to leave, and then there's an abortion and then a new job and then another man and nobody gives a fuck about her except to use her. (*Miller*, p.31)

In *Le Quai des brumes*, the butcher cum murderer talks of "une petite idée derrière la tête", an idea which makes us tick. He remarks: "Voilà ce qu'il faut éviter de trouver. Pour les uns c'est la femme..." (*Quai*, p.68). For the Vian of *L'Écume des jours*, this was very definitely the case. Now, however, the reader is confronted by a desert full of desires spinning and colliding, where the policy seems to be to 'love 'em and leave 'em'. And to say that the rugged Anne merely epitomizes this stereotype is, perhaps, to ignore the full story.

In *Le Quai des brumes*, the deserter who can no longer bear life amongst the people of the quay (the people of the froth), turns his head in the only direction he knows:

> Tantôt je parle du Maroc, tantôt du Tonkin, le cafard n'a pas de patrie, il ne connaît qu'une direction: le Sud... royaume, chimérique résultat de tous nos cafards réunis... (*Quai*, p.51)

For Vian, 'cafard' takes on first the shape of woman and then fades into an indistinct onrush of desire. Mac Orlan's deserter will turn to the Foreign

Legion. Where he will search again for his Southern lands such as Tonkin, where "l'un de nous mourut piqué par une mouche", Vian's "légionnaire" will seek his destiny in Pékin where the sting of model aircraft is equally deadly.

If Vian's travellers incarnate the spirit of 'la Légion', then Anne's desire can be interpreted rather differently. The cultural importance of the legionnaire which Adrian Rifkin is keen to stress is that of bisexuality. Of the popular song of the 1930s, 'Mon Légionnaire' by Raymond Asso and Marguerite Monot, he writes:

> 'Mon Légionnaire' takes place in a cinematic decor of the colonial desert - "il sentait bon le sable chaud", which fills out the essential quality of the fantasy in its distance from military reality as in its closeness to a literary tradition.[47]

This is a literary tradition into which *L'Automne à Pékin*, with its ideal setting, tries desperately to fit. Thus, when Anne tries to persuade Angel that they should go to Exopotamia alone ("Je vais m'embêter, dit Anne. Si tu viens avec moi, on pourra toujours se distraire." [*R*, p.244]), it is possible that he has the words of 'Mon Légionnaire' running through his head; in which case it is not simple comradeship that he desires:

> J'rêvais pourtant que le destin
> Me ramènerait un beau matin
>   Mon légionnaire
> Qu'on s'en irait loin, tous les deux,
> Dans quelque pays merveilleux
>   Plein de lumière.[48]

Anne, then, with his curiously feminine name and his ruthless exploitation of Rochelle (which makes Chick's 'loveless love' vis-à-vis Alise look like a show of chivalry), becomes the legionnaire and thereby reinforces the links between

---

[47] *Street Noises: Parisian Pleasure 1900-1940*, p.139.

[48] 'Mon Légionnaire', quoted in *Street Noises: Parisian Pleasure 1900-1940*, p.159.

L'Automne and the more traditionally Parisian novels. In the words of Adrian Rifkin:

> In the concealed reasons of the legionnaire the colonial situation is doubled back into becoming the exemplar of the city itself, now exaggerated and magnified in the colours of the desert, the blood, the boredom and the sunburned, tattooed skin stretched over male flesh.[49]

Rifkin continues to point out that the legionnaire's stereotypic representation in this particular literary tradition usually demands a similarly standard 'punishment':

> In this object-state, the legionnaire is an exaggerated form of the *voyou*. The latter excites disdain and hatred in the writers who most depend on him. Mac Orlan, Béraud or Warnod seem compelled to hate precisely to the extent that they cannot otherwise escape their fascination for him. Very often the act of their worship is terminated by one of brutal renunciation, their praise for his strength or mysterious viciousness withdrawn by a declaration of his weakness, his vanity and his femininity.[50]

Not to be outdone, and not to settle for an appraisal of Anne's bad points on the part of the desert's resident benign adults, Vian has Anne killed. The cleanup of Paris which he has seemingly parodied with, for example, his use of a declared homosexual as project leader, Vian now employs more directly. (The element of choice which Atha and Petitjean discuss following the death is, perhaps then, rather a 'closed choice', the author's manipulation of genre having already set in motion a certain degree of determination.)

To return to the influence of *Adolphe* upon the theme of 'usure', it is interesting to notice that although it is Anne who has the relationship with

---

[49] *Ibid.*, p.163.

[50] *Ibid.*

Rochelle, it is Angel who has the feelings of guilt and pity. The following lines of *Adolphe* serve to render this curious ménage à trois even more difficult to understand.

> «Adolphe, s'écriait-elle, vous ne savez pas le mal que vous faites, vous l'apprendrez un jour, vous l'apprendrez par moi, quand vous m'aurez précipitée dans la tombe.» Malheureux! lorsqu'elle me parlait ainsi que ne m'y suis-je jeté moi-même avant elle! (*Adolphe*, p.93)

To continue the tale of the legionnaire, Ellénore's words may echo the sentiments of Anne rather than Rochelle. It is certainly he who is *thrown* into his grave by Angel. And yet, Angel does administer death to Rochelle as well. Those wishing to see Anne and Rochelle as two alter egos of Angel, or, indeed, as the id and ego to his superego, may, alternatively, wish to extract from the above lines the idea that the two murders are stages in Angel's own suicide (or, at least, the ridding of parts of himself in a kind of therapeutic catharsis). In either case, Angel escapes with the independence for which Adolphe so desperately longed: "[...] Je n'espérais point mourir avec Ellénore; j'allais vivre sans elle dans ce désert du monde, que j'avais souhaité tant de fois de traverser indépendant." (*Adolphe*, p.105) Perhaps, Angel manages to go one step further than Adolphe thought possible. By a progressive elimination of his 'Others', he succeeds in freeing himself from his own bonds. Does *L'Automne*, then, rather than simply borrowing both Adolphe and Ellénore's suffering, reject Constant's statement (which he makes in the 'Réponse' at the end of *Adolphe*) that "c'est en vain qu'on brise avec les objets et les êtres extérieurs; on ne saurait briser avec soi-même" (*Adolphe*, p.114)?

Whatever his reasons for killing, whatever the nature of the victims, Angel does murder. And the death of Rochelle has the same literary heritage as the 'poetic' end of Anne who plummets down a long, dark hole[51]. Like Adolphe, Angel rejects the classically romantic suicide pact. To free himself from Rochelle, Angel finds his inspiration in *Le Quai des brumes*, where Rabe finally rids himself of Nelly's encroaching presence with a glass of wine: "Tiens, bois du vin, ma belle, nous avons encore passé à travers". This she

---

[51] The death of Anne is one which allows Angel access to another layer of the dream/text; as such let us consider the 'long, dark hole' in its Carrollinian sense, as Alice's entry into the dream, rather than in its Freudian overtones.

takes and consequently resolves: "[...] Il faut, moi aussi, que je cherche une chambre." (*Quai*, p.119)

And yet, the source which may be seen to set out most clearly Angel's reasons is again a poem from *Les Fleurs du Mal*. The following lines of "Le vin de l'assassin" (which blends both murders as one) need little commentary:

> Ma femme est morte, je suis libre!
> Je puis donc boire tout mon soûl.
>
> Je l'ai jetée au fonds d'un puits,
>
> Elle était encore jolie,
> Quoique bien fatiguée! et moi,
> Je l'aimais trop! voilà pourquoi
> Je lui dis: Sors de cette vie!

This poem appears to add the scene and motive to a crime which has has been grounded in the treatment of sexual desire and lustful pollution of the female body, as seen in *Tropic of Cancer*, and in the need for conquest of another's prize and the eventual fading of passion, as seen in *Adolphe*. As murder can be seen to be at the very heart of the novel, it is not surprising that there are also at its epicentre two intertexts which deal - precisely - with murder. The remaining sections will examine the exploitation by Vian of the genres of classic detective fiction as well as that of the 'Série noire', a genre being introduced at the time of the composition of *L'Automne* (and in which Vian played a leading role as translator) and which was, therefore, eminently fashionable.

Murder in Exopotamia

In "Le Vin de l'assassin" can be found motive and method (although the wine of Baudelaire's poem provides the oblivion into which the poet casts himself - giving another literary case for arguing that the murder is, in fact, a suicide). For setting we have to look elsewhere.

To suggest an alternative title for the novel, such as *Murder in Exopotamia*, is to make a step in the right direction. For the classic detective novel does play its part here. Gilbert Pestureau underlines the importance of the detective novels of Agatha Christie in Vian's fiction in his book *Les Vies parallèles*. Under the general heading "La saveur de la para-littérature", he cites as a source of influence Christie's *The ABC murders*.[52] In other novels, interesting links between the two authors may be found; for example, in *The Murder of Roger Ackroyd*, Poirot outlines what will become, in Vian, the 'Ouapiti syndrome':

> But can you figure to yourself, monsieur, that a man may work towards a certain object, may labour and toil to attain a certain kind of leisure and occupation, and then find that, after all, he yearns for the old busy days, and the old occupations that he thought himself so glad to leave? [...] We work to attain an object, and that object gained, we find that what we miss is the daily toil.[53]

But the Christie novel which exerts the most powerful influence upon *L'Automne* is *Murder in Mesapotamia*. It, too, is a carefully structured novel. Vian's lettered sections and his 'passages' are echoed, in *Murder in Mesopotamia*, by a foreword, a frontispiece and a chapter to introduce the narrator. When finally Christie plunges the reader into the novel, in which she readily admits the setting will pale into insignificance when compared with the intrigue, it is into the site of an archaeological dig. In this book, where the characters spend a deal of their time reparing pottery ("There was a lot of stuff lying about - mostly broken pots it seemed to me - or else ones that were all mended and stuck together"[54]), whilst Athanagore spends his breaking it, there can be found sufficient motive to account for the two murders of *L'Automne*.

As in Vian's novel, there are multiple levels (as well as the archaeological dig having different levels, there is also a line being traced:

---

[52] *Les Vies parallèles de Boris Vian*, p.252.

[53] Agatha Christie, *The Murder of Roger Ackroyd* (Glasgow: Fontana/Collins, 1981), p.20-21.

[54] Agatha Christie, *Murder in Mesopotamia* (Glasgow: Fontana/Collins, 1990), p.44. (Hereafter referred to as *Christie*).

"There had been two Frenchmen in the restaurant car the night before. And a party of three men whom I gathered... had to do with the Pipe line" [*Christie*, p.33]), and much that is important lies beneath the surface; as Poirot states: "From the very beginning I have felt that to understand this case one must seek not for external signs or clues, but for the truer clues of the clash of personalities and the secrets of the heart." (*Christie*, p.186) Thus, when one has discarded the peripheral characters such as Dr Reilly, who bears an uncanny ressemblance to the murderous, yet loveable Mangemanche ("We couldn't say anymore just then because Dr Reilly came in, saying jokingly that he'd killed off the most tiresome of his patients" [*Christie*, p.122]), one is left with a double crime which revolves around four central figures who are entangled in a web of love and hate.

Here too, the protagonists are thrown together. The house at Tell Yarimjah, with its inwardly facing windows, is rather like a Foucauldian Panopticon. Once again, when one is surrounded by 'les Autres', it is 'l'enfer', or as Christie puts it so *Englishly*: "If people are too much cooped up together it's got a way of getting on their nerves." (*Christie*, p.15)

There is Dr Leidner whose career as a famous archaeologist is a façade masking his tortured past. He is hiding a series of dualities; he is Eric Leidner, and he is also Frederick Bosner. Like Angel he is disillusioned by the failure of his love for the one woman he can desire. Like Angel, his change of identity also coincides with a train crash:

> To begin with, he loves his wife Louise with an overpowering passion such as only a woman of her kind can evoke. She betrays him. He is sentenced to death. He escapes. He is involved in a railway accident but he manages to emerge with a second personality... (*Christie*, p.211)

Anne and Angel are one in the same way as Bosner and Leidner: Anne is sentenced to death; Angel (because of Anne's death) escapes. His hatred of his wife for having wrenched him apart is equalled only by his love for her: "[...] I soon convinced myself that his love for his wife was the mainspring of his existence. He was a man torn and ravaged by grief." (*Christie*, p.197) But in the Mesopotamian desert Leidner has his 'Other in love'. Richard Carey suffers from the same duality the final outcome of which can only be imagined: "[...] And I was struck by the extraordinary look of strain on his face... This man was at the end of his tether. Very soon, something would snap." (*Christie*, p.37)

For Carey not only are his feelings mixed ("You shall have the truth! I hated Louise Leidner - there's the truth for you! I hated her like hell!" [*Christie*, p.148]), but the object of his emotions is also double. His love for Louise Leidner (which for Poirot is only confirmed by his affirmed hatred for her) can never win out because she is married to a man he greatly respects and admires:

> He has been a man torn by two opposing passions. He loved Louise Leidner - yes, but he also hated her. He hated her for undermining his loyalty to his friend. There is no hatred as great as that of a man who has been made to love a woman against his will. (*Christie*, p.202)

And there is still another candidate for the murder of Mrs Leidner, the woman at the meeting point of all these passions: Miss Johnson. She loves Dr Leidner; she cannot have him, however, because the love he shares with his wife blocks her path. Her jealousy is of Mrs Leidner (a jealousy shared by Carey who loves both parties of the Leidner marriage: "I've an idea *he* was jealous just like Miss Johnson" [*Christie*, p.116]).

Clearly, Louise Leidner, just as Rochelle, must die. Both have transgressed, they are fallen angels. Louise loves two men, and the two men she loves are each two men. She also fears two men. For Frederick Bosner, her first (and second) husband had a brother, William. Both have a reason to kill her, but only one will: "[...] He's going to kill me. It may be Frederick - it may be little William - but he's going to kill me." (*Christie*, p.60)

Poirot has the facts; his job is to discover the motives, and thence to find the killer. The reader of *L'Automne* is presented with all the motives and is challenged to work out what the resultant facts will be: "Sans préjuger de la suite des événements, on devrait enfin être en mesure de déterminer avec précision ce que va faire Angel." (*R*, p.385) The question is not who but how. This is also true in *Murder in Mesopotamia*. It is only when someone realises how the first murder was committed, that a second murder becomes necessary. Thus, in both books there are two murders: the siren is killed, by poison in Vian, and by a heavy blow in Christie. The other murders, which do not, at first, seem parallel, are linked: Christie's other victim is Miss Johnson, the slightly manly spinster who loves Dr Leidner, and whose Christian name is

Anne. She has to die because she realises that Mrs Leidner was killed as the result of the murderer causing an object to fall from a considerable height (just as Anne himself was murdered in *L'Automne*). The only person able to cause such a fall was Dr Leidner. He it is, then, who kills Anne by giving her acid to drink whilst she is half asleep. In his summation, Poirot shows why Dr Leidner had to kill. The motives cross perfectly across the borders of the two novels:

> He wishes to impress on his wife, once and for all, that Eric Leidner and Frederick Bosner are two different people.
> [...] If she belongs to any other man but him, he would kill her. And she has given herself to Richard Carey. (Christie, p.212)

Dr Leidner does not break down; rather he feels as if a huge weight has been lifted from his shoulders: "Then he said simply: 'I'm sorry about Anne. That was bad - senseless - it wasn't *me*! [...] I loved Louise and I killed her'." (*Christie*, p.215) In this outburst can be read the very duality which is at the heart of Angel: whether he can be said to have killed Anne or whether it was suicide depends very much on whether Anne is Anne, a separate identity, or whether he is just Angel's alter ego. All the motives, as well as the desert scene, which make up the core action of *L'Automne* can be found in *Murder in Mesopotamia*. But to concentrate solely on Agatha Christie is to not go far enough.

The flight of an angel

Thus, it can be seen that there is a real link between *L'Automne* and the classic detective novel. But what of 'la Série noire'? That Vian employs the 'hard boiled' style as well as that of which Christie is an exemplar has already been hinted at in such episodes as the arrest of Claude Léon. The intertextuality which links this genre to *L'Automne à Pékin* can also be matched with a specific text, just as the detective novel is represented by *Murder in Mesopotamia*. One only has to sift through the titles of novels from 'la Série noire' series which were being published in France at around the same time as *L'Automne* was being written to find one in which an angel takes centre stage. One of the earliest texts to be 'traduit de l'américain' for inclusion in 'la Série noire' is *Le Funiculaire des anges*, or *Flight of an angel*, by Verne Chute. As was suggested, at the very start of this chapter, what could be more appropriate than the title 'flight of an angel'?

In Chute's novel, the principal character, who is known more often than not as Jamey-Boy Raider, is battling with a disturbing case of amnesia. The story is, therefore, one of recovering a lost identity, whereas Christie's murderer had sought to conceal a past known only to himself. As each of Vian's characters have an experience of the Other, Raider learns of his own Otherness through the classic look in the mirror: "Le jeune homme détournait les yeux, surpris, lorsqu'il rencontra, au hasard d'une glace, à la devanture d'un magasin, sa propre image.[55]" His problems are not unlike those of Angel; both are lost geographically, both are lost in layers of consciousness, but, worst of all, neither of them knows himself. Chute writes: "Etre dans une ville inconnue à la recherche de son chemin, c'est déjà troublant, mais NE PAS SE RECONNAITRE SOI-MÊME, c'est vraiment terrifiant." (*Chute*, p.7)

The catalyst for Raider's discoveries is a funicular railway, the 'Vol des Anges'. It is via a flight in a cablecar that Raider must return to his past. His preliminary destination is 'Olive Street'. In this light, Angel's flight, too, can be read as a return to his past. Angel's childhood can be reflected in the mirror provided by the two children, Didiche and *Olive*. Raider receives his suggestion to ascend in a passage highly reminiscent of the concluding lines of *L'Automne*:

> L'homme l'entraîna sous l'auvent du magasin le plus proche. D'une main il indiqua la route à Raider:
> - C'est par là... tout en haut de Bunker Hill. Vous pouvez prendre les escaliers, mais le mieux, c'est encore d'attendre le 'Vol', là, au bout de la rue. (*Chute*, p.14)

Thus, one of the potential interpretations of Angel's flight is the desire to return to childhood. In such an interpretation can also be found a possible literary precursor of the island la Toupie, on which there is "un naufragé" (*R*, p.280). Although 'toupie' is a word in its own right (indeed, it is a word whose

---

[55] Verne Chute, *Le Funiculaire des anges* (Paris: Gallimard, 1994), p.7. (Hereafter referred to as *Chute*.)

literary heritage links it with voyages[56]), it is also important in its anagrammatical form 'utopie'. There is a feeling that the further one comes from the opening of *L'Écume des jours*, the more strongly a need is felt to return to childhood. Whilst remaining no more than a trauma for Angel, as well as a strong kinship with Olive and Didiche, this will become more pronounced in the novels which follow: in *L'Herbe rouge*, Wolf will appear to visit his childhood in a series of 'trips'; and in *L'Arrache-cœur*, the skies will play host to flying children.

The one person who, more than any other, may be said to be forever shipwrecked in the utopia of childhood is Peter Pan. In J.M. Barrie's own words: "To be born is to be wrecked on an island."[57] It is, perhaps, Vian's contention that we are all born of the froth, on the same island as Colin and Alise, the island which Barrie names the Neverland: "We too have been there; we can still hear the sound of the surf, though we shall land no more." The lapping of the waves against the shores of the Neverland can be heard in both *L'Écume des jours* and *L'Automne à Pékin*. For example, the tie which bites Chick is the same which all but bites Mr Darling:

> 'This tie, it will not tie.' He became dangerously sarcastic. 'Not round my neck! Round the bedpost! Oh yes, twenty times have I made it up round the bedpost, but round my neck, no! Oh dear no! begs to be excused! (*Peter Pan*, p.30)

---

[56] The word 'toupie' occurs in Baudelaire's poem "Le Voyage" (once again, *Les Fleurs du Mal*):

> Nous imitons, horreur! la toupie et la boule
> Dans leur valse et leurs bonds; même dans nos sommeils
> La curiosité nous tourmente et nous roule,
> Comme un Ange cruel qui nous fouette des soleils.

This, once more, underlines the importance exerted by these poems upon the whole novel...

[57] Quoted by Naomi Lewis in J.M. Barrie, *Peter Pan* (London: Penguin,1976), p.11. (Hereafter referred to as *Peter Pan*.)

By locking the tie in place with 'une bouteille de fixateur à pastel', Colin and Chick follow the advice which Mr Darling is too proud to take: "[...] But there were occasions when it would have been better for the house if he had swallowed his pride and used a made-up tie!" (*Peter Pan*, p.30).

In *L'Automne*, it is Peter's shadow, which he loses in the Darlings' playroom window before it is sown back onto his foot by Wendy, which reappears, dancing across the dunes:

> Leurs ombres progressaient avec eux, verticales et minuscules. Ils pouvaient les apercevoir en écartant les jambes, mais par un hasard curieux, celle de l'abbé était à la place de l'ombre de l'archéologue. (*R*, p.369)

It is worth mentioning that the dog (who has a name which means 'girl' in French, Nana) is not seen by the 'little angels' as a dog, but as a nurse. In *L'Automne*, Anne is not considered by the children (as by Angel for example) to be a man with a girl's name, but as a man with a dog's name: "C'est un nom de chien, répéta Didiche..."[58] (*R*, p.286)

As we have already seen, although *L'Automne*, like *Peter Pan*, is circular in nature, having the capacity to begin again an infinite number of times, it also reaches back into the past (*L'Écume*) and forwards into the future (*L'Herbe rouge* and *L'Arrache-cœur*). Thus, when Angel asks for the 'terminus', he may be asking to go back whence he has come, or he may be talking about a potential terminus where children will be in a position to respond directly to the conductor's order to fly. In *L'Arrache-cœur* (at the terminus of the tetralogy), the children will fly; Alise has already flown (leaving only her hair as testament to her flight); Wolf will fly (aided by a machine[59]); and Clémentine will clip her own wings whilst her children take to the air. Angel, who has the most appropriate name for doing so, does not fly in

---

[58] The 'nom de chien' reference may also point back to the island of another Utopian writer, H.G. Wells. In his *The Island of Dr Moreau*, there is, amongst the various products of vivisection, a 'dog-man'.

[59] One possible source of Wolf's machine comes in Kafka's *In the Penal Colony* which takes place on an island (and is an important intertext for *L'Herbe rouge*), thereby displaying further the importance of 'La Toupie' as a point of convergence for several intertexts.

the literal sense (even though he is actually told to do so). Angel's flight is metaphorical and, above all, intertextual.

Such is the role of an angel: to fly; to fly from the land of dreams into that of the waking world. This is a journey also made by a famous angel of English literature. Pestureau remarks: "Pour tout le monde, l'ange arrive du Pays des Rêves, *The Land of the Dreams*, alors que pour lui, c'est la terre qui lui semble un cauchemar."[60] For, however fitting this description may be for Vian's hero, so ill at ease in the desert, he is not talking about Angel, but Mr Angel, the fantastic visitor of H.G. Wells' novel, *The Wonderful Visit*. As is the case for Wolf, the central figure of *L'Herbe rouge*, Angel's foreign looking name is derived from a foreign literary source. Once again: "On peut noter que la majuscule - *Angel* - fréquente en anglais peut favoriser la transformation d'un nom commun en nom propre; d'où notre «Angel»...".[61]

Throughout *L'Automne à Pékin* Angel becomes disheartened by 'l'usure'; he becomes contaminated by humanity (les Autres) and experiences a desire to go back. H.G. Wells' own angel, during his 'wonderful visit', shares this experience during his stay on Earth. At length Mr Angel is so depressed that he even doubts his own angelic identity: "If you say there are no angels - clearly I must be something else. I eat - angels do not eat. I may be a man already."[62] (Angel's own doubts as to the reality of his earthly existence are expressed with similar syllogistic reasoning: "Est-ce que vous vous rendez compte que nous sommes dans un désert? - Non, dit Angel. Dans un vrai désert il n'y a pas de chemin de fer." [*R*, p.335]) Wells' angel is also advised to fly: "He turned suddenly on the Angel and said "Home!" He fancied that he might revive in the Angel some latent memory of his lost youth." (*Visit*, p.44)

Perhaps both Angel's murders were attempts to eradicate ageing itself by extinguishing two of its ugly manifestations. The desire to fly may also represent the desire to find love in the arms of Alise. This perfect love, which Vian would not allow Alise to share, is revealed to the angel of *The Wonderful Visit*, in the shape of Delia:

---

[60] *Boris Vian, les Amerlauds et les Godons*, p.298.

[61] *Ibid.*

[62] H.G. Wells, *The Wonderful Visit* (London: C. Arthur Pearson Ltd., 1902), p.44. (Hereafter referred to as *Visit*.)

> Then in a flash he saw it all, saw this grim little world of battle and cruelty, transfigured in a splendour that outshone the Angelic Land, suffused suddenly and insupportably glorious with the wonderful light of Love and Self-sacrifice. (*Visit*, p.114)

Delia exposes herself to fire to help the man she loves. But unlike Alise, who is rejected by Colin and fails to save Chick, Delia is not abandoned in her moment of glory. She is joined in love and her flight is shared: "But little Hetty Penzance had a pretty fancy of two figures with wings, that flashed up and vanished among the flames." (*Visit*, p.114)

Delia/Alise also appears in *Le funiculaire des anges*, this time as Violette who satisfies all the pertinent physical criteria:

> Il ne pouvait détacher son regard de ces cheveux blonds comme de l'or filé, de ces yeux d'un bleu inimaginable, d'un bleu à faire tourner toutes les têtes, de ce visage plein de douceur et de grâce. (*Chute*, p.21)

Violette is Raider's Alise because of her unspoilt love and willingness to sacrifice herself; she is also Rochelle in as much as she dies that he might live. Raider, angelic on account of the curious nature of his sudden entry into Violette's life, plays Wells' angel to her Delia:

> - Tu es un ange, mon cœur.
> - Ne sommes-nous pas tout près du «Vol des Anges»?
> [...] Et ici, je t'ai toujours trouvé merveilleux. Chaque minute de notre vie a été un paradis. [...] Tu es à moi... Tu es mon enfant trouvé. (*Chute*, p.58)

The angelic Violette has her counterpart on the other side of the Angel/Whore borderline, a girl called Butch. Butch exposes the glory of her body to Raider just as Alise does to Colin, in an attempt to conquer a heart with more 'human' weapons:

Puis, jeune et radieuse dans sa nudité, elle s'avança vers Raider...

Regarde, dit Alise. Elle se leva, tira le petit anneau de la fermeture et sa robe tomba par terre.

- Vraiment, je ne vous plais pas?
Le regard ébloui de Raider aurait suffi à lui répondre. Il murmura:
- Vous voulez rire...
Elle posa ses mains sur ses jeunes seins qui pointaient.

Ses seins paraissaient prêts à s'envoler et les longs muscles de ses jambes déliées, à toucher, étaient fermes et chauds.
- Je peux embrasser? dit Colin.

- Alors, il y a autre chose... C'est parce que je suis une... une... (*Chute,* p.151)

- J'aime mieux Chloé... maintenant. (*Ej,* p.182)

Butch has already sacrificed herself for her husband (buying a headstone for his grave and, thereby, driving herself to poverty and prostitution), and has taken the angels' flight 'au septième ciel' (a room on the seventh floor). And once she has fallen in love with Raider, he abandons her. His is truly the kiss of death ("Vous comprenez, je porte malheur à ceux que j'aime" [*Chute,* p.176-177]), and it is the girl's pledge of eternal love which seals her fate (Violette, who will die by a bullet with Raider's name on it, tells him that she will love him: "Aussi longtemps que je vivrai" [*Chute,* p.59]).

Having indirectly caused the death of Violette, and having broken the heart of Butch, Raider finally discovers the truth of his identity in the arms of the new love of his life. Merna, a pretty brunette, turns out to be none other than his wife. Thus it is that Raider turns full circle, ending up back where he started. The 'Vol des Anges' has been his means of travelling through time; its role as pathway is reflected in the suitable environment it provides for instances of objective chance. Like Nadja, Merna is a Surrealist love-object: "Mais, soudain, il se leva brusquement... se précipita au-dehors. Il descendit la rue en évitant de se heurter aux passants... C'est alors qu'il la vit debout, devant le café." (*Chute*, p.51)

Merna's part is comparable to that played, in *L'Écume*, by Chloé. She is not strikingly beautiful in the same way as an angel; she does not provoke the same carnal desire as the prostitute; and yet, she keeps her man. Despite the similarities between the love of Merna and Raider and that of Colin and Chloé, this time there is a 'happy ending'. The doctor who calls to treat Merna has better news than Mangemanche: "Il y a eu juste assez de résistance pour faire dévier la balle. C'était une balle de 45, qui a simplement déchiré la peau et entamé la chair." (*Chute*, p.213)

There are no such narrow escapes in Vian. Angel's return will not be to happiness in the arms of another woman. Love and death are too tightly bound. As Miller wrote, once more on the suject of Matisse:

> On the beach, masts and chimneys interlaced, and like a fuliginous shadow the figure of Albertine gliding through the surf, fusing into the mysterious quick and prism of a protoplasmic realm, uniting her shadow to the dream and harbinger of death. (*Miller*, p.167)

Raider has his own future with Merna. This fact he celebrates by presenting his wife with a bottle of perfume: "Oh! l'*Herbe bleue*... Jamey, il faut que je vous embrasse." (*Chute*, p.156) (My italics.) For his part, Angel must fly; and it is upon grass of a different hue that his wings will next alight.

In the second novel it can be seen that Vian's strategy has, whilst becoming tighter in structure, widened in scope. A complex intertextual link to Aragon served to expose the meaning of the death of the light in *L'Écume des jours*, whilst strengthening the links between the two Vian novels by maintaining a continuity of genre between their respective intertexts. Vian, thus, moves from the quasi random use of intertextuality of the first novel, where intertexts took the form of individual key texts, to a use of intertextuality where genre becomes the defining code. This gives intertextual breadth and depth of meaning within a more controlled structure. This structure does, however, remain visible at the level of textual organisation: the text is organised, as the sub-headed sections of this chapter reflect, into various passages which tend to signal the organisation beneath the textual level, at the level of the intertexts. In the novels which follow the structure is less punctuated at the level of the text (chapter headings will, for example, never again be so rigid), meaning becoming increasingly dependent on a coherent reading at the level of the intertexts: the sub-headings are fewer and more evenly spread in these chapters, being centred on the (intertextual) meaning, and becoming increasingly divorced from the apparent structure of the text itself.

The concept of Paris has remained at the forefront in a way which also parallels the intertextual techniques of *L'Écume des jours*. Just as Surrealism works in the text beneath the outer layers of Existentialism (in the name of Partre), Paris is concealed beneath the dunes of a desert and the name of Pékin. Paris remains the centre of the text through intertextuality: Parisian novels remain constant and ubiquitous. The relations with *L'Écume* are also maintained in the concept of Vian as experimenter with shades of light and dark, painting his text so that it resembles a Man Ray photograph, where, before, he composed it like a Duke Ellington arrangement.

L'Automne à Pékin, however, is not merely a retrospective text; it has the foresight to progress. In Vian's manipulation of genre, there is room for the next novels to be born: the concept of a tetralogy can be seen to be developing in Angel's survival and return from the cataclysm of the final pages of the story. His flight through the realms of detective fiction is parallel to the flight which rescues Alise from the cataclysm of *L'Écume*. And in the intertextuality between Vian and Wells, Angel becomes angel in more than name alone, setting his return for future adventures when another Angel will take to Vian's stage.

CHAPTER FIVE
L'Herbe rouge:
The problem with Science Fiction

Thus far this study of Vian's novels has exposed an increasingly complex use of intertextuality, from the innocuous-looking 'clins d'oœil' of *L'Écume des jours* to the harmonising of different genres in *L'Automne à Pékin*. Should the reader of the third of the four novels, *L'Herbe rouge*, not then expect a similar strategy to be at work in this the shortest of Vian's novels? The critical response to *L'Herbe rouge*, however, has been slightly perverse: despite picking up a plethora of references to other works, both novelistic and poetic, the text has tended to be regarded as lying within particularly narrow parameters. There have thus arisen two readings: according to the first *L'Herbe rouge* is a work of autobiography, and according to the second it is a classic example of Science Fiction. Before dispensing definitively with all forms of biographical criticism which go quite clearly against the grain of this particular analysis, it is worth noting that the further one comes, in terms of dates of publication, from *L'Écume des jours* the greater the tendency of the critic to elect the autobiographical approach; the figure of Clémentine, for example, has been seen as both Vian's own mother and, indeed, as his first wife, Michelle.[1]

What, then, of the Science Fiction reading? As the basis of much of the analysis of *L'Herbe rouge*, this would appear an ideal starting point, even more so because its origins are intertextual. In fact, the impetus of this reading can be seen to be derived from one source, an article which has remained unchallenged since its appearance in 1976[2]. It is, thus, in Jacques Aboucaya's "A propos de *L'Herbe rouge*" which this analysis of the text has its beginnings. Aboucaya's Science Fiction reading has its basis in two particular aspects of the text: the title and Wolf's machine.

---

[1] One 'biographical' detail which seems to contradict this trend is the fact that despite the late publication dates for *L'Arrache-cœur* (1953), all four novels were supposedly conceived between 1946 and 1947.

[2] Jacques Aboucaya, "A propos de *L'Herbe rouge*", *Obliques*, 8-9 (1976), 139-142.

The title of any novel is clearly significant. *L'Herbe rouge* has added significance as a title since the novel was originally conceived under the title *Le Ciel crevé*: its final election, therefore, may be seen to point to features lying peripheral to the basic plot line.[3] It has already been shown how the choice of the orthodox spelling of 'l'écume des jours' can be seen as symbolic as the beginning of a writing project which was to yield a sequence of novels. So too the fact that the events of the second novel take place in neither Autumn nor in Peking allows an understanding of writing techniques such as were seen in the last chapter. Thus Aboucaya begins his search for a fictional location for Vian's third novel:

> ET D'ABORD, L'HERBE ROUGE.
> Alors, il faut chercher ailleurs.
> Sur une autre planète.
> Et pourquoi pas sur Mars? Relisons Wells: " ...les semences que les Marsiens... apportèrent avec eux donnèrent toujours naissance à des pousses rougeâtres. Seule, la plante connue sous le nom populaire d'Herbe Rouge réussit à entrer en compétition avec les végétations terrestres."[4]

Vian's novel takes place, then, in the midst of flora sown by H.G. Wells in his *The War of the Worlds*: "C'est le locus où Vian situe son roman, sans le définir plus précisément, puisque, de toute évidence, cette caractéristique est suffisamment éclairante."[5] Enlightening this certainly is. It is a subtle reference which allows the reader to view Vian's text against the backdrop of an entire genre, a genre which will allow *L'Herbe rouge* a certain autonomy within the tetralogy. It has also been so generally accepted that Jacques Goimard, for example, includes *L'Herbe rouge* in his "Chronologie générale de la S.F." alongside such works as Ray Bradbury's *The Martian Chronicles*.[6]

---

[3] See Alain Calame, "Du Ciel crevé à *L'Herbe rouge*", in *Boris Vian: Colloque de Cerisy*, pp.351-363.

[4] "A propos de *L'Herbe rouge*", p.139.

[5] *Ibid.*

[6] Jacques Goimard, "Chronologie générale de la S.F.", *Europe: Revue littéraire mensuelle*, 580-

There is, however, one slight problem as regards the labelling of *L'Herbe rouge* as a piece of Science Fiction. In his article entitled "The Introduction of Science Fiction into France", Pascal Ory attempts to put precise dates to what seems to be a fairly amorphous mass of Science Fiction style writing:

> The 1929 term [i.e. 'science fiction'] was first used in France, almost certainly, in the middle of an article in the *Figaro Littéraire* of 8 April 1950 by a certain Claude Elsen who, having first of all presented it in italics as an untranslated anglicism, then dispensed with any attempt at translation.[7]

This may appear to be mere linguistic squabbling, since whether one uses the label Science Fiction or another, such as 'anticipation', the genre still exists as a potential provider of intertexts.[8] Nonetheless, given that *L'Herbe rouge* was completed by 1949, it is a point worth bearing in mind. (Michel Fauré, for instance, although keen to stress the attraction which Science Fiction held for Vian, is careful that his words should not be misinterpreted: "Boris Vian était d'ailleurs tellement préoccupé du futur que certaines de ses œuvres, comme *l'Herbe rouge*, sont très proches de la science-fiction."[9]) For the moment the term Science Fiction should be disregarded in order that *The War of the Worlds* may be considered as an intertext in its own right.

Wolf, it is claimed, walks straight into the world of H.G. Wells the very moment he leaves his house. In his notes to the text, Pestureau writes:

---

581 (1977), 159-69 (p.163).

[7] Pascal Ory, "The Introduction of Science Fiction into France", in *France and the Mass Media*, ed. by Brian Rigby and Nicholas Hewitt (London, Macmillan Academic and Professional Ltd., 1991), pp.98-110 (p.98).

[8] The inventory of books which Vian possessed compiled by Nicole Bertold of La Fondation Vian in Paris lists two under this latter title. It also lists, as a separate entry, six titles by H.G. Wells.

[9] *Les Vies Posthumes de Boris Vian*, p.265.

> Le Carré: Ce territoire de fiction est comme un carrefour poétique et mythique des deux extrêmes de la guerre froide: le *French Quarter* ou « Vieux Carré » de la Nouvelle-Orléans et le *Red Square*, place Rouge de Moscou que signale l'herbe rouge du roman, pourtant venue sans doute de H.G. Wells: après la défaite des « Marsiens » auprès de Londres, ils ont laissé une herbe rouge sur le sol anglais (*La Guerre des mondes*). (*R*, p.1311-1312.)

Thus, there is what might be called an 'interfloral' link that seems to bind the two novels.

> And speaking of the differences between the life on Mars and the terrestrial life, I may allude here to the curious suggestions of the red weed. [...] Apparently the vegetable kingdom in Mars, instead of having green for a dominant colour, is of a vivid blood-red tint. [...] It spread up the sides of the pit by the third or fourth day of our imprisonment, and its cactus-like branches formed a carmine fringe to the edges of our triangular window.[10]

It is interesting that the machine in *L'Herbe rouge* which lies across the square of red grass should also be constructed over a pit ("La cage était remontée, et entre les quatre pieds râblés béait un puits profond." [*R*, p.429]), and that Wolf's view is cut out against a triangular backdrop ("La machine, à cent pas, charcutait le ciel de sa structure d'acier gris, le cernait de triangles inhumains."). As mentioned earlier, the machine is of great importance for Aboucaya's reading:

> Machine cosmique, dont le prototype vient de Mars. La description qu'en donne Boris Vian ne laisse subsister

---

[10] H.G. Wells, *The War of the Worlds* (London: Everyman, J.M. Dent, 1993), p.121-122. (Hereafter referred to as *War*.)

> aucun doute: il parle de "quatre pieds râblés" disposés autour d'un puits profond, mentionne "les éléments destructeurs qui [viennent] s'ajuster automatiquement à la suite les uns des autres." Et il ajoute: "La machine avait l'air filiforme d'une toile d'araignée vue de loin."
> Wells, pour sa part, compare la machine des Marsiens à "une araignée métallique avec cinq jambes articulées, et de 'tentacules'. Même aspect général, chez l'un et l'autre: 'structure d'acier gris' chez Vian, 'reflets métalliques' chez Wells. Inutile de poursuivre plus avant: tout y est - à une jambe près. Il est clair que les deux descriptions s'appliquent à une seule et même réalité.[11]

Although it *is* clear that *The War of the Worlds* is intertextually bound to Vian's novel, a closer look at Wolf's entrance to the text reveals further intertextual implications in that first paragraph:

> Le vent, tiède et endormi, poussait une brassée de feuilles contre la fenêtre. Wolf, fasciné, guettait le petit coin de jour démasqué périodiquement par le retour en arrière de la branche. [...] Il descendit, se retrouva dehors et ses pieds prirent contact avec l'allée de briques, bordée d'orties bifides, qui menait au Carré, à travers l'herbe rouge du pays. (*R*, p.429)

What fascinates Wolf is the wind blowing outside his window; when he leaves the house he 'se retrouve dehors': both these signs indicate a certain strangeness of his environment. Then, to reach 'la machine', he follows a brick road across two types of unusual flora (only the second of which is 'l'herbe rouge'). If we substitute for Wolf the name Dorothy, then the implications of the red grass are rather different. Dorothy's house, in *The Wizard of Oz*, is picked up by an unusual (although quite natural, indeed terrestrial) wind and is relocated in what one might term another dimension. And if Dorothy's brick road was yellow, then there is no reason why, in that same dimension, Wolf's

---

[11] "A propos de *L'Herbe rouge*", p.140.

grass should not be red. The location of this other dimension is revealed at the end of *The Wizard of Oz* when Dorothy wakes up: it was all a dream. The reader of *L'Automne à Pékin* is already used to Vian's use of falling asleep as entry into the oneiric text; in *L'Herbe rouge* he is using what appears to be an opposite technique: Wolf wakes up into the text; and this concept is crucial to an understanding of it. Wolf will go on to explain how he has been 'robbed of his nights', as if he is a nocturnal animal who has been forced to live by day. Thus, when one reads 'wake up' one can, to all intents and purposes, infer 'go to sleep'. The novel is, then, once more located in Vian's dreamland. Such a relocation of the novel helps to tighten the intratextual links binding the tetralogy. *L'Écume des jours* opens with the words "Colin terminait sa toilette" (*R*, p.61); he emerges from his morning shower, thereby waking up into the story. Then in the second novel the principal characters are sent to sleep one after the other before penetrating the text proper. Angel wakes (from one dream level to another) by the same (perversely) hypnotic passing of branches against a window-pane: "A l'extrémité du couloir, un faible courant d'air agitait une lourde branche d'hépatrol devant la fenêtre. Angel eut de nouveau cette sensation de s'éveiller..." (*R*, p.319). Then, towards the end of the novel, Angel begins his ultimate return to the waking world:

> \- Vous pouvez tuer quelqu'un et vous ne pouvez pas vous réveiller?
> \- Ce n'est pas pareil. Je les ai tués en dormant.
> \- Mais non, dit Petitjean. Vous le dites mal. Ils sont morts pour vous réveiller. (*R*, p.413-414)

Wolf's awakening closes the circle; it is as if 'la barre difficile à franchir' has now been crossed twice. (The line which divides night and day, dream and non-dream is hazy: *L'Écume* is apparently a waking text, and yet, as shown before, Stanley Chapman, in his translation, renders the title *Froth on the Daydream*.) There is also, as shall be seen, a continuity of intertextuality which supports the father-son relationship between Angel and Wolf.

It is clear, therefore, that *L'Herbe rouge* is not the incongruous, 'problem child' novel which it has sometimes (perhaps understandably) been taken to be; although its main protagonist follows a solitary path, the novel is not alone. The visual effect of a skyline cut up into triangles, which seems to be generated from the act of looking at/through the machine (and, possibly, into *The War of the Worlds*), is also to be found in the Exopotamian desert:

"Le profil grêle des appareils de levage en poutrelles d'acier mince se dessinait au-dessus des tas de matériaux, découpant le ciel en triangles cernés de noir" (*R*, p.360). In *L'Automne*, the construction of lines (of which the railway is the ultimate example) could be seen to expose the underlying use of lines of intertextuality; the use of such similar visual imagery in the description of the machine permits the reader to anticipate its role as a centre of intertextuality in *L'Herbe rouge*.

In his article, "Un Théorème botanique" (which is an investigation of the intertextuality existing between *L'Herbe rouge* and Queneau's *Les Fleurs bleues*), François Naudin points to three further 'imports' from *The War of the Worlds* which it will be useful to look at: "De *La Guerre des mondes*, outre l'herbe rouge, Vian importe l'huis fermé sans bruit... l'attitude de Wolf dans la mort... et les bandes de nuages pourpres."[12] The first of these draws a parallel between Wolf's nervous descent from his bedroom ("il fit grincer la lame grinçante du parquet et ferma la porte silencieusement pour compenser." [*R*, p.429]) and the silent flight of Wells' principal character from the oncoming Martians:

> Down the road towards Maybury Bridge there were voices and the sound of feet, but I had not the courage to shout or to go to them. I let myself in with my latch-key, closed, locked and bolted the door, staggered to the foot of the staircase, and sat down. (*War*, p.46)

The feeling of a baleful presence beyond a window (that which draws Wolf from his bedroom and into the text), expressed in the eerie outline of a tree can also be felt in a later passage of *The War of the Worlds*:

> Through the aperture in the wall I could see the top of a tree touched with gold, and the warm blue of a tranquil evening sky... and then I advanced crouching and stepping with extreme care amid the broken crockery that littered the floor. (*War*, p.116)

---

[12] François Naudin, "Un Théorème botanique", *Europe: Revue littéraire mensuelle*, 650 (1983), pp.103-109 (p.107).

Naudin's second 'import' highlights the similarity between the final description of Wolf's lifeless body and that of a victim of the Martians:

> A quelques centaines de pas, vers l'ouest, le corps de Wolf, nu, presque intact, gisait la face tournée vers le soleil. Sa tête, pliée contre son épaule à un angle peu vraisemblable, paraissait indépendante de son corps. (*R*, p.530)

> Before I could distinguish clearly how the man lay, the flicker of light had passed. I stood over him waiting for the next flash. When it came, I saw that he was a sturdy man... his head was bent under his body, and he lay crumpled up close to the fence, as though he had been flung violently against it [...] He was quite dead. Apparently his neck had been broken. (*War*, p.45)

It is also worth noting that there is an electrical storm, of the kind which illuminates the body of the Martians' victim, directly after the death of Lazuli (and, therefore, directly before the final return of Wolf). This use of a common source of intertextuality at the start and end of *L'Herbe rouge* provides a sinister framing device: just as it is an alien presence which draws Wolf into the text, it is an alien presence which takes him from it. This intertextual framing device can also be extended, intratextually, to include the two 'framing' novels: both *L'Automne à Pékin* and *L'Arrache-cœur* have a major character called Angel (and both of these angels can be seen to descend from a common source: H.G. Wells' *The Wonderful Visit*). Wolf's position in the Vian novels, as both son and father of an angel, is, therefore, inextricably bound to the novels of H.G. Wells.

It is Naudin's third 'import' which raises certain questions about the whole issue of aliens. Their lethal weapon in *The War of the Worlds* is well documented: "The Martians are able to discharge enormous clouds of a black and poisonous vapour by means of rockets." (*War*, p.76) In *L'Herbe rouge* strange clouds appear to arise as a result of Wolf's gaze: "Wolf regardait par la fenêtre de l'Ouest. [...] Une à une, les bandes rouges des nuages s'éteignaient, avec un léger murmure, un friselis de fer chaud dans l'eau." (*R*, p.435) This appears to be more than just a sunset. It is as if these clouds are the product of Wolf's morbidity, and not the other way round (the act of looking "vers l'ouest" seems to indicate his sense of his own impending death). But if, for Wolf, meteorological phenomena are symptomatic of a kind of impulse towards death (for he is surely as destined to die as are Wells' Martians, overcome by a common bacterial infection), they are not the means by which he will die.

In his essay charting the 'genèse' of *L'Herbe rouge*, Pestureau also draws attention to the importance of another Wells novel: "[...] H.G. Wells pour «l'herbe rouge» venue des «Marsiens» de *La Guerre des mondes*, puis pour *La Machine à remonter le temps* lors de la recomposition..." (*R*, p.426). It is interesting that Aboucaya, having been the single most important source of the 'Martian grass' theory, is not so keen on time machines:

> Elle [la machine] constitue l'élément essentiel de ce paysage, et plusieurs hypothèses ont été avancées à son sujet. L'opinion couramment admise est qu'il s'agit d'une machine à explorer le temps. L'explication est commode - et puérile pour autant que subsiste dans la pensée de son auteur l'arbitraire distinction entre le temps et l'espace. [...] La machine est, tout simplement, un vaisseau cosmique, capable d'explorer l'espace, et, par là-même, le temps. D'où son utilisation par Wolf pour une plongée dans son propre passé, ou son propre avenir.[13]

By giving less emphasis to the idea of 'Dr Who'-style time travelling, Aboucaya allows us to pursue the idea of the literary time traveller. Thus, Wolf may cross textual space, exploring other literary dimensions, both inter- and intratextual. However, in whichever direction he goes, be it "dans son propre passé" (*L'Écume des jours, L'Automne à Pékin*), "ou son propre avenir" (*L'Arrache-cœur*), he faces dissolution. For, surely the most fundamental role of the machine is that of execution.

If one of the roles of the machine is the disposal of matter, be it metallic or human, then this leads to an examination of other fields of intertextuality: the Science Fiction reading hinges on the machine being of

---

[13] "A propos de *L'Herbe rouge*", p.139-140.

Wellsian origins, the vessel of the invading Martians for Aboucaya and a time machine for others (Pestureau notes this possible function). As a machine tailored towards a more personal death, the machine may be seen to draw on other, more nightmarish, genres. The whole feeling of an inexplicable and ineluctable pull towards death is one reminiscent of the novels of Franz Kafka. In *The Trial*, for example, K is drawn deeper and deeper into a nightmarish conspiracy which ends in the only way possible: his death. And yet, K dies at human hands whereas Wolf's demise is inextricably linked with the workings of the machine. An intertextual search for a machine of execution in the work of Kafka proves fruitful. Jacques Bens, in "Cinq livres Pères", draws a parallel between Wolf's machine and that of the 'Officer' in Kafka's short story, *In the Penal Colony* (in French, *La Colonie pénitentiaire*). In an article otherwise devoted to denying the importance of external influence upon Vian's work[14], he writes (in his section devoted to *La Colonie pénitentiaire* which, he reminds us, is cited in Arnaud's *Les vies parallèles* as being one of Vian's "grands cinq"): "On ne peut s'empêcher d'évoquer ici, bien sûr, la machine et la mort de Wolf, dans *L'Herbe rouge*."[15]

The story is set on an island where corporal punishment, although supposedly increasingly out of favour, is still very much the rule. The machine used to this end is intricate (and gruesome). As well as being complex and long-running, to the point of being almost self-reliant, it is, as is Vian's own machine, built over a pit. The pit is there to collect the blood as it flows from the convict who meets his end under the sharp needles of the machine. The officer in charge of the executions is as one with the machine; he displays it to the foreign explorer with clear pride, explains its workings by deciphering an obscure script (esoteric, if not actually illegible to an outsider) and finally is drawn himself into its fatal embrace: '"Then the time has come," he said at last...'.[16] These are almost exactly the words used by Wolf as he steps into the machine for the first time: "C'est l'heure? demanda Wolf. [...] C'est l'heure, dit Lazuli." (*R*, p.457-458)[17]. It is clear that the Officer is doomed from the outset

---

[14] Bens raises here the same sort of objection as Clouzet in his work on Vian. Both believe that the term intertextuality implies, per se, a denial of originality. It is worth restating that the very objective of this study is to show just how Vian's originality lies in his manipulation of intertexts.

[15] "Cinq Livres Pères", p.148.

[16] Franz Kafka, *In the Penal Colony*, in *Kafka*, pp.140-67 (p.160).

[17] This scene also clearly reminds the reader of the murder/suicide of Anne, and Angel's part

to die by the machine; and when he does the machine dies with him, its cogs being shed as its needles lacerate his skin. There is also a feeling that Wolf has a kind of kinship with his machine (which might offer an answer to Aboucaya's question, "Wolf est-il un être humain?"[18]). The supposed role of Wolf's machine is to use up surplus metal. There are some suggestions that Wolf, whom the machine uses up with deadly efficiency, is himself rather metallic: "Sa main, sur le commutateur, était blanche et dure comme le métal du miroir." (*R*, p.436.)

The Officer's face, contorted by the throes of death, is the very image of Wolf's:

> It was as it had been in life; no sign was visible of the promised redemption; what the others had found in the machine the officer had not found; the lips were firmly pressed together, the eyes were open with the same expression as in life, the look was calm and convinced, through the forehead went the point of the great iron spike. (*Kafka*, p.166)

When fused with the description given earlier of the mangled corpse of one of the victims of Wells' Martians, the product is as follows:

> [...] Le corps de Wolf, nu, presque intact gisait la face tournée vers le soleil. Sa tête, pliée contre son épaule à un angle peu vraisemblable, paraissait indépendante de son corps.
> Rien n'avait pu rester dans ses yeux grand ouverts. Ils étaient vides. (*R*, p.530)

Thus, whether the impulse which drives Wolf to his death is inter- or intratextual, his actual death is very much an intertextual one.

---

therein.

[18] "A propos de *L'Herbe rouge*", p.140.

The role of the visiting explorer is also interesting. Much has been said of the role of the double in Vian's fiction: here Lazuli and Wolf's mirror-image play parts parallel to Wolf's own. There is sufficient intertextual interaction here to suggest that, if Vian's protagonist descends from each of Kafka's central characters, then the explorer's departure from the island offers some hope for (at least some part of) Wolf. If he dies, then his spirit certainly crosses "la barre" into *L'Arrache-cœur*; if he is only dreaming (which alternative will concern the second part of this chapter), then he will reawaken in that same text.

Despite the proximity of *In the Penal Colony* to *L'Herbe rouge*, there has been a tendency to view Kafka's influence in much more general terms: "[Mais] cette imprégnation est sans doute demeurée superficielle, ne déterminant guère sa vision du monde", writes Lionel Richard[19]. It is true that Vian's view of the world was very much his own. It would be possible to ignore Kafka's machine and to suggest that Vian invented his machine with resort to no other influence that his own imagination. However, this would be to ignore two factors: firstly, the intertextual path left in this novel; secondly, the precedent set in the form of the 'pianocktail', a machine calqued on Huysmans' 'orgue à bouche'. Therefore, in spite of Richard's warning ("[Au-delà de ces suppositions,] il paraît bien risqué de se prononcer sur l'influence que les œuvres de Kafka ont exercée sur lui."[20]), these risks are worth taking.

Neither is this link with Kafka unique in the tetralogy. The theme of the pull towards death can be traced back, via Anne and Rochelle, as far as Chloé. In *L'Écume des jours*, the fate of the mouse, which seems somehow to provide a scale model for the deterioration in the relationship of Colin and Chloé, is based, as has been seen, on a Kafkaesque model. The teeth of the cat offer a killing machine not unlike Kafka's. And yet, there is more to it than that. *L'Écume des jours*, as seen from the perspective of the mouse, is an exact rewrite (apart from the reluctance on the part of Vian's cat) of Kafka's *A Little Fable*.

Through Kafka this chapter has now come some way from Wells' red weed. Perversely, it is now, by returning to the article by François Naudin, which draws so heavily upon *The War of the Worlds*, that this chapter will begin to move away from dependence upon the Martian theory.

---

[19] "Vian était-il kafkaïen?", p.27.

[20] *Ibid*.

Naudin's "Un Théorème botanique" seeks to bind *L'Herbe rouge* and *Les Fleurs bleues*; this he does by investigating the closeness of their titles. An examination of the titles in the catalogues of 'le Livre de poche' and 'la collection Folio' produced only three titles to meet the following criteria: "D (déterminant) + S (substantif) végétal + A (adjectif) de couleur", those being: "*Les Fleurs bleues* (Raymond Queneau), *Les Lauriers roses* (Joseph Kessel) et *L'Herbe rouge* (Boris Vian)."[21] The second he rejects because of the superfluousness of the adjective: "Les arbustes en tutu de Joseph Kessel, malgré leur forme D+S+A, sont aussi déterminés que le persil tout court ou la saponaire sans plus."[22] One might well ask if it is for the same reason that Naudin fails to cite *Le Mouron rouge*. No similar failing in Vian; for example, in *L'Écume des jours*: "Un chahut commençait à s'organiser dans le fond, quelques étudiants cherchant à semer le doute dans les esprits en déclamant à haute voix des passages tronqués dilatoirement du *Serment de la Montagne*, de la baronne Orczy" (*Ej*, p.108), about which Pestureau makes the following note: "La baronne Emmuska Orczy: 1865-1947, auteur de romans anglais sentimentaux dont *Le Mouron rouge* (*The Scarlet Pimpernel*) - encore une «herbe rouge» précédant celle de H.G. Wells dans *la Guerre des mondes*, et celle du roman de Vian..." (*Ej*, p.269).

The loss of an impossible love and the attainment of love undesired are two features of Vian's text which extend beyond the expected bounds of the Science Fiction text as, indeed, they go beyond the texts of Kafka which have been looked at. These elements, which are nonetheless manifest in *L'Herbe*, appear to have more in common with a 'sentimental novel' or love story. Although in Baroness Orczy's 'sentimental novel' love finally conquers, as is clearly not the case in *L'Herbe rouge*, the two texts do have some surprising similarities. The focus of the action in *The Scarlet Pimpernel* is the French Revolution; more precisely it is 'la Place de Grève', a square washed red with blood, the throne room of the infamous guillotine. And what purpose did this machine serve if not the removal of memories, the remembrance of centuries of repression. The knife of the guillotine is emblematic of vengeance: "Their ancestors had oppressed the people, had crushed them

---

[21] "Un Théorème botanique", p.103.

[22] *Ibid.*, p.104.

under the scarlet heels of their dainty buckled shoes...".[23] Blood avenges blood: red is the colour. In fact, the novel is at times very red indeed; in the space of two pages, the following descriptions can be found:

> [...] The red-tiled floor was as brilliant as the scarlet geranium on the window-sill...
>
> He [Mr Jellyband] wore the typical scarlet waistcoat...
>
> [...] The faces of Mr Jellyband's customers appeared red and pleasant... (*Orczy*, p.18-19)

In France, then, red signifies social upheaval and suffering, in England ruddy-cheeked contentment and social harmony and, between the two, the concealed figure constantly making the journey from one side to the other of the Channel ('la barre difficile à franchir'?). Escape must be made from la Place de Grève itself: "Every afternoon before the gates closed and the market carts went out in procession by the various barricades, some fool of an aristo endeavoured to evade the clutches of the committee of Public Safety." (*Orczy*, p.8) The enclosure of the two principal couples within 'le Carré' is somewhat like the imprisonment of the aristos. Wolf is himself at the beck and call of townspeople: "C'était le jour de l'inauguration et les Municipaux allaient attendre. Rapidement, il se mit à sa toilette." (*R*, p.454) The wall of his enclosure is pierced by the arrival of Monsieur le Maire; it is only after this hole has been made that Wolf can leave (in as much as he can be said to leave) in the machine.

> Derrière le mur du Carré, il y eut un vague bruit de musique [...] puis un pan de briques s'abattit sous la pression du défonce-murs municipal, piloté par un huissier barbu en habit noir et chaîne d'or. Par la brèche entrèrent les premiers représentants de la foule... (*R*, p.454)

---

[23] Baroness Orczy, *The Scarlet Pimpernel* (London: Hodder and Stoughton, 1980). (Hereafter referred to as *Orczy*.)

Just as this scene is the signal for Wolf to enter another level of the text, so too, in *L'Écume des jours*, a similar act of hole-punching permits Colin to complete his entry into the text: "Il vida son bain en perçant un trou dans le fond de la baignoire." (*Ej*, p.42)

The romantic climax of *The Scarlet Pimpernel* is the reunion of the two halves of the Sir Percy Blakeney-Marguerite St Just marriage. Each had been guilty of failing to understand the other: Lil seeks to learn her future by going to see 'la reniflante', but takes the destiny of 'le Sénateur' to be that of Wolf:

> Un grand bonheur pour une personne de votre maison. Elle va trouver ce qu'elle cherche depuis très longtemps après avoir été malade.
> Lil pensa que Wolf avait eu raison de construire la machine et qu'enfin ses efforts allaient être récompensés...
> (*R*, p.448)

Had she, like Marguerite, gone into her husband's inner sanctum, his office where his two disparate lives merge, she may have been able to piece together the puzzle that is Wolf. Whereas Marguerite has time to recognise her mistake ("her very blindness in not having guessed her husband's secret seemed now to her another deadly sin" [*Orczy*, p.170]), Lil does not. And neither does Wolf ever find the love that he had once thought he felt for Lil; his failure to understand women, and, thus, to love, is fatal: "[...] De ma vie, je n'ai pu lire quoi que ce soit dans un regard." (*R*, p.518) Although Sir Percy's problem is much the same, he finally realises Marguerite's fidelity and is able to right his mistake. Thus, *The Scarlet Pimpernel*, in the true tradition of the swashbuckling love story, ties all the knots and unites the correct halves of the respective love matches. *L'Herbe rouge*, in as much as it fails to respect this convention, cannot be said to be a sentimental novel in the classic tradition. It flits between genres, alighting and assuming a fleeting identity, but does not adhere to any of the labels offered so far. It can, however, be said that there is a potential for intertextuality between these two red-flowered novels. But what of the other novel, *Les Fleurs bleues*, the one which Naudin does not reject? He does not so much offer a direct line of intertextuality between the two novels, as juxtapose them in order to expose their similar usage of intertextuality. Had he sought to establish a line of intertextuality between the two novels, it would, given their respective years of publication (*L'Herbe rouge* 1949, *Les Fleurs bleues* 1959), have been running in the wrong direction; this despite his somewhat tongue-in-cheek declaration "*L'Herbe rouge* est un plagiat par anticipation des *Fleurs bleues*."[24] And yet, such intertextuality is manifestly present, and not simply between *Les Fleurs bleues* and *L'Herbe rouge*, but between *Les Fleurs bleues* and *L'Arrache-cœur* as well: not only does Cidrolin live on a barge within an area called 'le carré', but he is also the father of 'triplées" ("Je n'ai que mes triplées, ce qui est, je vous assure, un calvaire"[25]), just as Clémentine is devoted to her 'trumeaux'.

If it is the case that, this time, Queneau is drawing on Vian's work, then what should one infer from such intertextuality? It seems possible that, in much the same way as Vian offers a potential reading of *Le Chiendent* in *L'Écume des jours*, Queneau is offering a reading of *L'Herbe rouge*. Without wishing to enter here into a long analysis of *Les Fleurs bleues*, it is worth exposing some examples to give credence to what may seem a somewhat improbable statement. For, within Queneau's novel, a category can be glimpsed into which *L'Herbe* appears to fit more comfortably than any other. Both texts have an outward appearance of sentimentality, Vian's through the need for love shown by Wolf and his failure, despite everything, to make his marriage work, and Queneau's through its very title ('fleur bleue' means 'sentimental' in French). But, beneath this aspect, the novels both function on an oneiric level the realisation of which allows the Vian reader a fuller view of the strategies at work in *L'Herbe rouge*.

As suggested above, Queneau refers not only to *L'Herbe rouge* but to *L'Arrache-cœur* as well. In fact, in the course of *Les Fleurs bleues*, he draws on his intimate knowledge of all four Vian novels. For example, there is an apparent exploitation of that most famous of paragraphs from *L'Écume des jours* ("A l'endroit où les fleuves se jettent dans la mer..."): "Il [le duc d'Auge] alla pisser dans le fleuve et se réjouit en son cœur du bruit allègre du jet d'eau se brisant à la surface de l'eau." (*Fleurs*, p.235) Similarly, he captures the dual collapse of Pippo's hotel (which previously stood over a railway line) and the railway line (which was being constructed over a ley line) of *L'Automne à Pékin* in the collapse of his hotel which was being built next to Cidrolin's stretch of river: "Un immeuble en construction s'est écroulé, répondit un

---

[24] "Un Théorème botanique", p.105.

[25] Raymond Queneau, *Les Fleurs bleues* (Paris: Gallimard, 1994), p.24. (Hereafter referred to as *Fleurs*.)

passant qui venait en sens inverse. Il était inhabité, naturellement, puisqu'il était toujours en construction." (*Fleurs*, p.269)

The rapport with *L'Herbe rouge*, however, remains the most consistent. Vian's 'quartier des amoureuses' is twinned neatly with Queneau's 'ville capitale':

> - Tu ne vas pas encore me demander ce que je viens faire dans la ville capitale?
> - Nul besoin! Messire vient voir nos putains qui sont les plus belles de toute la chrétienté. (*Fleurs*, p.18)

And whilst Lil consults 'la reniflante', Russule consults 'l'astrologue' (*Fleurs*, p.146). Queneau even appears to exploit certain of Vian's intertexts; thus, in a novel satirising a novel which was influenced in part by Lewis Carroll's *Through the Looking-Glass*, it is not surprising that one should find a fine example of semantics reminiscent of Humpty Dumpty:

> - Vous êtes sûr que cela s'appelle comme ça?
> - Pour le moment, moi j'appelle ça comme ça, donc ça s'appelle comme ça et comme c'est avec moi que vous causez en ce moment et avec nul autre, il vous faut bien prendre mes mots à leur valeur faciale. (*Fleurs*, 30-31)[26]

It seems clear that Queneau has quite deliberately set his novel against the background of those of Vian. The question is, then, in what way can this knowledge shape a reading of *L'Herbe rouge*? The answer may be as simple as this: what Queneau is doing manifestly in his novel, Vian is doing tacitly in his. Above all, and in spite of its title, *Les Fleurs bleues* is a novel about dreaming. The implication is that, from the midst of an oneiric tetralogy, *L'Herbe rouge* is a novel about dreaming, about transportation via dreaming and where transportation signifies dreaming.

In *Les Fleurs bleues*, despite the continual jumping about in time, it is always apparent that the two principal characters, Cidrolin and le duc d'Auge,

---

[26] It is, of course, not entirely surprising to find allusions to Carroll in any work by Queneau who knew this English author particularly well.

are linked together in their dreams (hence the question which the text invariably provokes: who is dreaming whom?). The presence of a clock in 'le carré' is indicated more than once: "Cidrolin consulta l'horloge dans le carré..." (*Fleurs*, p.23). And what is a clock if not a time machine? But the clock is not the most important piece of equipment on board: "Il alla dans le carré regarder l'heure et, comme conséquence de cet examen, il s'étendit de nouveau sur sa chaise longue pour achever sa sieste interrompue." (*Fleurs*, p.39) The chaise longue is a sleeping machine, a means of entry into a dream.

Thus, via an article which was largely devoted to exposing the influence of *The War of the Worlds* on Vian's novel, one can arrive at a possible way of reading *L'Herbe rouge* which has nothing to do with Science Fiction. That such an outcome is possible is due both to the complexity and potentiality of the Vian text, and the weakness of any reading that attempts to classify it under any single heading. Thus, it is useful to recognise and expose the contribution of Wells' work, but it is not possible to say that *L'Herbe rouge* is simply a work of Science Fiction.

Who is Wolf?

Because the name 'Wolf' is not merely unusual, but foreign-sounding and 'alien' to the text, this can be said to work in favour of the 'Alien' analysis of the text. One does not have to search far, however, to find other Wolves; it suffices to read other texts to see that Vian's Wolf, although a lone figure, is not alone in modern literature. One does not need to seek his past in another galaxy; one must simply look to other texts. The weight of intertextuality existing between Wells and Vian drives Aboucaya to ask the following question: "Wolf est-il un être humain?" He suggests that his physical appearance makes it unlikely that he is a Martian. It is true that Wolf could not be said to come from the Mars of H.G. Wells; that of Ray Bradbury, however, would accomodate Wolf fairly well; in "The Third Expedition", for example, a group of astronauts find a planet resembling that of their childhood, only to discover that their relations are being impersonated by aliens.[27] In his conclusion, however, Aboucaya goes one step further:

---

[27] "April 2000 The Third Expedition", in Ray Bradbury, *The Martian Chronicles* (London: Flamingo Modern Classics, 1995).

> Alors un fait s'impose, qui devrait figurer dans les prémisses de toute étude sérieuse de *L'Herbe rouge*, et qu'on s'étonne de ne pas voir seulement envisagé: *Wolf est un mutant*.
>
> [...] On voit les dimensions que prend l'œuvre dès lors qu'on l'observe sous le seul éclairage qui lui convient.[28]

Aboucaya's point is pertinent; but it is certainly not the case that a mutant Wolf is necessarily the product of Science Fiction. In as much as Vian's principal characters champion the cause of the individual over that of society's masses, Wolf is the next in a line of social 'mutants' which includes both Colin and Angel. Literature teems with the tales of society's outcasts, hounded into exile and, so often, death (the resonance of Camus' *L'Etranger* has already been felt across the pages of *L'Automne à Pékin*). The name Wolf bears the stigma of this alienation: one may think, for example, of the proud and silent death of the wolf hunted down by men in Vigny's *La Mort du Loup*. The name of Vian's main protagonist is, however, not Loup, but Wolf; it seems likely that the reader is being asked to see the origins of this wolf in a text/texts written in a Germanic language (and, once more, not in that Anglo-Saxon genre that is Science Fiction). An analysis of Hermann Hesse's *Steppenwolf* yields some interesting similarities between that classic text and *L'Herbe rouge*.

> For he was not a sociable man, as a matter of fact, he was unsociable to a degree I had never before experienced in anybody. He really was a wolf of the steppes, as he called himself [...] Altogether he gave the impression of having come out of an alien world, from another continent perhaps.[29]

---

[28] "A Propos de *L'Herbe rouge*", p.142.

[29] Hermann Hesse, *Steppenwolf* (London: Penguin, 1965), p.7-9. (Hereafter referred to as *Hesse*.)

This is surely an aspect of 'mutation', another 'éclairage qui lui convient'. Another, but clearly not sufficient. Hesse was adamant, in the face of the mass of literary criticism which defined his novel as an attack on the bourgeoisie, that, of all his books, "Steppenwolf is the one that was more often and more violently misunderstood than any other." (*Hesse*, p.5) The same can also be said of Vian's third novel. It is in their reactions to their plight, to their alienation, that Harry Haller and Wolf are so tightly related. A cursory glance at Haller's descent into himself, his encroaching madness and his disappearance from the view of others will reveal an illumination of Wolf's story via which this chapter will be able to proceed.

Both texts are progressively introspective, and as Haller and Wolf descend further into themselves their stories become increasingly personal and less attached to 'reality'. The description of the Steppenwolf quoted above is offered by the nephew of Haller's landlady. Thus, the text opens with an external view of the hero, his 'être-pour-autrui', that from which Wolf, in particular, will flee. *Steppenwolf* plays on the theme of mirrors (and mirror-images), that which *L'Herbe rouge* picks up in a crucial scene. The mirror in Wolf's office parallels that which, in *Steppenwolf*, is THE mirror, the existence of which Haller both suspects and dreads:

> [...] To be able at last to dare to leap into the unknown a Steppenwolf must once have a good look at himself. He must look deeply into the chaos of his own soul and plumb its depths. [...] And he is aware of the existence of that mirror in which he has such bitter need to look and from which he shrinks in such deathly fear. (*Hesse*, p.68-69)

It is, indeed, into this mirror that he will look only when he has at last finished his descent (into madness). As Wolf is mirrored both by his own reflection and by Lazuli (who kills himself in an attempt to stab his own shadow), Haller is mirrored by the wolf and 'the girl', Hermine. All these dualities are expressed as Haller finally confronts himself, knife in hand (as Lazuli):

> I stood opposite the gigantic mirror. I looked into it. In the mirror there stood a beautiful wolf as tall as myself. [...] Again I looked into the mirror. I had been mad. There was no wolf in the mirror, lolling his tongue in his maw. It was I, Harry. [...]

> "Harry," I said, "what are you doing there?"
> "Nothing," said he in the mirror, "I am only waiting. I am waiting for death." (*Hesse*, p.237)

The landlady's nephew speculates that Haller's strange behaviour is the result of a harsh upbringing:

> Although I knew very little of the Steppenwolf's life, nevertheless, I have good reason to suppose that he was brought up by devoted but severe and very pious parents and teachers in accordance with that doctrine that makes the breaking of the will the corner-stone of education and up-bringing. (*Hesse*, p.15)

Wolf's early trips in the machine lead to the same conclusion. Such destruction of the spirit leads, in both cases, not only to the hatred of the external world, but to the hatred of self. So it is that Wolf's sorties in the machine, far from being pleasant day trips, take on a sado-masochistic aspect. And when he can no longer hurt himself, Wolf hurts others: for example, he deliberately smashes Lil's glass dish, and, finally, kills the old civil servant. Compare with this the desires of Haller:

> After a short time it [contentment] fills me with irrepressible loathing and nausea. Then, in desperation, I have to escape into other regions, if possible on the road to pleasure, or, if that cannot be, on the road to pain. [...] I have a mad impulse to smash something, a warehouse perhaps, or a cathedral, or myself, to commit outrages, to pull off the wigs of a few revered idols... (*Hesse*, p.34-35)

Thus, with a similar upbringing, with similar desires, Wolf and Haller both descend, firstly, from their room, and then, into their past:

> Thus I went down the steep stairs from my attic among strangers [...] I trod the moist pavements of the narrow

streets [...] The forgotten years of my youth came back to me. (*Hesse*, p.35-37)

The importance of the streets and of 'flânerie' in *Steppenwolf* is crucial as it introduces an oneiric edge to the text (as in *L'Herbe rouge* there is a strong case for suggesting that all that follows is a dream). Haller's memories are also induced by synaesthesia: firstly, he is transported by the music of a piano ("After two or three notes of the piano the door was opened all of a sudden to the other world." [*Hesse*, p.38]). Then, later, it is the taste of wine which recalls that music. In *L'Écume des jours*, the pianocktail is at the centre of synaesthetic transports; in *L'Herbe rouge* its place is taken by the machine.

As Steppenwolves, both Harry and Wolf share a love of the night (of which the latter, if his own 'memories' are to be trusted, has been deprived for sixteen years): "It was part of the Steppenwolf's aspects that he was a night prowler. [...] With this was bound up his need for loneliness and independence." (*Hesse*, p.56)

In *Steppenwolf*, as in Vian's novels, the oneiric centre is focussed on a woman, a woman Harry meets in a bar, as if pulled to her by 'le hasard objectif'. This androgynous figure, whose name, the reader later learns, is Hermine, reminds him of a childhood love, Rosa, and a friend, Hermann (in *L'Herbe rouge*, too, there is a fusion of memories and dreams). As does Folavril, Hermine induces sleep:

God knows where the girl got her voice; it was so deep and good and maternal. It was good to obey such a voice, I had found that out already. Obediently I shut my eyes... (*Hesse*, p.111)

Her objective appears at first to be to teach him to dance. However, it transpires that she wishes to put him in a position where he will fall in love with her and will yet be forced to kill her. For the reader of *L'Écume des jours* this sequence of events will be familiar: Colin, having encountered 'le biglemoi', falls in love with a girl who is always destined to die. In *L'Herbe rouge*, Wolf avoids dancing, but in doing so lies down with Folavril in a scene loaded with no less significance than the dancing of 'le biglemoi'. In one of his journeys into the past (which are exactly parallel to Wolf's trips in the machine), Harry recalls lying on grass with a girl; here, as in *L'Herbe rouge*, the scene appears naively touching; here, too, the role of violets is crucial:

> We [Harry and Rosa] were both still children and did not quite know what to do with each other. That Sunday we did not even kiss, but we were immeasurably happy. [...] Then Rosa said that she smelt violets and we knelt in the short spring grass and looked for them and found a few with short stalks and I gave her mine and she gave me hers, and as it was getting chilly and the sun slanted low over the cliffs, Rosa said she must go home. (*Hesse*, p.232-233)

In as much as Rosa and Hermine are one and the same, Hermine's request that she die at Harry's hands is rather a statement of fact. Once violets are exchanged death is inevitable. As centre of the text's surreality, coming and going much as Nadja, Hermine is like Chloé; as harbinger of death in the guise of violets, she is like Folavril. She also acts as 'agent provocateur' much in the same way as Isis during her party; encouraging Harry to seduce Maria, she says: "You ought to make love to her a little, Harry. She is very pretty and such a good dancer, and you are in love with her already, I know very well." (*Hesse*, p.149) For her part, Maria obligingly plays out the role of Chloé: "Again we fell asleep and again I woke to find my arm still about her, my beautiful, beautiful flower." (*Hesse*, p.164)

Hermine's most important role, however, is that of intermediary between Harry and the enigmatic musician, Pablo (both act as a mirror before his gaze: "Was it not, too, my own soul that contemplated me out of his black eyes like a lost and frightened bird, just as it had out of Hermine's grey ones?" [*Hesse*, p.203]). It is Pablo who offers Harry the chance to escape; in terms of *L'Herbe rouge*, he provides the machine.

> It is a pleasure to me, my dear Harry, to have the privilege of being your host in a small way on this occasion. You have often been sorely weary of your life. You were striving, were you not, for escape? You have a longing to forsake this world and its reality and to penetrate to a reality more native to you, to a world beyond time. [...] Only within yourself exists that other reality for which you

> long. [...] All I can give you is the opportunity, the impulse, the key. (*Hesse*, p.204)

This, as shall be seen, is precisely the role of the machine in *L'Herbe rouge*; Wolf's journey is exactly comparable to that of the Steppenwolf: it is a flight from his external reality, a journey to the centre of himself.

Having once more shown Harry the image of the Steppenwolf in a looking-glass, Pablo leads him into his theatre, a peep-show where every room casts a view over Harry's past, as it was, could have been or how he would have desired it to be. Each room is the same as a trip in the machine.

> You have no doubt guessed long since that the conquest of time and the escape from reality, or however else it may be that you choose to describe your longing, means simply the wish to be relieved of your so-called personality. (*Hesse*, p.206)

The release which Harry Haller finds in Pablo's theatre, Wolf finds in death. Although ostensibly different, Wolf's demise can be seen to be a perfect metaphor for the escape from the 'être-pour-autrui': he dies only before the gaze of *L'Herbe rouge*; his literary essence is liberated. Thus, there is continuity between Vian's novels, the death of one character allowing the birth of another.

It is also possible to find a logical progression within the tetralogy which results in the red grass of this text. Thus, red grass is also an intratextual entity. The grass in *L'Écume des jours* was lush, watered by the very frothiness of the text:

> C'était la bonne route, lisse, moirée de reflets photogéniques, avec des arbres parfaitement cylindriques des deux côtés, de l'herbe fraîche, du soleil, des vaches dans les champs... (*Ej*, p.103)

This is the idyllic picture of a time gone by, when love seemed possible and the sun still shone. At this point, *L'Écume des jours* was still clinging to the Pastoral tradition. With the decay of the light, the appearance of the dark zones, comes a gradual degradation of the landscape. The vision of love is now a dream at one remove. Anne's dream has little bearing on his actual existence:

> Il y a tant de choses. Rien que cette herbe verte et pointue. Rien que toucher cette herbe et craquer entre ses doigts une coquille d'escargot jaune, sur ce sable sec et chaud...
> (*R*, p.321)

In the space of a fleeting moment, when Wolf and Folavril share a moment of tenderness which reflects the eternal 'what might have been', the red grass sees its herbaceous qualities return: "Wolf se retourna lentement pour changer de position. Il ne voulait pas perdre une seconde le contact de l'herbe." (*R*, p.438) Wolf's regret at the loss of this grass is more poignant even than Anne's:

> Voyez-vous, Monsieur Brul, mon point de vue est simple: aussi longtemps qu'il existe un endroit où il y a de l'air, du soleil et de l'herbe, on doit avoir regret de ne point y être. Surtout quand on est jeune. (*R*, p.497)

The grass has wilted; exposure to the desert sun has burned it; now it has achieved the state of ultimate deformation: it is red. In these privileged lines of the tetralogy grass represents the flora of the dreamland. This decaying dream is now the title of the third novel. *L'Herbe rouge*, then, is a negative image of *L'Écume des jours*. Once again there is progression: the gradual extinguishing of the sun in *L'Écume des jours* is significant of a movement away from a realist art form (for example, the daydreamy feel running through it); the stark zones of dark and light of *L'Automne à Pékin* reveal the influence of artists such as Man Ray who, as has been seen, exposed their photographs to varying degrees of light to produce virtual negatives (just as Cuivre and Lavande are negative images of one another), thereby introducing the theme of entrance into the text via the dream; finally, in *L'Herbe rouge* Vian produces a 'negative novel' (for, red is the colour of grass as seen on the negative of a colour photograph). Thus, as day is the negative of night, and dream the negative of the waking moment, then Wolf's is a quest to reconquer the night, to return to the dream: for he does not regret having been deprived of the night per se; rather he seeks that essential dream quality which is particular to childhood:

> [...] Jamais vous ne saurez qu'il y a un moment, comme la mer s'arrête de descendre et reste, un temps, étale, avant de remonter, où la nuit et le jour se mêlent et se fondent, et forment une barre de fièvre pareille à celle que font les fleuves à la rencontre de l'océan. On m'a volé seize ans de nuit, Monsieur Brul. On m'a volé ça... (*R*, p.495-496)

Are we not once more in that area so sacred to the Surrealists, that area where "la beauté sera convulsive, ou ne sera pas"? This is the froth of days, that interstitial region where the dream zone becomes the location of 'real life'. To live 'la nuit' is to really live.[30]

A reading which views *L'Herbe rouge* through the perspective of Queneau's *Les Fleurs bleues*, is one which puts these privileged passages where they belong, in the foreground. Le duc d'Auge and Cidrolin dream each other together, fusing finally on board a barge, a vessel which, though moored, can move with the water. And this water is the canal, neither fast-flowing like a river, nor stagnant like a pond: it is "un endroit où...".

To consider *L'Herbe rouge* as an oneiric text is to introduce another set of intertexts. It is Pestureau, in his essay on the genesis of the novel, who supplies a possible answer to Aboucaya's question, "Wolf vient-il d'ailleurs?"[31]: " [...] Claude Farrère aussi, je crois, pour sa nouvelle "Où?" (1923), reprise dans *L'Autre Côté* (1928): pour parvenir "là-bas", il faut rêver et, pour revenir "ici", il faut "reculer dans le temps, d'abord; redevenir enfant" (*R*, p.426).

However, the instructions on how to get *there* and how to return *here* are not clear; neither is it clear what *there* and *here* are. If Aboucaya's *elsewhere* is read as the dream, it is, therefore, difficult to say whether Wolf goes *there* from *here*, or comes *here* from *there*. Farrère himself cannot locate

---

[30] This idea conjures up images such as those captured by the lens of Brassaï in his book, *Paris after Dark*.

[31] "A propos de *L'Herbe rouge*", p.140.

the two regions: "Où? - Je ne sais pas."[32], and, as does Breton, regards the two as parallel and equal, the dream, if anything, being *more* real than our reality: "Autre part. Pas dans cette apparence-là, où nous vivons. Dans une autre. Et des deux, la moins fausse pourrait bien être cette autre apparence: - là où c'est..." (*Farrère*, p.20). What is interesting is that Farrère includes his 'nouvelle', with its Science Fiction style title, in a book, the title of which would, similarly, not appear out of place amongst the novels of Ray Bradbury, under the heading, *Rêves*.

For the purposes of this study, *L'Herbe rouge* represents an oneiric novel within an oneiric tetralogy, a dream within a dream. Thus, the two regions will be read as being those of intertextuality and intratextuality. Both these possibilities will be dealt with in the following chapter.

---

[32] Claude Farrère, *L'Autre Côté* (Paris: Flammarion, 1928), p.19. (Hereafter referred to as *Farrère*.)

CHAPTER SIX
L'Herbe rouge:
Dreams or Memories

If Wolf is a dreamer and this novel is his dream, the intertextual nature of the text may lead the reader to consider the possibility of links between *L'Herbe rouge* and other more classically oneiric texts, those which herald their own relationship to the world of dreams. It will be the aim of this chapter first to situate *L'Herbe rouge* amongst such texts, and in so doing to analyse the contents of the text as if they were fragments of a dream; it will then remain to weigh the merits of an analysis less removed from the manifest content of the text: that of story as the unfolding of Wolf's memories.

Wolf as dreamer of the text

The main body of the dream section of Farrère's *L'Autre côté* is taken up by the 'nouvelle' *Où?*. Pestureau, as has been seen, is quite justified in indicating this tale as a possible source of influence, as its subject matter seems close to many of the concerns of Vian's novels. Not only does it suggest the existence of parallel worlds, *ici* and *là-bas*, it also states that to move from the one into the other: "il faut, d'abord, s'endormir; puis rêver." (*Farrère*, p.21) However, not merely does this recall Vian's general method of entering the text, once *là-bas*, Farrère's dreamer uses a means of transport with which the reader of *L'Automne à Pékin* cannot help but be familiar.

> Lors, le tram électrique accéléra soudain son allure. Et je
> me penchai vers l'homme qui donne les billets...
> Je lui demandai:
> - Quand arriverons-nous?
> Il me considéra:
> - Où? - dit-il.

> Je nommai la station que je croyais mon but:
> - A Fourvières?
> Il rit:
> - LA-BAS?... Peste! ce n'est pas ICI... Quand nous arriverons, mon pauvre monsieur? Mettons dans cent ans, par exemple... hein?
> Et il me tourna le dos, comme on fait aux mauvais plaisants. (*Farrère*, p.38)

Vian's conductor suggests that Angel fly; this, so it would seem, is how Wolf will make the journey outlined by Farrère's conductor. The journey from one land to another, across an unknown quantity of sand, is, thus, much the same as that which apparently spans time and space. Indeed, a description of a network of bridges *là-bas*, is much like that of Wolf's machine:

> Ils sont métalliques et tubulaires, tous. [...] Aériens, naturellement: on ne fait que les apercevoir en plein ciel, beaucoup plus haut que la cime des plus hauts arbres; ils s'élancent d'un horizon à l'autre, se croisant et s'entre-croisant, perpendiculaires, obliques ou parallèles, et couvrant toute la terre d'une toile d'araignée prodigieuse [...] Chaque pont repose sur piliers. Et chaque pilier n'est qu'un mât métallique, ajouré, mince à l'invraisemblable, jailli du sol du Parc, parmi les fûts de la futaie. (*Farrère*, p.43)

Not only do the bridges resemble a spider's web, they also, like the machine, reach the heights of the sky whilst remaining attached to the earth by slender threads: "La fuite vertigineuse du sol apparent lui coupa le souffle. Il [Wolf] était au centre d'un fuseau dont une pointe se perdait dans le ciel et dont l'autre jaillissait de la fosse." (*R*, p.459)[33]. Thus, it appears that *Où?* is not only a source of influence, but may, in fact, legitimately be read as an intertext for *L'Herbe rouge*.

---

[33] The step from the ladder of *Le Ciel crevé* to the machine of *L'Herbe rouge* is really not a big one...

Finally, there appear to be two cults in *Où?*; one from which Wolf, in particular, is excluded, and another with a more general bearing on Vian's tetralogy. The first is centred on a temple. It, too, is mysterious; the traveller knows little about it: "Mais c'est un culte assurément nocturne. Car tout le jour, et tous les jours, le Temple est muet, désert et clos." (*Farrère*, p.53) This is a cult which would appeal to Wolf, but one from which he has always been excluded ("On m'a volé seize ans de nuit..." [*R*, p.496.]). The traveller is also excluded: "Et c'est là qu'habitent les Étrangers, tel moi-même, ces voyageurs en visite LA-BAS, qui tout le jour peuvent à leur gré parcourir la Ville, mais qui n'ont point le droit d'y demeurer la nuit." (*Farrère*, p.59) The second, not stated explicitly as such, corresponds to that, in Vian, of 'la jolie fille'. The traveller is haunted by a male presence, 'le Cavalier' (not unlike Lazuli's 'homme vêtu de sombre') from whom will come, he feels sure, "un malheur"; he knows, however, that the advent of this apocalyptic knight will be signalled by a girl:

> La femme à côté de lui, elle, la détourna [la tête], et, naturellement, me vit. [...] Et je la reconnus.
> [...] Ce n'était pas celle que vous croyez, celle que je cherche, que je dois chercher, que je dois attendre, toute ma vie, en vain; celle qui ne viendra pas, jamais. [...] Non, c'en était une autre. Mais, pour moi, plus précieuse encore. La plus précieuse au monde...
> Une femme d'ICI... très blonde [...] Une femme violente et menue, que la vie a grandie en la brisant... (*Farrère*, p.64)

This makes for a fitting description of Alise, the centre of beauty (and blondness) in *L'Écume des jours*, and, as has already been suggested, of the entire tetralogy. As all beautiful blondes descend from Alise, in the same way male protagonists descend from Colin. Their ultimate failure to consummate their love is what lies behind the failure of those who follow them to find true love (this feeling of the eternally cursed pursuit of love is also in *Où?*: "Enfin je compris que j'étais là pour attendre [...] quelqu'un qui ne viendrait jamais... [...] Pour attendre, aux termes d'une condamnation ancienne, - originelle!" [*Farrère*, p.44]). There are two representatives of the Alisian cult in *L'Herbe rouge*: Folavril who, like Alise, is coupled with the other male lead and with whom Wolf shares one of those fleeting moments of intimacy, and Carla who will warn Wolf of his impending fate.

In *L'Autre Côté*, and within the section devoted to dreams, *Où?* is preceded by two short stories, the first of which will be dealt with in the third section. The second is entitled *Les deux sœurs irréprochablement vertueuses*. It is worthy of mention if only for the description of one of its two principal characters, 'le Roi du royaume Lou'. The name Lou is phonetically identical (/lu/) to Loup, or, in English, Wolf. Not interesting in itself, but more so when one notes the description of this dream king's vanguard: "Il montait la voiture rouge traînée par des chevaux roux à queue noire et il portait l'étendard de couleur incarnat. Il était vêtu de rouge, avec des rubis au bonnet et à la ceinture." (*Farrère*, p.13) Once more then, red is the colour of dreams.

In the light of the importance of *Nadja* and *Le Paysan de Paris* in *L'Écume des jours* and *L'Automne à Pékin* respectively, one may wonder if there is a Surrealist influence at work in the oneiric aspect of *L'Herbe rouge*. Of all Breton's work, the book which deals most fully with the importance of dreams, and, more precisely, with the passage into and out of the dream state, is *Les Vases communicants*. This study has already emphasized the importance of waking/falling asleep in terms of entry into the Vian text; *L'Herbe rouge* seems to introduce a series of particularly oneiric scenes (the trips in the machine and so on), which may be seen as self-consciously dream-like, into a text whose entirety may be seen as one long dream. This idea of the dream within a dream raises those questions which are central to Breton's work:

> Le débat me paraît ne pouvoir se centrer mieux qu'autour de cette pensée de Pascal: «Personne n'a d'assurance hors la foi s'il veille ou s'il dort; vu que durant le sommeil on ne croit pas moins fermement veiller qu'en veillant effectivement... De sorte que la moitié de la vie se passant en sommeil par notre propre aveu... qui sait si cette autre moitié de la vie où nous pensons veiller n'est pas un sommeil un peu différent du premier, dont nous nous éveillons quand nous pensons dormir?»[34]

The dream is not just part of life, it is also somewhere to go to when life is no longer enough. This is what the machine represents for Wolf. His

---

[34] André Breton, *Les Vases communicants* (Paris, Gallimard, 1955), p.145. (Hereafter referred to as *Vases*.)

life, his present and his past, is no longer enough. He must use the machine. We learn as early as the third page of the novel that the real function of the machine is to destroy memories (and not, as the Mayor will later announce, to get rid of excess metal):

> - Qu'est-ce que tu veux oublier? dit Lil maussade.
> - Quand on ne se rappelle rien, répondit Wolf, ce n'est sûrement pas pareil... (*R*, p.431)

This is, according to Breton, the very role of the dream:

> De même que derrière le rêve on ne découvre en dernière analyse qu'une substance réelle empruntée aux événements déjà vécus, l'appauvrissement extrême de cette substance condamne l'esprit à chercher refuge dans la vie de rêve. L'emmagasinement de nouveaux matériaux, comme au moment d'une faillite, n'est plus qu'une obligation dont l'homme s'acquitte à contre-cœur. Le passif est trop élevé; on ne sait si les nouvelles marchandises qui arrivent couvriront seulement les frais de leur magasinage. Il y a tendance à s'en débarrasser immédiatement. Le rêve, qui manque depuis quelque temps l'aliment, fait ici figure de liquidateur. Il tend à décharger l'homme à bas prix, de ce dont celui-ci n'espère plus avoir l'usage. Il obtient tout ce qu'il veut en me persuadant que, libéré de telle créance, je me découvrirai peut-être une nouvelle raison sociale, je pourrai recommencer à vivre sous un autre nom. (*Vases*, p.152-153)

And so it is that the act of dreaming is represented by the role of the machine. But what qualities does the machine bring to the novel which could not have been provided by the ladder (whose function was to allow Wolf another perspective, a view from up there) which was to be the centre-piece of *Le ciel crevé*? The answer is that the whole dream process, as described by Breton, makes physical demands which Vian's use of the machine allows him to develop. There is a great deal at stake, but it is a price which Wolf is willing to pay: "Une solution qui vous démolit vaut mieux que n'importe quelle incertitude." (*R*, p.436.) Thus, it is Wolf's dreaming which alienates him; as he reverts to the contemplation of his inner-self, he necessarily becomes detached from his worldly being: he becomes machine. As mentioned before, his physical kinship with the machine is striking: "Il s'approcha du tableau de commande et ses mains laminées éprouvèrent la solidité. (*R*, p.430)[35] And, to enter the machine, to journey to the centre of himself, is to take his own life's blood: "Le long du montant de droite, il aperçut soudain une traînée sombre, luisante, comme une coulée de grès fondu aux parois bombées d'une cruche de poterie. [...] C'était poisseux. [...] La figure de Wolf était moite et glacée." (*R*, p.459-460) Compare this with Breton's dream:

> Le mal sacré, la maladie incurable réside et résidera encore dans le sentiment. Le nier ne sert rigoureusement de rien; mieux vaut à tous égards en passer par ses accès brisants et tenter, de l'intérieur de la cloche à plongeur aux parois vibrantes qui sert à pénétrer dans sa sphère, d'organiser un tant soit peu le brillant désaccord auquel il se plaît. Ce n'est pas en vain que l'individu, par son intermédiaire, entrant en rapport avec le contenu de lui-même, éprouve d'une manière plus ou moins panique, qui le réchauffe ou le glace, que ce contenu se distingue de la connaissance objective extérieure. Tout doit continuer d'être entrepris pour essayer d'y voir plus clair et pour dégager, de la certitude irrationnnel qui l'accompagne, ce qui peut être tenu pour vrai et pour faux. (*Vases*, p.191)

There is a strong similarity between Breton's vision of the painful 'dive' into oneself and the pull which the machine exerts on Wolf. For Wolf, too, the attempt 'd'y voir clair' is worth the physical pain which the divorce of conscious and unconscious entails. As has been seen, he tries to explain this to his mirror image: "Une solution qui vous démolit vaut mieux que n'importe quelle incertitude." (*R*, p.436) That he fails to agree with the mirror can, perhaps, be explained in similar terms: the mirror reflects his outer-self, that

---

[35] This way of analysing Wolf's 'metallic' aspect seems more productive than the attempt to alienate him in the literal sense.

which others see, whereas the Wolf on this side of the mirror is already inverting, becoming like the machine (once again: "Sa main, sur le commutateur, était blanche et dure comme le métal du miroir." [*R*, p.436]).[36] Herein lies the role of the machine: it provides the link between the interior and the exterior (it is the communication between the 'vases communicants'). Only by making this link can Wolf make sense of his life as a whole, from an historical perspective ("[dès qu'] il s'agit, comme il continuera toujours à s'agir, de sonder la nature individuelle entière dans le sens *total* qu'elle peut avoir de son passé, de son présent et de son avenir." [*Vases*, p.192]).

The Farrère and Breton texts having enabled us to situate *L'Herbe rouge* in the dream, it is now possible to chart the novel more thoroughly in terms of its intertextuality. For it is into the realm of intertextuality that Wolf's dream takes him:

> Il tombait des régions supérieures de vagues traînées de poussières brillantes, insaisissables, et *le ciel fictif* palpitait à l'infini, troué de lueurs. [...] Il plongeait toujours plus avant, et devant lui se déroulaient la carte sonore à quatre dimensions de *son passé fictif.* (My italics) (*R*, p.460-461)

Wolf is an intertextual being, a fictitious character travelling through a sky behind every star of which there lies a story. This recalls the final pages of Queneau's *Le Chiendent* (the story of 'who's dreaming whom' par excellence) in which the main protagonists discover that they are just that:

> - C'est pas moi qu'ai trouvé ça, dit la reine. C'est dans le livre.
> - Quel livre? demandèrent les deux maréchaux errants.
> - Eh bien, çui-ci où qu'on est maintenant... (*Chiendent*, p.429)

---

[36] This reading of the mirror scene is the reverse of the more standard intertextual reading whereby the mirror image shows Wolf 'through the looking-glass', and, thus, in the dream state.

The novel reaches its conclusion by dissolving into 'le ciel fictif'; the story becomes cyclical, beginning again in itself and in other books:

> Un masque traversa l'air, escamotant des personnages aux vies multiples et complexes, et prit forme humaine à la terrasse d'un café. La silhouette d'un homme se profila; simultanément, des milliers. Il y en avait bien des milliers.
> (*Chiendent*, p.432)

L'Herbe rouge can also be read as a voyage across such a sky. Whereas *L'Automne à Pékin* used 'going to sleep' as its means of gathering its principal characters at the scene of the action (Exopotamia is a land conjured up by their common dream[37]), in *L'Herbe rouge* a similar sequence of entries actually *are* the action.

As has been shown, there is a strong case to be made for reading Wolf's awakening in the novel's opening paragraph as 'falling asleep'. The textual evidence provided by the opening paragraph (a mere eight lines) is two-fold. Firstly, there is the movement of the wind in the tree which holds his attention: this wind is 'tiède et endormi'. Rather than being simply 'warm and listless', this description is snug and sleepy, not the kind of gale likely to wake somebody up. The branch of the tree is likewise behaving in a way which goes against the reader's initial understanding: its movement is gentle and periodic, less arousing than hypnotic. Thus, when "Sans motif, il se secoua soudain, appuya ses mains sur le bord de son bureau et se leva" (*R*, p.429), there is as much reason to believe that this action is the entrance into a dream as the exit out of one (although he is said to get up from his desk, how do we know that he is not actually tucked up in bed?).[38]

One particularly famous dream involving wolves goes like this:

> I dreamt that it was night and that I was lying in my bed. [...] Suddenly the window opened of its own accord, and I

---

[37] In much the same way as the Park of 'Les Buttes-Chaumont' is a place where Aragon, Breton and Marcel Noll share a common Surrealist experience ("Le romanesque a pour eux le pas sur tout attrait de ce parc, qui pendant une demi-heure sera pour eux la Mésopotamie." [*Aragon*, p.165]).

[38] Note that the strength of the wind may depend on the nature of the dream: Dorothy dreamt of a wind so violent that it actually transported her, house and all, into another world.

was terrified to see that some white wolves were sitting on the big walnut tree in front of the window. There were six or seven of them. The wolves were quite white, and looked more like foxes or sheep-dogs, for they had big tails like foxes and they had their ears pricked like dogs when they pay attention to something. In great terror, evidently of being eaten up by the wolves, I screamed and woke up...[39]

This dream, as recounted to Freud by the Wolf Man (in the text which is the second of our Germanic titles about wolves), has four points of interest as far as *L'Herbe rouge* is concerned[40]: firstly, and obviously, that it is a dream; secondly, the focus on the window; thirdly, the view of the tree through the window; and lastly, the wolves themselves. As there are no animals sitting in the tree in Vian's account, and as the attention being paid is from the inside of the room, then the dreamer is the wolf, or simply Wolf.

Freud himself begins his analysis by making similar transpositions: he believes that the dream takes much of its subject matter from one of the patient's favourite childhood stories in which a tailor eludes some wolves by hiding in a tree and that, therefore, the place of the wolves and the human are reversed. Similarly, there is some play on the idea of the acts of waking and dreaming being equally confused:

> It [the opening of the window] must mean: "My eyes suddenly opened." I was asleep, therefore, and suddenly woke up, and as I woke I saw something: the tree with the wolves." No objection could be made to this; but the point could be developed further. He had woken up and had

---

[39] Sigmund Freud, *Case Histories II* (London: Penguin Freud Library Volume 9, 1991), p.259. (Hereafter referred to as *Wolf Man*.)

[40] Clearly, it would be possible to perform an analysis of the dreams in *L'Herbe rouge* following the methods outlined in this case history and in *The Interpretation of Dreams*. However, for the purposes of this study it is more useful to treat the Wolf Man's account at its face value, using it as intertext. Furthermore, its usefulness lies, here, in the key it provides for distinguishing between dream and non-dream in Vian's text, since it is not at all clear that the 'trips in the machine' are the only dreams in an otherwise 'waking' text.

seen something. The attentive looking, which in the dream was ascribed to the wolves, should rather be shifted on to him. At a decisive point, therefore, a transposition had taken place; and moreover this is indicated by another transposition in the manifest content of the dream. For the fact that the wolves were sitting on the tree was also a transposition, since in his grandfather's story they were underneath, and were unable to climb on to the tree.

What, then, if the other factor emphasized by the dreamer were also distorted by means of a transposition or reversal? In that case instead of immobility... the meaning would have to be: the most violent motion. That is to say, he suddenly woke up, and saw in front of him a scene of violent movement at which he looked with strained attention. In the one case the distortion would consist in an interchange of subject and object, of activity and passivity: being looked at instead of looking. In the other case it would consist in a transformation into the opposite; rest instead of motion. (*Wolf Man*, p.265-266)

Thus, it would appear that the manifest action of Vian's text, by just such a transposition, is of motion and of (wolf) man looking out (looking at, in Freud's example, the repressed material behind the dream: the primal scene). So, if in this case dreaming has been mistaken for waking moments, what is taking place is, in fact, stillness (falling into sleep) and Wolf's being observed (the idea of the 'être-pour-autrui' from which he must flee). Wolf's fear of being observed can be seen to be paralleled by a desire to observe from a position of safety. With regard to 'the big walnut tree', Freud notes: "[...] A high tree is a symbol of observing, of scopophilia. A person sitting on a tree can see everything that is going on below him and cannot himself be seen." (*Wolf Man*, p.275) It is worthy of note that the principal concept behind the original draft of *L'Herbe rouge* (under its initial title, *Le Ciel crevé*) was just that of 'scopophilia'; that elements of this remain in the finished product is quite clear. Departing from the concept of scopophilia the reader of Vian's novel is able to locate elements of the text, as is the case in the first two novels, within the Parisian cityscape; in so doing it is also possible to synthesize the two manifestly distinct lines of analysis that are the Science Fiction reading and the Parisian/Surrealist dream reading. If a Parisian wished to 'voir clair', to find a place from which he might make out all potential streets for his 'flânerie', where he might dream, his head in the clouds, the wind rushing through his hair, where would he go? It is more than feasible that he would elect a structure made of triangles and built upon four sturdy feet: in a word, the Eiffel Tower.[41] It is precisely in these triangles and in these feet that Aboucaya saw Wells' Martians. Vian's machine, within which Wolf is both on the ground and in the sky, is located in a field. So, too, the Eiffel Tower; in fact, 'la Tour Eiffel' surges up from no other field than 'le Champ de Mars'. The map of the 'Métropolitain' perfectly juxtaposes 'Champ de Mars' and 'Tour Eiffel'. The Paris of the 'Métro', as the Paris of Vian's novels, travels across the world; indeed, to travel from 'Place de Clichy' (where Vian lived, and where Bardamu begins his *Voyage au bout de la nuit*), to go to 'Tour Eiffel' one passes through 'Rome', skirting past 'Europe' and 'Argentine'. This strengthens the argument for locating Vian's novels within a Parisian context: 'Plan du Métro' as intertext, or flight of the angels as 'voyage au bout du Métro'.

The second reason for believing Wolf's initial descent from his room into the open air, the narrative locus of the novel, to be the first tentative steps into a dreamworld is the strange nature of 'le Carré'. Having already mentioned the similarities between Wolf's relocation and that of Dorothy, it is worth noting those that exist between 'le Carré' and 'le pré' in Breton's *L'Amour fou*.

> De ce paysage passionné qui se retirera un jour prochain avec la mer, si je ne dois enlever que toi aux fantasmagories de l'écume verte, je saurai recréer cette musique sur nos pas. Ces pas bordent à l'infini le pré magique qui cerne l'empire du figuier.[42]

L'Amour fou conjoins the idea of the dream with that of all-consuming love. The above quotation juxtaposes 'l'écume' and 'le pré magique', thereby endowing both with the properties of the surreal. To apply a similar rapprochement within the work of Vian (where 'l'écume verte' becomes

---

[41] The Eiffel Tower, as Surrealist enigma, both phallus and woman, is also a 'store of excess metal'; it is a massive collection of steel girders.

[42] André Breton, *L'Amour fou* (Paris: Gallimard, 1995), p.119. (Hereafter referred to as *Amour*.)

'l'écume des jours' and 'le pré magique' becomes 'le carré') is to trace a line of love between the first and third novels. However, whilst love is the cherished centre-piece of the work of both authors, in Vian it is its failure which drives the narrative. The last line of *L'Amour fou* reads, "Je vous souhaite d'être follement aimée." (*Amour*, p.176) If there is a character in Vian's world worthy of being put upon such a pedestal, it is Alise. She is certainly beautiful and pays the consequences ('la beauté sera convulsive ou ne sera pas'). And yet it is Partre who receives the purest form of 'amour fou' via Chick's compulsive book collecting, a passion which Colin can be seen to try to mimic in his love for Chloé. It is the failure of Colin to love Alise, and his persistent mastering of his feelings that pervades Angel's actions and, ultimately, destroys Wolf: "Vous avez toujours pu résister à vos désirs [...] Et vous pouvez toujours. C'est pour cela que vous mourrez déçu." (*R*, p.524) Wolf's is, indeed, a journey into himself. It seems, however, that it is also a search for love.

Breton's meadow is the sacred place where he wishes to walk eternally with the object of his 'amour fou':

> Car une femme et un homme qui, jusqu'à la fin des temps, doivent être toi et moi, glisseront à leur tour sans se retourner jamais jusqu'à perte de sentier, dans la lueur oblique, aux confins de la vie et de l'oubli de la vie, dans l'herbe fine qui court devant nous à l'arborescence. (*Amour*, p.119-120)

Place of inspiration in Breton, place only of hopes past in Vian. Anne's regret was to not be where the grass grew, and Wolf's fleeting glimpse of what might have been, in the arms of Folavril, will also happen on the grass. Breton sees in his grass potential for the rekindling of love:

> Mais quelle est donc cette herbe d'énigme... ? Le bruit court, plus léger qu'une onde sur elle, que c'est la *sensitive*. [...] J'ai à peine besoin de te toucher pour que le vif-argent de la sensitive incline sa harpe sur l'horizon. Mais pour peu que nous nous arrêtions, l'herbe va reverdir, elle va renaître, après quoi mes nouveaux pas n'auront d'autre but que te réinventer. (*Amour*, p.120-123)

There is no return to lush greenery in *L'Herbe rouge*; the novel ends with the departure of the girls, their hopes of love definitively abandoned, and with the resurgence of the red grass: "L'herbe rouge commençait à repousser partout où Wolf et Lazuli avaient dégagé le terrain..." (*R*, p.529).[43] Breton's grass seems to wilt and regrow with the comings and goings of the various loves of his life: desire itself is the focus of 'l'amour fou': "Le désir, seul ressort du monde, le désir, seule rigueur que l'homme ait à connaître, où puis-je être mieux pour l'adorer qu'à l'intérieur du nuage?" (*Amour*, p.129) And whom did Colin adore in the midst of a cloud if not Chloé, the reification of his desire? Little wonder, then, that Wolf's bid for the clouds (in as much as it signifies an attempt to retrieve the love of Alise) is doomed to fail. Wolf's quest is the most negative of all those undertaken by Vian's male leads; this because it is the most blatantly introspective (in this respect, Lazuli's fear of the 'regard' of the Other is an exact reflection of Wolf's need to abolish the outside world). The pernicious effects of an external eye upon man's ability to love also appears in *L'Amour fou*; under an unwelcome gaze, coming from another 'carré', a lover's tiff and the area in which it takes place become indissociable:

> Sans doute mon malaise atteignit son comble à découvrir
> dans l'enceinte même de ce fort deux ou trois hommes qui
> s'étaient arrêtés de faucher un carré de blé dérisoire pour
> nous suivre de l'œil alternativement. (*Amour*, p.154)

Fear of being watched, or of exposing oneself to public scrutiny (which 'le carré' could be said to represent in Breton and Vian) appears to be recurrent in dreamtexts.

Thus, in the first paragraph of *L'Herbe rouge* there already seems to be much to suggest that Wolf is treading the pathway into a dream. The second entry into the dream comes six pages later:

> Wolf... se glissa dehors pour entrer dans son bureau. Là,
> dans un coin, il y avait, sur quatre pieds, un grand miroir
> d'argent poli. Wolf s'approcha et s'étendit de tout son long,

---

[43] Note that the sado-masochistic relationship (whereby the men cut the grass which, in return, finally cuts them) that exists between the male characters and the grass is colour-coded: Lazuli (Lapis), or Saphir, is strictly blue, and thus diametrally opposed to the grass which is red.

> la figure contre le métal, pour se parler d'homme à homme.[44] (*R*, p.435-436)

The reference here is clearly to Lewis Carroll's story *Through the Looking-Glass*. In Western culture this is possibly the most classic example of the 'who is dreaming whom' trope. Thus, it would be plausible to argue that this is where Wolf's dream really begins. And yet, by going back to the Carroll text it can be seen that Alice, too, is already dreaming before passing through the looking-glass. Alice, like Wolf, is placed in snug, listless (and, thus, soporific) surrounds, the focus of which is again the view from a window:

> Do you hear the snow against the window-panes, Kitty? How nice and soft it sounds! Just as if someone was kissing the window all over outside. I wonder if the snow *loves* the trees and fields, that it kisses them so gently? And then it covers them up snug, you know, with a white quilt; and perhaps it says "Go to sleep..." (*Alice*, p.133-134)

In both stories, then, the act of passing through a mirror marks ascendance to another stage within the dream rather than entry into the dream itself. Of course, in Alice's case the mirror is the gateway *into* Looking-Glass House, whereas, for Wolf, it strengthens his resolve, by allowing insight into his duality, to go *out of* the house. For them both it is outside the house that the main dream action will take place; and they both enter into this action with the same purpose. Their paths each lead to a better view (Wolf's via the machine):

> "I should see the garden far better", said Alice to herself, "if I could get to the top of that hill: and here's a path that leads straight to it..." (*Alice*, p.143)

---

[44] The use of the verb 's'étendre', coupled with the position of the mirror (on four feet, and, thus, presumably horizontal), adds dual significance to this passage. Of the things which people can lie down on, two are particularly important: one lies down on a bed to sleep (and, thus, to dream), and one lies in one's coffin when one is dead.

> - Ici, dit Wolf, qu'est-ce que je vois? Des brumes, des yeux, des gens... des poussières sans densité... et puis ce sacré ciel comme un diaphragme. (*R*, p.436)

Thus, both leave the house and enter the story, Alice into the centre of the dream ("So, resolutely turning her back upon the house, she set out once more down the path, determined to keep straight on till she got to the hill." [*Alice*, p.143]), and Wolf into a machine from the inside of which he will be able to see. For his dreams are not only his own, he *sees* into others' dreams. His interior is, perversely, made up of others' lives; the oneiric centre of *L'Herbe rouge* depends largely on intertextuality. Through the machine Wolf can dream himself into other texts. Such is life for Breton as well: "[...] Qu'il y a là [entre le monde de la réalité et celui du rêve] une porte entr'ouverte, au delà de laquelle il n'y a plus qu'un pas à faire pour, au sortir de la maison vacillante des poètes, se retrouver de plain-pied dans la vie." (*Vases*, p.11)

The importance of *Through the Looking-Glass* does not end once the house is left; its influence can be felt throughout *L'Herbe rouge*. By entering through the looking-glass Wolf's dreams (within the dream) automatically take on the appearance of memories, and their effects are disorientating:

> [...] Saphir se pencha vers Wolf et l'aida à se relever. Pas à pas, ils le guidèrent dans l'ombre. Wolf marchait avec peine. (*R*, p.470)

> "That's the effect of living backwards" the Queen said kindly: "it always makes me a little giddy at first..." (*Alice*, p.181)

Dreams, memories and intertextuality mingle inexorably. Like the other novels, *L'Herbe rouge* leaves phrases which allow the reader to see past the pages of the novel in hand, and into the pages of other novels:

> Où étaient les souvenirs purs? En presque tous se fondent les impressions d'autres époques qui s'y superposent et leur donnent une réalité différente. Il n'y a pas de souvenirs, c'est une autre vie revécue avec une autre personnalité qui résulte pour partie de ces souvenirs eux-mêmes. On

n'inverse pas le sens du temps à moins de vivre les yeux fermés, les oreilles sourdes. (*R*, p.461)

Lazuli is removed from the text in the same way as are Wolf's 'memories'. It is interesting, therefore, to note that his death is intertextually ordered. He is killed, his existence removed by the same thunderstorm which undermines the identity of the White Queen:

> It was *such* a thunderstorm, you can't think! [...] And part of the roof came off, and ever so much thunder got in - and it went rolling round the room in great lumps - and knocking over the tables and things - till I was so frightened, I couldn't remember my own name! (*Alice*, p.240)

Following Lazuli's death at his own hand, a thunderstorm destroys his bedroom. In the following chapter Lil learns of what has happened from Folle as she wakes up. As Lil reconciles herself to the facts of what has happened, it is Folle who, ever more conscious, begins to doubt the story:

> - C'est la foudre... dit Lil. C'est la foudre qui a volatilisé Lazuli et sa chambre.
> - Non, dit Folavril.
> [...]
> - Ça a toujours été comme ça... se força-t-elle à dire. Il n'y avait pas de chambre, et Lazuli n'existe pas. (*R*, p.513-514)

The story is a dream, and one from which she is gradually waking up. Lazuli dies along with his name (that which is so crucial to one's autonomy); Folle who had been the only person to refer to him by his Christian name, Saphir, reverts to using his surname once he is dead (and his slender purchase on real existence is obliterated). Whilst the White Queen was first to make the link between fear and the loss of identity, in Vian the search for self becomes central.[45]

---

[45] The importance of colour coding becomes clear once again: whilst Alice joins the Red and

Of the three quests in *L'Herbe rouge*, all end in destruction. Misconceptions lie at the heart of the failure of Vian's quests. In a poem which counted amongst his favourites[46], Carroll's *The Hunting of the Snark*, there is much play on the possible outcome of the failure to recognise things for what they are:

> But oh, beamish nephew, beware of the day,
> If your Snark be a boojum! For then
> You will softly and suddenly vanish away,
> And never be met with again!

For Lazuli, 'l'homme vêtu de sombre' is clearly not the Snark he believes him to be: whereas the existence of this shadowy figure leaves him in no doubt, there is clearly nobody there. His attempt to hunt an illusion can but result in his death. Thus, he dies by a sword whose edge is doubly Carrollinian: the thunder rolls in through the looking-glass and the Snark turns out to be a boojum. For Wolf the boojum-factor is present in his realisation that his quest was misdirected: "J'ai toujours pu résister à mes désirs... [...] Mais je meurs de les avoir épuisés..." (*R*, p.528). And yet, the most intriguing example of the boojum-factor is the case of le Sénateur Dupont.

For le Sénateur, the quest is for a ouapiti. The ouapiti becomes emblematic of absolute happiness; it is also the end of life[47]. All of those characters who achieve their dream and who are then destroyed as a result (Colin is an obvious example[48]) are victims of the ouapiti syndrome. For le

---

White Queens, Lazuli, killed by the red grass, changes from a blue gem to a blue stone.

[46] Pestureau at one point refers to Vian as a "grand lecteur du *Snark*" (*Boris Vian, les Amerlauds et les Godons*, p.146).

[47] There is also a vision of a world under the reign of the ouapiti in H.G. Wells' *The Time Machine*: "For after the battle comes Quiet. Humanity had been strong, energetic, and intelligent, and had used all its abundant vitality to alter the conditions under which it lived. And now came the reaction of the altered conditions. [...] And in a state of physical balance and security, power, intellectual as well as physical, would be out of place." (In *H.G. Wells, Selected Short Stories*, [London, Penguin, 1958], pp.7-83 [p.33].)

[48] Colin sets the precedent. It is the contention of this book that it is his failure to love Alise, to allow the Snark to slip through his fingers, that is the origin of the myth of the ouapiti. For those who follow him the ouapiti will, as was Chloé, be a boojum.

Sénateur alone does the possession of that which one has always desired bring happiness. It is no less fatal. But he at least dies happy; his death is purely a loss of his mental capacity: he becomes senile. It is not so much that this real life ouapiti (as opposed to its ersatz rivals) turns out to be a Snark; rather his success lies in the fact that he was consciously hunting the boojum all along. In as much as he is ultimately realistic about the chance of happiness in a world ruled by days, he achieves a relative success: he aims low and secures his target. Indeed, if one's aim is death all along, one cannot fail to succeed. It is the failing of the human characters (even those called Wolf) that they do not adapt their ambitions to their real circumstances: they cannot see the Snark. Folavril is surely a Snark for him who would dare to hunt her, yet Lazuli, for all his efforts, can only catch a boojum. It is Lil who seems to understand that she is a boojum for Wolf:

> - Lil, dit Wolf. Je t'aime tant. Pourquoi est-ce que ça ne me rend pas aussi heureux que le Sénateur?
> - C'est que je suis trop petite, dit Lil en se serrant contre lui. Ou alors, tu vois mal les choses. Tu les prends pour d'autres. (*R*, p.501)

Both her suggestions are right: she is a boojum (and therefore his vision is obscured) and she is 'trop petite': she is Chloé, in whose words and body language she formulates her reply, and is therefore the bringer of doom.[49]

Given le Sénateur's exalted position in the text, it is possible to ask whether he may have some role in the dreaming process (he goes into a coma-like state once he finds his ouapiti). Similarly, one might ask the same question of the kitten in *Through the Looking-Glass*. The opening line of the story exposes its importance to the narrative: "One thing was certain, that the *white* kitten had nothing to do with it - it was the black kitten's fault entirely." (*Alice*, p.131) In light of this, and of the fact that Alice goes on to suggest that the kitten understands the game of chess, it is possible that the kitten is not the Red Queen, as Carroll suggests, but the Red King and, thus, dreamer of the text: "[...] You see, Kitty, it *must* have been either me or the Red King. He was

---

[49] The difference between Lil and Chloé lies in the way their respective partners see them: Wolf never actually tries to convince himself that Lil is a Snark.

part of my dream, of course - but then I was part of his dream, too!" This would account for the nature of much of the dream text:

> By the way, Kitty, if only you'd been really with me in my dream, there was one thing you *would* have enjoyed - I had such a quantity of poetry said to me, all about fishes! (*Alice*, p.254)

To follow this line is to open the potential reading of 'le Sénateur' as dreamer of the text.[50]

The next significant dream sequence is the scene shared by Wolf and Folavril. This scene is clearly of great importance, being an example of what has previously been described as the privileged passage. It fits into this as well as the next section of this chapter, being a node of inter- and intratextuality. The principal significance of this scene in terms of a dream reading is that it takes place at night. Wolf invites Folavril to join with him in a discovery of that of which his childhood was deprived. The night carries the same resonance as 'la barre difficile à franchir', shuddering as it does in full Surrealist convulsiveness; it is both late and early: "Il était tard, ou tôt, et la nuit ruisselait sur le toit de la maison avec des remous..." (*R*, p.437). Night also brings out the best in the grass which consequently is to be located at the centre of the dream as well as the Science Fiction reading. Thus, far from being 'earthy' or 'down to earth', the fact that Folle smells of the grass makes her essentially oneiric ("Folavril était tout près de lui et l'arôme de son corps se mêlait aux parfums de la terre et de l'herbe" [*R*, p.438]). Her very name suggests a connection with spring flowers. It also contains a form of the word 'fou' which may, or may not, connect her to Breton or to Freud. She certainly recognises the flowers of death upon which she is lying (which, given Chloé's literary parentage, makes the reader dubious as to the possible outcome of this dream): "Sous ma tête, ce sont des violettes de la mort..." (*R*, p.439). Breton himself comments on the colour violet in *Les Vases communicants*:

> J'éprouve, en effet, pour le violet une horreur sans borne, qui va jusqu'à m'empêcher de pouvoir séjourner dans une pièce où cette couleur, même hors de ma perception

---

[50] As Kitty resumes the role of cat once the dream (story) is at an end, so Le Sénateur Dupont's senility may be seen as a return to/assumption of his life of 'dog' and thus an end to the dream (story), and, hence, Wolf.

directe, laisse filtrer quelques-uns de ses rayons mortels.
(*Vases*, p.137)

If, then, this act of falling asleep in the flowers of death, indeed of sleeping with (or 'deflowering', in as much as Wolf takes one of her cherries) the girl who is a flower (it is possible that 'dormir' fulfills here a similar function to that of 'le biglemoi' in *L'Écume des jours*) represents the passage into another level of the dream, one may suspect that this is a dream from which safe exit is becoming unlikely: "Ils s'endormirent sans parler, le corps contre la terre chaude, dans le parfum des fleurs sanglantes." (*R*, p.439).

This level of the dream carries Wolf to the machine where he will go into the first of the most blatant dreams within the dream. There is, however, a slight fluctuation in the dream pattern which Wolf tries to avoid: "A moitié conscient, Wolf tenta un dernier effort pour arrêter la sonnerie de son réveil, mais la chose, visqueuse, lui échappa..." (*R*, p.453). The particular dream (or sub-dream) in which he attempts to remain is one which sees him plummeting into the darkness, the stench of death and flowers in his nostrils ("[...] L'odeur du cœur en feu des reines-marguerites..."). It is as if his desire for Folavril, the flower-girl, is pushing him down ("[...] Wolf s'enfonçait dans le noir..."), this dream acting as a microcosm of the main dream which he will enter through the machine.

The first trip leads Wolf to a place not unlike 'le Carré': "Devant Wolf, une allée allait en pente douce." (*R*, p.463). This similarity tends to suggest that he is 'following the same path': this *is* 'le Carré'; this, too, is a dream. The first person that Wolf meets is a bearded old man. Pestureau, in his notes to the Livre de Poche edition of *L'Herbe rouge* points out a link between this gentleman and the old man of Hugo's poem "Booz endormi": as Vian's character is "vêtu de lin" (*R*, p.462), Booz is "Vêtu de probité candide et de lin blanc"[51]. He also notes a rapprochement between the two texts in an earlier note, where he uses Folavril's use of the word 'asphodèle' as intertextual clue (a line in Hugo's poem reads: "Un frais parfum sortait des touffes d'asphodèle"): "[...] Poème [Booz endormi] dont la situation présente quelque analogie avec le passage de *L'Herbe rouge*: un homme dort près d'une jeune fille et le ciel est plein d'étoiles sur un paysage idyllique."[52] It is clear that the

---

[51] Cited in *L'Herbe rouge* (Paris: Le Livre de Poche, 1992), p.188.

[52] *Ibid.*, p.186.

dream that is the flight in the machine is bound, intertextually, to the two other dream levels. Certain other segments of this dream poem reveal a use of 'dream vocabulary' common to that in the Vian text. Take the following two lines as an example:

> La respiration de Booz qui dormait,
> Se mêlait au bruit sourd des ruisseaux *sur la mousse*
> [...]
> Ruth songeait que Booz dormait; *l'herbe était noire*;
> [...]
> (My italics)

Everything points to the fact that what Wolf experiences is a dream, and as has already been indicated these dreams are intertextual; they appear as memories, but they do not come straight from Wolf's mind. The stories he tells, the people he meets are filtered through from other texts, or more precisely, given that the main bulk of the intertextuality seems to set up, and not occur in, the trips in the machine, through a suggestion of other texts. The main aim of this chapter was to establish the oneiric nature of *L'Herbe rouge*, to present the possiblity of a dream reading. This having been achieved it only remains to look briefly at some of the possible sources of Wolf's memories.

Wolf's discussion with M. Perle, his first interlocutor 'on the other side', touches on his attitudes towards his parents. It is here that his problems begin; it is due to his upbringing that his inner desires have never been given free expression, that his fear of others' 'regard' has always equalled his own will to succeed:

> Ils avaient toujours peur pour moi, dit Wolf. [...] Il suffisait qu'il y ait un peu de vent pour qu'on me mette ma peau de bique et, hiver comme été, je ne quittais pas mon gilet de laine [...] Jusqu'à quinze ans je n'ai pas eu le droit de boire autre chose que de l'eau bouillie. [...] A force je finissais par avoir peur moi-même, par me dire que j'étais très fragile, et j'étais presque content de me promener, en hiver, en transpirant dans douze cache-nez de laine. Pendant toute mon enfance, mon père et ma mère ont pris sur eux de m'épargner tout ce qui pouvait me heurter.

> Moralement, je ressentais une gêne vague, mais ma chair
> molle s'en réjouissait hypocritement. (*R*, p.466-467)

This diatribe recalls the outpourings of the Wolf Man. However, it also closely resembles a Sartrean text. Indeed, all that passes between Wolf and M. Perle, and subsequently M. Brul and l'Abbé Grille, can be located in a Sartrean framework: Wolf's 'être-pour-soi' will always be equally matched (and moulded) by his 'être-pour-autrui'. For 'l'enfance d'un Wolf' (a wolf, from the outset, in sheep's clothing ["en douze cache-nez de laine"]) one may read "L'Enfance d'un chef".[53] The young Lucien, despite his desire to do that which he is not supposed to do ("Il demanda de l'orangeade parce qu'elle était glacée et qu'on lui avait défendu d'en boire"[54]), is never happier than when he is fulfilling the expectations of others: "Elle [Mme Besse] renversait Lucien, elle le chatouillait en disant: «Ma petite poupée.» Lucien était ravi, il riait d'aise et se tortillait sous les chatouilles... comme un poupon de caoutchouc." Thus, it is a show of bravado, which he tries to see as the expression of his desire, that leads him (via various experiences of homosexuality at the hands of a character clearly calqué upon André Breton[55]) to join a fascist organisation and, eventually, to physically attack a Jew[56]. By this stage it has become clear

---

[53] The Freudian and Sartrean intertexts run in parallel throughout the 'trips' into the past: this may be largely due to the fact that Sartre's text has as much to do with Surrealism and psychoanalysis as it has to do with Existentialism. As was seen in Chapter One, where *Le Chiendent* and *La Nausée* run simultaneously through *L'Écume*, the host text can imply external rapprochements between the intertexts as well as the reverse.

[54] Jean-Paul Sartre, "L'Enfance d'un chef", in *Le Mur* (Paris: Gallimard, 1992), pp.151-245 (p.152). (As with "Érostrate", referred to as *Mur*.)

[55] There is a neat reversal here. Vian, who seems closest to Breton when he revelling in the virtues of heterosexual love and constructing his altar to beautiful girls, is perhaps returning Sartre's caricature with his own 'clin d'œil'.

[56] It is worthy of note that Wolf's dual sadistic and masochistic tendencies (and more especially those of Lucien: "Il était beaucoup plus amusant d'arracher les pattes d'une sauterelle [...] [Il] aurait bien voulu faire souffrir une de ces bêtes qui crient lorsqu'elles ont mal, une poule, par exemple, mais il n'osait pas les approcher." [*Mur*, p.160.]) have a possible source, once more, in Freud's account of the Wolf Man:

> He also felt fear and loathing of beetles and caterpillars.
> Yet he could also remember that at this very time he

that Lucien's life, in terms of the projection of his 'être-pour-soi', is effectively finished. Wolf's murder of the old 'fonctionnaire' is meant as a release of his pent-up desires ("Pour la première fois. [...] Vous allez voir se déchaîner une passion dominante de mon existence: la haine de l'inutile." [*R*, p.526]), and yet it is in no way cathartic. He still dies from the loss of his desire.

Wolf continues to journey through the dreams of others even between his trips in the machine. Between the discussion with M. Perle and that with M. Brul, he and Lazuli visit 'le quartier des amoureuses'. Rich though this passage is (in terms of the quasi onanistic sexual encounter and the sadistic games played by the sailors), its primary intertextual importance can be seen through the dreams of one man. Pestureau, in the 'Livre de Poche' edition of *L'Herbe rouge*, notes:

> Ce «Quartier réservé» évoque à la fois des décors de science-fiction (pierres précieuses, gaz parfumé, «télévoyance»...) et une architecture urbaine utopique comme celle de Claude-Nicolas Ledoux (1736-1806) pour les Salines d'Arc-et-Senans, avec le plan en forme de sexe du quartier des plaisirs.[57]

Ledoux had a dream; it is a dream which is in almost perfect harmony with the novelistic project of Vian:

> Avant que la nuit ne recouvre de son voile obscur le vaste champ où j'ai placé tous les genres d'édifices que réclame l'ordre social, on verra des usines importantes, filles et mères de l'industrie, donner naissance à des réunions

---

> used to torment beetles and cut caterpillars to pieces. Horses, too, gave him an uncanny feeling. If a horse was beaten he began to scream, and he was once obliged to leave a circus on that account. On other occasions he found himself beating horses.
> (*Wolf Man*, p.244.)

(Note also the similarity to Jacquemort's reaction upon seeing a horse being crucified in *L'Arrache-cœur*.)

[57] *L'Herbe rouge* (Livre de Poche), p.188.

> populeuses. Une ville s'élevera pour les enceindre et les couronner. Le luxe vivifiant, ami nourricier des arts, y montrera tous les monuments que l'opulence aura fait éclore. Ses environs seront embellis d'habitations consacrées au repos, aux plaisirs, et plantés de jardins rivaux du fameux Éden.[58]

This vision can be seen to be the same as the dream which conjured up the Paris of *L'Écume* (Ledoux's dream city includes 'une forge à canons') and the dunes of *L'Automne*. It is also a dream that is turning sour. Ledoux's words, taken from his introduction to «L'architecture considérée sous le rapport de l'art, des mœurs et de la législation», is headed by the words *omnia vincit amor*. It is the very failure of these words to come true which condemns Wolf. Thus, it is apt that he should glimpse what might have been in a dream; he and Lazuli will find love in the arms of the sleeping women precisely because they are asleep, because they are part of the dream.

In Ledoux's dream "un édifice destiné aux récréations" rises up from the middle of a lawn: "[...] On voit une riante pelouze, au milieu de laquelle s'élève un bâtiment dédié à la gaieté..." (*Ledoux*, p.114). The recreational activities on offer correspond well with those played in Vian's quartier (as well as with what is known of Wolf's views on education which he would like to see replaced by more vigorous exercise: "[...] Parlez-moi d'un bon match de boxe..." [*R*, p.499]): "La Lutte, Le Pugulat, Luttelitique, Le Javelot" feature amongst other attractions. Of course, the pleasure capital of both authors' cities is the monument to love. Where Ledoux uses his landscaping skills to generate the atmosphere in his "oikema" ("[...] Le vallon qui supporte cet édifice est entouré de prestiges séducteurs; un vent doux caresse l'atmosphère; les variétés odoriférantes de la forêt, le thym, l'iris, la violette, la menthe soufflent leurs parfums sur ces murs..." [*Ledoux*, p.118]), Vian uses women; as well as the naturally fragrant Folavril, whose violets disséminate their perfume throughout the dream, the prostitutes entice the senses in a synaesthetic onslaught: "Celles qui n'opéraient pas étaient devant leurs portes, dans des niches de cristal où ruisselaient des jets d'eau de rose pour les détendre et les adoucir." (*R*, p.475) These dream women are, indeed, reminiscent of those in

---

[58] Jacques Ohayon, ed., *L'Œuvre et les rêves de Claude-Nicolas Ledoux* (Paris: Sté Nle des Éditions du Chêne, 1971), p.39. (Hereafter referred to as *Ledoux*.)

Ledoux's vision, but what of those who are not? It is on those other women that the remainder of this section will concentrate.

Before Wolf's final vain gesture of defiance, the last three people with whom he talks on his travels in the machine are all female. Mademoiselle Héloïse and Mademoiselle Aglaé are there to talk of love. There is an obvious parallel between these two old ladies and their two young counterparts in the other dream zone. Whilst Wolf explains his incapacities in love, Lil and Folavril are becoming increasingly disillusioned by the lack of love which they are receiving. If the influence of the Carroll text suggested the possibility of positing le Sénateur Dupont as dreamer of *L'Herbe rouge*, perhaps there is room for two more dreamers? As old women Aglaé and Héloïse may be seen as projections (into a possible future beyond the dream - suggesting their survival of its conclusion) of Lil and Folavril. In *L'Écume* a vision of an old woman was seen wearing Chloé's clothes; there, that premonition heralded the decay of Colin's love (given that Chloé was more the reification of his desire than an actual physical being); here the departure of the girls from a dream which they may in part be dreaming will bring Wolf's destruction. It is time for them to dream another dream:

> [...] Il [Wolf] ne reviendra pas. D'ailleurs on n'a plus besoin de lui.
> - Mon rêve, dit Folavril en réfléchissant, mon rêve ça serait d'épouser un pédéraste avec plein d'argent. (*R*, p.529)

It is interesting that their new vision should be one where men play little real part. Is Folavril's dream to be realised in *L'Arrache-cœur*?

The final female character has little more than a cameo role and is, perhaps, all the more enigmatic because of it. Carla emerges from the water. The significance of water is clearly manifold: on the one hand it represents amniotic fluid, on the other its significance is intratextual, the crossing into the dream being across 'la barre difficile à franchir' of *L'Écume*. It is with "les cheveux frisés d'une fille brune à qui le soleil avait fait un teint d'or foncé" (*R*, p.523) that she emerges from the water. It was water, in the form of froth, which lay behind *L'Écume des jours*, and it was water which Angel had to cross in order to enter Exopotamia. Thus, it is adorned with the mantle of her female predecessors (so many women spurned) that this 'golden girl' penetrates *L'Herbe rouge*. As such her criticism is all the more damning: "[...] Vous étiez plus affectueux, autrefois." (*R*, p.524.) Wolf's forefathers may have been more affectionate, but their amorous designs were ill-directed and, ultimately, disastrous. It is not only for his own sins (his inability to love, itself an intratextual curse), but for the sins of his past incarnations that he must die "déçu".

The sea from which Carla emerges is also representative of the evolution of the text itself: the water (froth) is a place of intertextuality. Carla recalls the water nymph of a novel which featured as an intertext in relation to *L'Automne à Pékin*. In Camus's *L'Etranger*, Meursault, universally misunderstood, finds love in the water: "J'ai retrouvé dans l'eau Marie Cardona..." (*Camus*, p.34). All the physical sensations which he enjoys are united in this scene, and the girl fits in. Meursault puts the two together and decides that he probably does love Marie. This honest appraisal of his feelings is what will cost him his life. Meursault swims after Marie just as Wolf follows Carla:

> Quand le soleil est devenu trop fort, elle a plongé et je l'ai suivie. (*Camus*, p.34)

> Elle nageait, à brassées rapides, vers le rivage - il fit demi-tour et la suivit. (*R*, p.523)

Carla's criticisms are at once the regrets of Marie and the attacks of the prosecution in *L'Etranger* which will condemn Meursault for not being able to love normally (neither his mother, at whose funeral he does not cry, nor Marie, with whom he does not talk the language of love): "Et, bien sûr, vous n'avez jamais su lire dans un regard" and "Vous avez toujours pu résister à vos désirs, dit-elle. Et vous pouvez toujours. C'est pour cela que vous mourrez déçu" (*R*, p.524), respectively. Wolf's subsequent reflections on his relationship with Lil ("Pour elle, avait-il été d'autre qu'un étranger?" [*R*, p.525]) and his killing of the old man ("Ils avançaient dans le sable, la main de Wolf crispée comme une serre sur le cou du vieil homme... Le soleil de plomb tombait comme une masse sur Wolf et son compagnon." [*R*, p.527]) have clear intertextual resonance.

The increasing closeness felt between Lil and Folavril also has echoes in another 'Existentialist' text. Between them they will decide to move on to another life/dream. When Folavril is upset because Lazuli is seemingly impotent, it is as if her dreams (of him) control his reality:

> Des rêves couraient devant Folavril; au passage, elle y accrochait ses yeux; paresseuse, elle ne les suivait jamais jusqu'au bout. A quoi bon rêver puisque Lazuli viendrait, qu'il n'était pas un rêve. Folavril vivait réellement. (*R*, p.505)

Thus, when he dies, it is as if she has ceased to dream him, has left him. Her tears are like those shed by Lulu, the woman who leaves her husband in Sartre's "L'Intimité". Where Rirette's comforting arms belie her true intent, Lil's tenderness is typical of the emotions shown by Vian's more two-dimensional characters (Lil is more a Chloé than an Alise, even though the role of comforter may seem more Alisian):

> Lulu se plia en deux et se mit à sangloter. Rirette la prit dans ses bras et la serra contre elle. De temps à autre, elle lui caressait les cheveux. Mais, au-dedans, elle se sentait froide et méprisante.[59]

> Maintenant, Folavril reposait sur le lit de son amie. Lil, assise près d'elle, la regardait avec une pitié tendre. Folavril pleurait encore un peu, reniflant à gros sanglots oppressants et tenait la main de Lil. (*R*, p.512)

Over the course of Vian's novels the female characters, through persistent disappointment (and, indeed, mistreatment), have become more resilient. Lil and Folle feel pain, but they survive. Although this is not necessarily a trait of any particular literary genre, there are some interesting links between Vian's women and the women of certain works of American detective fiction. It should not really come as any surprise that 'la Série noire', certain characteristics of which were so discernible in *L'Automne à Pékin*, should continue to exert its influence in *L'Herbe rouge*. Thus it is that Folavril leaves, as has been seen, dressed like a dame: "Folavril portait un tailleur noir très strict et un chemisier à jabot mousseux, avec de longs gants noirs et un

---

[59] Sartre, "L'Intimité", in *Le Mur* (Paris: Gallimard, 1992), pp.103-48 (p.134).

chapeau noir et blanc." (*R*, p.529). She does not so much leave as 'take a run-out powder'. Her plain talking about love and men leads Lil to ask Folavril: "Où avez-vous pêché tout ça?" (*R*, p.504) An obvious answer would be in the pages of Beauvoir whose work *Le Deuxième sexe* is contemporaneous with *L'Herbe rouge*. But the pages of American detective fiction abound with plain-talking ladies. For example, in Vian's own translation of Peter Cheyney's book *Dames don't care* (*Les femmes s'en balancent*), Lemmy Caution and a 'dame' discuss the fine points of matrimony:

> [...] Je suppose que toutes les femmes qui épousent un type faible se disent qu'elles vont l'améliorer. Nous sommes toutes des prosélytes en puissance.
> [...]
> C'est pour ça que les mauvais garçons ont tant de succès. Si un gars est un gars bien, les femmes ne s'y intéressent guère. Si c'est un salopard, alors elles se disent qu'elles vont essayer de l'amender.[60]

What is important is that the girls do not just leave the text, they also leave the dream. There is one classic novel of the 'Série noire' genre in which the act of leaving, at the end of the story, is not only highly charged emotionally, but also linked to the final explanation of a dream; the novel in question is Dashiell Hammett's *The Glass Key*, itself widely read in France at the time of the composition of *L'Herbe rouge*.[61] At the very end of the story the main female protagonist, Janet Henry, explains that she had lied about a dream which she had recounted to Ned Beaumont. In it they had supposedly entered a cabin by means of a glass key (the key to the dream and to the text) and had avoided hundreds of snakes in order to reach a table full of food. She explains that this dream of 'happy endings' was false:

> In that dream - I didn't tell you - the key was glass and shattered in our hands just as we got the door open,

---

[60] Peter Cheyney, *Les Femmes s'en balancent* (Paris: Gallimard, 1982), p.122.

[61] It had been read even before then, as is testified in the *Journal* of André Gide.

because the lock was stiff and we had to force it. [...] We couldn't lock the snakes in and they came out all over us and I woke up screaming.[62]

The end of the story brings about the realisation that she has also misread a man, Paul Madvig, a man who loves her and whose love she has returned with hatred. Her recounting of the true events of her dream coincides with her exit from the nightmare that has been the story. Ned and Janet leave town and leave Paul Madvig broken.

When Lil and Folavril leave they too leave a silent victim; they fail to notice Wolf's broken body. In *The Glass Key*, Taylor Henry, Janet's brother, is left dead in the street, his neck broken. This rapprochement of the two texts allows the reader a privileged insight into Wolf's motivations at the time when he (seemingly callously) inflicts pain upon the woman whose love he cannot return:

> - Donne-moi le grand saladier de cristal, dit-elle.
> C'était une vaisselle à laquelle Lil tenait énormément. Une grande chose claire et travaillée, assez lourde.
> Wolf se baissa et prit le saladier. [...] Et puis ça l'ennuyait et il le lâcha. Le saladier tomba sur le sol et se réduisit en poussière blanche crissante, avec une note aiguë. (*R*, p.522)

It is he who breaks the glass dish, and it is he who first leaves ("Je l'ai fait exprès, et je vois que ça m'est égal. [...] Alors je m'en vais. il est temps."), and yet it is she who will leave the dream alive.

The girls leave the text in a surge of female solidarity which will continue to develop in the next novel. This is the same kind of solidarity shown by the Queens who come together for Alice's coronation:

> *Hush-a-by lady, in Alice's lap!*
> *Till the feast's ready, we've time for a nap.*

---

[62] Dashiell Hammett, *The Glass Key*, in *Dashiell Hammett: The Four Great Novels* (London: Picador, 1982), p.781.

> *When the feast's over, we'll go to the ball -*
> *Red Queen, and White Queen, and Alice, and all! (Alice,*
> *p.241-242)*

Thus, when Lil and Folavril leave they pass one last time through the looking-glass.

Memories as the last testament of a dying wolf

In this final section the dreams of Wolf will be given the status which they are ostensibly given in the novel: they will be treated as memories. To this end certain intertextual evidence will be sifted in the form of texts which link dreams and death. These will be seen to have the oneiric feel of memories played back before the eyes of a dying man. Also certain intratextual elements will be investigated in an attempt to show how the memories of the main protagonist of this third novel reach back into events located in the preceding two.

One of the texts analysed in the course of the chapters on *L'Automne à Pékin*, *Le funiculaire des anges*, told the story of Raider, a man searching for his past, trying to recover his memories. Raider's aim is ostensibly the opposite of Wolf's: Vian's hero devotes his energies to extinguishing his memories in order that he may see things unburdened by his past. Both men use a machine: for Raider it is a funicular railway, for Wolf, simply, 'la machine'. Raider's quest begins when he experiences a pain in his neck which he attempts to alleviate by means of a massage. It is through memories of former neck pains brought on by this massage that his memory starts to return. It is interesting, then, that Wolf's recollections (the memories have to be recalled in order to be erased) induce a pain akin to that so central to Raider's quest:

> - Ça me fait peur, murmura Wolf. La façon dont on repense aux choses là-dedans...
> Il eut une crispation de déplaisir dans la région du cou. (*R*, p.501)

Wolf's memories are located 'on the other side'; but what does his journey into his memories actually entail? As has already been shown, the process relies heavily on the dream techniques established, in particular, in *L'Automne à Pékin*. By returning to one of the dream intertexts of the second section of this chapter, it may be shown that to dream can also be to die. In Claude Farrère's *L'Autre Côté*, Van Mitten, the protagonist of the first 'conte insolite' of the section entitled *Rêves* realises the full implications of his dream:

> Ah çà? - fit-il... Ah çà?... Je suis mort... là-dessus, nul doute. Je suis mort tout de bon. [...] Je ne vois plus, je n'entends plus, je ne sens plus, je ne me souviens plus... Ah çà! ah çà, qu'est-ce que je sais? qu'est-ce que j'étais? d'où est-ce que je viens? [...] Ma mémoire! elle est restée là-bas... (*Farrère*, p.11)

Wolf realises that he is to die, but does not seem to consider the possibility that he may be already dead. His aim is to leave his memory 'là-bas' just as has Van Mitten, and death is the path which he must take. His journey is, then, a kind of oneiric suicide. In attempting to see more clearly by leaving his memory on the other side, Wolf exposes an answer to one of the questions asked by Van Mitten: in as much as his suicide recalls that of Anne (Angel sends him to his doom in the same way that Lazuli sends Wolf into the machine), Wolf can be said to 'come from' *L'Automne* (and as Van Mitten is reborn as someone else's baby, Wolf's spirit will return in *L'Arrache-cœur*).

There is certainly sufficient textual evidence to suggest that Wolf is alone in his failure to realise that his trip to the other side is one from which he will not return alive:

> [...] Quoi de plus seul qu'un héros?
> - Quoi de plus seul qu'un mort? (*R*, p.469)

> [...] Et quoi de plus tolérant qu'un athée?
> - Un mort... (*R*, p.491)

> - Quoi de plus stable... commença Monsieur Brul... puis il regarda Wolf d'une façon bizarre, et ne dit rien de plus. (*R*, p.493)

Is Wolf dead before the end of the text? Is he dying from the start, and if not, at which point does his descent begin? The sheer number of entries and exits in the text make this question almost impossible to answer. However, attempts to establish some intertextual evidence for Wolf's death can shed some light. As Hugo's poem "Booz endormi" can be used to suggest that Wolf is dreaming the text, another poem, this time by Rimbaud, can be seen to run parallel, but with opposite consequences. The second and final verses of "Le Dormeur du Val" are very similar to two passages from *L'Herbe rouge*:

> Un soldat jeune, bouche ouverte, tête nue,
> Et la nuque baignant dans le frais cresson bleu,
> Dort; il est étendu dans l'herbe, sous la nue,
> Pâle dans son lit vert où la lumière pleut.
> [...]
> Les parfums ne font pas frissonner sa narine;
> Il dort dans le soleil, la main sur sa poitrine
> Tranquille. Il a deux trous rouges au côté droit.

In the lines of "Le Dormeur du Val" Wolf's ineluctable drive towards oblivion and his tendency to dream finally find their synbook. The final verse of Rimbaud's poem shows a corpse, its serenity spoilt only by two red holes in its side. The word 'trou', in fact, provides a framing device for the poem, the opening line reading: "C'est un trou de verdure où chante une rivière". The reddening of 'trou' is reflected in Vian by the reddening of 'l'herbe'. This would suggest that Wolf has been dead from the very beginning of the text, his blood seeping out and staining the grass around him until he is but a husk ("Rien n'avait pu rester dans ses yeux grands ouverts. Ils étaient vides." [*R*, p.530]). The second verse (the first of those quoted above) tends, on the other hand, to locate the death scene at a point some way into the text; it is alongside Folavril that Wolf falls asleep on the grass.

This passage is a focal point, not only of the novel, but of the entire tetralogy. It plays on the similarity between Folavril and Alise, thereby establishing the latter as the ultimate recipient of Wolf's love. It also (in accordance with the general degrading of love since Alise's was spurned) develops her role to that of executioner. When they 'sleep together' it is as if this act is the consummation of the love which slipped past Alise and Colin, a love which now disguises death. The intratextual roots of this passage are not only in *L'Écume* but in *L'Automne* as well. Their falling asleep together, like two babes in the wood, recalls the suicide pact which takes Rochelle (to Angel's suggestion that they should die together, "Mourir ensemble. L'un près de l'autre", Rochelle makes the following alteration: "Cela serait si beau, s'endormir maintenant" [*R*, p.410/411]), but on which Angel reneges. Folavril's exit from the text shows that she follows the same path, and, thus, reneges on the deal. Whereas Angel gives Rochelle a bottle of poison to put her to sleep, Folle uses fruit:

> Il sentit les doigts frais lui caresser le visage, cherchant sa bouche, et lui glisser une cerise entre les lèvres. Il la laissa tiédir quelques secondes avant de la croquer et rongea le noyau mobile. (*R*, p.438)

Immediately his head begins to swim as he is engulfed by her entrancing fragrance: "Folavril était tout près de lui et l'arôme de son corps se mêlait aux parfums de la terre et de l'herbe." So, the red grass becomes symbolic not only of the passage into the dream, but also of the passage into death: as Lil, who could not 'smell' its danger during her trip to 'la reniflante', finally says, "Cette herbe rouge... c'est sinistre." (*R*, p.514) If this is the moment of Wolf's death then the first memory which flies before his eyes is that of Alise:

> - Tu sens bon, Folle, dit-il. J'aime ton parfum.
> - Je n'en mets pas, répondit Folavril. (*R*, p.438)

Wolf combines with Folle and slumps into her very nature. One of the questions the novel raises is that of madness. Le Sénateur Dupont goes, to all intents and purposes, mad once he has found his 'ouapiti' (at the very least he shows signs of advanced senility). Wolf will go on to deny that his own malaise is a symptom of madness: "Je le suis naturellement. Pas exactement fou mais mal à mon aise." (*R*, p.443) If his natural disposition is not madness, Folavril's, on the other hand, is; her very name indicates as much (especially when shortened to Folle). In her, madness and death coincide: the second half of her name being 'avril' which corresponds nicely with her floral fragrance. Her spring flowers are, as has been seen, 'les violettes de la mort'. It is precisely these flowers which will lead us into the final intertext.

Once again Queneau's *Les Fleurs bleues* provides the link. In his article "Échange de fleurs", Alain Calame raises the question, "D'où viennent ces fleurs bleues?"[63] A similar question has been asked by many Vian critics about the provenance of 'l'herbe rouge', and it is the same question which prompted François Naudin to make his remark, "L'Herbe rouge *est un plagiat par anticipation des* Fleurs bleues."[64] Calame endorses this remark when, having stated that they are the flowers of intertextuality ("leur origine est intertextuelle bien plus que personnelle"), he shows how one can read a text through the eyes of a later one:

> Ne méconnaissons pas, non plus, l'effet rétroactif des Fleurs bleues sur leur source. Aussi bien, pourrait-on tout autrement lire *la Fleur de Coleridge* [a text which Calame asserts is an important influence for Queneau's work]... Effet dénoncé par Borges lui-même dans une formule célèbre: "Un grand écrivain crée ses précurseurs."[65]

One of the key precursors of *Les Fleurs bleues*, according to Calame, is George Du Maurier's *Peter Ibbetson*. His résumé of the story suggests that it may also be a precursor of *L'Herbe rouge*:

> Raymond Queneau publie, en 1956, chez Gallimard, la traduction du roman onirique de Georges du Maurier [*sic*]: *Peter Ibbetson*, dont un film, et les surréalistes avaient fait la réputation.[66] La donnée essentielle de la trame, on s'en souvient, réside dans la possibilité pour

---

[63] Alain Calame, "Échange de fleurs", *Europe: Revue Littéraire Mensuelle*, 650 (1983), 29-38 (p.29).

[64] "Un Théorème botanique", p.105.

[65] "Échange de fleurs", p.30.

[66] Nb. on page 113 of *L'Amour fou*, Breton says of *L'Age d'or*, "Ce film demeure à ce jour, la seule entreprise d'exaltation de l'amour total tel que je l'envisage...". He appends a footnote to this, however: "Non plus la seule, mais une des deux seules depuis que m'a été révélé cet autre film prodigieux, triomphe de la pensée surréaliste, qu'est *Peter Ibbetson*."

> deux êtres physiquement séparés, de se retrouver chaque nuit dans un rêve qui leur est commun et dont le lieu est le passé. Le rêve partagé est aussi voyage dans le temps... Le narrateur étant interné, son témoignage serait suspect et sujet à caution s'il ne pouvait produire des preuves de la réalité de ces rencontres oniriques.[67]

To read the scene between Wolf and Folavril through the perspective outlined in the above quote is extremely tempting: the story not as the dream of a single person but a joint dream serving as a form of communication between them and signifying their love. In *Peter Ibbetson*, however, the dream is located in a lived past; it is the manipulation of memories of an idyllic childhood with which the adult world could never compete. The memories of *L'Herbe rouge* are two-fold; there are those which Wolf recounts to the people on the other side; there are also those lived in the previous Vian novels: this can be seen in the text as memory as intratextuality.

The beloved woman in Du Maurier's novel sends proof of their supernatural communication in the form of violets. Calame signals the importance of this (although, clearly, in the context of *Les Fleurs bleues*):

> Lors de leur premier rêve partagé, la duchesse de Towers promet à Peter, le narrateur, de lui faire parvenir, dès le lendemain, une enveloppe contenant quelques violettes [...] Le billet est écrit à l'encre violette (identité de couleur) sur une feuille de papier parfumé au santal (permanence du parfum).[68]

Folle is the 'violet girl', at once the object of love and, like so many of her literary predecessors, the harbinger of death (and, as for her perfume, Lil's trip to 'la reniflante' is testimony to its importance). The proof of this reading lies in a series of intratextual rapprochements, but does Wolf himself provide any proof? Curiously, it is the machine, whose nature it is to destroy memories,

---

[67] "Échange de fleurs", p.31.

[68] *Ibid.*

which attests to the reality of Wolf and Folle's encounter: the ground surrounding it retains the imprint of Folle's body as well as a floral reminder:

> Le sol, facile, portait encore l'empreinte du corps élégant de Folavril et l'œillet qu'elle avait tenu dans ses lèvres était là, mousseux et dentelé, déjà rattaché à la terre par mille liens invisibles, des fils d'araignées blanches. (*R*, p.454)

The flower remains embedded in the past, and, by the use of vocabulary such as 'mousseux', into former novels. Proof of a past meeting, but also proof that Wolf, on Folle's exhortation, has passed on; his trace does not remain in the grass: he himself is now but a memory.[69]

It can be seen that *Peter Ibbetson* provides a way of reading Vian's novel. It is also interesting as an intertext in its own right. The story opens with the following lines by Lamartine by way of an epigraph which, in turn, may remind the Vian reader of Alise's flight into *L'Automne à Pékin*:

> O toi qui m'apparus dans ce désert du monde,
> Habitante du ciel, passagère en ces lieux![70]

The primacy of girls in the novel, outlined even before the first page, is similar to that of her role in Vian's tetralogy: women will come and go, apparitions of beauty, taking to the skies before love can flourish. The failure of this love is paralleled in the moving away from the state of potentiality. In Vian this state has its purest manifestation in *L'Écume des jours*; the distance which the tetralogy has come from those 'days' can be inferred from the nature of Wolf's recall. His memory of his old school can be given an intratextual interpretation. His desire to run in order that he should not miss his classes is strangely like the desire which Colin felt to run back to Chloé. These

---

[69] Here, then, the dual significance of violets is exploited: the dream and the death of Wolf merge into one. The concept of madness is also present, i.e. the proof that he was (in one sense) 'not dreaming' is a flower given by and emblematic of a girl whose name is Folle. Thus, in wearing her flower he assumes not only her dream and her death, but also her essential madness.

[70] George Du Maurier, *Peter Ibbetson* (London: James R. Osgood, McIlvaine & Co., 1896). (Hereafter referred to as *Ibbetson*.)

memories must be excavated: the school, representative of the decayed apartment block where it all began, is like the site of an archaeological dig:

> Les pas de Wolf résonnaient dans le couloir et il avait envie de courir comme il courait lorsqu'il était en retard, autrefois, quand il passait par la loge du concierge après la fermeture de la grande grille bardée de tôle opaque. Le sol de ciment grainé était coupé au droit des colonnes qui soutenaient la voûte, de bandes de pierre blanche plus usées que le reste, où l'on distinguait des traces de coquillages fossiles. (*R*, 487-488)

If the trip to see M. Brul sends the reader back into the realm of Athanagore and l'Abbé Petitjean, then that which takes Wolf to M. Perle is similarly a step back into *L'Écume* and *L'Automne*. The first outing in the machine sends Wolf back to the time of Colin and to that of Angel, the two resembling one another like two sides of the same coin (this is quite in line with our analysis of *L'Automne* which exposed it as an alternative way of viewing *L'Écume*, a relocation of Paris into the desert):

> Les lambeaux du temps jadis se pressaient autour de lui, tantôt doux comme des souris grises, furtifs et mobiles, tantôt fulgurants pleins de vie et de soleil - d'autres coulaient tendres et lents, fluides sans mollesse et légers, pareils à la mousse des vagues. (*R*, p.460)

Are these, then, his real memories? He goes on to say how representations of the past cannot be 'real' (one of the discoveries made throughout the course of the story is the extent to which a change of perspective discolours our memories to the extent of altering the past itself):

> Certains avaient la précision, la fixité des fausses images de l'enfance formées après coup par des photographies ou les conversations de ceux qui se souviennent, impossibles à ressentir à nouveau, car leur substance s'est évanouie depuis longtemps. (*R*, p.460)

If the 'images de l'enfance' which Wolf is about to experience are equally 'fausses', then the masks of their actors must be removed. The first line depicting the world of the other side is significant: "Il faisait un léger soleil d'automne..." (*R*, p.462). A Carrollinian analysis of the name of Wolf's bearded interlocutor exposes a truly autumnal identity. M. Perle is keen that Wolf should know his full title: "C'est moi Monsieur Perle... Léon-Abel Perle." (*R*, p.462) This is a portmanteau word as developed by Humpty Dumpty in the course of *Through the Looking-Glass*. In his "Preface to *The Hunting of the Snark*", Carroll explains exactly in what a portmanteau word consists:

> For instance, take the two words "fuming" and "furious". Make up your mind that you will say both words, but leave it unsettled which you will say first. Now open your mouth and speak. If your thoughts incline ever so little towards "fuming", you will say "fuming-furious"; if they turn, by even a hair's breadth, towards "furious", you will say "furious-fuming"; but if you have that rarest of gifts, a perfectly balanced mind, you will say "frumious".[71]

Whether or not Wolf's mind can be said to be 'perfectly balanced', the name Léon-Abel Perle is the result of a frumious collision of Claude Léon and L'Abbé Petitjean, two of the principal characters of *L'Automne à Pékin*.

In *Peter Ibbetson*, the story begins with an account of Peter's childhood followed by the dream journeys which, as an adult, he makes back into that childhood. Yet, as in Wolf's case, the truth of what actually took place in the past is distorted by perspective; the story is passed on by a relative of Peter after his death. Even as he wrote his tale (which he does from within a lunatic asylum) his memories are those of a dying man: "And just as when a man is drowning, or falling from a height, his whole past life is said to be mapped out before his mental vision as in a single flash..." (*Ibbetson*, p.25). Both novels end with the image of the dead dreamer; but where Wolf is forgotten by Lil and Folle, Peter lives on in the memory of his cousin:

---

[71] *The Complete Works of Lewis Carroll* (London: The Nonesuch Library, 1939), p.678.

> I had the melancholy satisfaction of seeing him in his coffin. [...] The most magnificent human being I had ever beheld; and the splendour of his dead face will haunt my memory till I die. (*Ibbetson*, p.381)

Peter's victory in death is the result of the final consummation, in his dreams, of his childhood love. As it is the smell of the grass and of Folavril which sends Wolf into his dream, for Peter too, the entrance into the dream is linked to a scent:

> And here, as I write, the faint, scarcely perceptible, ghost-like suspicion of a scent - a mere nostalgic fancy... an olfactory symbol of the "Tout Paris" of fifty years ago, comes back to me out of the past; and fain would I inhale it in all its pristine fulness and vigour. For scents, like musical sounds, are rare sublimators of the essence of memory... (*Ibbetson*, p.59)

Only in his subconscious 'dream' thoughts does Wolf make the connection between the smell of the grass and the smell of 'l'écume'. In the same way he makes no conscious connection between the face of Folavril and that of the beloved girl of his Parisian past. It is Peter's ability to 'dream true', to recognise and love the 'girl of his dreams' which allows him to achieve happiness:

> Prostrate with emotion and fatigue... that haunting, beloved face, with its ineffable smile, still printed on the retina of my closed eyes, I fell asleep. And then I dreamed a dream, and the first phase of my inner life began! (*Ibbetson*, p.183-184)

Only in a dream can he find his beloved, and only in her arms can he put an end to his desire for otherness (that which Wolf, despite his discussion with the mirror, never masters):

> Oh that alternate ebb and flow of the spirits! It is a disease... And from that dreary seesaw I could never

escape, except through the gates of dreamless sleep, the death in life; for even in our dreams we are still ourselves. [...] I passionately longed to be somebody else; and yet I had never met anybody else I could have borne to be for a moment.

Through the dream his being is invaded by her spirit; he is made whole: "[...] A heavenly sense had come over me that at last my periphery had been victoriously invaded by a spirit other than mine - a most powerful and beneficent spirit." (*Ibbetson*, p.188) Wolf declines, in true Existentialist style, Lil's offer to enter into her skin, to become whole within her: "[...] On ne peut pas être dans la peau d'un autre. Ça fait deux. Tu es complète." (*R*, p.501) The only time that Wolf finds coincidence with another being is in sleep, first with Folle and then with the girl in 'le quartier des amoureuses': "Il s'étendit contre la rousse tout près de lui. Elle était chaude de sommeil et n'ouvrit pas les yeux. Ses jambes se réveillèrent jusqu'à son ventre. Le haut continuait à dormir pendant que Wolf, bercé, redevenait jeune comme tout." (*R*, p.477) This is more than Existentialist rape, more than simply using a sightless female body lacking in consciousness, this is conjoining with a woman in the dream.

As has already been shown, for dream one can read death. Peter dies happy because only in death can he finally be with his beloved Duchess of Towers. His dreams show him the way to his death. At the end of Wolf's dream, he too realises its full oneiric implications: "Un mort... c'est bien. C'est complet. Ça n'a pas de mémoire. C'est *terminé*. On n'est pas complet quand on n'est pas mort." (*R*, p.527) Wolf desires in death that which his conscious mind refused him; for, just as Colin's love for Alise was given voice in Freudian slips, Wolf cannot let go of his inhibitions: "Une ou deux fois même, il tenta d'incorporer au passage l'effigie de Folavril, mais une honte à demi formulée lui fit éliminer ce montage." (*R*, p.449-450) There is, thus, in *L'Herbe rouge*, an inexorability about Wolf's death. The memory reading depends as much upon this fatalism as the Science Fiction reading, which sends him to his end crushed and mangled by Martians. And the intertexts of memory are interwoven with the theme of the dream, which also tends to push for death. This chapter shows that there is more than one approach to this novel; there is, however, one single outcome. The weight of the whole novel drives the narrative beyond the limits of the pages of *L'Herbe rouge* and into the next awakening: *L'Arrache-cœur*. With Wolf's death the story turns full circle. Wolf's body is emptied and its spirit can fly on.

CHAPTER SEVEN
L'Arrache-cœur:
Revenge

As has been seen in the preceding two chapters, an analysis of the lines of intertextuality and intratextuality running through *L'Herbe rouge* allows the successful location of that particular text within the structure of this book. This is possible despite the apparently incongruous nature of this third novel. The last of the four novels is *L'Arrache-cœur*. This seems, *a priori*, to be axiomatic: it is the fourth and final of the 'romans signés Vian' to be published (in 1953). It does not, however, logically follow that because a novel is the last of four to go into publication it is, and was always intended to be, the closing chapter of a unified and coherent tetralogy. From a biographical view-point, there is evidence both for and against the tetralogy theory.

In *Les Vies parallèles de Boris Vian*, Noël Arnaud defines a chronology of the conception of the individual novels:

> *L'Arrache-Cœur* [sic] naît, s'impose à l'esprit de Boris, alors que l'écriture de *l'Automne à Pékin* [sic] est toute fraîche et susceptible encore de ratures et de remaniements, avant même que ne soient publiés *Vercoquin* et *l'Écume des jours* [sic]. *L'Arrache-Cœur* est, devait être le troisième roman de Boris Vian, après *Vercoquin* et *l'Écume*, ou plutôt après *l'Écume* et *l'Automne* (*Vercoquin* étant, au jugement de Boris, antérieur, non certes renié mais préliminaire, à son œuvre de romancier). C'est dans cette succession que Boris prévoyait *l'Arrache-Cœur*. Quant à la date de conception du roman, nous la connaissons avec une exactitude rigoreuse. C'est le 16 janvier 1947...[1]

---

[1] *Les Vies parallèles de Boris Vian*, p.230.

As evidence, then, to support this book, Arnaud provides a double-edged sword: *L'Arrache-cœur* does, indeed, follow on from *L'Automne à Pékin*, but is not influenced by *L'Herbe rouge*, being itself "le Roman III ou R 3".[2] It is, once again, within the texts themselves that the evidence to substantiate the tetralogy theory is to be found. The textual evidence is available to show that *L'Arrache-cœur* does, in fact, progress from the pages of *L'Herbe rouge*, and that this final novel maintains especial links with the first, *L'Écume des jours*, in the sense that it both provides a perfect cadence to the series of novels (despite the biographical evidence that it was, until a relatively late stage (1951), considered as the first part of a work in two volumes ("[...] C'est texte de *l'Arrache-Cœur* sous le titre: *les Fillettes de la Reine. Tome 1: Première manche. Jusqu'aux cages.*"[3]), and the apparently imperfect cadence of the novel itself) and completes the circle, bringing the reader back to the founder or, perhaps more appropriately, mother text.

There is then, at the start of this chapter, the question of whether the sequence of publication of the last two novels coincides with the sequence of their composition, if not of their conception. As has already been implied, it is by no means generally accepted that the four novels were conceived in the order in which they were finally published. Again it is Noël Arnaud who argues, this time in the preface to *Conte de fées à l'usage des moyennes personnes*, that *L'Arrache-cœur* is the third novel; furthermore, he makes explicit reference to the place in the series of *L'Herbe rouge*: "A son sentiment [à celui de Vian], *l'Ecume* [sic] aura été son premier roman, *l'Automne à Pékin* [sic] le deuxième et le troisième *l'Arrache-coeur* [sic] qui a précédé *l'Herbe rouge* [sic], quoiqu'édité trois ans après."[4] Whether or not Vian ever actually stated this categorically, there is evidence within the texts themselves that would, in fact, appear to suggest that this is not the case. Indeed, it is the aim of the remaining chapters to establish the place of *L'Arrache-cœur* as the concluding section of a tetralogy of novels. Despite the conflicting opinions on the sequence of conception of the novels, the textual evidence, which is the only evidence truly germane to this study points, as shall be seen, clearly to a position for *L'Arrache-cœur* subsequent to that of *L'Herbe rouge*.[5] In terms of

---

[2] *Ibid.*

[3] *Ibid.*, p.226.

[4] Boris Vian, *Conte de fées à l'usage des moyennes personnes* (Paris: Pauvert, 1997), p.8.
[5] Nicole Bertolt, in the course of the second of the interviews already cited, agreed that the

publication, *L'Herbe rouge* comes third (1950) and *L'Arrache-cœur* fourth (1953). This is the sequence of composition which this chapter will aim to substantiate, and this, then, by means of analysis of the texts themselves. Within the text there will be shown to be lines of intratextuality which extend out of *L'Herbe rouge*. In terms of intertextuality, there is also a pre-defined corpus of intertexts from which *L'Arrache-cœur* appears to depart. In an essay which he includes by way of an introduction to the novel in *Boris Vian: Romans, Nouvelles, Œuvres Diverses*, Pestureau writes:

> Si la maison sur la falaise transpose sans doute la villa de vacances des Vian dans le Cotentin, l'inspiration semble se rattacher aussi à des lectures: à Richard Hughes [*A High Wind in Jamaica*] on ajoutera Gracq (*Au château d'Argol*) pour le début, Carl Sandburg (*Le Pays de Routabaga*) et les enfants qui volent, Queneau (*Saint Glinglin*) pour le village et ses mœurs, Sartre (*Les Mouches*) avec l'homme qui prend en charge la honte de la communauté [...], Beauvoir (*Le Deuxième Sexe*) pour des conduites maternelles ou mystiques de fierté et d'avilissement [...]. *Le Kalevala* enfin [...] qui, conjugué à *L'Ève future* de Villiers de L'Isle-Adam et à *Metropolis* de Lang, annonce le maréchal-ferrant et son androïde. (R, p.534)

This list is extremely useful in that it recognises the importance (and, indeed, the reality) of the role of intertextuality in Vian's oeuvre. Pestureau also states, with an air of nonchalance, that intertextuality does not deny originality, something which this study has been at pains to emphasise: "Mais toutes ces traces intertextuelles recensées, *L'Arrache-cœur* est un des romans les plus puissamment originaux de Vian...". He does not, however, go as far as to suggest that the novel's originality lies in its (exploitation of) intertextuality.

In order to deal with the major applications of intertextuality at work within the fourth novel systematically, and in such a way as to expose its status as the final phase of a tetralogy, this chapter takes as its basis the following question: what is 'l'arrache-cœur'? It is a question which, although of obvious and primordial importance, seems to have been overlooked. In its role as a weapon it is notable for its absence in the text. Its presence, therefore, is

---

sequence of conception tallied with the sequence of publication.

primarily conceptual. Firstly, as a woman's weapon (that wielded by Alise), it is a symbol of matriarchal dominance and, thus, of revenge; secondly, it represents commitment to a cause and, thus, sacrifice; and thirdly, it signifies return and remembrance of that which has gone before.

As a weapon of revenge, be it as a physical entity or as a symbol, 'l'arrache-cœur' must have someone to wield it. In its original usage, as part of the apocalyptic finale of *L'Écume des jours*, it served the needs of the archetypal (within the tetralogy) avenging angel: "Alise rassembla ses forces, et, d'un geste résolu, elle planta l'arrache-cœur dans la poitrine de Partre." (*Ej*, p.190) Alise is not just a 'woman'; she is not a female agent provocateur. As woman and active protagonist, she is unique to the first three novels. The search for a character within the final novel who has taken up the weapon (thus assuming the role of Alise) must start at the door of a character who is both female and a central character. In Clémentine the reader finds both leading lady and main protagonist. Indeed, as she exacts her own revenge she becomes the eponymous hero of *L'Arrache-cœur*. It is precisely by analysing in what Clémentine's revenge consists that one is able to get a clearer idea of *who* she actually is.

To stress that Clémentine is main protagonist of this Vian's final novel may appear to be labouring the point. However, it is a point which criticism often overlooks. Arnaud, whilst not himself subscribing to either camp, names the two most popular candidates for the woman behind the mask:

> Avant même la découverte du manuscrit et parce qu'on n'ignorait pas que le roman avait été présenté à Gallimard en 1951, pour tous, Clémentine, la mère abusive qui par excès d'amour devient la geôlière et le bourreau de ses enfants, c'était à la fois Mme Vian mère et Michelle Léglise-Vian, à doses variables selon les commentateurs, un peu de l'une, beaucoup de l'autre, ou le contraire.[6]

Julia Older, in the introduction to her translation of Vian's short stories *Blues for a Black Cat and Other Stories*, places herself amongst those who would refute any debt to biographical material within Vian's fiction:

---

[6] *Les Vies parallèles de Boris Vian*, p.226.

> Some critics have speculated that Vian's novel *Heart-snatcher* (L'Arrache-coeur), which portrays an overprotective mother who builds a wall around the house and puts her children in a cage, depicts his own sheltered childhood. Reductive analysis of this kind seems to ignore completely Vian's fertile imagination. Any author who has an eel slipping out the bathroom tap to snitch the toothpaste, or a piano that mixes a certain cocktail when "Mood Indigo" is played can't be counted on for true-to-life personal disclosures.[7]

Such criticisn also ignores his 'fertile' usage of intertextuality. Arnaud himself goes on to crush such biographical criticism (from within his own biographical study):

> Très bien, à cette réserve près - capitale - que Clémentine est Clémentine et nulle autre mère, et *l'Arrache-Cœur* un roman, donc un *fait*, eût dit Vian, qui se suffit à lui-même et doit s'apprécier dans l'ignorance nécessaire de toute référence extérieure.[8]

This is, indeed, crucial: that Clémentine is a character in a novel above all. She is not Vian's mother, but a mother born of the text. But as with the texts themselves, she has a heritage. It is through Vian's own testimony that Clémentine's status as literary mother may be reviewed. Pestureau notes:

> Il semble que seul François Billetdoux ait parlé du roman après sa publication, avec faveur et rapportant une conversation avec Vian qui disait avoir voulu faire un

---

[7] Boris Vian, *Blues for a Black Cat and Other Stories*, trans. by Julia Older (Lincoln: University of Nebraska Press, 1992), p.x.

[8] *Les Vies parallèles de Boris Vian*, p.229.

«anti-Bazin» - Hervé Bazin dont *Vipère au poing* avait
paru avec succès en 1948. (*R*, p.534)

It is precisely within Bazin's novel that a Clémentine, or, perhaps, an «anti-Clémentine», may be found.

The title *Vipère au poing* signifies revenge. The act of crushing a viper is symbolic of the desire of the main protagonist, Jean Rezeau, to destroy his nemesis, in this case his mother. Thus, it is an act prior to the main storyline which stands as symbol and as title. In *L'Arrache-cœur*, the same is true: the act of revenge which lies behind the violence of the fourth novel can be seen to be located in the first novel of the tetralogy. In the eyes of the snake Jean makes out the hatred which will drive the entire narrative:

> Elle avait de jolis yeux, vous savez, cette vipère... des yeux de topaze brûlée, piqués noir au centre et tout pétillants d'une lumière que je saurais plus tard s'appeler la haine et que je retrouverais dans les prunelles de Folcoche...[9]

In Bazin's novel, as well as in Vian's, hatred is a captivating force. It is insufficient to say that Folcoche (the name which the three Rezeau brothers give to their mother) and Clémentine have a love-hate relationship with their respective offspring; on both sides there is an intense form of Schadenfreude. Examples of Clémentine's sadism can be seen reflected in the expressions of pure hatred which abound in *Vipère*: "La haine, beaucoup plus que l'amour, ça occupe." (*Bazin*, p.68) Thus, when Clémentine gives birth, that which she brings into the world (novel) is not merely intratextually ordered (via, for example, the reappearance of Angel), but intertextually as well. When, for example, she teases Noël, it is not only his torment, but her enjoyment of it which perturbs her. Her abuse of one 'salopiot' is immediately followed by an experience of complicity, and, indeed, sexual communion with another, Citroën this time. It is in his gaze that she reads her own mind, through his otherness (he is distinct from the 'jumeaux', and as such comparable with Jean

---

[9] Hervé Bazin, *Vipère au poing* (Paris: Le Livre de Poche, 1996), p.6. (Hereafter referred to as *Bazin*.)

whose intense and prolonged staring at Folcoche becomes a game called 'la pistolétade': "Je te fixe donc, je te fixe éperdument" [*Bazin*, p.29]) that she receives a dawning sense of her intertextuality:

> Il cria de plus belle. Clémentine était intéressée. Elle recommença. Quatre fois. Fou de rage, Noël prenait une teinte violette. [...] Clémentine eut une peur terrible, subite, et le secoua. [...]
> Lorsqu'elle prit le dernier, elle s'aperçut qu'il la regardait. Avec ses cheveux frisés et ses yeux bien ouverts, il était inquiétant, profond comme un petit dieu étranger. Il souriait d'un drôle de sourire de connivence.
> Il but sa tournée. De temps en temps, il s'arrêtait, la regardait et, continuant à la fixer, gardait, sans avaler, le bout du sein dans sa bouche. (*R*, p.562)

The attraction which Jean and Folcoche have for one another derives from more than just a common 'love of the game'. They simultaneously fight against and revel in their own similarity to the extent that when Folcoche exclaims, "Tu me détestes, je le sais. Pourtant je vais te dire une chose: il n'y a aucun de mes fils qui me ressemble plus que toi" (*Bazin*, p.63), her sexual pleasure is scarcely veiled. Clémentine, on another occasion attempts to seduce Citroën by making him jealous: "Clémentine, parfois, lui lançait un regard ironique et affectait d'embrasser Noël et Joël." (*R*, p.577) Thus it is that Clémentine escapes into sleep. But, as for her predecessors, the act of 'slipping into a dream' is rarely innocuous. It is further into the world of Folcoche that her dream takes her: "Encore perturbée, elle s'étira et se remit au vague. Des trois maillots montait l'odeur aigre de la sueur. Elle fit un mauvais rêve."

Such is Clémentine's backround: she is mother by weight of intertextuality. When Folcoche (re)enters the life of her two eldest sons, who have been in the care of their paternal grandmother, the concept of mother has little meaning for them. A neighbour explains, "Une maman, c'est encore bien mieux qu'une grand-mère!" (*Bazin*, p.20) Their innocence will soon be shattered, and it is an innocence of which 'les salopiots' are deprived even before their conception. Mother stands for curtailment and infliction of pain:

> Le tour de vis fut donné, progressivement, au fur et à mesure des inspirations maternelles. Affirmer son autorité

> chaque jour par une nouvelle vexation devint la seule joie de Mme Rezeau. Elle sut nous tenir en haleine, nous observer et détruire nos moindres plaisirs. (*Bazin*, p.35)

In *L'Arrache-cœur*, the infliction of pain such as that administered by Folcoche becomes a universal modus vivendi. Folcoche's first expression of maternal generosity is to squash her sons under the weight of her suitcases. This, and the particular brand of encouragement which she administers sets a precedent for the treatment of Vian's 'apprentis': "Celle [la valise] qui m'échut était beaucoup trop lourde pour mes huit ans. Un coup de talon dans le tibia me donna des forces." (*Bazin*, p.22) This violence is taken to another level by Vian, to the extent that the treatment of André appears almost charitable: "Il [le forgeron] lui décocha un grand coup de pied parce qu'André ne se pressait pas assez..." (*R*, p.687).

The maternal violence of *Vipère* does not simply filter into *L'Arrache-cœur* as a general theme: it is interesting to note that, in order to construct his «anti-Bazin», Vian uses several examples straight from Bazin's text.

> Le premier droit qui nous fut retiré fut celui de l'*ourson*... ou petit tour... Nous avions jusqu'alors licence de nous promener dans le parc, à la seule condition de ne pas franchir les routes qui le bordent. [...] Elle nous parquait ainsi dans un espace de trois cents mètres carrés. (*Bazin*, p.35-36)

Folcoche's attempts to hem her children in, to attack their living space, heralds the most central theme of Vian's novel. It is also, perversely, on this point that Vian's novel becomes an «anti-Bazin». Clémentine puts barriers between the outside world and 'les salopiots' because she *loves* them. Her love, however, in its hegemonic desire to control becomes difficult to distinguish from hatred, her cry of anxiety ("Il faut éviter à tout prix qu'ils ne sortent du jardin" [*R*, p.632]) indistinguishible from the command of a tyrant. Wearing the guise of Bazin's notorious matriarch, Clémentine seeks to protect her young from the dangers of the outside world[10]. In so doing, however, she actually becomes the

---

[10] One of the children's favourite activities is digging for 'cailloux'. Clémentine fears the many potential accidents which could befall them, and so closes the garden off. It is interesting to note that Folcoche, by way of torturing her children, sets them to work in the garden, weeding and,

very reification of those dangers. In this respect, her actions can also be seen as the natural extension of an intratextual pathway. Since love died in *L'Écume des jours*, personal space has been under attack: Colin was literally squeezed out of his diminishing apartment; the vast space that is the desert became so cramped, in *L'Automne à Pékin*, that a railway line had to pass through a hotel; Wolf, in *L'Herbe rouge*, ran from the outside world into himself until he was quite literally crushed; and, finally, life and love converge in the form of the mother.

Not only are 'les salopiots' confined to the area within the garden walls, (which is gradually reduced until they are put into cages in the house), their feet are forced into little metal shoes, as if to restrict their physical development. Jacquemort is sent to the village to order some to be made especially by the 'le maréchal-ferrant'. This punishment, too, comes straight from the pages of *Vipère*:

> Et, maintenant, voici l'invention des sabots. [...] Papa résista quelques semaines [...] Mais, comme toujours, il céda. Nous dûmes porter les sabots, que Mme Rezeau commanda spécialement au sabotier du village. Et non pas des sabots de fermière, relativement légers, recouverts de cuir, mais de bons gros sabots des champs, taillés en plein hêtre et ferrés de clous en quinconce. (*Bazin*, p.37-38)

This decision to force the boys to wear 'sabots' is made primarily to humiliate them. Although Clémentine hides her children away (and, therefore, cannot expose them to public ridicule, something which Folcoche particularly enjoys), her motives do appear to be the same, as well as her tone of voice:

> - Pourquoi tenez-vous à ce qu'ils soient élevés comme les gosses des paysans?
> - Pourquoi pas? dit Clémentine sèchement. Ça vous gêne?
> - Ça me gêne, répondit Jacquemort.
> - Snob! dit Clémentine. Mes enfants seront simples. (*R*, p.586)

---

therefore, playing around amongst the 'cailloux' ("[...] Nous étions *autorisés* à gratter les allées du parc." [*Bazin*, p.36]), something which they find unbearable.

Since the children's world is to become self-contained, when discussing plans for their education, Jacquemort makes the following suggestion: "Faites venir un précepteur à domicile..." (*R*, p.648). Given the long succession of tutors whose task it is to educate the boys in *Vipère*, this idea can also be seen to be intertextually generated. It is certainly the case that one of Folcoche's tutors bears more than a passing ressemblance to Jacquemort himself: "Madame mère le soutenait malgré la qualité médiocre de son préceptorat et le zèle fâcheux qui le poussait vers les filles de ferme." (*Bazin*, p.48) Clémentine makes clear her disapproval of Jacquemort's own 'ancillary loves'.

Jacquemort's role in the children's upbringing is interesting in as much as it is also intertextually ordered. His very name suggests that he is reincarnated, a former character come back from the dead. His most obvious direct predecessor is Wolf whose empty eyes are the gaze of death itself. From death to life, from desire to be empty to the desire to be (re)filled, the progression from Wolf to Jacquemort is a logical step. This link with death/the dead accounts for the 'mort' part of the latter's name. But what of 'Jacque'? Jacques Rezeau is the official head of the household in *Vipère*. It is his sanction that Folcoche needs in order to carry out her plans. Since there is no obvious reason for Clémentine to rely upon Jacquemort[11], or, indeed, for him to be there at all, it is all the more interesting that an order may be found outside the text itself. As has been seen in the case of the 'sabots', Jacques' approval was necessary. Again, in the case of the garden, Folcoche looks to her husband: "Non, mais je pense qu'il devient nécessaire de leur interdire de dépasser les barrières blanches. [...] Vous n'êtes pas de mon avis, Jacques?" (*Bazin*, p.36)

The link between the father and the principal son is also similar in both novels (Angel and Jacquemort both taking elements from Jacques Rezeau). In a rare fit of rebellion, Jacques dares to ally himself to his children

---

[11] F. Sucarrat suggests, in "Clémentine, qu'est-ce que c'est? Possibilités sémiotiques du personnage de *L'arrache-cœur* de Boris Vian" [*Information littéraire*, 45 (1993), 10-23 (p.12)], that the exercise of her power over Jacquemort is a form of self-affirmation: "Il s'agit là d'une façon non négligeable de s'affirmer. Toutes les étapes de la destruction du monde extérieur seront commandées au-delà du jardin par Jacquemort mais sur l'ordre de Clémentine...". If 'l'arrache-cœur' may be seen as an act of revenge against man, then the subjugation of Jacquemort is as important as either her rejection of Angel, or her violence against her children.

against his wife: "Je dis que tu nous casses les oreilles. Laisse ces enfants tranquilles et fous-moi le camp dans ta chambre." (*Bazin*, p.46) Folcoche's dominance lies in her ability to get her own way: she softens her tone, and Jacques loses his impetus: "Déjà M. Rezeau regrettait ses cris." (*Bazin*, p.46) In a comparable instance, Angel finally asserts his right to father his children:

> - Je te demande de quel droit tu as fait goûter ces enfants, dont il est entendu que tu n'as pas à t'occuper?
> Avant qu'elle ait eu le temps de refermer la bouche, les gifles arrivèrent à toute volée. Elle chancela sous le choc. Angel, blanc comme un drap, tremblait de rage. (*R*, p.603)

The violence inherent in the Clémentine-Angel marriage is more blatant than the insidious manoeuvring for power in *Vipère*. Angel's anger also wanes instantly. Clémentine's reaction, however, is more primitive (she is wholly mother, she knows no artifice). Thus, although his first reaction is that of Jacques, his decision to rebel is ordered by another level of inevitability:

> - Je regrette, dit-il enfin, mais tu vas trop loin.
> [...]
> - En fait, continua-t-il, je ne regrette pas. Je regrette de ne pas avoir tapé plus fort. (*R*, p.603)

In *Vipère*, Jean's bitterness is directly proportional to his father's weakness. Citroën (who sticks a nail into Angel's leg) is more enigmatic, but, although his anger is manifestly opposite to that of Jean (he takes his mother's side), his stare is, nonetheless, tinged by a sad fatalism: "De temps en temps, Citroën se retournait et lançait à son père un regard noir. Angel restait songeur." Jean and Jacques have a certain complicity, but it is tainted by their shared knowledge that the latter is too weak to save the former. Jean's own 'regard noir', then, expresses the same emotions as that of Citroën:

> Il [Jacques] trouva seulement le courage de me sourire. Les dents serrées, les yeux durs, je le fixai longuement dans les yeux. Ce fut lui qui baissa les paupières. Mais,

quand il les releva, je lui rendis son sourire, et ses moustaches se mirent à trembler. (*Bazin*, p.48)

There are clearly many points where the two novels coincide. Their potential opposition resides, as has already been intimated, in Clémentine's saintliness. If Clémentine is masochistic, Folcoche is clearly sadistic: whereas Clémentine lives off the scraps left by her children, Folcoche not only feeds her brood on burnt offerings, but actually steals the food parcels sent to them by their maternal grandmother. The stock of provisions which Folcoche finds hidden in Frédie's bedroom is a possible source of inspiration for that which Clémentine keeps in her own room; both have a similar odour:

> Pendant votre absence, dit-elle sans préambule, j'ai découvert dans la chambre de Frédie une cachette contenant des victuailles et de l'argent. C'est une forte odeur de pourriture qui m'a mis la puce à l'oreille. Les œufs s'étaient gâtés. (*Bazin*, p.110)

> Dans l'armoire, ça sentait mauvais. Ça sentait la charogne, très exactement. Il y avait une boîte à chaussures en carton d'où venait l'odeur. [...] Dans la boîte, sur une soucoupe, un reste de bifteck achevait de se putréfier. (*R*, p.629-630)

The first example shows a tyrant; the second seems to show a martyr. (Jacques uses this word when the upbringing of his sons is called into question: "Dites que nous les martyrisons!" [*Bazin*, p.64]) It is, however, in her very saintliness that Clémentine becomes indistinguishable from her would-be nemesis. Jacquemort eloquently sums up this paradox:

> - Vous avez une drôle de conception du monde, dit-il.
> - C'est ce que je pensais de vous. La mienne n'a rien de drôle. Le monde, c'est eux.
> - Non, vous confondez, dit Jacquemort. Vous souhaitez d'être le leur. Dans ce sens-là, c'est destructif. (*R*, p.684)

The inevitable result of such repression as experience both sets of boys is escape, or more appropriately 'flight'. It has been seen how the need to escape from oneself (as displayed by Wolf, for example) can be associated with scopophilia. The flight of 'les salopiots' is an extension of this phenomenon; where Wolf's and Angel's flight was intertextual, that of the children is quite literal. The same rebellion occurs in *Vipère*. Jean says of the early stages of their rebellion: "Nous n'en étions pas encore au stade du vol domestique." (*Bazin*, p.38-39) Allowing for a play on the double meaning of the word 'vol', this phrase, if taken 'au pied de la lettre', that is to say to make a play on words out of it in the style so often exhibited by Vian himself, may be seen as an intertextual link as important as any from a work such as *Peter Pan*. As Jean begins to gain the upper hand, his ascension finds its apotheosis in a tree:

> Et je comprends soudain ce que représente pour moi le taxaudier, cet arbre fétiche, le symbole de mon indépendance, planté, fiché tout droit dans cette glaise craonnaise qui le nourrit, mais lancé aussi, lancé en flèche vers un ciel où courent librement les nuages, venus d'ailleurs et repartant ailleurs. (*Bazin*, p.176)

It was a tree which brought Wolf into *L'Herbe rouge*; and the concept of being at once rooted to the ground and extending into the sky is that of 'la machine'. Citroën leads his brothers into the clouds, so that, in their scopophilia, they assume the primary function of 'la machine': the escape from the violence of the external reality which, in the final novel, is 'l'arrache-cœur'. This weapon, once of Alise, and now of Clémentine, destroys its target, but brings destruction also to its bearer. It signals apocalypse. Folcoche's apparent defeat is also that of Jean; in *Vipère*, too, one finds the mark of 'l'arrache-cœur':

> [...] Ce don de seconde vue que tu possèdes à certains moments, cette prescience, qui n'est donnée qu'aux anges et aux démons, te permet de bien augurer de mon avenir. Tu as forgé l'arme qui te criblera de coups, mais qui finira par se retourner contre moi-même. Toi qui as déjà tant souffert pour nous faire souffrir, tu te moques de ce que je te réserve, pourvu que mûrisse ce que je me réserve à moi-même. (*Bazin*, p.184-185)

The extent to which the violence of these two matriarchs can be said to be that of saint or sinner is open to debate. In both cases, one thing is certain: theirs is the behaviour of a mother. In "Clémentine, qu'est-ce que c'est? Possibilités sémiotiques du personnage de *L'arrache-cœur* de Boris Vian", F. Sucarrat writes:

> Les quatre premiers chapitres ne désignent le personnage que comme «la mère», ou moins souvent «la femme». Elle ne devient Clémentine qu'à travers Angel, son mari... Tant qu'elle accouche elle n'est pas elle, elle n'a pas de personnalité propre, à la limite elle est une non-personne. La récupération comme quelqu'un se fait à travers un personnage interposé, son mari. Ceci en dit long sur le statut de la femme dans nos sociétés...[12]

An allusion is being made here to a text approximately contemporaneous with *L'Arrache-cœur*, a text written to dispel the myths surrounding woman and the reasons for her secondary status. If Clémentine is 'mère' and 'femme mariée', what can be learned about her from the corresponding chapters of Beauvoir's *Le Deuxième Sexe*? The introspection of *L'Arrache-cœur*, that which has grown throughout the tetralogy to the point where Clémentine has made the banishment of the outside world her goal, can be seen as a woman's trait:

> La vocation du mâle, c'est l'action; il lui faut produire, combattre, créer, progresser, se dépasser vers la totalité de l'univers et l'intimité de l'avenir; mais le mariage traditionnel n'invite pas la femme à se transcender avec lui; il la confine dans l'immanence.[13]

---

[12] "Clémentine, qu'est-ce que c'est? Possibiltés sémiotiques du personnage de *L'arrache-cœur* de Boris Vian", p.10-11.

[13] Simone de Beauvoir, *Le Deuxième Sexe II* (Paris: Gallimard, 1985), p.228. (Hereafter referred to as *Beauvoir*.)

As Sucarrat notes, "[Mais] Comparée à Angel, elle choisit l'intimité alors qu'Angel, lui, choisit l'extériorité."[14] Is it this tendency, that society sees as woman's nest-building instinct, which is being parodied in Clémentine's efforts to make a world within her house, and ultimately to 'mean the world' to her children?

> [Au lieu que] La femme est enfermée dans la communauté conjugale: il s'agit pour elle de changer cette prison en un royaume. Son attitude à l'égard de son foyer est commandée par cette même dialectique qui définit généralement sa condition: elle prend en se faisant proie, elle se libère en abdiquant; en renonçant au monde elle veut conquérir un monde. (*Beauvoir*, p.230)

A hybrid of 'la femme mariée' and Folcoche, she drives away that which she wishes to retain around her. Her violence is that of wife, although it is clear that her role as mother has the upper hand since she consciously drives Angel from the house. The flight of 'les salopiots' is not merely an allegory of the utopia of childhood, it is a reaction against Clémentine's desires:

> Les enfants plus encore que le mari souhaitent dépasser les limites du foyer: leur vie est ailleurs, devant eux; l'enfant désire toujours ce qui est autre. La femme essaie de constituer un univers de permanence et de continuité: mari et enfants veulent dépasser la situation qu'elle crée et qui n'est pour eux qu'un donné. C'est pourquoi, si elle répugne à admettre la précarité des activités auxquelles toute sa vie se dévoue, elle est amenée à imposer par la force ses services: de mère et de ménagère elle se fait marâtre et mégère. (*Beauvoir*, p.246)

Not only is the weight of her intertextually-inherited social status sufficient to make her a tyrant before her husband and children, it can also explain her abuse of herself. Her craving to eat rotten meat, her pleasure in the disfiguring

---

[14] "Clémentine, qu'est-ce que c'est? Possibilités sémiotiques du personnage de *L'arrache-cœur* de Boris Vian", p.18.

effects of childbirth (which transform her visibly, and, thus, textually from female character to mother) are exaggerated forms of that which every housewife feels:

> [...] Souvent la ménagère le subit [son triste destin] dans la rage. Bachelard prononce à son propos le mot de «méchanceté»; on le trouve aussi sous la plume des psychanalystes. Pour eux la manie ménagère est une forme de sado-masochisme... (*Beauvoir*, p.237)

This all-consuming pressure of domesticity is not only responsible for bursts of sado-masochism; it also causes a deal of anxiety, culminating in paranoia. In Clémentine's case, fear of dust and stress when confronted by a battle which can have no end are replaced by blind panic as to the dangers threatening 'les salopiots'. Thus, the following passage showing the housewife at her wits' end is a fitting description of the pressures which force Clémentine to lock her children away for their own safety:

> Elle voudrait empêcher son entourage de respirer: le moindre souffle est menace. Tout événement implique la menace d'un travail ingrat: une culbute de l'enfant, c'est un accroc à réparer. A ne voir dans la vie que promesse de décomposition, exigence d'un effort indéfini, elle perd toute joie à vivre; elle prend des yeux durs, un visage préoccupé, sérieux, toujours en alerte; elle se défend par la prudence et l'avarice. Elle ferme les fenêtres car, avec le soleil, s'introduiraient aussi insectes, germes et poussières; d'ailleurs le soleil mange la soie des tentures... Cette défiance tourne à l'aigreur et suscite de l'hostilité à l'égard de tout ce qui vit... (*Beauvoir*, p.237)

This preoccupation with things adjacent to one's life, one's 'être-pour-soi', Beauvoir calls "fuite indéfinie loin de soi-même" (*Beauvoir*, p.239). On one level, this is, indeed, true for Clémentine; for Sucarrat, she only begins to assume her own identity long after childbirth, via her acts of violent self-assertion. There is also, however, a case to be heard for her flight *into* herself. As Wolf fled the outside world, she, too, assumes an inner identity which has more to do with finding her 'être-dans-d'autres-textes' than creating her own novelistic identity. To charge her with *mauvaise foi* would be harsh since, in Vian's tetralogy, the weight of one's literary past, both intra- and intertextual, is difficult to disregard. That said, in Clémentine's case there seems to be a far more conscious decision to become the role that her intertexts have dictated she have (since Alise, Vian's characters have tended to sleep themselves in and out of the text).

Clémentine's strained relationship with herself may also be responsible for her idiosyncratic sexual behaviour. The masturbatory frenzy into which she works herself upon the coffee table seems far removed from more traditional forms of 'housework':

> [...] Cette fuite, ce sado-masochisme où la femme s'acharne à la fois contre les objets et contre soi, a souvent un caractère précisément sexuel. «Le ménage qui exige la gymnastique du corps, c'est le bordel accessible à la femme», dit Violette Leduc. (*Beauvoir*, p.239)

When she says to Jacquemort, "Je croyais bien pouvoir m'en passer" (*R*, p.602), it is not, in fact, clear if she can cut herself off from expressions of her sexuality or not. The 'en' is ambiguous: if it refers to sexual satisfaction, be it through masturbation and fantasy or through the intermediary of various sexual substitutes, such as looking after the kids, then, indeed, she cannot do without it; if, on the other hand, it refers to sex with a man then she *can* do without it (in the sense that contact with Angel now appals her), and, perversely, *cannot* do without it (to the extent that another man figures largely in her fantasies). The nature of love and sex in *L'Arrache-cœur* is extremely complex, and much hinges on one's interpretation of Clémentine's relationship with 'le maréchal-ferrant'. The one thing that can be said with a degree of certainty is that she does away with sex with her allotted husband. In this respect, *Le Deuxième Sexe* has something to say:

> Cette brutale satisfaction du besoin ne suffit d'ailleurs pas à assouvir la sexualité humaine. C'est pourquoi il y a souvent dans ces étreintes qu'on regarde comme les plus légitimes un arrière-goût de vice. Il est fréquent que la femme s'aide de fantasmes érotiques. Stekel cite une femme de 25 ans qui «peut éprouver un orgasme léger

> avec son mari en s'imaginant qu'un homme fort et plus âgé la prend sans le lui demander de façon qu'elle ne puisse se défendre». Elle se représente qu'on la viole, qu'on la bat, que son mari n'est pas lui-même, mais un *autre*. (*Beauvoir*, p.227)

If one accepts the reading that Clémentine is having sex with 'le maréchal-ferrant', through the intermediary of 'l'androïde', then, following the above outline given by Beauvoir, it is her imagination, her fantasy which animates her metallic alter ego[15]. Thus, her flight from herself could be said to be quite literal, allowing her to manifest herself in another being, or, at least, to invest another body with her desires. The blacksmith's role is simple: he is the other, the one outside the marital nest. However, to follow this model closely is to change the structure of the married couple; Jacquemort himself plays out the husband's role:

> Le mari se fait voyeur: il a besoin de voir sa femme ou de la savoir couchant avec un amant pour retrouver un peu de sa magie; ou il s'acharne sadiquement à faire naître en elle des refus, de manière qu'enfin sa conscience et sa liberté lui apparaissent et que ce soit bien un être humain qu'il possède. Inversement, des conduites masochistes s'ébauchent chez la femme qui cherche à susciter chez l'homme le maître, le tyran qu'il n'est pas; j'ai connu une dame élevée au couvent et fort pieuse, autoritaire et

---

[15] Sucarrat is in no doubt as to the identity of the android:

> En effet, Clémentine a un double physique parfait, à son image, un double extérieur créé par le désir d'un homme, à la fois rustre et «drôlement civilisé»: l'androïde. C'est par cette image posée hors de Clémentine, hors du monde dans lequel elle vit et veut vivre, que la beauté, jusque-là escamotée, surgit. [...] Clémentine n'est donc qu'un androïde. Il est difficile d'être plus objectivée. Il est difficile d'être moins soi. ("Clémentine, qu'est-ce que c'est? Possiblités sémiotiques du personnage de *L'arrache-cœur* de Boris Vian", p.11.)

dominatrice pendant le jour, et qui la nuit adjurait passionnément son mari de la fouetter, ce dont il s'acquittait avec horreur. (*Beauvoir*, p.227-228)

Both Jacquemort and Clémentine have their part to play: he is present to witness, as voyeur, her writhing on the table and the corresponding activity of the blacksmith. When she is sure that Jacquemort has witnessed her display, Clémentine says: "J'ai fait un rêve" (*R*, p.601). It is a dream into which he is only too willing to be drawn; his trips to the village, carried out at her instigation, lead him to the dream that is their fantasy, the place where their desires can meet. It is at the wall of the blacksmith's bedroom (where he has been doing with the other's maid what he wants to do with Clémentine) that the link is made: "Depuis le jour où il l'avait surprise dans la salle à manger, tous les jours, à quatre heures et demie, Clémentine se retirait dans sa chambre pour faire, disait-elle, un petit somme." (*R*, p.618) This is the same coquetry in which the sexual act has been veiled since the dancing of 'le biglemoi'; the appeal of the sleeping beauty is that which enabled Wolf and Lazuli to 'be themselves', to become one with their fantasies.

To trace these dreams and fantasies to a source of intertextuality is to open the relationship which exists between Clémentine and Jacquemort, and, indeed, between her and the rest of the tetralogy, to a multitude of potential readings. To suggest, as does Sucarrat, that she is an android is to beg the question: who is her creator? It is clear that Vian himself is creator, but he is only following others' plans. The android walks into the text a gleaming construction, made of the same materials as Wolf's machine (from which his own man-of-steel appearance made him, at times, indistinguishable): "C'était, vêtu d'une robe de piqué blanc, un merveilleux androïde de bronze et d'acier, ciselé à l'image de Clémentine, et qui marchait vers le lit d'un pas irréel." (*R*, p.617) Thus, she can be seen to be a progression of the tetralogy, a logical progression of love in the Vian novels: sex has become progressively onanistic, the feel of the texts more metallic. Once again, if in *L'Écume des jours* the stuff of day-to-day life, which was reified in the metal of foundries and arms factories, snuffs out desire, then *L'Arrache-cœur* offers, in the form of this metallic lover, a synbook of love and days. In terms of intertextuality, Pestureau considers that the android is made of the same stuff as that of *The Kalevala*. He seems justified in his assessment of the limited value of an intertextual study in that direction, but his cursory rejection of *L'Ève future* is more surprising:

> L'inspiration de cette amante mécanique, très cohérente avec le monde de la fiction scientifique, peut venir, sans remonter à Hoffmann, de *L'Ève future* de Villiers de l'Isle-Adam [...] mais elle semble surtout tributaire du *Kalevala* [...] où le forgeron Ilmarinen, «habile batteur de fer» et veuf, se forge «une femme d'or, une fiancée d'argent» qu'il couche dans son lit; mais la comparaison s'arrête ici car elle ne lui rapporte qu'un froid glacial alors que l'amante-robot du maréchal-ferrant l'échauffe considérablement! (*R*, p.1313)

If, however, one looks into Villiers' text, one finds, if not the answers to the question "what is 'l'arrache-cœur'?", then, at least, several lines of hypobook.

L'Ève future teems with women and representations of women, the former usually more artificial than the latter. This already recalls Vian, whose women vary in degrees of reality and artificiality. Lord Ewald offers a vision of beauty in the shape of the statue, "la *Vénus victrix*"; she is beauty itself, an essence to be translated into desire by those who encounter her:

> La déesse est voilée de minéral et de silence. Il sort de son aspect ce verbe-ci: "Moi, je suis *seulement* la Beauté même. Je ne pense que par l'esprit de qui me contemple. En mon absolu, toute conception s'annule d'elle-même, puisqu'elle perd sa limite. Toutes s'y abîment, confondues, indistinctes, identiques, pareilles aux vagues des fleuves à l'entrée de la mer. Pour qui me réfléchit, je *suis* telle qu'il peut m'approfondir."[16]

If one returns to that point in *L'Écume* where "les fleuves se jettent dans la mer", one finds that, there too, beauty is in the eye of the beholder. Is that not precisely what Chloé represents? She is the very expression of Colin's desire. This desire, however, is not pure; rather, as the expression of Colin's desire for

---

[16] Villiers de l'Isle-Adam, *L'Ève future* (Paris: Gallimard, 1993) p.93. (Hereafter referred to as *Villiers*.)

Alise, Chloé is impure, a fact constantly reiterated through her artificial attributes. If the reader of Vian follows Lord Ewald's plan, Alise is Venus. And yet, as centre of a cult of love, she is misplaced in *L'Écume des jours*. Colin is part of the froth of days in which the objects of our desires are 'jolies filles'; as such, Alise makes her entrance (at least, she has the right clothes: she is dressed almost identically to Isis). But it is Chloé who lies at the centre of the cult of 'la jolie fille'; she it is who receives the adulation that rightfully belongs to 'la fille aux cheveux d'or'. This is why Alise's sacrifice on the altar of a failed love becomes the very symbol of the triumph of days (life) and of the ultimate failure of love itself. Love of woman, in as much as she is not beauty itself, becomes fatal: it is her status as artificial object of desire which destroys the life which Colin has built around himself:

> Chose à déconcerter la raison, l'axiome qui ressort de ces féminines stryges, qui marchent de pair avec l'homme, c'est que leur action fatale et morbide sur LEUR victime est en raison directe de la quantité d'artificiel, au moral et au physique, dont elles font valoir, - dont elles repoussent, plutôt, - le peu de séductions naturelles qu'elles paraissent posséder. (Villiers, p.196)

Ewald puts the sanity of him who finds the beautiful 'jolie' into question: "Vous connaissez l'adage: l'amour du Beau, c'est l'horreur du Joli. [...] Simple question: l'homme qui trouverait "jolie" la *Vénus victrix* serait-il intelligible?" (*Villiers*, p.92) Ewald's dilemma (he feels strong sexual desire for a woman, Miss Alicia Clary, whom he compares, physically, to Venus, but he does not *love* her since life has endowed her with human traits which he finds insufferable) is that of Colin: the desire of both of them for beauty has resulted in their coupling with 'une jolie fille'.[17] Both become desperately unhappy, but Ewald is given a chance: Edison plans to reverse the process to make the beautiful out of the pretty - hence, the android. This offer, then ("[...] Je vous offre, moi, de tenter la même expérience sur cette ombre de votre esprit extérieurement réalisée, voilà tout." [*Villiers*, p.131]), although ostensibly parallel to that which Isis makes to Colin - a satisfaction of his internal desires through their external projection - can be seen to be entirely opposite.

---

[17] Although the name Alicia recalls Alise, it is not in her, but elsewhere in Villiers' text that an incarnation of Colin's true love may be found.

Goddesses find difficult the role of woman on earth. If Venus (Villiers seems to be referring to Milo's version) were to be given arms, what would her earthly incarnation resemble?

> Mais comment comprendre une Vénus victorieuse qui, ayant retrouvé ses bras au fond de la nuit des âges et apparaissant au milieu de la race humaine, renverrait au monde éperdu qui viendrait lui offrir son éblouissement le coup d'œil rêche, oblique et retors d'une matrone manquée dont le mental n'est que le carrefour où toutes les chimères de ce faux Sens-commun [...] tiennent, gravement, leur oiseux conseil? (*Villiers*, p.93)

Is this not how Clémentine appears, the deity that she is drowned in the anxieties of earthly motherhood? The arms that she has reassumed, are they not symbolised by 'l'arrache-cœur'? If such is Clémentine, then she only becomes herself (Alise) by doffing the garb of Isis and assuming the 'pas irréel' of the android; this she does by shutting her eyes and dreaming (assuming in the dream the conditions of both her intra- and intertextuality):

> Ce sens de la statue que *Vénus victrix* exprime avec ses lignes, Miss Alicia Clary, debout sur le sable, devant l'Océan, pourrait l'inspirer comme son modèle, - si elle se taisait et fermait les paupières. (*Villiers*, p.93)

There is, in *L'Arrache-cœur*, a character whose eyelids are firmly closed: this is 'la couturière'. She it is who, on one level, links 'le maréchal-ferrant' to Clémentine, copying her clothes so that he can dress his android in her likeness. According to our intertextual model of events, however, she is the link between Clémentine and the android, taking her clothes[18] so that she may enter her dream naked and, once inside the dream, remove them again, this time before the blacksmith, so becoming the android. Thus, through the intervention of characters who, endowed with intra- and intertextual

---

[18] At one stage (i.e. when she is *not* dreaming) Clémentine accuses Jacquemort of interfering with her washing, although no further acknowledgement is made as to any tampering with clothes.

significance, guide her into the dream that links the novels, Clémentine is able to assume 'l'arrache-cœur'. This interpretation exposes her intentions as a new, and much more indirect, attempt to find love. Love must be located in that "endroit où" where love and days become intertwined: 'l'arrache-cœur' is a sublimation (Edison wants to create Platonic essences out of a contingent being: "Enfin, cette sotte éblouissante sera non plus une femme, mais un ange: non plus une maîtresse, mais une amante; non plus la Réalité, mais l'IDÉAL." [*Villiers*, p.108]); it is also untenable.

Whatever 'l'arrache-cœur' is, it is clear that it is not wielded in a void. The men in Vian's novel are not only potential victims of its curse, they also play a part in its actualisation. In *L'Ève future*, Edison believes that he is in control, that it is male desire which is the dominant force: "Tenez, mon cher lord, à nous deux, nous formons un éternel symbole: moi, je représente la Science avec la toute-puissance de ses mirages: vous, l'Humanité et son ciel perdu." (*Villiers*, p.136) There are obvious similarities between this male partnership and that of Jacquemort (psychiatrist) and Angel (father, flown in from Exopotamia). And yet, explanations of 'l'arrache-cœur' which turn around the supremacy of scientific man tend to be unconvincing. Edison stakes his claim: "Je me sens, aujourd'hui, la faculté d'émettre, à distance, une somme d'influx nerveux suffisante pour exercer une domination presque sans limites sur certaines natures..." (*Villiers*, p.333). His power is not enough, however. He relies, at one point, on the psychic powers of Miss Hadaly, the raw material, as it were, for the android: "Puisque vous avez... la seconde vue, Miss Hadaly... seriez-vous assez aimable pour regarder comment elle [Miss Alicia Clary] est vêtue?" (*Villiers*, p.254) Miss Hadaly, then, resembles Vian's 'couturière', who is similarly seen as an underling, this time serving the blacksmith:

> A ce moment, Jacquemort constata que la vieille couturière avait effectivement de faux yeux peints sur ses paupières fermées. Le maréchal suivait son regard. [...] On a tort de dire les yeux fermés [...] On n'a pas les yeux fermés parce qu'on met des paupières devant. (*R*, p.613)

Edison himself must rely on seamstresses, amongst others, to help him construct the android: "[...] Pendant les dites séances, des couturières, gantières, lingères, corsetières, modistes et bottières [...] prendront le double exact de toute la toilette de Miss Alicia Clary..." (*Villiers*, p.143). It has already been suggested that Clémentine's act of closing her eyes can be seen as a return to the original state of beauty; 'la couturière', it would seem, is symbolic of that state. Although it appears that Clémentine is receiving her sexual satisfaction from the blacksmith through an act of coition instigated by him, and channelled through the android (this is, indeed, what our previous analysis of *Le Deuxième Sexe* supported), closer analysis of *L'Ève future* throws this into doubt. The proposed model for the creation of Villiers' 'andréïde', therefore, reads: Edison takes an inanimate structure, adds the desire of Lord Ewald for Alicia (divested of her human characteristics), creates 'l'andréïde' (beauty itself). When translated directly into *L'Arrache-cœur*, this pattern yields the following: the blacksmith takes an inanimate structure, adds his desire for Clémentine, creates 'l'androïde'. This is too simplistic; it does not, for example, account for the desires of Clémentine, for her decision to 'enter into the dream' is not dictated by the blacksmith. There is also something lacking in the model of *L'Ève future*: that something is Any Sowana.

Any Sowana is a person of history who has entered into the body of an old friend of Edison known as Mistress Anderson. Anderson, on the death of her husband, became ill and now exists in a kind of dream state in which Sowana reassumes her voice. What Edison does not know is firstly who Sowana actually is/was, and secondly that she has entered into the body of Hadaly, investing it with a spirit and putting the android beyond his control. In terms of Vian, this scenario allows the reader to fill in the missing gaps by putting a name to the person behind the symbols, inside the android and, thus, in control of 'l'arrache-cœur': that name is Alise.

Alise and Mistress Anderson have much in common; the men they have loved have both been driven to destruction, having first been taken from them by a 'pretty little thing', in each case a master of artifice:

> *Mais celles-là seules qui peuvent avilir à ce point et jusqu'à ce dénouement un homme tel qu'Anderson,* ne peuvent pas être *belles* [...] Car le *joli* de leurs personnes ne tarde pas à devenir d'une qualité le plus souvent *artificielle*, et TRÈS ARTIFICIELLE entre-temps. (*Villiers*, p.195)

The result of such devastation is the fading away of the victim, the passing into the state of sleep.

> Sous le coup de la triste mort et de la ruine de son mari, Mistress Anderson [...] fut, tout d'abord atteinte d'un mal qui la réduisit à l'inaction complète, - d'une de ces grandes névroses reconnues incurables, celle du Sommeil. (*Villiers*, p.331)

Alicia Clary, who sees Sowana in her role as sculptor, offers of her a description befitting Venus as well as Vian's 'couturière':

> [...] Une femme très pâle, *entre deux âges*, peu parleuse, toujours en deuil, ayant dû être fort belle: ses yeux sont constamment fermés, au point que la couleur en demeure inconnue. Cependant elle y voit clair... (*Villiers*, p.330)

The Anderson/Sowana pairing can be seen to be directly comparable to that of Alise/Venus in Vian. As Anderson she returns in the role of 'la couturière', and as Sowana she inserts herself into the body of the android (this would offer a potential explanation for Jacquemort's crucial role as voyeur: his presence, as descendant of Colin, is needed as witness to the fruition of Alise's sexuality). This is her revenge. When Edison explains his plans to create an android to Anderson/Sowana, her joy testifies to her need for pay-back: she will take over the project, wield 'l'arrache-cœur':

> En même temps, je lui communiquai l'esquisse déjà très nette, de ma conception de Hadaly. Vous ne sauriez croire avec quelle joie sombre, nouvelle et comme vengeresse, elle accueillit et encouragea mon projet! (*Villiers*, p.335)

Thus, 'l'arrache-cœur' is revenge of love (twisted though it may be) over days. It is the victory of an ineffable mysticism over science: man's control has led to disappointment and destruction; Clémentine is the symbol of Alise's return, and of woman's ascendancy.

Through Clémentine, woman can be seen to be rebelling against her secondary position. For, in terms of the intertextual links with *Le Deuxième Sexe*, she is not merely mother and wife; she also assumes many of the other traits which Beauvoir catalogues under the heading 'woman'. In the chapter devoted to *La Lesbienne* one can discover the reasons behind Clémentine's need to dress in traditionally masculine clothes. Firstly, her trousers symbolise her active role within the text; not content to lie back and take it, she accepts responsibility and drives the narrative: "Rien n'est moins *naturel* que de s'habiller en femme; sans doute le vêtement masculin est-il artificiel lui aussi, mais il est fait pour favoriser l'action au lieu de l'entraver..." (*Beauvoir*, p.190) Nowhere is Clémentine's decision to take hold of the world in her own hands, and the power with which this decision endows her, better portrayed than in the scene in which she climbs the mountain; and it is no ordinary mountain that she conquers, it is 'l'Hömme de Terre: "Aujourd'hui, elle devait se donner à fond. Pas une prise, rien sous la main que le flanc de l'Hömme, le granit lisse et compact." (*R*, p.582) Hers is a battle to find a hand-hold, on man and on the world. Her attitude in this respect is, once again, akin to that of Beauvoir's lesbian:

> Un grand nombre de sportives sont homosexuelles; ce corps qui est muscle, mouvement, détente, élan, elles ne le saisissent pas comme une chair passive; il n'appelle pas magiquement les caresses, il est prise sur le monde... (*Beauvoir*, 177)

And yet, her lovers are not women. Her active sexuality is aimed directly at men. Whether 'l'Hömme' is mankind in general, a man in particular or, simply, a rock (i.e. whether her agression is vented through sex or through masturbation), the role she assumes is that which has been man's from the outset of Vian's tetralogy. She is now in control of her own body; power and pleasure are hers: "Clémentine rejeta sa tête en arrière, regarda l'angle et ronronna doucement de plaisir. Elle était mouillée entre les jambes." (*R*, p.583) Beauvoir herself admits that sexual dominance need not be achieved through the compliance of another woman: "Il faut remarquer cependant que les femmes les plus volontaires, les plus dominatrices, hésitent peu à affronter le mâle: la femme dite «virile» est souvent une franche hétérosexuelle."(*Beauvoir*, p.177)[19]

---

[19] It is worth noting that Clémentine's 'displays' before Jacquemort can, by application of Beauvoir's writing on the lesbian, be interpreted as inner turmoil as well as inner strength: "Souvent la lesbienne essaiera de compenser son infériorité virile par une arrogance, un exhibitionnisme qui manifestent en fait un déséquilibre intérieur." (*Beauvoir*, p.179)

Pestureau notes the influence of *Le Deuxième Sexe*, pointing out the similarities between the masochism of Clémentine and that of certain saints whom Beauvoir mentions:

> A propos des déviations mystiques, ses remarques sur sainte Marie Alacoque qui nettoya de sa langue les excréments d'un diarrhéique ou sur sainte Thérèse qui témoignait de possession à la fois divine et sexuelle ne sont pas sans faire penser au comportement de Clémentine... (*R*, p.1313)

Such displays of mysticism do, indeed, recall Clémentine; they also recall Alise. By exposing the complex ghostly incarnations and psychic control of the other in *L'Ève future*, it has been shown how Alise makes her appearance in the text through Clémentine. The visions of the mystic being sexually orientated, the behaviour of Clémentine may be seen as the transcendance of the more truly saintly Alise. Beauvoir's chapter entitled *La Mystique* shows a woman who believes herself to be on a holy mission slipping into delirium:

> Il y avait là des jeunes docteurs qui voulaient refaire le monde: dans mon cabanon, je sentais leurs baisers sur mes doigts, je sentais dans mes mains leurs organes sexuels; une fois, ils m'ont dit: «Tu n'es pas sensible, mais sensuelle; retourne-toi»; je me suis retournée et je les ai sentis en moi: c'était très agréable... (*Beauvoir*, p.509)

Intratexually speaking, Alise reaches her climax (as saint and as sexual being) through the possession of Clémentine. Thus, too, can the reader understand the importance (for Clémentine) of Jacquemort in the text. His task is to listen, a task which Beauvoir assures is that of God on Earth:

> C'est surtout le confesseur qui occupe entre ciel et terre une place équivoque. Il écoute avec des oreilles charnelles la pénitente qui lui exhibe son âme, mais c'est une lumière surnaturelle qui brille dans le regard dont il l'enveloppe; c'est un homme divin, c'est Dieu présent sous l'apparence d'un homme. (*Beauvoir*, p.510)

It is, indeed, with "oreilles charnelles" that Jacquemort listens to his patients: Culblanc and Nëzrouge are right when they understand 'sex' and 'sodomy' when he says the word 'psychoanalysis'. His look it is that exposes Clémentine's inner self, the mystical woman beneath. Sucarrat notes that it is in the memories of Jacquemort that Clémentine is dressed like a woman. These are memories of a time gone by, memories of Alise:

> Dans les retours en arrière de Jacquemort, comment apparaît-elle? Souvent en robe. Ce qui tendrait à prouver que ce qui la féminise c'est le regard de Jaquemort tandis qu'elle-même ne s'assume pas du tout comme femme. Jacquemort la revoit en robe, je souligne *la revoit* car il s'agit toujours d'un souvenir et non pas d'une vision directe...[20]

However, it may be argued that through Jacquemort the reader is offered not his view of Clémentine, but a glimpse of who she really is. For when she appears at the end of the novel an all-conquering *Vénus victrix*, it is not before the eyes of Jacquemort, but before those of a young boy: "Il y avait devant lui une dame assez grande dans une très belle robe. [...] Elle vous regardait d'une façon qui serrait un peu la gorge." (*R*, p.687) For at the end her sexual sublimation[21] is complete, she has 'l'arrache-cœur', she assumes 'le regard'. Through the intermediary of Clémentine, the pain felt by Alise when her love was spurned is turned into sexual pleasure. In "la célèbre vision de sainte Thérèse", as quoted by Beauvoir, the whole story of the love of Colin and Alise, their frustration on Earth and their flight to the realm of angels, is reduced to a symbol: 'l'arrache-cœur':

> L'ange tenait dans ses mains un long dard doré. De temps en temps, il le plongeait dans mon cœur et le poussait dans mes entrailles. Lorsqu'il retirait le dard, c'était comme s'il

---

[20] "Clémentine, qu'est-ce que c'est? Possibilités sémiotiques du personnage de *L'arrache-cœur* de Boris Vian", p.11.

[21] For Beauvoir mysticism can be pure sexuality: "Les textes de sainte Thérèse ne prêtent guère à équivoque et ils justifient la statue du Bernin qui nous montre la sainte pâmée dans les excès d'une foudroyante volupté; il n'en serait pas moins faux d'interpréter ses émotions comme une simple «sublimation sexuelle»... (*Beauvoir*, p.512)

allait m'arracher les entrailles et j'en restais tout enflammé d'amour divin... Ce dont je suis certaine, c'est que la douleur pénètre jusqu'au fond même des entrailles et il me semble que celles-ci se déchirent lorsque mon époux spirituel retire la flèche sur laquelle il les a transpercées. (*Beauvoir*, p.511)

This revenge by appropriation of sexual pleasure, this entry into the male domain, clearly demands a deal of sacrifice on Clémentine's part. The following chapter will consider the concept of a return to the beginning of the first novel and the symbol of sacrifice, and, in particular, that of the male characters.

CHAPTER EIGHT
L'Arrache-cœur:
Sacrifice and Return

This final chapter will follow the lines of inter- and intratextuality which lead the male characters both into (for example, *Au Château d'Argol* in the case of Jacquemort) and out of (*L'Écume des jours,* in the case of Angel) the text. The role of intratextuality within all the preceding Vian novels will be considered in terms of a return to the beginning of the tetralogy, but a case will be made for *L'Écume des jours* as key intratext. And, just as Clémentine's role as avenging angel was made by an examination of the intertextuality comprising her character, the sacrificial role of Angel and Jacquemort will be made by an examination of intertexts of sacrifice, namely Sartre's *Les Mouches* and Queneau's *Saint Glinglin*.

Sacrifice

The theme of sacrifice can be seen as early as the birth of the 'salopiots'. Their entrance into the text is heralded by a loss of light which has distinctly religious undertones.

> - Il faut qu'elle perde les eaux, dit-elle.
> Jacquemort, sans réagir, approuva. Puis, frappé, il releva la tête. La lumière baissait.
> - C'est le soleil qui se cache? demanda-t-il. (*R*, p.543)

Darkness is cast upon the scene only to be lifted on the arrival of the last of the three: "Comme le troisième bébé arrivait, il le saisit adroitement, aida la femme. [...] La nuit se déchirait sans bruit, la lumière entrait dans la chambre..." (*R*, p.544). There are two elements at work here: clearly the reader is, on the one hand, reminded of the crucifixion of Christ, the original sacrifice; and, on the other hand, the casting of the beginning of this final novel into darkness serves also to reinforce its links to the mother text. *L'Écume des jours* is, by this stage of the tetralogy, invested with a kind of biblical significance, Alise's death in the flames being itself an original sacrifice. The birth of Citroën sees the return of light, the resurrection from the dead, not after three days, but after the delivery of the third child. If Alise's acceptance as deity casts a heavenly aura around Clémentine, it leaves Jacquemort and the other male protagonists in a rather more existential struggle. That is not to say that the role of religion in the text ends here. Jacquemort's first encounter with La Gloïre is juxtaposed with his first view of the church: "Encore cinquante mètres et, assez loin devant lui, surgit l'église. Et, sur le ruisseau rouge, une barque immobile." (*R*, p.565) If one puts the rather crass religious symbolism (the red river as blood of Christ and the image of the fisherman gathering in the sins of the world) to one side, these glimpses of God and His estate on Earth still function as markers, underlining important passages in the text. To ignore their value is to be working on the wrong hermeneutic code: here, the cult is that of the gods of *L'Écume*.

The true religion in the text is not to be confused with the caricatures of 'le curé' and his 'sacristain', whose value is more traditionally comic[22]. And yet, even here, the same textual strategies are in play. As in *L'Écume*, the men of the cloth have intertextual origins. The passage describing the boxing match between the two religious figures can be seen to have resonance (as was the case with Alise and *La Petite Sirène*) in the fairy tales of Hans Andersen. The following passage taken from *Grand Claus et Petit Claus* shows a member of the Church being taken to be the Devil:

- Dis donc, demanda-t-il, ton magicien peut-il aussi évoquer le diable? En ce moment je me sens si bien et de

---

[22] Typical analysis of 'religion in Vian' tends to heap all the priests together as representative of the author's dislike of the Church, this often, in classically anarchistic style, side by side with a similar review of his military characters. Note that in Michel Gauthier's excellent 'profil' of *L'Écume des jours* a section entitled *Contre le goupillon* is followed directly by one entitled *Contre le sabre*.

si bonne humeur, rien ne me divertirait mieux que de voir maître Belzébuth faire ses grimaces.

- Oh! oui, répondit Claus, mon sorcier fait tout ce que je lui demande. N'est-il pas vrai? continua-t-il, en heurtant son sac du pied. Tu entends, il dit oui. Mais il ajoute que le diable est si laid, que nous ferions mieux de ne pas demander à le voir.

- Oh! je n'ai pas peur aujourd'hui, dit le fermier. A qui peut-il bien ressembler, Satan?

- Il a tout à fait l'air d'un sacristain.

- Ah! dit le paysan. Dans ce cas, il est affreux, en effet. Il faut que tu saches que j'ai les sacristains en horreur. Tant pis, cependant; comme je suis prévenu que ce n'est pas un vrai sacristain, mais bien le diable en personne, sa vue ne me fera pas une impression trop désagréable. [...]

Le paysan leva un peu le dessus [de la caisse] et regarda.

- Oh! s'écria-t-il en faisant un saut en arrière. Je l'ai vu, cet affreux Satan. En effet, c'est notre sacristain tout vif. Oh! quelle horreur![23]

Similarly, the crowd assembled to see the entertainment provided by 'le curé' are less frightened by the apparition of the Devil than they are angered by the representatives of the Church who are presented in the following manner:

- Aujourd'hui, annonça-t-il [le curé] sans préambule, je combattrai devant vous en dix reprises de trois minutes, avec vigueur et fermeté, contre le diable!

[...]

- Il y a huit jours, annonça le curé, j'ai découvert ceci: mon sacristain, c'était le diable.

Le sacristain cracha négligemment un assez beau jet de flamme. Malgré sa longue robe de chambre, on voyait très bien les grands poils de ses jambes et ses sabots fourchus. (R, p.639)

---

[23] Hans Andersen, *Grand Claus et Petit Claus*, in *Andersen Contes* (Paris: Librairie Gründ, 1995), pp.178-87 (p.182).

In the first text, then, a priest is mistaken for the devil, and, in the second, the devil, long taken to be a priest, is exposed in all his diabolical splendour.

In *L'Arrache-cœur*, the grandiloquent ramblings of 'le curé' may be seen as an appeal for a luxurious reading of the text:

> [...] Quiconque en cette circonstance refusera d'agir luxueusement recevra le châtiment des méchants qui rôtiront éternellement en enfer sur de misérables feux de charbon de bois, de tourbe et même *d'argol*, si ce n'est pas d'*herbe sèche*. (*R*, p.637)

My italics highlight respectively an intertextual and an intratextual marker. In his own list of intertexts, Pestureau mentions Julien Gracq's *Au Château d'Argol* "pour le début". Jacquemort's approach to the house on the cliffs is, indeed, much like Albert's route to 'le manoir d'Argol'.

> Quoique la campagne fût chaude encore de tout le soleil de l'après-midi, Albert s'engagea sur la longue route qui conduisait à Argol. Il s'abrita à l'ombre déjà grandie des aubépines et se mit en chemin.[24]

> Jacquemort avançait sans se presser et regardait les calamines dont le cœur rouge sombre battait au soleil. A chaque pulsation, un nuage de pollen s'élevait, puis retombait sur les feuilles agitées d'un lent tremblement. (*R*, p.539)

Both are drawn by a sense of recognition. The house to which Jacquemort is being pulled is one containing a character who is no stranger to the reader: here, for 'manoir d'Argol', read 'maison d'Angel'. Albert, Jacquemort's intertextual counterpart, is himself somewhat other-worldly: "[...] Telle était cette figure angélique et méditative: un air venu des régions supérieures..." (*Gracq*, p.18). Albert has further characteristics which point, intertextually, to Jacquemort's intratextual past; his behaviour vis-à-vis women is such that: "[...] les plus hardies... le laissaient quoique à regret poursuivre ailleurs une

---

[24] Julien Gracq, *Au Château d'Argol* (Paris: José Corti, 1996), p.15. (Hereafter referred to as *Gracq*.)

carrière toujours nomade et nonchalante." (*Gracq*, p.16) This past is implied by the intratextual marker found in the speech of 'le curé': for *herbe sèche*, read *herbe rouge*. It is in the shadow of Wolf's death that Jacquemort begins his journey into the text. Further on in his tract, 'le curé' adorns his imagery with jewels taken from *two* previous texts: "[...] Dieu est un œil de saphir dans un triangle étincelant, un œil de diamant au fond d'un pot de chambre d'or..." (*R*, p.638). Here are recalled Saphir Lazuli and 'les triangles inhumains' of *L'Herbe rouge* as well as the eye in a pot found by Athanagore in *L'Automne à Pékin*. In as much as it was his attempt to flee his 'être-pour-autrui' which killed him and Lazuli, this eye is the view into Jacquemort's past life.

The dominance of *L'Herbe rouge* over the entrance into the text is marked, the first paragraph immediately offering a vista of dead flora which can be seen to recall the final lines of the previous novel in which Wolf's corpse lies prostrate on the red grass:

> Le sentier longeait la falaise. Il était bordé de calamines en fleur et de brouillouses un peu passés dont les pétales noircis jonchaient le sol. Des insectes pointus avaient creusé le sol de mille petits trous; sous les pieds, c'était comme de l'éponge morte de froid. (*R*, p.539)

Jacquemort himself idles his way into the text as if carried on a wash of memories: "[Il] regardait les calamines dont le cœur rouge sombre battait au soleil." Once again, death and red are juxtaposed, and hearts are again exposed, this time by the rays of the sun and not X-rays. The death contained in his very name implies a kinship with Wolf which, in turn, suggests that this novel, like those that precede it, is set against the backround of a land of the dead or, given the soporific droning of the bees, a land of dreams. Whichever it is, Jacquemort is to live as Wolf died: empty.

Throughout *L'Herbe rouge,* Wolf is gradually emptied; to follow the analysis of the previous chapter, this occurs either as he dreams himself away or as he is, quite literally, drained of his life's blood. In the course of his dreams, he conversed with various interlocutors in the manner of a patient talking to his psychoanalyst. Jacquemort picks up this thread. To empty oneself one reclines as analysand, to fill oneself up one assumes the position of the analyst: such is Jacquemort. He is born with a label which indicates his role in the text: "J'avais... une notice à côté de moi, dit Jacquemort. «Psychiatre. Vide. A remplir.» Une notice! C'est indiscutable. C'est imprimé." (*R*, p.551) As well as being a lampoon of bureaucracy (that same thing against which Wolf strove with the last breath in his body), the idea that Jacquemort's being is encapsulated within 'une notice' stands to reinforce the position of the author. This may be seen as the voice of Vian as creator, stating that Jacquemort is devoid of personality (he was, by his own admission, which depends again on a notice, in the form of a birth certificate, born only a year ago) since he is, first and foremost, a character in a novel. The reader is, thus, alerted to the need for him to assume his identity by taking that of other characters; Jacquemort's analysis is a metaphor for intertextuality.

His emptiness is actual: he is, at times, quite transparent. He gradually gains solidity at the expense of other characters, notably La Gloïre:

> - Votre tête grossit, remarqua Clémentine. [...]
> - C'est possible, dit Jacquemort. Lui [La Gloïre], en tout cas, devient vraiment très transparent... (*R*, p.646)

This solidity is accompanied by a beard which calls to mind, on one level, Sigmund Freud and, from within the tetralogy, M. Perle, the first of Wolf's interlocutors. Jacquemort's ontological stability becomes a parody of Existentialism. As a character (a contingent being) one can (and, indeed, must) be free. It seems, from the debate between himself and Angel, that Jacquemort's freedom hinges on whether or not his desire to have desires counts, itself, as a desire:

> - Alors vous voyez bien que ça ne vient pas de moi, ce désir de me remplir, dit Jacquemort. Que c'était joué d'avance. Que je n'étais pas libre.
> - Mais si, répondit Angel. Puisque vous avez un désir, vous êtes libre.
> - Et si je n'en avais pas du tout? Pas même celui-là?
> - Vous seriez un mort. (*R*, p.551)

The inevitable last line of this exchange was scrupulously avoided by those in *L'Herbe rouge* who wished to spare Wolf the knowledge that he was dead, a realisation which he finally makes himself: "[...] Je meurs de les avoir épuisés [mes désirs]" (*R*, p.528). Where there is 'être-pour-soi' (which Angel calls "le désir qui vient de vous" [*R*, p.551]), there is life. The grass around them seems to testify to this fact: "Des deux côtés croissait une herbe cylindrique, *vert foncé...*" (my italics).

Psychoanalysis and Existentialism remain caricatures, always restrained by the power of the tetralogy. Sex itself, so germane to the theories of psychoanalysis and such a key factor in the struggle for dominance of the Other, follows the logical progression of the novels. Whereas Clémentine's control over her own sexuality has increased, that of the male characters has not simply decreased, rather it has degenerated into bestiality. In *L'Écume des jours*, sex was intended as an expression of love; in *L'Automne à Pékin* it became brutal, a way of degrading and suppressing women; in *L'Herbe rouge* it became masturbatory, depending less on woman's presence than on her (conscious) absence; finally, in *L'Arrache-cœur*, sex has entered into the animal kingdom. The manner of fornication displayed (the maids can only conceive of sex as an exercise in being dominated, taken from behind) seems to derive from the swapping of roles between humans and beasts: 'un maquignol' sells people, horses are crucified, pigs and goats hitch-hike and Culblanc has a strong odour and tosses her head when she is mounted. The words which Culblanc chooses to describe herself expose her transition from woman to horse: "Je ne sais pas parler, mais je ne suis pas assez *bête* pour vous laisser vous moquer de moi." (*R*, p.579, my italics.) Jacquemort's taste alters accordingly: "On venait de le passer [le cheval] à la tondeuse [...] et Jaquemort admira ses belles fesses rondes, son dos un peu en creux, son poitrail puissant et sa crinière..." (*R*, p.592). Jacquemort himself elects a cat to be his 'être-en-animal', the very animal which brought the first novel to its close.[25] It is against the backdrop of this pervasive animality that Clémentine's own majesty shines forth. It is little wonder that André is entranced by her; he himself has become a horse: "André tremblait entre ses brancards. Il aurait voulu être un cheval pour aller plus vite. Il allait plus vite. Son cœur battait presque trop fort." (*R*, p.686) It can be seen, then, that corruption of an ideal of love has taken place progressively over the course of the four novels. There is, therefore, intratextuality. But when one considers the sacrifice which Jacquemort makes (although Wolf also sacrifices himself to novelistic ends), it is the intertextual reading which is the more useful.

Pestureau's list of intertexts yields a work which embodies a sacrifice inextricably linked to an examination of freedom: "[...] Sartre (*Les Mouches*)

---

[25] In reply to a question about mice as part of the feline diet, Jacquemort remarks: "Purement distrayant... Mais pas bon." (*R*, p.607) Perhaps it is a lack of flavour which explains the reluctance of the cat of *L'Écume des jours* to eat the mouse?

avec l'homme qui prend en charge la honte de la communauté - sans préjudice du rôle évangélique de confesseur-rédempteur joué par le psychiatre à la barbe rousse..." (*R*, p.534). This thematic coincidence is backed by textual evidence in the form of the recurrence of the word 'mouches':

> - Jacquemort écarta une grosse mouche qui bourdonnait en cercle autour de la tête pâle de l'enfant mort. (*R*, p.564)
>
> - S'élever, telle une mouche le long du mur. (*R*, p.583)
>
> - Déjà des mouches excitées par le sang venaient s'engluer les pattes autour des clous. (*R*, p.590)
>
> - Jacquemort se gratta le menton, regarda le plafond ventru et décoré de mouches mortes sur des rouleaux gluants. (*R*, p.612)

Whilst Pestureau makes a connection between a novel in which a character accepts the guilt of a community and a play where a character attempts to do the same thing, it is interesting to see how *L'Arrache-cœur* is constructed around this link (once again, Pestureau tentatively suggests what he would describe as influence, whilst leaving the onus of interpretation very much in the court of the intertextual analyst). In Sartre's play Jupiter, the god travelling incognito, explains the significance of the flies to the two travellers ("[...] C'est un symbole."[26]). A conspiracy of silence reigns in the town of Argos. With their king murdered and his throne usurpé, the citizens, who said nothing at the time, cannot bear even to mention this crime for which they all share the guilt. A woman passes by dressed in black. Before Jupiter's explanations of her mourning, the woman responds in a manner which, when translated into the typical violence of Vian's novels, parallels the reaction of the villagers to the word 'honte':

> [Jupiter] - Le costume d'Argos? Ah! je comprends. C'est le deuil de ton roi que tu portes, de ton roi assassiné.

---

[26] Jean-Paul Sartre, *Les Mouches* (Paris: Gallimard, 1989), p.113. (Hereafter referred to as *Mouches*.)

> [la vieille] - Tais-toi! Pour l'amour de Dieu, tais-toi!
> (*Mouches*, p.113)

Guilt, then, refers back, across generations, to an event which took place some years before: "[...] Et mon petit-fils, qui... est sage comme une image, tout blond et déjà pénétré par le sentiment de sa faute originelle." (*Mouches*, p.115) This is to the utmost satisfaction of the gods ("[...] Voilà de la bonne piété, à l'ancienne, solidement assise sur la terreur." [*Mouches*, p.115]). Électre desires revenge for the murder of her father; deliverance she imagines in the shape of her brother. To her mind, to fail to act would be to live in shame; talking hypothetically to Oreste, whom she does not yet recognise, she employs the word so often on Jacquemort's lips:

> Tu as préféré la honte au crime, libre à toi. Mais le destin
> viendra te chercher dans ton lit: tu auras la honte d'abord,
> et puis tu commettras le crime, en dépit de toi-même.
> (*Mouches*, p.172-173)

Silence, in the face of outrage, is both crime and punishment. Jacquemort is beaten for speaking out; the people of Argos hold their tongues, for that is what they have always done: "Et quand ils ont vu Clytemnestre lui tendre ses beaux bras parfumés, ils n'ont rien dit." (*Mouches*, p.111-112)

This determined silence can also be found in the novel *Saint Glinglin* which is one of those to which Pestureau refers: "[...] Queneau (*Saint Glinglin*) pour le village et ses mœurs..." (*R*, p.534). A close examination of this text reveals that Pestureau's juxtaposition of it with *Les Mouches* says, perhaps, more than he intended. Although, he lists them back to back he suggests that their 'influence' is different. In fact, both texts function, intertextually, in a very similar manner. Certainly, both texts hinge upon a common usage of guilt and sacrifice (they also both function intertextually in terms of the customs of Vian's townspeople). And both texts are linked intertextually to *L'Arrache-cœur* through their application of these twin concepts. To a large extent, since Queneau's novel bears more than just a passing resemblance to Sartre's play, the two intertexts may be read as one. In *Saint Glinglin* the silence is that of Hélène, the sister of Queneau's 'frères Nabonide', who repeatedly asserts "Je n'ai jamais crié". Pierre and Jean Nabonide (who seem to represent the two aspects of Oreste) both desire the overthrow of their father Mayor Nabonide, the former because he hates him, the latter because he loves their sister who has been locked away by him. Oreste has just returned to Argos (whence he was carried off as a child); Pierre has just returned from 'la Ville Etrangère' (where he was sent by his father to learn the language[27]). Jean, too, has just returned from a spell in the desert (like Jesus, but also like Angel); his goal is to liberate his sister who has suffered ignominious treatment at the hands of the despotic patriarch[28]. Nabonide in his flight from his sons falls into a lake and is turned to stone. Pierre leaves, with his brother's encouragement and warning, to accept, like Oreste, the weight of his destiny: "Ta vengeance accomplie, tu hérites d'un dieu terrible qui ne pardonne pas...".[29]

Pierre Nabonide also inherits a sense of shame: his father's disgust with his enlightenment vis-à-vis life and troglodytic fish spreads to the community at large, which dares not speak out against its Mayor, making Pierre a pariah before he even returns:

> - Je suis une honte et une dégénération. [...]
> - Ils me prendront pour un honteux, pour un qui devrait
> avoir honte. (*Glinglin*, p.40-41)

Jean, too, knows that he will receive similar treatment from the townspeople: "[...] D'autres [prétendent] que j'insultais la face de la lune éblouissante et que je défiais cette étoile dont les paysans ne veulent pas dire le nom." (*Glinglin*, p.43)

The brothers are not the only characters from *Saint Glinglin* who resemble Jacquemort; Dussouchel is a stranger to the town, an ethnographer by trade. His study of foreign cultures, however, is only as professional as Jacquemort's psychoanalysis:

---

[27] Various plays on words reveal that this town is England - Pierre's sojourn is, therefore, the same as that endured by Ferdinand in Céline's *Mort à Crédit*. In fact, Queneau's text, as well as being a rewriting of Greek myth, is a work of intertextuality in the same way as *L'Arrache-cœur*.

[28] Although parallel in significance to Électre's treatment by her parents, Hélène's incarceration relies, for its description, on Gide's text *La Séquestrée de Poitiers* (Paris: Gallimard, 1930).

[29] Raymond Queneau, *Saint Glinglin* (Paris: Gallimard, 1992), p.124. (Hereafter referred to as *Glinglin*.)

> Dussouchel examina la fille. Un bon spécimen de pucelle urbinatalienne, lui sembla-t-il. Il eut envie de l'essplorer. Quelques détails folkloriques pouvaient émerger de cette confrontation. (*Glinglin*, p.174)

Thus, for 'essplorer' read 'psychanalyser' read 'danser le biglemoi'; as Jacquemort has feelings for Clémentine which are transposed into desires for housemaids, Dussouchel has feelings for his beautiful travelling companion which are similarly redirected. His travelling companion is none other than screen starlet Alice Phaye. It is this love which explains the inability of both men to fulfil their professional duties:

> Mais il ne cherchait qu'Alice, non d'ailleurs qu'il espérât qu'elle se révélassassât à lui avec des lépidoptères sur des cuisses de soie noire, mais il s'apercevait simplement, tout simplement qu'il avait de la déperdition quant à son objectivité scientifique. (*Glinglin*, p.177)

Having been to see Pierre, now Mayor, who is about as popular with the townspeople as 'le curé' with the villagers, Dussouchel feels a little more local colour in the form of an interrogation:

> Sur ce, il reçut un formidable coup de pied dans le cul fort sévèrement décoché. [...] Des Urbinataliens s'intéressaient. Les Touristes ont toujours droit à de bénignes brimades. (*Glinglin*, p.179)

Attitudes towards strangers and women in *L'Arrache-cœur* can, then, be traced back to *Saint Ginglin*. The animal in even the mayor is aroused by the scent of a young woman:

> [...] Nabonide s'appuya contre le chambranle de la porte-fenêtre, en se cachant la face d'une main dans la paume de laquelle il flaira la trace du parfum d'Éveline. (*Glinglin*, p.94)

Jacquemort, too, retains the scent, in this case of Culblanc:

> [...] Il fallait l'odeur de ses mains, l'odeur du sexe de cette fille [...] Il flaira sa paume, il se revit en pensée guidant sa possession et l'affermissant - à ce souvenir, sa chair s'émouvait presque malgré sa lassitude. [...] Furtivement, tournant dans une allée, il respira ses doigts. L'odeur tenait. (*R*, p.594)

Here, Jacquemort's olfactory passion is kindled by virtue of the nature of the analysis which he is imposing upon Culblanc; he is attempting to integrate her personality into his own. She represents horse; he desires horse. When he analyses the cat, his nose leads him to fish. Try as he might to, as it were, follow his nose, the weight of intertextuality, in the form of *Les Mouches* and *Saint Glinglin* determines that these preliminaries will lead him to his ultimate analysand: La Gloïre. He attempts, therefore, to fill his void, as did Oreste, with a sacrifice. As do the other 'angels' of the tetralogy, he floats, from one text to another. What he feels is a need to shackle his freedom, to fix himself in time and space:

> Tiens, un esclave, lorsqu'il passe, las et rechigné, portant un lourd fardeau... il est dans sa ville [...] Argos est autour de lui, toute pesante et toute chaude, toute pleine d'elle-même; je veux être cet esclave, Électre, je veux tirer la ville autour de moi et m'y enrouler comme dans une couverture. (*Mouches*, p.177)

The slave who, in *L'Arrache-cœur*, wishes to snuggle into a cosy existence away from the burdens of the world is André:

> Ça devait être merveilleux de rester tous ensemble comme ça [les salopiots], avec quelqu'un pour vous dorloter, dans une petite cage bien chaude et pleine d'amour. (*R*, p.688)

As 'les salopiots' are luckier than André, so is he luckier than Jacquemort. Happiness, here, is defined by restriction of freedom and withdrawal away from the outside world. This is the nihilistic philosophy which finished by crushing Wolf. Such is Pierre Nabonide's discovery: that 'poissons cavernicoles' live without contact with other existents, thus with no conception of fear (from the binary that is with fear/without fear, Pierre approaches a theory of parallel lives, waking life/sleeping life, again not unlike Wolf's situation). How this revelation, which Pierre calls 'le vertige' can bring happiness to man, however, remains unclear. This fear of the 'être-pour-autrui' is a form of existential anxst, and Jupiter of *Les Mouches* also talks of it in terms of 'vertige': "Moi aussi, j'ai mon image. Crois-tu qu'elle ne me donne pas le vertige?" (*Mouches*, p.201) It is due to his illumination that Pierre is, once more, cast out:

> - Tu peux t'en aller, mon enfant, dit Nabonide avec douceur. Il n'y a pas de place dans cette maison pour les gens qui ont le vertige. (*Glinglin*, p.53)

As his own quest changes from one of appropriating others' memories to the adoption of a town's guilt, Jacquemort goes into exile. His sacrifice is, therefore, no act of altruism; as such, it parallels the project of Oreste whose original complaint is that he has no memories:

> Ah! s'il était un acte... qui me donnât droit de cité parmi eux; si je pouvais m'emparer, fût-ce par un crime, de leurs mémoires, de leur terreur et de leurs espérances pour combler le vide de mon cœur, dussé-je tuer ma propre mère...
>
> - Écoute: tous ces gens qui tremblent dans des chambres sombres, entourés de leurs chers défunts, suppose que j'assume tous leurs crimes. Suppose que je veuille mériter le nom de «voleur de remords» et que j'installe en moi tous leurs repentirs... (*Mouches*, p.126 & 182)

Jacquemort, it is true, does not leave the village dragging off guilt as a kind of Pied piper/flycatcher; rather, he stays and fishes for guilt. His method of 'fishing' tangible lumps of guilt from the river into which they have been thrown is not so clichéd. Instead, he adopts a method of retrieval which recalls that seen in a famous Parisian text which has already been seen to function as an intertext of *L'Automne à Pékin*. He adopts the appearance of the lock-keeper, emerging out of the pages of Eugène Dabit's *L'Hôtel du Nord*:

> [...] Des curieux sont déjà attroupés devant le bateau-lavoir. Aidés de longues gaffes, deux mariniers cherchent à attirer vers la rive une masse noire qui flotte à la surface de l'eau. [...] Julot [l'éclusier], qui aide au repêchage, saute dans une barque, donne quelques coups de rames vigoureux et saisit le noyé par un bras; il a une grimace; puis il empoigne une jambe, soulève le corps et le fait passer tout entier dans la barque. (*Dabit*, p.84)

Électre begs Oreste to reconsider. The exchange between Jacquemort and Angel encapsulates the options open to Oreste. Jacquemort, who is shown by Angel that if he had no desire at all he would not exist, continues to see in that state freedom itself. Both he and Oreste seek to justify their existence with one sacrifice; they both act in bad faith: "Bien, dit Angel. Je suis heureux de voir que vous êtes de mauvaise foi et insensible à l'évidence." (*R*, p.552) This is confirmed by the following statement which effectively seals his fate: "Après tout, le rôle d'un psychiatre, c'est clair. C'est de psychiatrer". (*R*, p.553) Here, he displays a classic example of 'mauvaise foi' in that he is trying to justify himself and his actions through his professional title, his job description. Jacquemort must take the path to sacrifice daily (in a sense, then, he is, despite himself, a hero until the moment when he finally commits existential suicide in 'le ruisseau rouge'), as his is the path which Oreste himself finally chooses:

> Zeus, faut-il vraiment qu'un fils de roi, chassé de sa ville natale, se résigne saintement éxil et vide les lieux la tête basse, comme un chien couchant?
>
> Je te dis qu'il y a un autre chemin... mon chemin. Tu ne le vois pas? Il part d'ici et il descend vers la ville. (*Mouches*, p.178 & 180)

It is against a backround of such ignominious exile that Pierre and Jean Nabonide make their sacrifice. Paul, too, makes a sacrifice. He spurns political status for love. The woman with whom he leaves 'la Ville natale' bears a remarkable resemblance, both in name and past deeds, to Alise. Paul sees Alice Phaye's image at the cinema: "La seconde fois que je la vis, je la remarquai uniquement. Elle n'a que le second rôle, mais comme je la préfère."[30] (*Glinglin*, p.137) Second to Chloé was the part Alise played for Colin, despite his preference for her. And, as Alise, Alice exposes her body in the hope that she may receive love for who, and not what she is:

> A chacune de ses apparitions, je découvre un peu plus son corps, son visage, son regard; entre chacune s'étend la nuit. Je n'admire pas seulement ses jambes (qu'elle ne cache point), ses hanches (que dessinent ses robes), sa bouche illuminée d'un sang chimique... je me prends de sympathie pour son rôle et, derrière lui, derrière l'hypocrisie, à cause d'elle, pour elle-même. (*Glinglin*, p.137)

As does Alise's spell in *L'Écume des jours*, Alice's part ends in the loss of her love and acceptance of second best:

> Aussi, lorsque à la fin du film, son personnage est déformé (l'homme qu'elle aime lui préfère une milliardaire, et elle, elle finit par consentir à donner son numéro de téléphone à l'ignoble milliardaire de père de la jeune fille rivale), je m'indigne... (*Glinglin*, p.137)

This is doubly poignant since it recalls both elements of Alise's dual betrayal: Colin accepts an ersatz lover (thus removing love which Alise feels); Chick prefers to her the writer, Partre (thus removing love felt for Alise). The name of the film in which Alice Phaye is the star is *Incendie de la ville*, a possible alternative title of the story in which Alise (Ange) is heroine:

---

[30] It should be noted that Alice *Faye* did, indeed, star in a film where she played a role second only to that of the giant ape in *King Kong*. Here, the significance of the name can also be seen to draw upon the concept of Alice as *Fée*; Carroll's Alice is a constant source of influence and intertextuality throughout Queneau's work, and is clearly not without bearing on Vian's Alise.

> Le dernier soir je restai même pour la scène finale afin de voir encore celle qui allait disparaître. [...] Ces affiches représentaient Alice Phaye vêtue d'une sorte de maillot de soie noire, ornée sur la cuisse gauche d'un papillon brodé. Derrière elle s'allumait l'incendie d'une ville. (*Glinglin*, p.137-138)

Paul feeds off his love for this heroine (two-dimensional at this stage), making himself prime material for 'le hasard objectif': "Je détachai cette beauté déjà libérée d'une présence réelle pour me l'inoculer, pour m'en nourrir, pour m'en consumer." (*Glinglin*, p.138) Thus, in *Saint Glinglin* the reader is presented with a model for Alise's 'original' sacrifice. The sacrifice of the men within this novel resembles *L'Arrache-cœur* itself.

Pierre, as mayor, sacrifices his position for an ideal. In his love for aquatic life he decides to dismantle the 'chasse-nuages', thus bringing rain and going directly against the wishes of his citizens:

> - Ne suis-je pas le maire?
> - Plus quand il pleut, dit Le Busoqueux. Quand il pleut, on
> en change. C'est une coutume.

In *L'Arrache-cœur*, 'le curé' goes against the express desires of his flock by *refusing* to make it rain (a decision which their violent protests force him to reconsider, in both texts popular custom being exploited in order to undermine the power of figures of authority).

Jean's sacrifice is the giving of his life that 'le beau temps' may return. In doing this, he becomes the eponymous hero of the novel, just as Alise's weapon, symbol of her sacrifice, gives Vian's final text its title. In *L'Arrache-cœur*, however, there is a change of perspective: the angel of the froth does influence the final novel, but 'le beau temps', which marked the beginning of the tetralogy, does not return:

> Des fêtes furent instituées en l'honneur de Jean que l'on surnomma saint Glinglin (sans doute parce que, lorsqu'il empêche de pleuvoir - ce qu'il fait toujours - il cingle un

grain; mais comment ce terme de marine est-il venu en ces régions?) (*Glinglin*, p.267)[31]

'L'arrache-cœur' (a term which has come from the froth) can, thus, be seen to represent sacrifice. This sacrifice, although one made equally by Jacquemort, Clémentine and, indeed, Angel, is an ultimate sacrifice for the men only. Clémentine survives the novel. Whilst the others are banished from the text, she remains, an angelic figure bathed in light. For, although, as we have just said, the tetralogy has fallen from grace, the naivety of the mythological opening lost forever, there is a final glimpse of illumination:

> La lumière allumée dans le living-room ruisselait sur les marches par les vitres aux volets ouverts. La porte n'était pas fermée. André, timidement, toqua.
> - Entrez! dit une voix douce. (*R*, p.687)

The intertexts of sacrifice also paint a picture of Clémentine's anguish; her actions are as we have seen determined by Alise's original sacrifice. Électre, after Oreste's revenge is taken, is torn by remorse. If 'les mouches' are the reification of one's guilt, then the speech of 'la première Érinnye' strikes the same chord as that inside Clémentine, driving her to self-abuse:

> Tu as besoin de nos ongles pour fouiller ta chair, tu as besoin de nos dents pour mordre ta poitrine, tu as besoin de notre amour cannibale pour te détourner de la haine que tu portes, tu as besoin de souffrir dans ton corps pour oublier les souffrances de ton âme. (*Mouches*, p.224)

For Oreste his sacrifice forces his own exile. To Jupiter he cries:

---

[31] There is a feeling, at the end of Queneau's text, that the whole novel has been written in order to deliver this play on words. The symbol which brings back 'le beau temps' is, like 'l'arrache-cœur', a hyphenated word: "L'ensemble du mât et de la momie fut dénommé nasse-chuages, puis, par contrepetterie, chasse-nuages." The significance of 'l'arrache-cœur', as play on words, may be that not only is the first novel one which 'arrache le cœur au lecteur', but so is the whole tetralogy.

> Je ne reviendrai pas à ta nature: mille chemins y sont tracés qui conduisent vers toi, mais je ne peux suivre que mon chemin. Car je suis un homme, Jupiter, et chaque homme doit inventer son chemin. (*Mouches*, p.237)

Such is the course which Jacquemort and Angel must take. In terms of intratextuality, both men return into the tetralogy. Jacquemort follows the trail set by Wolf (who also left the way clear for his female conterparts); where Wolf chose the red grass, Jacquemort chooses the red river.[32] Angel, for his part, returns to the froth. Although it concords with Clémentine's wishes that he leave,[33] it is finally his decision. It is interesting that his mode of transport (because Angel never walks when there is a train, car or boat available) is intertextually generated. As does Väinämöinen, the mythical hero of *The Kalevala*[34], Angel builds a boat. And this boat has feet ("Onze pairs de pieds articulés en sortaient sur toute la longueur." [*R*, p.608]). This stands to reason, for if it had none it could not walk. Or so goes the nursery rhyme found in *Peter Ibbetson*:

> *Maman, les p'tits bateaux*
> *Qui vont sur l'eau.*
> *Ont-ils des jambes?*
>
> *Eh oui, petit bêta!*
> *S'ils n'en avaient pas*

---

[32] The potential intertextuality to be found on the silver screen should not be underestimated. There is a destiny to be followed in *Red River* (1948), the western starring John Wayne which was contemporaneous with Vian's last two novels. Regarding *L'Automne à Pékin*, Pestureau notes the similarity of the western *Duel in the Sun* (1946).

[33] As Beauvoir relates in *Le Deuxième Sexe*, the marital bed can be a place of intense disappointment. The following quotation, taken from the confession of a young fiancée, portrays the sentiment that will be felt by Clémentine: "A peine déshabillé, il éteignit la lumière. M'ayant à peine embrassée, il essaya tout de suite de me prendre. J'avais très peur et lui demandai de me laisser tranquille. Je désirais être très loin de lui." (*Beauvoir*, p.223)

[34] *The Kalevala* was a constant source of word play and repartee between Boris and Michelle (see *Les Vies parallèles de Boris Vian*).

Ils n'marcheraient pas. (Ibbetson, p.224)

Clémentine's path is equally solitary. Hers is also an escape from the outside world, protection not only of her 'être-pour-les-enfants', but of her 'être-pour-soi'. Électre, before her wish for matricide is fufilled, wishes similar escape from 'le regard': "M'enfermer dans une grande tour, tout en haut? Ça ne serait pas une mauvaise idée, je ne verrais plus leurs visages." (*Mouches*, p.130) The concept of incarceration which links all three texts recalls the sequestration of a young girl as recorded by Gide in his *La Séquestrée de Poitiers*. Here, Melanie Bastian seems to enjoy the squalid conditions in which she is kept: when she is released she talks of her prison in the fondest terms ("[...] Lorsqu'on lui servait du poulet, elle disait: «On m'en donnait aussi dans mon cher grand fond Malampia.»"[35]). In the same way, Clémentine develops a real taste for rotten meat. Once again, Vian leaves a marker indicating the link with the intertext: "[...] Dieu, c'est... les cent mille bagues des courtisanes de Malampia" (*R*, p.638). Queneau's *Saint Glinglin* relies heavily on *La Séquestrée de Poitiers* as a model for Hélène's incarceration; the following description, from Queneau, could just as easily be taken from Gide: "Sur le sol pourrissaient des nourritures et des vers grignotaient la viande crasse..." (*Glinglin*, p.102). And yet, it is Hélène's prison, and not that of Melanie Bastian, that most closely resembles Clémentine's house:

> Nabonide avait isolé sa fille du monde, il lui avait construit un destin heureux
> Là-haut près des montagnes à la limite de l'herbe et des pierres. (*Glinglin*, p.110)

The power which places Clémentine's house on the cliffs next to rocks and grass is not so much patriarchal as intratextual; the situation of the house reflects the position of the novel within the tetralogy: it follows *L'Herbe rouge* and brings the reader back to *L'Écume*. The ruling deities are, however, inter- as well as intratextual.

---

[35] André Gide, *La Séquestrée de Poitiers* (Paris: Gallimard, 1930), p.67.

The rotten meat which Clémentine reserves for herself is given by Électre to Jupiter:

> Tiens: voilà des épluchures... et de vieux bouts de viande grouillants de vers, et un morceau de pain souillé, dont nos porcs n'ont pas voulu, elles aimeront ça, tes mouches. (*Mouches*, p.127)

Although it is Clémentine who eats the 'food of the gods', it is Jacquemort, with his famous red beard, who resembles Jupiter: "De ma vie je n'ai jamais vu pareille barbe, si j'en excepte une, de bronze, qui orne le visage de Jupiter Ahenobarbus, à Palerme." (*Mouches*, p.108) Jupiter's own account of what God is concords closely with the bombastic eulogies poured out by 'le curé':

> [...] Le monde est bon; je l'ai créé selon ma volonté et je suis le Bien. [...] Le Bien est partout, c'est la moelle du sureau, la fraîcheur de la source, le grain du silex, la pesanteur de la pierre... (*Mouches*, p.233)

As does Oreste, Jean Nabonide turns his back on the patriarchal omnipotence that is God; this he does by watching him turn into a rock: "Je quitte ce Grand Homme, ce Grand Minéral informe, ce négalithe véritable." (*Glinglin*, p.124) Clémentine refuses to accept the patriarchal system in the same way that the villagers will not admit the power of the Church, nor the townsfolk of 'la Ville Natale' the power of the mayor: as Jean and Pierre, she quite literally petrifies it, climbing over man's estate, in the form of 'l'Hömme de Terre'.

Clémentine's rise to power, a progression of that of Lil and Folle, represents a return to a matriarchal system at the spiritual head of which is Alise. In *Saint Glinglin*, Paul rejects the office of mayor in favour of union with Alice, who is a living 'star'. About her image she says:

> - Universelle... Quelle femme, de plus, que moi?
> - Déesse, répliqua Dussouchel.
> - Sans doute, et qui bouge. Pas une manifestation occulte ou symbolique, de temps à autre, mais la continuité de mouvements.
> - Forme sans matière.

> - Forme de lumière.
> - Et d'ombre.
> - Ces atomes de temps qui défilent, c'est moi. (*Glinglin*, p.170)

Alise has, herself, flitted through the novels heedless of time, casting light and shadow according to her caprices. With the restoration of power (and real novelistic identity) to woman, there is restoration of light. As Alise, who was recognisable by her natural perfume, Alice, too, is distinctly fragrant; although her perfume is worn, rather than emanated, it has, by a reversal of the natural-artificial polarity, the same impact as the Alisian variety: "[...] Il percevait cependant le parfum [d'Alise Phaye] surajouté, mais fin plus qu'aucune odeur naturelle à la Ville Natale." (*Glinglin*, p.169)

The real power at work in *L'Arrache-cœur* is that of the mother text. In these two intertexts there is a common theme of return. For return home in these texts, one can read return to the mother text in Vian. For example, *Les Mouches* opens with Oreste's return to Argos, his home town. His return is to a town which is his own, but which he cannot remember: "Je suis né ici et je dois demander mon chemin comme un passant." (*Mouches*, p.106) This is similar to Jacquemort's entrance into *L'Arrache-cœur*, a text in which, as part of a tetralogy, he has an heredity, which is perceived, through textual evidence, more as an instinct than as a conscious memory. If the house on the cliffs is another relocation of the Paris of *L'Écume*, then it is a Paris unlit by the benevolent twin suns which once illuminated Colin's steps. The light in the streets of Argos is also harsh: "Ces rues désertes, l'air qui tremble, et ce soleil... Qu'y a-t-il de plus sinistre que le soleil?" (*Mouches*, p.106) In *Saint Glinglin*, too, there would appear to be glimpses back to Vian novels prior to *L'Arrache-cœur*; Pierre's journey back to 'la Ville Natale' seems to resemble a move away from the emptiness of *L'Herbe rouge* (on a travelling machine, this time in the form of a bicycle), away from the (distant) happiness of the froth towards the sacrifice of *L'Arrache-cœur*:

> Je méditais ainsi sur l'ocre d'un gazon mourant; il y traînait quelques paquets de cigarettes vidés, quelques tickets d'autobus usagés, quelques autres débris; ma bicyclette s'était fidèlement couchée près de moi. [...] [Je compris] qu'il y avait deux vies [...] Et je vis que l'une était de

l'avenir et s'appelait la Gloire, et que l'autre, du passé, se nommait le Bonheur. (*Glinglin*, p.38-39)

Then, once he has returned to 'la Ville Natale' (i.e. has reached *L'Arrache-cœur*), there can be seen to be a return to *L'Écume* (this in the form of a funeral exactly like that of Chloé, pre-empted by a play on words parallel to one made in *L'Automne à Pékin*). The grandmother of the Nabonide brothers is not 'ensablée' as she would be in the exopotamian desert, rather she is 'embourbée': "Tout le monde était à la fête. Il fallait attendre pour l'embourber." (*Glinglin*, p.240) The path to the cemetery embodies a return, from the arid desert, to the original froth:

> Ils descendirent le long de la gorge sèche où gisaient les marécages du fourre-tout [...] Ils pataugeaient dans la marmelade fangeuse où pourrissaient [*sic*] ce qui ne vivait plus de la Ville Natale. Les quatre garçons choisirent un endroit qui leur parut plutôt creux et bousculant la civière y jetèrent leur fardal. La grand'mère enveloppée de son linge ultime fit floc, puis le ballot taché de gouttes de boue s'enfonça lentement... (*Glinglin*, p.252-253)

Return

The symbol of return functions, as do those of revenge and sacrifice, on two levels which, once again intertwine. Thus, there are intertexts of return and there is return to the previous novels of the tetralogy via remembrance, this in the form of intratextuality.

One text which symbolizes the entire concept of return is Pierre Mac Orlan's *La Maison du retour écœurant*. In this early novel (1912), Mac Orlan produces a work of rich humour which had a marked influence on Vian (Gilles Costaz, for example, speaks of it as "un livre qui enthousiasma Boris Vian et l'influença"[36]). As well as having a heart-rending title (arrache-cœur/écœurant), this novel has as its node, around which all banishment and return are centred, a house; but this is no ordinary house:

> [Et] l'histoire commença au 7 de la rue principale de Truchebœuf, dans une maison normande ou anglaise, toute semblable à ces jolies maisons à colombages que les vieilles estampes de sport ont popularisées.[37]

As Noël Arnaud would have us believe[38], Clémentine's house is designed around the Vian family holiday home in Normandy. If this is, indeed, the case, then Vian's attention may well have been drawn to the house of Mac Orlan. There are, however, more tangible textual links between *La Maison du retour écœurant* and Vian's tetralogy.

To begin with *L'Arrache-cœur*, there are in Mac Orlan's text examples of words being adorned with supererogatory accents (presumably, in order to give a more exotic flavour to the concept of voyage), for example: "le portrait du Gallois Joë" and "Mac Doë".(*Maison*, p.58 & 67)[39] Such accents are ubiquitous in *L'Arrache-cœur*. The texts to which *L'Arrache-cœur* marks the return are also represented. Dreaming of his return to the house at Truchebœuf, Paul, the principal character, says: "Je l'embellirai, cette maison, je l'embellirai de mes souvenirs." (*Maison*, p.213) Although the houses in *L'Herbe rouge* and *L'Arrache-cœur*, where the destruction and acquisition

---

[36] Gilles Costaz, "Mac Orlan, poète mal entendu", *Tendances*, 68 (1970), pp.729-743, (p.732).

[37] Pierre Mac Orlan, *La Maison du retour écœurant* (Paris: Collection littéraire de la Renaissance du Livre, 1924), p.13. (Hereafter referred to as *Maison*.)

[38] "Nous avions identifié la maison de *l'Arrache-Cœur* et la villa des vacances à Landemer." (*Les Vies parallèles de Boris Vian*, p.226)

[39] It is worthy of note that Villiers de l'Isle-Adam was also fond of this (over)use of accents. Alan Raitt remarks: "Quant au tréma dont Villiers décore le mot [Salëm], on sait que c'est un signe pour lequel il nourrissait une prédilection extrême, surtout quand il translitère des mots étrangers. Dans les noms juifs de *L'Annonciateur* (*Contes cruels*), leur nombre est tel qu'il a suscité chez Max Daireaux le commentaire suivant: «Sur tout cela les trémas pleuvent comme si, aux yeux de Villiers de l'Isle-Adam, ils ajoutaient encore à la somptuosité des syllabes qu'ils couronnent»." (*Villiers*, p.399)

respectively of memories are paramount, witness rather negative alterations, the texts are embellished by the presence, both inter- and intratextual (as memory), of other texts.

In *La Maison du retour écœurant* can also be found a progression from railway lines to dancing negroes; this is a progression from *L'Automne à Pékin* to *L'Herbe rouge*:

> Mac Guldy le géant se traînait péniblement couché en angle droit, à tel point que, trop vieux pour piocher le long des lignes de chemins de fer, il servait de table à thé chez un grand danseur nègre, qui jouait comme ombre chinoise sur un écran de toile blanche. (*Maison*, p.187)

In fact, *La Maison du retour écœurant* shares much common ground with *L'Automne à Pékin* (for Angel, the second novel is certainly a journey with a difficult return). Vian's hotelier makes an appearance, although, in Mac Orlan's novel, his is the name of a boat:

> Les frères Mac Guldy avaient frêté un ancien aviso de la marine américaine pour les besoins de leur contrebande et cet aviso, qu'ils avaient appelé *la Pipe*... (*Maison*, p.3)

And in this case it is not la Pipe who is decapitated; rather it is the owners of 'la Pipe' who wish to decapitate Thomas (Paul's uncle): "Il y a des chances... que si je rencontre ce crétin... ce soit pour lui couper la tête au ras de la ceinture." (*Maison*, p.3) Thomas, not unnaturally, alarmed at this prospect eventually suffers bizarre consequences:

> [...] L'oncle Turnlop, sous le coup de la peur, avait vu ses cheveux, jadis noirs, blanchir instantanément, mais par contre le noir de sa chevelure s'était répandu sur sa peau lui donnant toutes les apparences du noir le plus attaché aux traditions dermiques de sa race. (*Maison*, p.22)

The negative image of himself which Thomas becomes is a perfect reflection of the negative images which Cuivre and Laverne offer of one another.

As was shown in the second chapter of this book, the Exopotamian desert can be understood as an oneiric relocation of Paris. For, to follow the syllogistic reasoning of *L'Automne à Pékin,* if a desert cannot be a desert if it has a railway line, then Paris cannot be Paris if it has camels roaming its streets:

> Quand les chameaux eurent pris place dans les prés de l'oncle Turnlop qui ne se doutait de rien, on leur fit boire à chacun cent vingt litres de Calvados et, sous le prétexte de les utiliser au transport de colis sans importance, on les introduisit tous les six dans Paris... (*Maison*, p.26)

Finally, the 'raccourci' taken by Amadis Dudu, through the blue lanterns of the brothels, and which ultimately takes him overland to Exopotamia, can be traced to a street in *La Maison du retour écœurant*:

> Avant de prendre son billet pour le paquebot qui devait l'emmener vers l'Amérique, Paul Choux alla rôder dans les bars soigneusement cachés aux yeux des familles en de petites rues obscures mais sales. L'une d'elles, plus sombre que les autres, attira le jeune homme. Des femmes en corsage jaune clair, vert pâle, rose tendre se dressaient dans l'encadrement des portes. C'était dans toute la ruelle noire sous un ciel de velours bleu foncé, comme des lanternes vénitiennes de 14 juillet. (*Maison*, p.57)

The intertextuality in Mac Orlan's novel extends from *L'Arrache-cœur* right back into *L'Écume des jours* (that is, when considered from the perspective of the former). In the opening pages the story is set in the froth of the high seas: "A vingt-sept ans, alors que les frères Mac Guldy écumaient la Mer Jaune..." (*Maison*, p.14). From froth, the story passes via mechanised animals, like the pill-producing, half-metal rabbits of *L'Écume*[40], to a state of

---

[40] "[...] Des quatre vaches à vapeur qui donnaient par jour deux cents litres de lait chaud." (*Maison*, p.32)

general sadness and degradation, the effects of which on the 'villa' are the same as those of the death of the sun in Vian's world:

> Et [pourtant] une tristesse légère, mais pénétrante comme une pluie d'octobre, transperçait l'oncle et tout le monde dans le villa. Et nulle courtepointe, nulle douillette, nul pyjama, fourrure, imperméable ou pardessus à taille, ne paraissaient capables de protéger le cœur et les os contre cette mélancolique. (*Maison*, p.86)

The reason, in a roundabout way, for this misery is Thomas' taking of the wrong woman as his wife, once again marking a parallel with *L'Écume*. This is not the only instance of marriage in *La Maison du retour écœurant* which recalls the situation of Colin and Alise:

> Elle s'appelait Alice, c'était une Anglaise et son amie qui est devenue ma femme s'appelait Anna, Anna Boulumay. [...] Anna Boulumay, quand je la connus, présentée par Alice... (*Maison*, p.119)[41]

From *L'Arrache-cœur* to *L'Écume des jours*, the whole text seems geared towards this return; Jacquemort's desire for memory reflects the remembrance of the novel itself. Clémentine only senses victory (the victory of Alise) once Angel has left. His departure, although similar to that which he effected at the end of *L'Automne à Pékin*, is, this time, more definitive. Whereas, on board the bus out of the desert his instructions were to fly (and one can imagine that this airborne angel is bound to alight again, like H.G. Wells' Mr Angel, on human, that is to say textual, ground), this time he returns to the mythological spawning ground that is the froth: "Lorsqu'il [le bateau d'Angel] fut à son plein régime, il parut, léger et grêle, marcher sur l'eau calme au milieu d'une gerbe d'écume." (*R*, p.620) Once again, as already discussed,

---

[41] Anna, who also has a tendency to 'rougir' resembles, in this scenario, Chloé. Alice (although, here, more in the role of Isis) is another potential model for Alise. Note that Mac Orlan's Alice, like Queneau's Alice Phaye, is English; she is, thus, a recollection of Lewis Carroll's Alice, who is, herself, not without influence over the work of Vian.

the lines left by Max Jacob in the *Livre de bord* of Montmartre's *Le Lapin Agile* reveal their importance:

> La Seine qui passe,
> O Tavernier du Quai des brumes,
> T'apporte sa gerbe d'écumes.

The water which flows through the Parisian novel that is *L'Écume des jours* is the same water which returns for Angel, calling him back to the froth. In a dignified manner, worthy of an angel, he cedes the novelistic space to Clémentine; he crosses 'la barre difficile à franchir' back into 'l'écume'. Thus, for him 'the flight of the angel' comes full circle. This, Clémentine knows: "Elle sentait déjà ce que signifiait l'incendie sans avoir besoin de vérifier. Son dernier obstacle s'envolait." (*R*, p.622) Whilst the word 's'envolait' shows that Angel's novelistic identity is no secret to her, the word 'incendie' is more pertinent to her own heredity. The fire, which lifted Alise from the froth, has now reclaimed an angel, bringing an end to the limbo which has only allowed glimpses of Alise since the end of the first novel. For the angels of the tetralogy, then, the 'wonderful visit' appears to be almost at an end.

Once again, Wells' text *The Wonderful Visit* has an influence over the characters of Vian's novel. All the main characters, including, this time, 'les salopiots', have angelic traits. Of all the characters, 'les salopiots' are the least human. As Pestureau points out[42], Richard Hughes, in *A High Wind in Jamaica*, his novel about a fantastic sea voyage undergone by a group of children, declares that: "[...] Children are human (if one allows the term 'human' a wide sense) [...] Babies of course are not human - they are animals, and have a very ancient and ramified culture...".[43] This is truly the culture of 'les salopiots'. As well as being conversant in the ways of magic, they are also, of all Vian's creations, the most ostensibly angelic. For, rather than flying in a

---

[42] "[...] Comme le disait bien Richard Hughes dès 1929 dans *Un Cyclone à la Jamaïque*, les bébés sont des mutants..." (*R*, p.533) And in Vian's texts, what does 'human' signify if not a baby who has been overexposed to 'jours': angels and mutants both stand in the same opposition to humans.

[43] Richard Hughes, *A High Wind in Jamaica* (London: Harvill, 1994), p.158.

symbolic, metaphorical sense, they are the very reification of 'the flight of an angel'. It is the accumulation of days which makes people increasingly less angelic and correspondingly more human. Thus, it stands to reason that babies should fly. Wells' angel enters his novel via accounts of a "Strange Bird":

> At first he [the solicitor's clerk] thought it was an eagle he saw. It was near the zenith, still incredibly remote... and it seemed as if it fluttered and beat itself against the sky, as an imprisoned swallow might do against a window pane. [...] It seemed larger than a man. (*Visit*, p.15)

So, too, 'les salopiots' seem larger than birds ("Tout à coup, il aperçut dans la direction de la mer, trois oiseaux un peu plus grands qui volaient si vite qu'il ne put distinguer leur espèce." [*R*, p.667]), imprisoned as they are in this human (non-angelic) world, from which Angel has already taken his final leave. The flight of the children, although more concrete than that of their intratextual predecessors, does follow a similar pattern. When instructing his brothers on flight procedures, Citroën lies flat on the grass: "Il s'étendit à plat ventre sur l'herbe et, par un mouvement imperceptible des mains et des pieds, s'éleva à trente centimètres du sol." (*R*, p.663) This recalls both Wolf's night on the grass with Folavril (which may be interpreted as flight) and the recumbent position which he assumes on his mirror (another example of flight). Their flight also follows a vision of an Alisian figure:

> [...] Une petite fille avec de longs cheveux blonds. [...] Elle dansa quelques minutes, sans jamais sortir du triangle. Et puis, brusquement, elle s'arrêta, regarda le ciel et s'enfonça dans le sol aussi rapidement qu'elle était sortie. (*R*, p.644)

Although this passage could be subjected to almost any number of interpretations (including that of the entry of Alice into Wonderland), it does seem to be a premonition of the children's flight and, perhaps, of their subsequent 'grounding', all this under the sign of Alise.

Jacquemort, for his part, enters into the text in time to witness a kind of eclipse. Darkness it is which pulls Wells' angel out of the angelic world and into the text: "[...] And suddenly everything went dark and I was in this world of yours." (*Visit*, p.71) A description of the world from which he has come seems to confirm Jacquemort's intratextual provenance. When Wolf slept on the ground with Folle, there was, she assured him, asphodel beneath them ("[...] Près de mon autre main, il y a des asphodèles."[*R*, p.439]); this is how angels sleep: "*We* never double ourselves up. We lie about on the asphodel when we want to rest." (*Visit*, p.33)

Once on Earth, the angel's path is the 'road to humanity: "He had eaten and slept and learnt the lesson of pain - had travelled so far on the road to humanity." (*Visit*, p.110) This is the path which Jacquemort, too, will take; as the wings of Wells' angel recede ("[...] These excrescences of yours don't seem nearly so large as they did yesterday" [*Visit*, p.71]), so Jacquemort's beard continues to grow. Both make trips to a village and a forge, receiving similarly harsh treatment on account of their difference. The result of these trips to the village is the same for both: it is that typically human desire, the desire to inflict pain. Mr Angel says of this feeling: "I am indeed becoming tainted and coloured altogether by the wickedness of this world." (*Visit*, p.92) Jacquemort eventually gives in to his human side: "Il avait encore envie de se battre. Il cogna dans ce qu'il vit. Il cogna et ça le soulageait énormément de cogner sur des adultes." (*R*, p.642)

As has been seen in chapter two, the sacrifice of the maid, Delia, made for the love of Mr Angel, is parallel to that made by Alise. Wells describes how (Alisian) love is natural to the human heart, but that it is suffocated beneath the weight of daily life ('jours'):

> She [Delia] had all that wonderful emotional tenderness, that subtle exquisite desire for self-sacrifice, which exists so inexplicably in a girl's heart, exists it seems only to be presently trampled under foot by the grim and gross humours of daily life... (*Visit*, p.95)

(The other side of maidservants (popular opinion, at least, as to their character), presented in Vian by the behaviour of Culblanc and Nëzrouge, is alluded to by Wells in an ironic apology for Delia; a servant, he admits, ought to behave with: "[...] A cheerful readiness to dispose of [her] self-respect for half-a-crown." [*Visit*, p.96])

The act of giving birth seems to give Clémentine the humanity necessary for successful vengeance. This access to anger is an aspect of 'l'arrache-cœur', the desperation of an angel who gives over to all that is human within him/her. Angel, when pushed too far, strikes Clémentine; Jacquemort learns the joy of inflicting pain; and Clémentine becomes the very symbol of revenge, an avenging angel. So, too, Mr Angel:

> He made one step towards him, with the whip raised, and then something happened that neither he nor the Angel properly understood. The Angel seemed to leap into the air, a pair of grey wings flashed out at the Squire, he saw a face bearing down upon him, full of the wild beauty of passionate anger. (*Visit*, p.111)

This quotation from Wells is particularly expressive of the enigmatic figure that is Clémentine: she is a vision of womanhood, at once beautiful and terrible, and, in as much as she is descended from, or is a reincarnation of Alise, an angel both at the apogee of her powers and the end of her reign. For, *L'Arrache-cœur* is both the end of the novels and the return to the froth.

The final intertext with which this section has to deal is one built entirely around the concept of remembrance. It is a novel similar to *L'Arrache-cœur* not only due to its preoccupation with retrospection, but also due to its evocation of certain of Vian's characters. The text in question is Thomas Wolfe's *Look Homeward, Angel*. Not only does the title bear the name of a character who will appear in Vian's novels on two separate occasions, but the name of the author himself is phonetically identical to that of the hero of *L'Herbe rouge*. First published in the United States in 1929, *Look Homeward, Angel* is a reminiscence, a series of glimpses into a collective past. Its very title reads like a plea for a return to the angelic land (and its author sounds, for all the world, like the hero of *L'Herbe rouge*). In Wolfe's text, the union that is family appears more as a coincidence of solitary lives. Similarly in Vian, the visits of angels into the texts are like prison sentences, periods of solitary exclusion:

> Naked and alone we came into exile. In her dark womb we did not know our mother's face; from the prison of her flesh have we come into the unspeakable and incommunicable prison of this earth. [...] Which of us has not remained forever prisonpent? Which of us is not

forever a stranger and alone? [...] O lost, and by the wind grieved, ghost, come back again.[44]

This poignant passage, when put into the context of Vian's tetralogy, becomes an ode to (an) angel, a voice pulling the characters back across the texts to a common ground. Angels are destined to be peripatetic; whilst both Angel's appearances have symbolised exile and voyage (back) and whilst Wolf ran out of journeys, the final text seemingly draws characters in for the express purpose of sending them home, back to the mother text. In *Look Homeward, Angel*, Eugene's grandfather begins a similar legacy:

> He [Gilbert Gant] left five children, a mortgage and - in his strange dark eyes which now stared bright and open - something that had not died: a passionate and obscure hunger for voyages. (*Wolfe*, p.12)

Moments of rest, alighting in the world/text are marked by the sign of (what one would refer to within the vianesque as) 'l'arrache-cœur'. Thus, Gant is dogged by remembrance of a former wife:

> [...] But sick with fear and loss and penitence, he wilted under the town's reproving stare, becoming convinced, as the flesh wasted on his own gaunt frame, that Cynthia's scourge was doing vengeance now on him. (*Wolfe*, p.13)

In *Look Homeward, Angel* as well as in *L'Arrache-cœur*, birth puts an end to marriage, in the sense that it drives a wall between mother and father. From that moment on they will always be *absent* for each other. Returning drunk, Gant is excluded from the bedroom/delivery-room:

> They heard a chair fall heavily below, his curse; they heard his heavy reeling stride across the dining-room and

---

[44] Thomas Wolfe, *Look Homeward, Angel* (London: Penguin, 1984), p.10. (Hereafter referred to as *Wolfe*.)

up the hall; they heard the sagging creek of the stair-rail as his body swung against it.
"He's coming!" she whispered, "He's coming! Lock the door, son!" (*Wolfe*, p.33-34)

Later he is forcibly ejected from the room in order to prevent him from harming Eliza with a poker which he is drunkenly wielding. The violence, in the comparable scene from *L'Arrache-cœur*, is, from the outset, controlled by Clémentine. Angel may only penetrate her sanctum on her terms:

> - Vous voulez voir votre mari? demanda-t-il [Jacquemort]
> - Oh! oui, répondit-elle. Mais donnez-moi d'abord le revolver... (*R*, p,542)

In the eyes of their sons (Eugene and Citroën) the two mothers see the same destiny. Once again, it is Clémentine who, of the two, acts to curtail the child's need for freedom. Eliza, although torn inside, lets Eugene go:

> Something taut snapped in her: she remembered his furtive backward glance [as he goes to school for the first time], and she wept. And she did not weep for herself, but for him: the hour after his birth she had looked in his dark eyes and had seen something that would brood there eternally, she knew, unfathomable wells of remote and intangible loneliness: she knew that in her dark and sorrowful womb a stranger had come to life, fed by the lost communications of eternity, his own ghost, haunter of his own house, lonely to himself and to the world. (*Wolfe*, p.84)

Here, Clémentine draws the line. With her the loneliness must end.
Eugene embarks, from the moment of his birth, upon a voyage, not of discovery, but of rediscovery:

> He had been sent from one mystery into another: somewhere within or without his consciousness he heard a great bell ringing faintly, as if it sounded undersea, and as

he listened, the ghost of a memory walked through his mind, and for a moment he felt that he had almost recovered what he had lost. (*Wolfe*, p.44)

In *L'Arrache-cœur*, voyages of (re)discovery revert the reader's attention to former texts. Remembrance and return coincide. As Jacquemort steps into the text, the resonance is immediately intratextual. The tide of *L'Écume des jours* is already eroding the bedrock of the text: "Du pied de la falaise s'élevait le bruit doux et rauque des vagues. [...] De l'écume tremblait dans le creux des roches..." (*R*, p.539). To reach the house, he has to cross the limits of *L'Herbe rouge*. All is red ("ròc rouge", "falaise rouge"), and yet he is already separated from that text ("Jacquemort se pencha sur l'étroit rebord qui le séparait du vide [...] s'agenouilla sur l'herbe terreuse...") moving as he is both forwards (to what remains of the tetralogy) and even further backwards (to the mother text itself). He begins to run, pulled by the same force which drew Colin to the ailing Chloé: "Il accéléra l'allure, et se trouva brusquement dans l'ombre car les rayons du soleil ne parvenaient plus à le suivre." (*R*, p.540)

When Jacquemort arrives at the house, both of these former texts are again signalled. When the light is lost, there remains a glimmer of *L'Herbe rouge*: "Dans la chambre, on ne distinguait rien qu'une phosphorescence autour du miroir de la cheminée. [...] Il montait de la fenêtre une odeur d'herbes amères..." (*R*, p.543). The passage back in time is further reinforced, when, as the light returns, it does so in a 'frothy' manner: "Pas un bruit dans la chambre. Sauf, par moments, le clapotis du soleil au bas des rideaux." (*R*, p.547)

The path on which he embarks finally leads Jacquemort to replace La Gloïre. On one level this is a sacrifice as final as death itself. Gray's *Elegy* (as quoted in *Look Homeward, Angel*) describes the terminal nature of sacrifice:

> Await alike th'inevitable hour,
> The paths of glory lead but to the grave. (*Wolfe*, p.70)

The grave for Jacquemort is the collective past. There is a suggestion made by La Gloïre that he has followed a similar path to that of Jacquemort, and that his replacement will permit his return to Alise: "Ma mère n'était pas d'ici." (*R*, p.567) His too, then, is a return to the mother text.

The return accomplished in *L'Arrache-cœur* represents a sort of atonement for a past crime which has cast its shadow over all the tetralogy. In Wolfe's text, too, a mythological sin can have infinite knock-on effects:

> The seed of our destruction will blossom in the desert, the alexin of our cure grows by a mountain rock, and our lives are haunted by a Georgia slattern because a London cut-purse went unhung. (*Wolfe*, p.191)

Clémentine's fears are governed by a sentiment of inherited guilt (like that passed on in *Les Mouches*). She, indeed, fears that the fruits of original sin, which flourished in the Exopotamian desert, will result in an apocalyptic victory of the froth of days: "[...] Et les embruns, sur la falaise, montent, montent, et la terre, comme du sucre, s'amollit sous leur manteau d'écume, et comme du sucre, elle fond, elle fond et s'effondre et coule..." (*R*, p.669). And yet, she represents 'the alexin of [their] cure'. For, in this world where one is gradually 'de-angelised', woman has, through solidarity (beginning, unnoticed, with Alise and then with Lil and Folle), finally reversed the process. Both these concepts (the base contingency of the world and female solidarity within it) are to be found in *Look Homeward, Angel*. Eugene floats, in his daydreams, on the edge of the angelic land, only to be pulled back, down to earth:

> As he entered the office and drank in the warm tides of steel and ink that soaked the air, he awoke suddenly, his light-drugged limbs solidifying with a quick shock, as would some aerial spirit, whose floating body corporealises the instant it touches earth. (*Wolfe*, p.289)

Given the near sibling relationship which exists between Lil and Folle, the moment of intimacy shared by Eliza and her daughter, Helen, on the death of Ben (one of Eugene's brothers), can be compared to the solidarity which spurs on Vian's would-be heroines:

> They thought of sons and lovers: they drew closer in their communion, they drank the cup of their twin slavery as they thought of the Gant men who would always know

> hunger, the strangers on the land, the unknown farers who had lost their way. (*Wolfe*, p.283)

In Wolfe and Vian remembrance is tinged with sadness, since it is in retrospect that one realises what one has lost. For Colin, realisation of his mistake comes too late to alter events. For Eugene, love will come in the form of remembrance:

> He was in the lure of her subtle weariness: she gave him comfort and he never touched her. But he unpacked the burden of his heart, trembling and passionate. She sat beside him and stroked his hand. It seemed to him that he never knew her until he remembered her years later. (*Wolfe*, p.421)

This is not 'la douce souvenance' of Du Maurier's *Peter Ibbetson*; this is bittersweet memory tinged with regret. Angel's inability to love Cuivre, Wolf's failure to love Lil, these are twinges of the collective memory of the tetralogy. But, with the end of *L'Arrache-cœur*, all is returned to the froth. An approaching storm heralds the climax of the Vian novels ("La haute rumeur de la mer mousseuse engourdissait l'oreille. La grêle ne cédait pas." [*R*, p.680]). Clémentine is able to put her struggle into the wider perspective of the weight which Alise has borne over the entire course of the tetralogy:

> - J'ai l'impression d'être tout près du but, dit-elle. C'est extraordinaire. Ça me soûle un peu.
> [...]
> - Si vous avez la patience de supporter cette sujétion...
> - Ça ne sera plus rien, conclut-elle. A côté de ce que j'ai enduré!... (*R*, p.681)

Thus, when Jacquemort walks to the beach to cast a look over the sea which took Angel, he discovers that the froth has already covered his tracks:

> Laissant derrière lui la grille d'or, il descendit le chemin de la falaise et gagna la grève, et les cailloux humides à l'odeur fraîche avec leur frange d'écume fine. (*R*, p.682)

The return is complete.

CONCLUSION

It has been shown, over the course of the eight chapters of this book, that there are many lines of intertextuality coursing through Vian's novels. It has also been shown that these are far from being purely aesthetic in purpose; the 'clins d'œil' of *L'Écume des jours* have been shown to be indicators of potential lines of analysis, providers of meaning rather than simple plays on words. From this first text, Vian's manipulation of genre and increased complexity of intertextual strategy produced in *L'Automne à Pékin* a method of analysing this novel both as an autonomous work and as a continuation of a dynasty rooted in *L'Écume des jours*. From these beginnings, the novels of Vian attain a different level of textual organisation where intertextuality can be used as a key to a variety of readings which enable the reader, not only to understand the veiled layers of meaning, the intertexts forming a continuous meta-language in which the texts can be reread, but to build up an idea of a tetralogy. The concept of the four novels being read as one is, thus, shown to be viable not only due to their common intertextual drive, but also by a system of links which extend between the novels themselves, forming an intratextual pathway. This intratextuality becomes necessarily more prevalent as the volume of preceding material, to which it can refer, grows in size. By *L'Arrache-cœur*, therefore, intratextuality, both as direct textual signposting and through intertexts of retrospection (such as *Look Homeward, Angel* and *La Maison du retour écœurant*), is so dominant that the concept of the tetralogy is no longer reliant on a vague notion of an Alisian mythology dependent on a specific reading of *L'Écume des jours*; the tetralogy reading becomes, rather, an ineluctable response to an accumulation of textual indicators.

The four novels, when read in sequence, do, then, form a cycle. The tetralogy reading finds firm footing in the structures behind the narrative drive of each individual member text. There are, in addition, certain intertexts within which the integrity of the tetralogy can be seen to be preserved. Mac Orlan's *La Maison du Retour écœurant* is therefore an example of an intertext which has influence over each of the constituent Vian novels. Another example of a text which appears to be intertextually linked to the whole of Vian's tetralogy is Marcel Aymé's *Les Jumeaux du Diable*.

The very title of Aymé's novel of 1928 reminds the Vian reader of Clémentine's offspring. For 'jumeaux' one might happily substitute 'trumeaux', and the latter certainly have extra-terrestrial, if not necessarily diabolical, qualities. In *Les Jumeaux du Diable* the two brothers, both called Louis (although one is renamed Norbert at an early stage for the ease of fellow protagonists and reader alike), fall instantly in love with one woman. There is, then, a love triangle, and it is of the same sort as has been seen time and time again within the Vian texts. To continue the links with *L'Arrache-cœur*, Louis is, like Angel, possessor of the beloved; Norbert, like Jacquemort, desires the other's prize. It might be suggested that this is a scenario played out more clearly in *L'Automne à Pékin*. This is indeed true, but what is interesting is the solace which Norbert finds in the arms of a serving wench:

> Renversée sur son bras, tête en arrière, elle riait. Le rire plissait ses joues grasses, son corsage s'ouvrait sur un amas de chair rose et molle de cochon de lait. Elle exhalait une odeur de sueur et d'étable. Mais ça ne lui faisait rien, à Norbert.[45]

The heady equine odour and appearance of Culblanc actually excite Jacquemort, who becomes progressively masochistic throughout the text.

There is also a discreet foretaste of Wolf: Norbert takes up music "Par une habitude de sa vie souvenue d'étudiant" (*Aymé*, p.87). The connotations of this word 'souvenue' are instantly grasped by the reader of Aymé who is fully briefed as to Norbert's past which categorically does not exist. Norbert was 'made man', his past is just a dream (one which he shares with his twin). The implications of Wolf's memories can only be understood when they have been recognised, via analysis of the pertinent intertexts, as fundamentally oneiric.

The birth, as men, of the twins marks both the start of *Les Jumeaux* and the start of Vian's tetralogy. Both stories begin in the water. Colin emerges from a shower, whilst the brothers Louis begin life in the sea: "Maintenus par leurs ceintures de sauvetage, deux hommes flottaient sur l'océan calme qu'éclairaient les premières lueurs de l'aube." (*Aymé*, p.13) In *L'Écume*, Alise

---

[45] Marcel Aymé, *Les Jumeaux du Diable* (Paris: Éditions de la Nouvelle Revue Française, 1928), p.42. (Hereafter referred to as *Aymé*.)

is equally part of this Olympian birth; she, too, is born of the froth. Her equivalent in *Les Jumeaux*, the girl whom Norbert loves but may never possess, is aptly called Marie du Môle. She is born of an act of sacrifice (like that which will mark Alise's exit from the first text, but which will ensure her return); by her prayers and dancing in the midst of a storm, a shipwreck is miraculously avoided: "[...] Sur la pierre glissante du parapet étroit, dans l'écume et dans le vent, je dansai la danse de la mer." (*Aymé*, p.54) And her love for Louis is inspired because he, too, comes from the froth: "Et toi, Louis, je t'aime parce que tu viens de la mer." (*Aymé*, p.55)

The ensuing tug of love is reminiscent, above all, of *L'Automne à Pékin*. The children of the froth are brought into the real world with the same results as in Vian's second novel. Both brothers are, just like Anne and Angel, engineers. Once again there is fusion of the Vian texts within Aymé's own: it is on a train - motif of *L'Automne* - that Norbert discusses his position: "Je suis ingénieur en bâtiments, je dispose d'un capital de deux cent mille francs..." (*Aymé*, p.47). Colin's supply of 'doublezons' is also finite. Both brothers are also, just as Anne and Angel, divided by one woman: "[...] Et la jeune inconnue était entre eux comme un trait d'union." (*Aymé*, p.47) Their destiny is linked ("[...] La destinée de Louis lui semblait contenue dans la sienne propre." [*Aymé*, p.51]), and woman is the centre-piece: whereas Rochelle dreams that two men are fighting over her, it is, in *Les Jumeaux*, Norbert who dreams of such chivalrous pursuits: "Madame, nous sommes pareils, nous n'avons qu'une âme et qu'une image pour les deux. Vous me devez le même intérêt qu'à lui-même. Nous nous battrons..." (*Aymé*, p.51).

In *L'Écume des jours*, Chloé is 'arranged' in such a way as to provide a passive receptacle for Colin's desire to be in love. In *Les Jumeaux*, Marie models her beloved into an object of desire, shaping him to fit her precise requirements. He becomes what she wants him to be: "[...] Une divinité indolente, amoureuse d'aimer et d'accepter, qu'elle réduisait parfois, dans une contraction synthétique de pensée, à un simulacre phallique." (*Aymé*, p.63) Her mistake is to force her love upon him, and he will pay the price. She is also guilty of Clémentine's sin: she makes *him* her world. He becomes the passive waif that she desires: "Lorsque Marie crut soupçonner... que cette pâleur était l'indice d'un mal de poitrine, Louis eut de petits accès de toux... une toux mince qui était pour charmer." (*Aymé*, p.64) But, although this pulmonary infection is feigned, the resulting disease of their loving union is real enough: "Louis est miné par une affection de poitrine dont il est trop facile, hélas! de prévoir le fatal dénouement..." (*Aymé*, p.104). However, their love is saved by a sudden surge in Louis' activity: he shakes off his (signs of) illness in a way which leads the reader of Vian to wonder whether, had Colin seized Alise, letting passion tear through the moral dilemma, all might have turned out differently. His ascent is paralleled, as must always be the case, by a decline in Norbert, who becomes convinced that if he is the same as his brother, and if his brother is terminally ill, then he must be too. Every turn of the narrative pushes towards a climax in which the wills of the two brothers will meet head on.

As in *L'Automne à Pékin*, murder becomes a form of renaissance. Anne died that Angel might live on. Thus, Norbert (whom the reader initially identifies as the 'good' twin) begins to plan his redemption:

> Sans oser se l'avouer formellement, si folle était l'idée, Norbert avait acquis la conviction irraisonnée, physique pour ainsi dire, que la mort de son frère singulier lui restituerait sa vigueur et qu'il entrerait ainsi en possession de tout le bien de vie dont Louis était l'un des tenants. Il était si ferme dans cette superstition que la certitude de renaître en santé eût suffi, le cas tombant que son désir de vengeance se refroidît, à entretenir ses ardeurs meurtrières. (*Aymé*, p.176)

The ending is one of return to the water. It is, thus, akin to the endings of both *L'Automne à Pékin*, as ineluctable dissolution of an impossible situation and liberation of the central character who will continue his flight to the next level of the text, and *L'Arrache-cœur*, as end of the tetralogy and return to the froth. Norbert pushes Louis to his death:

> Les choses se passèrent simplement. Norbert dit: «Je suis ton frère», et poussa Louis dans la mer. Le décor, profil noir des rochers sur la mer unie, avait une certaine importance. (*Aymé*, p.215)

Thus dies Anne. Then it is Marie's turn. She dances her way to death, in a suicide as that of Rochelle, and in a gesture of defiance like Alise's flight from *L'Écume*:

> Marie dansa des pas qu'elle n'avait jamais dansés. Puis elle s'arrêta, face à la mer sans fin. Levée sur la pointe des pieds, les mains jointes au-dessus de la tête, elle s'offrit en ogive sur le ciel. A pas légers, elle glissa sur la roche plate et Marie du Môle descendit dans la mer. (*Aymé*, p.216)

It is his own return to the froth which Norbert does not manage to seal. His own death is more like that of Wolf; he dies alone:

> Norbert fit un bond qui le précipita dans le vide. Des rochers saillants à flanc de falaise l'arrêtèrent au milieu de sa chute et Norbert, les membres brisés, les côtes enfoncées, hurla toute la nuit sa souffrance. [...]
> - Mon frère Louis, laisse-moi vous rejoindre, laisse-moi entrer dans la mer où c'est doux [...]
> Un râle monotone sortait de sa gorge serrée. Sans interrompre sa plainte, il murmurait:
> - Je suis tout seul, je vais mourir tout seul... (*Aymé*, p.216-217)

Quotations such as this show how Aymé's text can be considered as playing host to a fusion of the concepts which will drive Vian's tetralogy, and not least of which are the concepts of the birth in the froth and the return to it. Thus it is, through its rich web of intertextuality, that Vian's tetralogy outlives the tide of days being laid to rest, as it was born, in the froth.

Through texts like *Les Jumeaux du Diable* as well as all those referred to over the course of this book, inter- and intratextuality become intertwined, at times almost indistinguishable from each other. For it is clearly not intratextuality alone in *L'Arrache-cœur* which promotes return; and neither is return merely reflected or paralleled in the nature of such intertexts as *Les Jumeaux du Diable*, *La Maison du retour écœurant* or *Look homeward, Angel*; return is determined in a key intertext broached in the first chapter. It is none other than the story of *La Petite Sirène*, which was seen to be emblematic of the failure of Alise and Colin's love. This tale not only determined that their love should die, thereby focussing the intertextual strategies which served to ensure the victory of days; it also decreed that this victory would be transient, and that Alise would rise again. Like the little mermaid's, however, Alise's victory would have to wait for another place, another time (another text). *La Petite Sirène*, as a text, is interesting in that it represents an example of intertextuality which promotes intratextuality, resulting finally in intertextual confirmation of the tetralogical status of the four novels. This is because Andersen's text lies at the very heart of the mythology which is born in *L'Écume*. Jeanne-Marie Baude alludes to the quasi Olympian feel of *L'Écume des jours*; in "L'Espace vital", she writes: "[Il] [Colin] naît seul dans sa salle de bains, comme Vénus de l'Écume."[46] There is, however, little place for Alise in Baude's mythology. Colin it is who, in her version, is cast out from the kingdom of the gods, the mythological reading depending not on intertextuality, but on socio-economic factors: "Colin chassé du paradis terrestre. Le terme de «paradis terrestre» semble d'autant plus justifié qu'à cette expulsion correspond, comme dans la Genèse, la découverte du travail."[47] To use terminology which has been used in the chapters on *L'Arrache-coeur*, Baude is describing the ascension of days. Such ascension there clearly is; application of an intertextual reading, via Andersen's tale, shows that this ascension of days is at the expense of love. To read Colin as fallen angel and neither to pick up the other examples of angels (or Angels) who have quite literally fallen, nor to decipher the role of Alise as mermaid is to see only half the story. For Baude does accept that Colin's mistake is to marry Chloé:

> Le mythe de Prométhée est donc inversé: fin du règne de la tecknè, triomphe de l'anankè, affaissement de l'homme incapable de ranimer le feu vital. La seule faute de Colin a été de se marier, c'est-à-dire de se rendre dépendant de la durée porteuse de la mort, donc de l'anankè.[48]

---

[46] "L'Espace vital", p.79.

[47] *Ibid.*, p.121.

[48] *Ibid.*, p.123.

It is Alise, with her blaze of golden hair, who represents this "feu vital". And she it is who sacrifices all, just as the little mermaid who forgoes her life in the froth in order to expose herself to oblivion all for the love of a man. Acceptance of Chloé by Colin implies, through the story of the little mermaid, rejection of Alise. Thus, Andersen's tale not only allows the reader to carry out an intertextual analysis of *L'Écume des jours*, disclosing the meaning behind Alise's sacrifice, but it extends forward into further texts giving a mythological framework to which intratextual links may be pinned.

The most animated declaration of Alise's potential as heroine of *L'Écume* is that of Michel Maillard in his article, "Colin et Chick ou la quête impossible":

> Mais presque tous [les lecteurs] ont oublié Alise. La belle, la merveilleuse Alise s'est évanouie comme de la fumée dans les feux qu'elle avait allumés. La meurtrière de Partre est morte sans laisser de traces.[49]

Maillard, despite the vigour of his eulogy, sees no trace of Alise in the novels which follow *L'Écume des jours*. He does see in her blondness, and in the proliferation of textual evidence, such as words of kissing, loving and looking, that she is the true object of (Colin's) love. He also goes on to discuss how the love scenario is always the same in Vian (the male lead desiring the second male's partner), but does not pursue this analysis to its full, intratextual conclusion: the scenario is the same because the people are the same, if present in different bodies.

The key to understanding the primacy of *La Petite Sirène* in the intertextuality reading lies in the fact that the mermaid must fly, becoming other than she has been, until such time as her good deeds, together which her original sacrifice, will have earned her the right to have a soul. Thus Alise flies. Flight is more than just a leitmotiv throughout the tetralogy, it is the very force which drives each narrative and ensures progression from one text to another. Alise's destiny can be traced in the following passage taken from *La Petite Sirène*:

---

[49] Michel Maillard, "Colin et Chick ou la quête impossible", in *Lecture plurielle de 'L'Ecume des jours'*, pp.194-286 (p.195).

> Une sirène n'a pas d'âme immortelle, ne peut jamais en avoir, à moins de gagner l'amour d'un homme. C'est d'une volonté étrangère que dépend son existence éternelle. Les filles de l'air n'ont pas non plus d'âme immortelle, mais elles peuvent, par leurs bonnes actions, s'en créer une. [...] Toi, pauvre petite sirène, tu as de tout cœur cherché le bien comme nous, tu as souffert et supporté de souffrir, tu t'es haussée jusqu'au monde des esprits de l'air, maintenant tu peux toi-même, par tes bonnes actions, te créer une âme immortelle dans trois cents ans. (*Andersen*, p.50-51)

The intertextuality which lies between Andersen's tale and the story of Alise is two-fold: it is a story of love lost, but also a glimpse of a vague and distant redemption. Thus intertextuality it is which pushes us towards a reading of *L'Écume des jours* through *La Petite Sirène*, and which, through the establishment of an Alisian mythology, makes the link with Clémentine's ultimate victory in *L'Arrache-cœur*. The internal keys to this reading are also present in both the first and last texts, and only a close reading of one can allow the other to be understood. The retrospection of *L'Arrache-cœur* picks up the predictions of *L'Écume des jours*. For, as Alise left the froth she was always destined to return; as intertextual being, as mermaid she represents, within the Vian tetralogy, both voyage and return. By applying the Andersen text to that most enigmatic of paragraphs, it can be seen that Alise it is who swims in the foam where the rivers meet the sea:

> A l'endroit où les fleuves se jettent dans la mer, il se forme une barre difficile à franchir, et de grands remous écumeux où dansent les épaves. Entre la nuit du dehors et la lumière de la lampe, les souvenirs refluaient de l'obscurité, se heurtaient à la clarté et, tantôt immergés tantôt apparents, montraient leur ventre blanc et le dos argenté (*Ej*, p.122)

In this paragraph, then, lies the key to not only *L'Écume des jours*, but to the whole tetralogy. In understanding that Alise is a mermaid, the reader understands that the memories are of her, and thus that hers is the "ventre blanc et le dos argenté"; she is the glimmer amid the frothy eddies of the "endroit où". She is an intertextual being, in that she is not only a mermaid, but Andersen's little mermaid; and as such she is a changeling, swimming out of the froth, into the text, and then flying onwards. She is journey and return; this much she hints in her final words to Colin as she sets out on her final journey in her Alisian form: "Peut-être je reviendrai te voir, dit Alise." (*Ej*, p.184) This she will do in another time, another place. Their future meetings will be reserved for other texts. As Alise stands for intertextuality and intratextuality (voyage and return), she represents the evolution of the texts themselves, texts which through their common narrative drive become, ultimately, as one.

BIBLIOGRAPHY

Existing bibliographies of Boris Vian

Caradec, François, "Pour une bibliographie de Boris Vian", *Dossiers Acénonètes du College de 'Pataphysique*, 12 (1960), 111-138

Caradec, François, "Pour une bibliographie de Boris Vian (suite)", *Dossiers Acénonètes du Collège de 'Pataphysique*, 18-19 (1962), 123-127

Caradec, François, "Petite bibliographie portative", *Bizarre*, 39-40 (1966), 187-203

(Documentation section in) Rybalka, Michel, *Boris Vian: essai d'interprétation et de documentation* (Paris: Minard, 1984)

For a listing of works translated by Vian (both with and without the cooperation of Michelle Vian), see Marc Lapprand, "Les Traductions parodiques de Boris Vian", *French Review*, 65 (1992), 537-546

WORKS OF BORIS VIAN

Boris Vian: Romans, nouvelles, œuvres diverses, ed. by Gilbert Pestureau (Paris: Le Livre de Poche, 1993)

L'Écume des jours, ed. by Gilbert Pestureau and Michel Rybalka (Paris: Bourgois, 1994)

Novels signed 'Vian'

Vercoquin et le plancton (Paris: Gallimard, 1946)

L'Écume des jours (Paris: Gallimard, 1947)

L'Automne à Pékin (Paris: Scorpion, 1947)

L'Herbe rouge (Paris: Toutain, 1950)

L'Arrache-cœur (Paris: Vrille, 1953)

Trouble dans les Andains (Paris: La Jeune Parque, 1966)

Novels signed 'Sullivan'

J'irai cracher sur vos tombes (Paris: Scorpion, 1946)

Les morts ont tous la même peau (Paris: Scorpion, 1947)

Et on tuera tous les affreux (Paris: Scorpion, 1948)

Elles se rendent pas compte (Paris: Scorpion, 1950)

Plays and operas

Fiesta (Paris: Heugel, 1958)

Les Bâtisseurs d'empire (*Collège de 'Pataphysique*, 86, 1959)

Théâtre 1: Le Dernier des métiers; L'Équarrissage pour tous; Le Goûter des généraux (Paris: Bourgois, 1971):
    -*L'Équarrissage pour tous* (Paris: Toutain, 1950)

-*Le Dernier des métiers* (Paris: Toutain, 1950)
-*Le Goûter des généraux* (*Collège de 'Pataphysique*, 89, 1962)

Théâtre 2: Tête de méduse; Le Chasseur français; Série blême (Paris: Bourgois, 1971)

Le Chevalier de neige, ed. by Noël Arnaud (Paris: Bourgois, 1974)

Opéras, ed. by Noël Arnaud (Paris: Bourgois, 1982)

Poetry: anthologies

Barnum's Digest (Paris: Aux deux menteurs, 1948)

Cantilènes en gelée (Paris: Rougerie, 1949)

Je voudrais pas crever (Paris: Pauvert, 1962)

Chansons et poèmes (Paris: Tchou, 1967)

Cent sonnets (Paris: Bourgois, 1984)

Nouvelles: collections

Les Fourmis (Paris: Scorpion, 1949)

Les Lurettes fourrées, in *Romans et nouvelles* (Paris: Pauvert, 1962)

"Le Danger des classiques [Nouvelle inédite présentée par François Caradec]", in Noël Arnaud and François Caradec, eds., *Littérature illettrée ou la littérature à la lettre* (Paris: Pauvert, 1964), pp.95-105

Le Loup-garou (Paris: Bourgois, 1970)

Le Ratichon baigneur (Paris: Bourgois,1981)

Screenplays etc.

Zoneilles (*Collège de 'Pataphysique*, 89, 1962)

Petits Spectacles (Paris: Bourgois, 1977)

Marie-toi. Scénarios, tome 1 (Paris: Bourgois, 1989)

Rue des ravissantes. Scénarios, tome 2 (Paris: Bourgois, 1989)

On music

En avant la zizique (Paris: Le Livre Contemporain, 1958)

Chroniques de jazz (Paris: La Jeune Parque, 1967)

Derrière la zizique (Paris: Bourgois, 1976)

Other (Including the articles and letters published by Vian in his lifetime)

Textes et chansons (Paris: Juillard, 1966)

Chroniques du menteur (Paris: Bourgois, 1974)

Manuel de Saint-Germain-des-Près (Paris: Le Chêne, 1974)

Cinéma/Science-Fiction (Paris: Bourgois, 1978)

Traité de civisme (Paris: Bourgois, 1979)

Écrits pornographiques (Paris: Bourgois, 1980)

La Belle Époque (Paris: Bourgois, 1982)

Boris Vian: Chansons, ed., by Georges Unglik (Paris: Bourgois, 1984)

Conte de fées à l'usage des moyennes personnes (Paris: Pauvert, 1997)

In translation

Blues for a Black Cat and Other Stories, ed., and trans. by Julia Older (London: The University of Nebraska Press, 1992)

"Blues for a Black Cat [trans. by Julia Older]", in *New Directions in Prose and Poetry. No.38*, ed. by J. Laughlin with Peter Glassgold and Frederick R. Martin (New York: New Directions Publishing Company, 1978), pp.119-131

Chansons, Satiren und Erzählungen, ed. by Klauss Völker (Berlin: Wagenbach, 1978)

"*L'Écume des jours* [extracts] presented by Graeme Watson", in George Lannois, ed., *Pages Françaises* (London: Pergamon Press, 1969), pp.127-139

Froth on the Daydream, trans. by Stanley Chapman (London: Rapp and Carroll, 1967)

Mood Indigo, trans. by John Sturrock (New York: Grove Press, 1968)

Round about Close to Midnight: The Jazz Writings of Boris Vian, trans. and ed. by Mike Zwerin (London: Quartet, 1988)

Teatro, trans. by Massimo Castri & Maria Grazia Tapognani (Turin: Einaudi, 1978)

Vercoquin e il plancton, trans. by Fabio Ragghianti (Milan: Dall'Oglio, 1980)

Articles by Boris Vian (Published posthumously)

"Pas d'explication", *Avant-Scène*, 406 (1968), 8-9

"Boris Vian: 'Ma Belle Époque'", *Point*, 6 May 1974, pp.156-161, 163, 165-166, 168-169, 171

"Une Lettre inédite à Gaston Gallimard [1er oct. 1946]", *Monde [des Livres]*, 13 August 1976, p.7

"L'Amélioration de Paris", *Obliques*, 8-9 (1976), 296-298

"Barnum's digest. 10 monstres fabriqués par Jean Boullet, traduits de l'américain par Boris Vian", *Obliques*, 8-9 (1976), 45-49

"Brevet d'invention", *Obliques*, 8-9 (1976), 240-241

"Les Confessions du Méchant Monsieur X", *Obliques*, 8-9 (1976), 314

"*Conte de fées*. Deuxième version (inachevée)", *Obliques*, 8-9 (1976), 90-96

"Le Cow-boy de Normandie", *Obliques*, 8-9 (1976), 305-312

"*Les Fillettes de la Reine* (projet d'une suite à *L'Arrache-cœur*)", *Obliques*, 8-9 (1976), 16-18

"Le Goûter des généraux", *Obliques*, 8-9 (1976), 116-118

"Le Jazz est dangereux", *Obliques*, 8-9 (1976), 153

"Lettre à Queneau", *Obliques*, 8-9 (1976), 160-161

"Lettre du major", *Obliques*, 8-9 (1976), 185-187

"Mes Deux points de vue", *Obliques*, 8-9 (1976), 43-44

"Notice biographique", *Obliques*, 8-9 (1976), 299-302

"Panégyrique du savant Cosimus", *Obliques*, 8-9 (1976), 63-64

"Le Poème du major", *Obliques*, 8-9 (1976), 182

"Poésie", *Obliques*, 8-9 (1976), 223-236

"Projet d'une suite au *Conte de fées*", *Obliques*, 8-9 (1976), 105-108

"Qu'est-ce que la 'Pataphysique'?", *Magazine Littéraire*, 320 (1994), 95-104

SECONDARY MATERIAL

Books

Anglard, Véronique, *Vian: Grandes œuvres, commentaires critiques* (Paris: Nathan, 1993)

Ansel, Yves, *'L'Écume des jours' de Boris Vian* (Paris: Pédagogie Moderne, 1979)

Arnaud, Noël, ed., *Boris Vian de A à Z*, [special edition of] *Obliques*, 8-9 (1976)

Arnaud, Noël, *Boris Vian. Présentation et choix [de textes] par Noël Arnaud* (Paris: Horay, 1970)

Arnaud, Noël, ed., *Le Dossier de l'affaire "J'irai cracher sur vos tombes"* (Paris: Bourgois, 1974)

Arnaud, Noël, *Les Vies parallèles de Boris Vian* (Paris: Bourgois, 1981)

Arnaud, Noël; Baudin, Henri, eds., *Boris Vian: Colloque de Cerisy/1* (Paris: U.G.E., 1977)

Arnaud, Noël; Baudin, Henri, eds., *Boris Vian: Colloque de Cerisy/2* (Paris: U.G.E., 1977)

Arnaud, Noël; d'Dée; Kübler, Ursula, *Images de Boris Vian* (Paris: Horay, 1978)

Baudin, Henri, *Boris Vian, humoriste* (Grenoble: Presses Universitaires de Grenoble, 1973)

Baudin, Henri, *La Poursuite de la vie totale* (Paris: Éditions du Centurion, 1966)

Bens, Jacques, *Boris Vian* (Paris: Bordas, 1976)

Birgander, Pia, *Boris Vian romancier: Etude des techniques narratives* (Lund: Gleerup, 1981)

Boggio, Philippe, *Boris Vian* (Paris: Flammarion, 1993)

Buffard-O'Shea, Nicole, *Le Monde de Boris Vian et le grotesque littéraire* (New York: Lang, 1993)

Caradec, François, *Boris Vian en verve*, présentation et choix de François Caradec et de Noël Arnaud (Paris: Horay, 1970)

Cismaru, Alfred, *Boris Vian* (New York: Twayne, 1974)

Clouzet, Jean, *Boris Vian: Une étude de Jean Clouzet. Avec un choix de textes, une bibliographie* (Paris: Seghers, 1971)

Costes, Alain, ed., *Lecture plurielle de 'L'Écume des jours'* (Paris: U.G.E., 1979)

De Vree, Freddy, *Boris Vian, essai* (Paris: Le Terrain Vague, 1965)

Dickhoff, Herbert, *Die Welt des Boris Vian* (Frankfurt: Lang, 1977)

Duchateau, Jacques, *Boris Vian* (Paris: La Table Ronde, 1969)

Duchateau, Jacques, ed., *Boris Vian* (Le Revest-Saint-Martin: Le Jas, 1984)

Emili, Ennio, *Arthur Adamov e Boris Vian* (Umana, 1972)

Fauré, Michel, *Les Vies posthumes de Boris Vian* (Paris: U.G.E., 1975)

Gauthier, Michel, *'L'Écume des jours'. Boris Vian. Analyse critique* (Paris: Hatier, 1973)

Héchiche, Anaïk, *La Violence dans les romans de Boris Vian* (Paris: Publisud, 1986)

Lapprand, Marc, *Boris Vian: La vie contre: Biographie critique* (Ottawa: Les Presses de l'Université d'Ottawa, 1993)

Lapprand, Marc, ed., *Vian, Queneau, Prévert: Trois fous du langage* (Nancy: PU de Nancy, 1993)

Lippi, Furio, *Vian il disertore* (Rome: Stampa Alternativa, 1993)

Meakin, David, *Boris Vian : 'L'Écume des jours'* (Glasgow: University of Glasgow French and German Publications, 1996)

Noakes, David, *Boris Vian* (Paris: Éditions Universitaires, 1964)

Pestureau, Gilbert, *Boris Vian, les Amerlauds et les Godons* (Paris: U.G.E., 1978)

Pestureau, Gilbert, *Dictionnaire des personnages de Vian* (Paris: Bourgois, 1985)

Renaudot, Françoise, *Il était une fois Boris Vian* (Paris: Seghers, 1973)

Roubichou, Gérard, *'L'Écume des jours' de Boris Vian* (Paris: Hachette, 1974)

Rybalka, Michel, *Boris Vian: essai d'interprétation et de documentation* (Paris: Minard, 1984)

Tenot, Frank, *Boris Vian: Le jazz et Saint-Germain* (Paris: Du May, 1993)

Vie et survie de Boris Vian (Paris: Magazine Littéraire [numéro spéciale, no.17], 1968)

Les vies parallèles de Boris Vian. Textes et documents inédits, études et témoignages recueillis et mis en ordre par Noël Arnaud [numéro spécial de *Bizarre*, 39-40] (Paris: Pauvert, 1966)

Völker, Klaus, *Boris Vian: Der Prinz von Saint-Germain: Ein Leser und Bilderbuch* (Berlin: Wagenbach, 1989)

Vree, Freddy, de, *Boris Vian* (Paris: Le Terrain Vague, 1965)

Vree, Freddy, de, *Blues pour Boris Vian* (Anvers: De Tafelronde, 1961)

Westerweller, Ulla, *Surrealistische Elemente in den Romanen von Boris Vian* (Heidelberg: Winter, 1992)

Articles in journals/newspapers

- "A l'Olympia Taverne (T.T.X. 75): Boris Vian chez Coquatrix", *Lettres Françaises*, 1373 (1971), 17

- "A vingt ans Boris Vian", *Nouvel Observateur*, 89 (1966), 29

- "Bibliographie", *Monde [des Livres]*, 20 November 1970, p.21

- "Bibliographie de *Sémantique générale*", *Obliques*, 8-9 (1976), 158

- "Bizarre Boris Vian", *Monde*, 19 March 1966, p.13

- "Boris Vian et Alain Tercinet: *Et on tuera tous les affreux*", *Magazine Littéraire*, 12 (1967), 58

- "Boris Vian: Chroniques du jazz", *Magazine Littéraire*, 12 (1967), 55-56

- "Boris Vian dans le collège de 'Pataphysique", *Dossiers Acénonètes du Collège de 'Pataphysique*, 12 (1960), 3-34

- "Boris Vian pornographe", *Monde*, 30 January 1973, p.13

- "Boris vu par sa bande", *Magazine Littéraire*, 17 (1968), 26-27

- "Le Cinquième anniversaire de la mort de Boris Vian", *Monde*, 17 June 1964, p.14

- "Deft and Dense", *Times Literary Supplement*, 8 January 1971, p.30

- "Le Dossier. Vian et les siens", *Nouvelles Littéraires*, 2544 (1976), 13-16

- "Épiphanies rhinocérotiques et schmürzicales", *Dossiers Acénonètes du Collège de 'Pataphysique*, 13 (1960), 67-70

- "Etude: Le phénomène Boris Vian", *Monde [des Livres]*, 20 November 1970, p.20

- "Hot Pursuit", *Times Literary Supplement*, 8 September 1966, p.798

- "Un inédit de Boris Vian: Petite géographie humaine de Saint-Germain-des-Prés: Quelques autochtones authentiques", *Arts & Loisirs*, 24 (1966), 66-68

- "M. Vian's Generals Fail to Survive Carnage", *The Times*, 12 November 1966, p.13

- "Man from Exopotamia", *Times Literary Supplement*, 5 May 1966, p.386

- "Paris Enjoys Vian's Fun at Generals' Expense", *The Times*, 16 February 1966, p.17

- "Paris met à l'affiche Boris et Ursula Vian", *Paris-Match*, 9 March 1968, pp.94-95

- "Poet pataphysician", *Times Literary Supplement*, 12 March 1971, p.289

- "Poignant", *Times Literary Supplement*, 2 November 1967, p.1029

- "Repères biographiques", *Monde [des Livres]*, 20 November 1970, p.20

- "Rêve, utopie et réalité chez Boris Vian", *French Studies in Southern Africa*, 7 (1978), 68-80

- "Tirages actuels", *Monde [des Livres]*, 25 April 1975, p.21

A., L., "Les anciens combattants contestent Vian à Toulouse", *Monde*, 23 January 1973, p.22

Aboucaya, Jacques, "A propos de *l'Herbe rouge*", *Obliques*, 8-9 (1976), 139-140

Albérès, R.-M., "Voyage littéraire dans un passé ambigu", *Nouvelles Littéraires*, 2449 (1974), 4

Alègre, Jacques, "Boris Vian", *Education Nationale*, 20 October 1966, p.25

Amelung, Anna D., "De la quête du moi à l'univers socialisé: une étude des structures de *L'Arrache-cœur* et des *Bâtisseurs d'empire*", *Chimères*, 11 (1978), 16-25

Ammendola, Rosine, "Boris Vian toujours vivant", *Cri du Monde* (March 1970), 53-57

Andersen, Ida, "En analyse af *Le Déserteur* af Boris Vian", *(Pré)publications*, 71 (1982), 9-22

Andouard, Yvan, "Boris Vian parmi nous", *Canard Enchaîné*, 20 September 1967, p.7

Andouard, Yvan, "Non, non, non, Boris Vian n'est pas mort puisque Prévert scande encore...", *Canard Enchaîné*, 2 March 1966, p.6

Arnaud, Noël, "L'Adolescence", *Bizarre*, 39-40 (1966), 9-11

Arnaud, Noël, "*L'Automne à Pékin*", *Obliques*, 8-9 (1976), 5-7

Arnaud, Noël, "Les Ballets", *Bizarre*, 39-40 (1966), 167-168

Arnaud, Noël, "Bibliographie", *Magazine Littéraire*, 270 (1989), 43-44

Arnaud, Noël, "Boris Vian", *Magazine Littéraire*, 270 (1989), 17-18

Arnaud, Noël, "Boris Vian: *Adolphe* à la modernité", *Obliques*, 8-9 (1976), 143-146

Arnaud, Noël, "Boris Vian, célèbre et méconnu...", *Paris-Théâtre*, 224 (1965), 22-27

Arnaud, Noël, "Boris Vian de A à Z", *Obliques*, 8-9 (1976), 1-2

Arnaud, Noël, "Boris Vian et Vernon Sullivan", *Magazine Littéraire*, 87 (1974), 21-23

Arnaud, Noël, "Boris Vian, la musique et l'opéra", *Magazine Littéraire*, 87 (1974), 16-20

Arnaud, Noël, "Ça c'est un monde", *Obliques*, 8-9 (1976), 244

Arnaud, Noël, "Capbreton", *Bizarre*, 39-40 (1966), 15

Arnaud, Noël, "Les Casseurs de colombes", *Bizarre*, 39-40 (1966), 45-50

Arnaud, Noël, "Les Chansons [avec les souvenirs de Henri Salvador, Jacques Canetti et Alain Gouragues]", *Bizarre*, 39-40 (1966), 153-166

Arnaud, Noël, "Le Chroniqueur", *Bizarre*, 39-40 (1966), 87-92

Arnaud, Noël, "Le Cinéma [déclaration de Pierre Kast avec des textes inédits de Boris Vian]", *Bizarre*, 39-40 (1966), 109-120

Arnaud, Noël, "Le Conférencier", *Bizarre*, 39-40 (1966), 93-94

Arnaud, Noël, "Contre la légende", *Magazine Littéraire*, 17 (1968), 24-25

Arnaud, Noël, "Le Directeur artistique [avec des témoignages de Denis Bourgeois et Jacques Canetti]", *Bizarre*, 39-40 (1966), 173-184

Arnaud, Noël, "Les Divertissements de Ville-d'Avray", *Bizarre*, 39-40 (1966), 23-27

Arnaud, Noël, "L'École Centrale", *Bizarre*, 39-40 (1966), 13-14

Arnaud, Noël, "Un Écrivain qui s'en remet aux mots", *Monde [des Livres]*, 20 November 1970, pp.20-21

Arnaud, Noël, "L'Enfance", *Bizarre*, 39-40 (1966), 5-8

Arnaud, Noël, "Le Figurant", *Bizarre*, 39-40 (1966), 43

Arnaud, Noël, "L'Homme du monde", *Bizarre*, 39-40 (1966), 103-106

Arnaud, Noël, "L'Ingénieur", *Bizarre*, 39-40 (1966), 29-34

Arnaud, Noël, "*J'irai cracher sur vos tombes*", *Bizarre*, 39-40 (1966), 57-66

Arnaud, Noël, "Le Major", *Bizarre*, 39-40 (1966), 17-22

Arnaud, Noël, "La Maladie et le mort", *Bizarre*, 39-40 (1966), 185-186

Arnaud, Noël, "Le Musicien", *Bizarre*, 39-40 (1966), 35-42

Arnaud, Noël, "Note sur *Conte de fées à l'usage des moyennes personnes*", *Obliques*, 8-9 (1976), 86-89

Arnaud, Noël, "L'Opéra", *Bizarre*, 39-40 (1966), 169-172

Arnaud, Noël, "La Passion du cinéma", *Magazine Littéraire*, 270 (1989), 38-39

Arnaud, Noël, "Le Pédagogue", *Bizarre*, 39-40 (1966), 97-102

Arnaud, Noël, "Le Poète", *Bizarre*, 39-40 (1966), 121-125

Arnaud, Noël, "Le Problème du style", *Bizarre*, 39-40 (1966), 95-96

Arnaud, Noël, "Le Romancier", *Bizarre*, 39-40 (1966), 79-81

Arnaud, Noël, "Saint-Germain-des-Prés", *Bizarre*, 39-40 (1966), 51-55

Arnaud, Noël, "Le Traducteur", *Bizarre*, 39-40 (1966), 85

Arnaud, Noël, "Le Traité de civisme", *Bizarre*, 39-40 (1966), 145-151

Arnaud, Noël, "Les Vacances", *Bizarre*, 39-40 (1966), 107

Arnaud, Noël, "Les Variétés amusantes", *Bizarre*, 39-40 (1966), 67-77

Arnaud, Noël, "Vian, côté ombre", *Magazine Littéraire*, 320 (1994), 89-93

Arnaud, Noël, "Les Vies de Vian", *Magazine Littéraire*, 182 (1982), 16-29

Arnaud, Noël, "Les Vies parallèles de Boris Vian", *Bizarre*, 39-40 (1966), 2-3

Arnaud, Noël; Bens, Jacques, "*L'Arrache-cœur* à la scène", *Obliques*, 8-9 (1976), 16-18

B., J., "Du côté de chez Sullivan", *Cahiers du Cinéma*, 192 (1967), 7

B., W.E., "The Individual is Always Right", *New Worlds*, 199 (1970), 30

Báccolo, luigi, "Boris Vian rescoperto", *Mondo*, 16 November 1965, p.9

Balakian, Anna, "Threnody in blue", *Saturday Review*, 28 December 1968, pp.34-38

Baratay, Pierre, "La Mythologie romanesque", *Obliques*, 8-9 (1976), 183-197

Baronian, Jean-Baptiste, "Vianomanie", *Magazine Littéraire*, 270 (1989), 8

Batlay, Jenny, "La Chanson d'Hamour de Boris Vian: La valse dingue", *Obliques*, 8-9 (1976), 319-322

Bauchère, Jacques, "Boris Vian: *Les Bâtisseurs d'empire*, ou l'angoisse à l'état pur", *Confluent*, 8 (1960), 477-478

Baudin, Henri, "Le Double et ses métamorphoses dans les romans de Boris vian", *Bizarre*, 39-40 (1966), 82-84

Baudin, Henri, "Le Double masculin et ses métamorphoses", *Obliques*, 8-9 (1976), 198-200

Bell, Sheila M., "*Boris Vian. Essai d'interprétation et de documentation.* By Michel Rybalka", *French Studies*, 26 (1972), 361-362

Bellosta, Marie-Christine, "Boris Vian, Colloque de Cerisy", *Revue d'Histoire Littéraire de la France*, 80 (1980), 147-149

Bens, Jacques, "Boris Vian p.p.a?", *Magazine Littéraire*, 182 (1982), 39

Bens, Jacques, "Cinq livres pères", *Obliques*, 8-9 (1976), 143-150

Bens, Jacques, "Le Frère jumeau de Boris Vian", *Le Monde [des Livres]*, 24 September 1993, p.35

Bens, Jacques, "Plaidoyer pour les bâtisseurs", *Magazine Littéraire*, 270 (1989), 29-30

Besse, Jean, "Boris Vian au Théâtre Populaire de Lorraine", *Lettres Françaises*, 1182 (1967), 24-25

Billetdoux, François, "Boris Vian et le 'Schmürz'", *Obliques*, 8-9 (1976), 271-275

Billetdoux, François, "Une Variété d'hippocampe", *Nouvel Observateur*, 4 March 1965, pp.20-21

Birgander, Pia, "Un Double univers", *Magazine Littéraire*, 270 (1989), 26-29

Bjürstrom, Carl-Gustav, "Boris Vian traducteur de Strindberg", *Obliques*, 8-9 (1976), 291-294

Borde, Dominique, "Le Souffle de Vian", *Le Figaro*, 24 June 1984, p.30

Bordillon, Henri, "*L'Écume des jours* et son public", *Obliques*, 8-9 (1976), 201-216

Bornu, Jacques, "Les Métamorphoses entre objets et êtres animés", *Obliques*, 8-9 (1976), 201-216

Bost, Jacques-Laurent, "Les Masques de Boris Vian", *Nouvel Observateur*, 16-22 February 1966, pp.32-33

Bott, François, "Un Certain Boris de Ville-d'Avray", *Le Monde [Livres-Idées]*, 18 October 1991, p.18

Boyer, Régis, "Mots et jeux de mots chez Prévert, Queneau, Boris Vian, Ionesco: Essai d'étude méthodique", *Studia neophilologica*, 40 (1968), 317-358

Brincourt, André, "Masque et visage de Boris Vian", *Figaro Littéraire*, 11-12 September 1976, [1] p.11

Broadridge, Judith, "'Travail, famille, patrie' dans *L'Écume des jours* de Boris Vian", *Modern and Contemporary France*, 2 (1994), 291-??

Bruno, Yvette, "Sartre encore et toujours", *Lingue de Monde*, 47 (1982), 250-256

Bryden, Ronald, "Generals at play", *Observer*, 21 August 1966, p.16

Cajoulet-Laganière, Hélène, "Etude de la structure et du contenu de vocabulaire de *L'Automne à Pékin*", *Revue de l'Association Québécoise de Linguistique*, 3 (1984), 105-122

Cantaloube-Perrieu, Lucienne, "Marc Lapprand: *Boris Vian: La vie contre: Biographie critique*", *Littératures*, 29 (1993), 214-215

Caradec, François, "Boris Vian au contraire", *Obliques*, 8-9 (1976), 57-59

Caradec, François, "La Norme Vian", *Dossiers Acénonètes du Collège de 'Pataphysique*, 16 (1961), 53-56

Caradec, François, "Petite bibliographie portative", *Bizarre*, 39-40 (1966), 187-203

Caradec, François, "Pour une bibliographie de Boris Vian", *Dossiers Acénonètes du Collège de 'Pataphysique*, 12 (1960), 111-138

Caradec, François, "Pour une bibliographie de Boris Vian (suite)", *Dossiers Acénonètes du Collège de 'Pataphysique*, 18-19 (1962), 123-127

Castelli, Laurenne, "Planétarium", *Arc*, 90 (1984), 92-97

Cauvin, Claire, "Boris Vian", *Tendances*, 63 (1970), 1-16, 97-112

Chapuis, Bernard, "Boris Vian, l'homme orchestre", *Nouvelles Littéraires*, 2665 (1978), 9

Chauvin, Jacques, "Boris Vian Sketch", *Le Français dans le Monde*, 168 (1982), 87-88

Chavance, Louis, "Boris Vian", *La Rue*, 6 (1969), 39-42

Chénetier, Marc, "Harmoniques sur l'irrespect littéraire: Boris Vian et Richard Brautigan", *Stanford French Review*, 1 (1977), 243-259

Christensen, Bente, "Boris Vian som romanforfatter", *Vinduet*, 32 (1978), 20-27

Christin, Pierre, "Gloire posthume et consommation de masse: Boris Vian dans la société française contemporaine", *Esprit Créateur*, 7 (1967), 135-143

Cismaru, Alfred, "Antimilitarism in Boris Vian's First Play", *South Atlantic Bulletin*, 40 (1975), 24-32

Cismaru, Alfred, "Boris Vian's Reproof of History", *Bulletin of the Rocky Mountains MLA*, 28 (1974), 49-56

Cismaru, Alfred, "Boris Vian's *Vercoquin et le plancton*", *South Central Bulletin*, 34 (1974), 146-149

Cismaru, Alfred, "Boris Vian's Views on Education", *Ball State University Forum*, 18 (1977), 44-50

Cismaru, Alfred, "Boris Vian: The Circle of Exchange and Recognition", *Nimrod*, 19 (1974), 31-41

Cismaru, Alfred, "The Death of Existentialism: Boris Vian's Prediction Materializes a Quarter of a Century Later", *American Society Legion of Honor magazine*, 47 (1976), 9-22

Cismaru, Alfred, "Gilbert Pestureau: *Boris Vian, les Amerlauds et les Godons*", *French Review*, 53 (1980), 621

Cismaru, Alfred, "An Introduction to Boris Vian", *Critique*, 25 (1973), 17-25

Cismaru, Alfred, "An Introduction to Boris Vian", *Critique*, 14 (1972), 17-26

Cismaru, Alfred, "Jean-Paul Sartre: A Belated Obituary", *San Jose Studies*, 7 (1981), 94-99

Cismaru, Alfred, "Two representative short stories of Boris Vian", *French Literature Series*, 2 (1975), 117-126

Cismaru, Alfred, "'Vercoquin et le plancton'", *South Central Bulletin*, 33 (1973), 124

Clouzet, Jean, "Boris Vian et le Jazz", *Cahiers du Jazz*, 14 (1966)

Cocteau, Jean, "Salut à Boris Vian", *Avant-Scène*, 406 (1968), 8

Constantin, Philippe, "Un Chroniqueur au vitriol", *Magazine Littéraire*, 17 (1968), 23

Contat, Michel, "Vian, le jazz et moi", *Arc* (1984), 64-68

Cornu, Daniel, "Boris Vian: 'Laisse-moi courir les rues'", *Journal de Genève*, 20-21 February 1965

Costes, Alain, "Boris Vian: approche psychanalytique de son œuvre et de la 'paralittérature'", *Information Psychiatrique* (1993), 551-560

Costes, Alain, "Pour une esthétique romanesque du contraste", *Obliques*, 8-9 (1976), 53-68

Costes, Alain, "Psychanalyse du Schmürz", *Magazine Littéraire*, 270 (1989), 30-34

Costes, Alain, "Vian et le plaisir du texte: Essai d'une lecture globale de l'œuvre de Boris Vian", *Temps Modernes*, 349-350 (1975), 130-158

Crichfield, Grant, "'La Carte n'est pas le territoire', ou l'espace 'patafantastique' des *Bâtisseurs d'empire* de Boris Vian", *Degré second*, 9 (1985), 43-49

D., L., "Un *Goûter des généraux* trois écrans", *Monde [des Arts et des Spectacles]*, 26 January 1973, p.16

Dadoun, Roger, "Numéro-Jazz pour Homme-Orchestre", *Arc*, 90 (1984), 3-4

D'Alessandro, Maria Grazia, "Pia Birgander: *Boris Vian romancier: Etude des techniques narratives*", *Rivista di Letteratura Moderna e Comparate*, 35 (1982), 84-86

Darnal, Jean-Claude, "Adieu à Boris", *Cahiers des Saisons*, 18 (1959), 324-325

Davies, Russell, "Champion and Scourge", *Times Literary Supplement*, 24 July-4 August 1988, p.829

Décaudin, Michel, "Gilles [sic] Pestureau: *Dictionnaire des personnages de Vian*", *Information Littéraire*, 39 (1987), 134

Degliane-Fouche, Marcel, "Vian sur la ligne Maginot", *Magazine Littéraire*, 182 (1982), 40-41

De Rossitt, James, "Boris Vian: *Blues for a Blood Cat and Other Stories*", *Review of Contemporary Fiction*, 13 (1993), 258-259

Doucelin, Jacques, "Boris Vian à l'opéra", *Le Figaro*, 11 March 1986

Drachline, Pierre, "La Plume fantasque de Boris Vian", *Monde [des livres]*, 18 December 1981, p.24

Dubuis, Catherine, "*Lecture plurielle de 'L'Écume des jours'*, collectif dirigé par Alain Costes", *Etudes de Lettres*, 4 (1980), 67-69

Duchateau, Jacques, "Attention: romans piégés", *Magazine Littéraire*, 182 (1982), 30-32

Duchateau, Jacques, "Petite histoire - portative - du roman français de *La Princesse de Clèves* à Boris Vian", *Arc*, 90 (1984), 7-17

Duchateau, Jacques, "Pierre Kast - Paul Braffort: Dialogue pour servir de Préface", *Arc*, 90 (1984), 5-6

Dulac, Philippe, "Colloque de Cerisy, *Boris Vian*", *Nouvelle Revue Française*, 304 (1978), 118-121

Durozoi, Gérard, "Boris Vian et ses critiques", *Monde*, 3 September 1966, p.9

Durozoi, Gérard; Gauthier, Philippe, "Notes sur *l'Automne à Pékin*", *Obliques*, 8-9 (1976), 5-15

Dutourd, Jean, "Faut-il apprendre à lire dans Boris Vian?", *Paris-Match*, 7 December 1974, p.11

Enard, Jean-Pierre, "La fête à Boris", *Arc*, 90 (1984), 70-72

Ernoult, Claude, "Enfance, irréalité, 'pataphysique dans les œuvres de Vian", *Dossiers Acénonètes du Collège de 'Pataphysique*, 12 (1960), 83-86

Etienne, Luc, "Le Gidouillographe de Boris Vian", *Dossiers Acénonètes du Collège de 'Pataphysique*, 12 (1960), 105-109

Etienne, Luc, "Le Gidouillographe de Boris Vian", *Obliques*, 8-9 (1976), 110-113

Fauré, Michel, "Boris Vian d'aujourd'hui", *Magazine Littéraire*, 87 (1974), 7-10

Fauré, Michel, "Propos sur quelques mises en scène de Boris Vian", *Obliques*, 8-9 (1976), 281-289

Fauré, Michel, "Sa Seconde vie", *Magazine Littéraire*, 182 (1982), 42-44

Fernández Molina, Antonio, "Boris Vian", *Poesía Española*, 184 (1968), 11-14

Fernández Molina, Antonio, "Boris Vian, poesía y furia de vivir", *La Torre*, 64 (1969), 100-108

Ferry, Jean, "Le Pataphysicien", *Bizarre*, 39-40 (1966), 127-134

Ferry, Jean, "Le Théâtre", *Bizarre*, 39-49 (1966), 135-143

Fiorioli, Elena, "Boris Vian, dix ans après", *Culture Française* (January-February 1970), 7-13

Foote, Audrey C., "Pretty Girls and Dixieland: That is All Ye Need to Know", *Chicago Tribune Book World*, 2 March 1969, p.10

Freixas, Ramón, "Una lógica extramuros: *Las Hormigas* de Boris Vian", *Quimera*, 30 (1983), 73

Gabriel, Jacques, "Angels à géométrie variable", *Arc*, 90 (1984), 39-42

Gainsbourg, Serge, "J'ai pris la relève", *Arc*, 90 (1984), 61-63

Galey, Matthieu, "Un Anarchiste sentimental: Boris Vian et sa légende", *Monde [hebdomadaire]*, 16-22 October 1969, p.13

Gaume, Myriam, "Double lecture", *Arc*, 90 (1984), 43-46

Gauvin, Claire, "Vian", *Tendances* (1970), 97-111

Gayot, Paul, "Boris le satrape", *Magazine Littéraire*, 182 (1982), 37-38

Gerrard, Charlotte Frankel, "Anti-Militarism in Vian's Minor Texts", *French Review*, 45 (1972), 1117-1124

Gerrard, Charlotte Frankel, "Satirical Letters by Cyrano de Bergerac and Boris Vian", *Papers on Language and Literature*, 12 (1976), 327-332

Gerrard, Charlotte Frankel, "Vian's Priest as Showman in *Le Dernier des métiers*", *French Review*, 47 (1974), 1123-1127

Giardina, Calogéro, "La Création lexicale dans *L'Écume des jours* de Boris Vian", *Banque des Mots*, 43 (1992), 63-83

Gibson, Anne L., "Boris Vian's *Le Goûter des généraux* or Word Battles in Wonderland", *Modern Languages*, 60 (1979), 203-210

Glende, Anne Margrethe, "Au Pays de Merveilles de Boris Vian", *Narcisse*, 14 (1992), 54-
64

Godard, Colette, "*Les Bâtisseurs d'empire* en Bourgogne", *Monde*, 27 February 1974, p.33

Goimard, Jacques, "Comment on devient un classique", *Monde [des Livres]*, 20 November 1970, pp.20-21

Goldschmidt, Bernard, "Défense de Boris Vian", *Arts & Loisirs*, 29 (1966), 2

González Gómez, Xesús, "Boris Vian: no vinte cabodano da súa morte", *Gnal*, 17 (1979), 471-477

Gouanvic, Jean-Marc, "Vian and SF", *Science Fiction Studies*, 7 (1980), 225

Goulemot, Jean-Marie, "Dans les défilés de l'université", *Arc*, 90 (1984), 76-81

Grainville, Patrick, "Dix livres pour l'an 2000: *L'Écume des jours* de Boris Vian", *Evénement du Jeudi*, 314 (1990), 124-125

Grenier, Roger, "La Revanche de Roger Sullivan", *Nouvel Observateur*, 7 January 1965, p.20

Grojnowski, Daniel, "L'Univers de Boris Vian", *Critique*, 212 (1965), 17-28

Guegan, Gérard, "Tout Minuit jamais n'abolira Boris", *Arc*, 90 (1984), 74

Guerini, Rosalba, "Boris Vian fut toujours futur...", *Culture Française*, 23 (1976), 107-111

Hâa, J., "Quelques éléments pour *L'Herbe rouge*", *Subsidia Pataphysica*, 6 (1968), 95-99

Haenlin, Lydie J., "Les Comparaisons de Boris Vian: Eléments d'une rhétorique de dissuasion", *French Review*, 50 (1976), 278-283

Hahn, Otto, "Boris Vian, cinq ans après: Un inédit de Boris Vian", *Express*, 18 June 1964, p.22

Haineault, Doris-Louise, "Boris Vian: Peintre verbal de *l'Écume des jours*", *Obliques*, 8-9 (1976), 129-135

Hanoteau, Guillaume, "Un Mythe de St. Germain des Prés", *Magazine Littéraire*, 17 (1968), 11-13

Hanrez, Marc, "Les Mini-textes de Boris Vian", *Quinzaine Littéraire*, 368 (1982), 8

Heiney, Donald, "Boris Vian, the Marx Brothers and Jean-Sol Partre", *Books Abroad*, 49 (1975), 66-69

Heist, Walter, "Ein neuer Auftakt? Boris Vian: *Die Gischt der Tage*", *Frankfurter Hefter*, 33 (1978), 66-70

Hope-Wallace, Philip, "The Generals' Tea-Party", *Guardian*, 12 November 1966, p.6

Hope-Wallace, Philip, "Intellectual Grand Guignol", *Manchester Guardian Weekly*, 9 August 1962, p.13

Hurtin, Jean, "'Le Déserteur' à l'Olympia", *Magazine Littéraire*, 17 (1968), 22

Husson, Claudie, "Marc Lapprand: *Boris Vian: La vie contre*", *Revue d'Histoire Littéraire de la France*, 5 (1994), 895

James, Carol P., "Vian, Boris: *Rue des ravissantes et dix-huit autres scénarios cinématographiques*", *French Review*, 65 (1991), 333-334

Jarry, André, "De la Représentation de la mort à la pulsion de mort: *L'Écume des jours* de Boris Vian", *Psychanalyse à l'Université* (juin 1983), 385-406

Jaubert, Jacques, "Un Guide 'rétro' à l'ombre de l'abbaye", *Figaro Littéraire*, 25 May 1974, [4] p.14

Jean-Nesmy, C., "Boris Vian, le révolté [chronique]", *Livres et Lectures* (June 1970), 261-265

Jones, Mervyn, "Exponent of the Absurd", *Tribune*, 26 (1962), 7

Juin, Hubert, "De Ville-d'Avray à la 'pataphysique", *Lettres Françaises*, 1371 (1971), 4-5

Kalck, Philippe, "Boris Vian et le modèle américain", *Silex*, 20 (1981), 7-13

Kast, Pierre, "Notes sur les œuvres de Boris Vian", *Obliques*, 8-9 (1976), 218

Kauffmann, Judith, "*L'Écume des jours*: Un nénuphar et l'amour", *Littératures*, 6 (1982), 83-94

Kay, Penelope, "Letters to the Editor", *New York Times Book Review*, 16 March 1969, pp.22-24

Kemp, John, "Chaos and Confusion", *Literary Review* (January 1989), 10

Klooke, Kurt, "Boris Vian: *L'Herbe rouge*", *Romanische Forschungen*, 94 (1982), 420-432

Knapp, Bettina L., "Boris Vian: *Théâtre inédit*", *French Review*, 45 (1971), 219

Koechlin, Philippe, "Le 'New' deux fois ressucité", *Nouvel Observateur*, 2-8 September 1968, p.35

Kohtes, Michael, "Ein Deserteur des Malheurs. Über Boris Vian (1920-1959)", *Orte-Schweitzer Literaturzeitschrift*, 77 (1991), 46-47

Konopnicki, Guy, "Vian à Douaumont!", *Arc*, 90 (1984), 74-75

Kool-Smit, J.E., "Opineur Boris Vian", *Tirade*, 8 (1964), 500-501

Koster, Serge, "Des Méchancetés à l'oreille", *Arc*, 90 (1984), 73

Kubler, Arnold, "Boris Vian au fil du souvenir", *Dossiers Acénonètes du Collège de 'Pataphysique*, 12 (1960), 91-104

Kubler, Arnold, "Boris Vian au fil du souvenir", *Obliques*, 8-9 (1976), 263-268

L., B., "Surréaliste. Mis en images par Pierre Kast, l'univers fantastique et quotidien, spirituel et amer de Boris Vian", *Le Figaro*, 11 September 1985, p.38

Labarthe, André S., "Boris Vian à cent à l'heure", *Matin de Paris*, 4 March 1977, p.26

Lafontaine, Cécile, "*Boris Vian romancier: Études des techniques narratives*. By Pia Birgander", *Romantic Review*, 75 (1984), 396-398

Laforêt, Guy, "On n'est pas des Schmürz", *Obliques*, 8-9 (1976), 269-277

Laforêt, Guy; Mignien, Alain, "A propos de Boris Vian et de sa *sémantique*", *Obliques*, 8-9 (1976), 156-157

Lambert, J.W., "Vian not Viable", *Sunday Times*, 13 November 1966, p.25

Lapprand, Marc, "Le Discours politique de Boris Vian: Référence et contre-référence", *Australian Journal of French Studies*, 28 (1991), 69-79

Lapprand, Marc, "Le Procès de la psychanalyse", *Magazine Littéraire*, 270 (1989), 22-26

Lapprand, Marc, "Les Traductions parodiques de Boris Vian", *French Review*, 65 (1992), 537-546

Lapprand, Marc, "*Vercoquin et le plancton* comme pré-texte de *L'Écume des jours*: Naissance de l'écrivain Boris Vian", *Texte: Revue de Critique et de Théorie Littéraire*, 7 (1988), 249-266

Latis, "Considérations de 'pataphysique doctrinale à propos de la grande et bonne presse et des *Bâtisseurs d'empire*", *Dossiers Acénonètes du Collège de 'Pataphysique*, 13 (1960), 72-78

Lazar, André, "Du Vianisme oriental", *Obliques*, 8-9 (1976), 220-222

Le Bris, Michel, "En effeuillant le nénuphar", *Nouvel Observateur*, 764 (1979), 64

Le Bris, Michel, "Le Romancier de la mort", *Magazine Littéraire*, 17 (1968), 14-16

Lebrun, Michel, "Mister Sullivan", *Magazine Littéraire*, 182 (1982), 33-34

Le Clec'h, Guy, "Boris Vian est devenu l'écrivain du futur", *Figaro Littéraire*, 17 February 1966, p.8

Le Clec'h, Guy, "Les Vingt-cinq ans de Saint-Germain-des-Prés: Boris Vian", *Figaro Littéraire*, 25 May 1974, [1] p.4

Leegaint, Jean-Pierre, "Un Cadavre", *Arc*, 90 (1984), 89-91

Lefèbvre, Franz, "Boris Vian: Un brise-divan? Ou le thème de la psychanalyse dans L'Arrache-cœur", *Nouvelle Revue Française*, 383 (1984), 64-68

Lemarchand, Jacques, "Un Bon goûter chez Boris Vian", *Figaro Littéraire*, 20 January 1973, pp.13-17

Lemarchand, Jacques, "*L'Equarrissage pour tous*", *Obliques*, 8-9 (1976), 76

Lemarchand, Jacques, "*L'Equarrissage pour tous* de Boris Vian, au théâtre des Hauts-de-Seine", *Figaro Littéraire*, 8 April 1968, pp.35-36

Lemarchand, Jacques, "*Le Goûter des généraux* de Boris Vian à la Gaîté-Montparnasse", *Figaro Littéraire*, 7-13 October 1965, p.14

Lenski, Branko Alan, "Michel Rybalka: *Boris Vian. Essai d'interprétation et de documentation*", *French Review*, 44 (1970), 442-444

Lenski, Branko Alan, "Noakes, David: *Boris Vian*", *French Review*, 39 (1968), 816

Lerner, Michael G., "Boris Vian's *L'Arrache-cœur*: Some Comments on his Style", *Neophilologus*, 57 (1974), 95-98

Leroyer, Patrick; Pontoppidan, Jeanne, "L'Inscription castration; un assemblage des
morceaux; deux lectures", *(Pré)publications*, 51 (1979), 9-21

Loriot, Marie-Christine, "Le Langage de Boris Vian", *Nouvelle Critique*, 175 (1966), 34-41

Loriot, Patrick, "Un Arracheur de Vian", *Nouvel Observateur*, 13-19 August 1973, p.49

M., G., "Joli, joli Vian", *Express*, 20-26 January 1969, pp.52-53

Macaigne, Pierre, "Boris Vian sur la voie royale des classiques", *Figaro*, 12-13 April 1975,
p.26

Mac Orlan, Pierre, "Une préface inédite de Mac Orlan: La petite copine de Boris", *Monde [des Livres]*, 20 November 1970, p.20

Malson, Lucien, "Boris Vian vingt ans après: Les amis veillent", *Monde [Aujourd'hui]*, 24-25 June 1979, p.17

Maillé, Bruno, "*L'Automne à Pékin*: Un roman surréaliste?", *L'Atelier du Roman*, 9 (1996), 115-122

Malson, Lucien, "Les Bonnes idées de Boris Vian", *Monde [des Arts et Spectacles]*, 5 November 1981, p.16

Mangan, Gerald, "Fatalistically Frothy", *Times Literary Supplement*, 17 July 1992

Marcoux, Bondfield, "Boris Vian", *Action Nationale*, 56 (1966), 81-83

Marjoral, Pierre, "De Vernon Sullivan à Chandler", *Magazine Littéraire*, 17 (1968), 20-21

Mathis, Ursula, "*Le Déserteur* von Boris Vian: Eine Fallstudie zum französischen Chanson mit einer musikalischen Analyse von Kurt Neuhauer", *Sprachkunst* (1er semestre 1984), 118-133

Matignon, Renaud, "Le *Chasseur français*: Un coup de Vian", *Figaro*, 2 January 1976, p.11

Matignon, Renaud, "Laissez Boris Vian dormir dans sa tombe", *Arts & Loisirs*, 25 (1966), 8-10

Medici-Skobwell, Henri, "Un Vian(taire)!", *Arc*, 90 (1984), 33-34

Michaelis, Rolf, "Vians Totentanz", *Theater Heute*, 8, 12 (1967), 46-47

Michel, Natacha, "Le Sudiste de *L'arrache-cœur*", *Arc*, 90 (1984), 69-70

Milhaud, Gérard, "A la Recherche de Boris Vian", *Europe*, 604-605 (1979), 199-202

Millar, Ruby, "Death to Jean Pulse Heartre", *Times Literary Supplement*, 13 June 1968, p.612

Murciano, Carlos, "...y sangriento", *Nueva Estafeta*, 17 (1980), 81-82

Nazikian, Paul, "Boris Vian et les jeunes", *Quinzaine Littéraire*, 19 (1967), 12-13

Nores, Dominique, "Boris Vian au Théâtre de Bourgogne", *Quinzaine Littéraire*, 184 (1974), 29

Nores, Dominique, "*Les Bâtisseurs d'empire* par les Tréteaux de Bourgogne", *Les Lettres Françaises*, 1230 (1968), 22

O'Connor, Garry, "Letter from Paris: New Vian in Old Bottles", *Financial Times*, 5 February 1971), p.3

O'Nan, Martha, "Names in Boris Vian's *Les Bâtisseurs d'empire*", *Literary Onomastic Studies*, 7 (1980), 149-159

Ory, Pascal, "Tentative d'explication d'une légende", *Arc*, 90 (1984), 85-88

Ossona de Mendez, Raphaël, "Deux goûters des généraux", *Dossiers Acénonètes du Collège de 'Pataphysique*, 18-19 (1962), 61-64

Pastorello Scarpari, Zilia Mara, "Uma leitura do interdito no maravilhoso de *A Espuma dos dias*", *Revista Letras*, 36 (1987), 180-191

Pérez Minik, Domingo, "*La Hierba roja* de Boris Vian", *Insula*, 35 (1980), 46-54

Pestureau, Gilbert, "Boris Vian, témoin anarchiste de la Libération", *French Cultural Studies*, 5 (1994), 293-300

Pestureau, Gilbert, "Souvenirs de lectures anglo-saxonnes", *Obliques*, 8-9 (1976), 165-280

Phelps, Robert, "Mood Indigo", *New York Times Book Review*, 26 January 1969, p.5

Philidor, "Boris Vian au temps de la tompette", *Monde [des Livres]*, 27 September 1967, p.2

Pia, Pascal, "Un Univers en expansion", *Dossiers Acénonètes du Collège de 'Pataphysique*, 12 (1960), 77-82

Picard, Michel, "Michel Rybalka: *Boris Vian. Essai d'interprétation et de documentation*", *Revue d'Histoire Littéraire de la France*, 71e année (1971), 138-139

Pinkernell, Gert, "Boris Vians Tragigroteske *Les Bâtisseurs d'empire* als Chronik der Ära Mollet (1956/57)", *Romanistische Zeitschrift für Literaturgeschichte / Cahiers d'Histoire des Littératures Romanes*, 8 (1984), 448-472

Poehr, V., "*L'Arrache-cœur* de Vian", *Recherches sur l'Imaginaire*, 13 (1985), 225-244

Poirot-Delpech, Bertrand, "*Les Bâtisseurs d'empire* de Boris Vian", *Monde*, 20 May 1967, p.12

Poirot-Delpech, Bertrand, "Comment l'esprit vient à un quartier: *Manuel de Saint-Germain-des-Prés* de Boris Vian", *Monde [des Livres]*, 12 July 1974, p.11

"Comment l'esprit vient à un quartier: *Manuel de Saint-Germain-des-Prés* de Boris Vian", *Monde [hebdomadaire]*, 18-24 July 1974, p.20

Pos, Sonja, "De late roem van Boris Vian", *Litterair Paspoort*, 203 (1967), 25-29

Pouilliart, Raymond, "Michel Rybalka: *Boris Vian. Essai d'interprétation et de documentation*", *Lettres Romanes*, 25 (1971), 83-85

Poulet, Robert, "Boris Vian, classique involontaire", *Spectacle du Monde*, 158 (1975), 93-98

Prévert, Jacques, "Lettre à Boris Vian", *Dossiers Acénonètes du Collège de 'Pataphysique*, 12 (1960), 72-74

Price, R.G.G., "New Fiction", *Punch*, 1 November 1967, p.680

Provence, Myriam, "Ascendance Boris Vian: Sans tabou ni trompette", *Généalogie Magazine*, 92 (1991), 32-36

Quatrezoneilles, "*L'Equarrissage pour tous*: Une rencontre avec Boris Vian", *Dossiers Acénonètes du Collège de 'Pataphysique*, 12 (1960), 87-90

Queneau, Raymond, "Boris Vian satrape mutant", *Dossiers Acénonètes du Collège de 'Pataphysique*, 12 (1960), 75-76

Queneau, Raymond, "Lettre à Boris Vian", *Obliques*, 8-9 (1976), 238

Rabourdin, Dominique, "En avant la zizique...", *Magazine Littéraire*, 182 (1982), 35-37

Rameil, Claude J., "Bibliographie", *Obliques*, 8-9 (1976), 22-43

Renaud-Chamska, Isabelle, "La Musique dans *L'Ecume des jours*", *Ecole des Lettres II*, 82 (1990), 11-20

Revol Cappelletti, Mireille, "Titoli e paratitoli nei romanzi di Boris Vian", *Micromégas* (1989), 141-150

Revol Cappelletti, Mireille, "Usure, vide, vent, etc.... Finir à la Boris Vian", *French Cultural Studies*, 5 (1994), 287-311

Rey, Henri-François, "Jules Bounot, Boris Vian et moi", *Magazine Littéraire*, 87 (1974), 14-15

Reynaert, François, "Les Vies retrouvées de Boris Vian", *Le Nouvel Observateur*, 30 September-6 October 1993, pp.54-55

Richard, Lionel, "Vian était-il Kafkaïen?", *Arc*, 90 (1984), 26-28

Rinaldi, Angelo, "Boris Vian: Feuilles mortes", *Express*, 19-25 August 1974, p.14

Roberts, Carolyn, "Boris Vian and the Libretto", *Comparison*, 5 (1977), 92-125

Rodríguez Rochette, Virginia, "La traducción de los neologismos en *L'Arrache-cœur* de Boris Vian", *Actas del I Coloquio International de Traductología (Valencia)* (1991), pp.181-182

Romi, Yvette, "Le Pianocktail sur le plateau", *Nouvel Observateur*, 3-10 May 1967, p.28

Rosine, Josiane, "Écumes du refoulé", *Arc*, 90 (1984), 35-38

Roskoff, Liliane, "La Drôle de tragédie: Boris Vian romancier", *Revue de Belles-Lettres*, 95e année (1971), 62-67

Roubichou, Gérard, "*L'Écume des jours*: La mort et la souris", *Enseignement du Français aux Étrangers*, 214 (1974), 2

Russo, M.T., "Per une rilettura di Boris Vian", *Quaderno*, 25 (1988), 55-71

Rybalka, Michel, "A Cerisy, la qualité Vian", *Monde [des Livres]*, 13 August 1976, p.7

Rybalka, Michel, "Baudin, Henri: *La poursuite de la vie totale*; Clouzet, Jean: *Boris Vian. Etude, choix de textes et bibliographie*", *French Review*, 41 (1967), 165-166

Rybalka, Michel, "Boris Vian: Le double et l'homme sans visage", *Temps Modernes*, 260 (1968), 1277-1290

Rybalka, Michel, "Boris Vian et le monde sensible", *French Review*, 41 (1968), 669-674

Rybalka, Michel, "Letters to the editor", *New York Times Book Review*, 16 March, 1969, p.24

Rybalka, Michel, "Le Phénomène Boris Vian", *Monde [des Livres]*, 25 April 1975, p.21

Rybalka, Michel, "Plaidoyer pour Vernon Sullivan", *Monde [des Livres]*, 20 November 1970, p.20

Rybalka, Michel, "Regards obliques sur Boris", *Monde [des Livres]*, 13 August 1976, p.7

Rybalka, Michel, "Vers une méta-méga-bibliographie de Boris Vian", *Subsidia Pataphysica*, 6 (1968), 81-94

Sarraute, Claude, "Au Théâtre de Plaisance: Boris Vian", *Monde*, 18 October 1967, p.14

Sénart, Philippe, "La Revue théâtrale", *Nouvelle Revue des Deux Mondes*, 5 (1982), 444-452

Shorley, Christopher, "*Boris Vian: 'L'Écume des jours'*. By David Meakin", *French Studies*, 52 (1998), 113-114

Shorley, Christopher, "*Boris Vian romancier: Etude des techniques narratives*. By Pia Birgander", *French Studies*, 38 (1984), 99

Shorter, Eric, "French Establishment as Butt of Satire", *Daily Telegraph*, 18 August 1966, p.17

Siclier, Jacques, "*Écume des jours*, Salle Favart: Au temps de 'Jean-Sol Partre'", *Le Monde*, 19 March 1986, p.18

Simmonet, Dominique, "L'Écume d'une vie", *L'Express*, 11 November 1993, p.63

Simsolo, Noël, "Dé«polar»isation", *Arc*, 90 (1984), 52-55

Simsolo, Noël, "Musique et chansons", *Magazine Littéraire*, 270 (1989), 40-43

Slonim, Marc, "Boris Vian", *New York Times Book Review*, 12 March 1967, p.22

Smith, Viviane, "La Musique et *L'Écume des jours*", *Australian Journal of French Studies*, 19 (1982), 204-222

Sobrero, Ornella, "Boris Vian 'sterpacuore'", *Fiera Letteraria*, 40, 46 (1965), 5

Starre, E. van der, "Boris Vian en de muzick", *Rapports - Het Franse Boek*, 3 (1974), 65-79

Stivale, Charles, "Desire, Duplicity and Narratology: Boris Vian's *L'Écume des jours*", *Studies in Twentieth Century Literature*, 17 (1993), 325-348

Stivale, Charles, "Of *Schmürz* and men: Boris Vian's *Les Bâtisseurs d'empire*", *Cincinnati Romance Review*, 7 (1988), 97-112

Sucarrat, Francine, "Clémentine, qu'est-ce que c'est? Possibilités sémiotiques du personnage de *L'Arrache-cœur* de Boris Vian", *Information Littéraire*, 4 (1993), 10-23

Sucarrat, Francine, "Rabelais dans les romans de Boris Vian: Quelques aspects sémantiques de l'intertexte", *Cuadernos de Filología Francesa*, 6 (1992), 171-187

Suñen, Luis, "Narrativa", *Estafeta Literaria*, 556 (1975)

Surugue, Daniel, "*Tête de méduse* de Boris Vian", *Avant-Scène Théâtre*, 640 (1978), 43-45

Tercenet, Alain; Romer, Jean-Claude, "Boris Vian et le cinéma", *Obliques*, 8-9 (1976), 69-79

Toledano, Francisco, "Novelista de fuera", *La Estafeta Literaria*, 425 (1969), 24

Trewin, J.C., "Making it up", *Illustrated London News*, 11 August 1962, p.226

Trewin, J.C., "Theatre", *Illustrated London News*, 19 November 1966, p.37

Trystram, Florence, "Un Sens aigu de la liberté", *Arc*, 90 (1984), 82-84

Tufveskeg, Kettil, "Suède, Finlande, Belgique célèbrent *Les Bâtisseurs d'empire*", *Dossiers Acénonètes du Collège de 'Pataphysique*, 13 (1960), 70-71

Unglik, George, "Discographie", *Obliques*, 8-9 (1976), 22-42

Unglik, George, "Yvette et autres chansons: Nomenclature des chansons de Boris Vian", *Obliques*, 8-9 (1976), 315-318

Vaquin, Agnès, "Boris Vian et Samuel Beckett", *Arc*, 90 (1984), 18-25

Vasseur, Nadine, "Jusqu'où va la zizique à Vian", *Arc*, 90 (1984), 56-60

Vaugeois, Gérard, "La passion du cinéma", *Arc*, 90 (1984), 47-51

Varenne, François, "V... comme Vian", *Figaro*, 14 March 1975, p.29

Venault, Philippe, "Un Théâtre profanatoire", *Magazine Littéraire*, 17 (1968), 17-19

Vermeulen, Jan, "Boris Vian: *Textes et chansons*", *Litterair Paspoort*, 204 (1967), 65

Vivier, Annick, "Du Bon usage au calembour", *Magazine Littéraire*, 270 (1989), 34-38

Vree, Freddy de, "Boris Vian", *Puits de l'Ermite*, 4 (1965), 4-5

Walters, Jennifer, "Death and Boris Vian", *Papers on Language and Literature*, 8 (1972), 97-101

Walters, Jennifer, "The Disquieting Worlds of Lewis Carroll and Boris Vian", *Revue de Littérature Comparée*, 182 (1972), 284-294

Weightman, John, "Two Cult-Figures from France", *Observer*, 5 November 1967, p.27

Westerweller, Ulla, "Surréaliste dans l'anticléricalisme", *Magazine Littéraire*, 270 (1989), 19-22

Whale, D.F., "A la Recherche de Boris", *Guardian*, 30 May 1988, p.10

Whitley, John, "Tea-Time with the Particular", *Sunday Times*, 12 November 1967, p.56

Wolfromm, Jean-Didier, "Mort trop tôt dans un monde trop vieux", *Magazine Littéraire*, 17 (1968), 8-10

Yaguello, Marina, "Linguiste malgré lui?", *Arc*, 90 (1984), 29-32

Zampa, Sergio M., "*L'Écume des jours* di Boris Vian: favola o incubo", *Quaderni di Filologia e Lingue Romanze*, 4 (1982), 129-144

Zappalà-Rivoire, Marguerite, "L'Actualité de Boris Vian", *Culture Française*, 23 (1976), 220-227

Zappalà-Rivoire, Marguerite, "Les Préoccupations métalinguistiques et métasémiotiques de Vian", *Culture Française*, 26 (1979), vol.1, 13-19; vol.2, 48-53

Ziel, Bernard, "L'Interférence des règnes animal, végétal et humain (Les associations impossibles)", *Obliques*, 8-9 (1976), 201-207

Zimmerman, Paul D., "Beauty under Size", *Newsweek*, 72 (1968), 56

Zoppi, Sergio, "Vian, la poesia dello sberleffo", *Tuttolibri*, 36 (1976), 9

Articles/chapters in books

- "Envoi: vers d'autres lectures de *L'Écume des jours*", in Alain Costes, ed., *Lecture plurielle de 'L'Écume des jours'* (Paris: U.G.E., 1979), pp.455-458

- "Vian", in Peter Schofer, Donald Rice and William Berg, eds., *Poèmes, pièces, prose: Introduction à l'analyse des textes littéraires français* (New York: Oxford University Press, 1973), pp.441-487

Adler, Marie-Hélène, "Espace, existence et satire dans *L'Arrache-cœur*", in Marc Lapprand, ed., *Vian. Trois fous. Queneau. Du langage. Prévert* (Nancy: Presses Universitaires de Nancy, 1993), pp.73-80

Andrevon, Jean-Pierre, "Boris Vian, Salut!", in *Passions d'auteurs* (Paris: Presses de la Renaissance, 1986), pp.77-79

"Aux miroirs de Vian", in Jacques Duchateau, ed., *Boris Vian* (Le Revest-Saint-Martin: Le Jas, 1984), pp.69-75

Baude, Jeanne-Marie, "De la vraisemblance dans l'œuvre de Boris Vian", in *Le génie de la forme: Mélanges de langues et littérature offerts à Jean Mourot* (Nancy: Presses Universitaires de Nancy, 1982), pp.633-643

Baude, Jeanne-Marie, "L'espace vital", in Alain Costes, ed., *Lecture plurielle de 'L'Écume des jours'* (Paris: U.G.E., 1979), pp.70-124

Baude, Jeanne-Marie, "Histoire du texte de Jeanne-Marie Baude", in Alain Costes, ed., *Lecture plurielle de 'L'Écume des jours'* (Paris: U.G.E., 1979), pp.438-440

Baude, Jeanne-Marie (et al.), "Consonances et dissonances du discours critique I. Questions de méthodologie critique", in Alain Costes, ed., *Lecture plurielle de 'L'Écume des jours* (Paris: U.G.E., 1979), pp.360-377

Baude, Jeanne-Marie (et al.), "Consonances et dissonances du discours critique II. Problèmes d'interprétation", in Alain Costes, ed., *Lecture plurielle de 'L'Écume des jours'* (Paris: U.G.E., 1979), pp.378-400

Baude, Jeanne-Marie (et al.), "Consonances et dissonances du discours critique III. Problèmes de lisibilité", in Alain Costes, ed., *Lecture plurielle de 'L'Écume des jours* (Paris: U.G.E., 1979), pp.401-407

Blondin, Antoine, "Boris Vian fait l'inventaire de Saint-Germain-des-Prés", in Antoine Blondin, *Ma vie entre les lignes* (Paris: Gallimard, 1984), pp.420-424

Bonaldi, Jacques-François, "L'Échec de Boris Vian", in *Vingt ans d'action littéraire. Les meilleures pages des 'Cahiers des Jeunesses littéraires de France'* (Paris: Le Cercle d'Or, 1976), pp.96-99

Bruézière, Maurice, "L'Existentialisme et ses séquelles: Boris Vian", in Maurice Bruézière, *Histoire de la littérature contemporaine. Tome II* (Paris: Berger-Levrault, 1976), pp.244-249

Buffard-O'Shea, Nicole, "Convergence textuelle chez Vian et Queneau", in Marc Lapprand, ed., *Vian. Trois fous. Queneau. Du langage. Prévert* (Nancy: Presses Universitaires de Nancy, 1993), pp.37-42

Calonnec, Geneviève, "Une Lecture de *L'Écume des jours* de Boris Vian", in *Mythe-rite-symbole: 22 essais littéraires. Recherches sur l'imaginaire. Cahier XIII* (Angers: Université d'Angers, U.E.R. des Lettres et des Sciences humaines, 1985)

Campbell, James, "We Will Spit on Boris Vian", in James Campbell, *Paris Interzone. Richard Wright, Lolita, Boris Vian and others on the Left Bank 1946-1960* (London: Seker & Warburg, 1994), pp.91-94

Canetti, Jacques, "Boris Vian", in Jacques Canetti, *On cherche jeune homme aimant la musique* (Paris: Calmann-Lévy, 1978)

Cantaloube-Ferrieu, Lucienne, "Boris Vian", in Lucienne Cantaloube-Ferrieu, *Chanson et poésie des années 30 aux années 60: Trenet, Brassens, Ferré... ou les "enfants naturels" du surréalisme* (Paris: Nizet, 1981), pp.492-531

Castelli, Laurence, "Planétarium", in Jacques Duchateau, ed., *Boris Vian* (Le Revest-Saint-Martin: Le Jas, 1984), pp.92-97

Cau, Jean, "Boris Vian", in Jean Cau, *Croquis de mémoire* (Paris: Juillard, 1985), pp.47-50

Cohn, Ruby, "*The Knacker's ABC (L'Equarrissage pour tous)*, Boris Vian", in Ruby Cohn, *From 'Desire' To Godot: Pocket Theater of Post-War Paris* (Los Angeles; London: University of California Press, 1987), pp.79-88

Contat, Michel, "Vian, le jazz et moi", in Jacques Duchateau, ed., *Boris Vian* (Le Revest-Saint-Martin: Le Jas, 1984), pp.64-68

Costes, Alain, "Approche psychanalytique de l'œuvre de Boris Vian et la 'paralittérature'", in Marc Lapprand, ed., *Vian. Trois fous. Queneau. Du langage. Prévert* (Nancy: Presses Universitaires de Nancy, 1993), pp.229-243

Costes, Alain, "L'Écume du corps", in Alain Costes, ed., *Lecture plurielle de 'L'Écume des jours'* (Paris: U.G.E., 1979), pp.127-163

Costes, Alain, "Histoire du texte d'Alain Costes", in Alain Costes, ed., *Lecture plurielle de 'L'Écume des jours'* (Paris: U.G.E., 1979), pp.441-443

Costes, Alain, "Les Notes préparatoires à *L'Écume des jours*", in Alain Costes, ed., *Lecture plurielle de 'L'Écume des jours'* (Paris: U.G.E., 1979), pp.9-26

Dadoun, Roger, "Numéro - Jazz pour homme - orchestre", in Jacques Duchateau, ed., *Boris Vian* (Le Revest-Saint-Martin: Le Jas, 1984), pp.3-4

De Hoest, Henriette, "Univers et langage dans *L'Écume des jours* de Boris Vian", in *Analyses de textes* (Groningen: Institut voor Romanse Talen, 1982), pp.41-60

Duchateau, Jacques, "Petite histoire portative du roman français de *La Princesse de Clèves* à Boris Vian", in Jacques Duchateau, ed., *Boris Vian* (Le Revest-Saint-Martin: Le Jas, 1984), pp.7-17

Duchateau, Jacques, "Pierre Kast - Paul Braffort: Dialogue pour servir de préface", in Jacques Duchateau, ed., *Boris Vian* (Le Revest-Saint-Martin: Le Jas, 1984), pp.5-6

Dumur, Guy, "Un Boris Vian ça trompe", in Gilbert Ganne, *Interviews impubliables* (Paris: Plon, 1965), pp.79-85

Dutourd, Jean, "*Le Goûter des généraux* (Gaîté-Montparnasse)", in Jean Dutourd, *Le Paradoxe du critique suivi de sept saisons. Impressions de théâtre* (Paris: Flammarion, 1972), pp.150-151

Essif, Les, "L'espace surréaliste et la mort hypersubjective dans *Les Bâtisseurs d'empire*", in Marc Lapprand, ed., *Vian. Trois fous. Queneau. Du langage. Prévert* (Nancy: Presses Universitaires de Nancy, 1993), pp.83-87

Gabriel, Jacques, "Angels à géométrie variable", in Jacques Duchateau, ed., *Boris Vian* (Le Revest-Saint-Martin: Le Jas, 1984), pp.39-42

Gainsbourg, Serge, "J'ai pris le relève", in Jacques Duchateau, ed., *Boris Vian* (Le Revest-Saint-Martin: Le Jas, 1984), pp.61-63

Gaume, Myriam, "Double lecture", in Jacques Duchateau, ed., *Boris Vian* (Le Revest-Saint-Martin: Le Jas, 1984), pp.43-46

Gobin, Pierre, "Vian ou l'invention d'une dramaturgie autre: La subversion des catégories d'Aristote", in Marc Lapprand, ed., *Vian. Trois fous. Queneau. Du langage. Prévert* (Nancy: Presses Universitaires de Nancy, 1993), pp.55-66

Goulemot, Jean-Marie, "Dans les défilés de l'Université", in Jacques Duchateau, ed., *Boris Vian* (Le Revest-Saint-Martin: Le Jas, 1984), pp.76-81

Haineault, Doris-Louise, "Auto-critique de la critique", in Alain Costes, ed., *Lecture plurielle de 'L'Écume des jours'* (Paris: U.G.E., 1979), pp.412-435

Haineault, Doris-Louise, "L'écume, complicités", in Alain Costes, ed., *Lecture plurielle de 'L'Écume des jours'* (Paris: U.G.E., 1979), pp.165-192

Jay, Salim, "Les Cocktails Gallimard", in Salim Jay, *Les Écrivains sont dans leur assiette* (Paris: Éditions du Seuil, 1991), p.150

Jeandillou, Jean-François, "Vernon Sullivan", in Jean-François Jeandillou, ed., *Supercheries littéraires: La vie et l'œuvre des auteurs supposés* (Paris: Usher, 1989), pp.353-369

Kolstrup, Søren, "Boris Vian", in Hans Boll Johansen, ed., *Den moderne roman i Frankrig* (Copenhagen: Akademisk Forlag, 1970), pp.52-60

Lapprand, Marc, "Boris Vian: Le manipulateur manipulé", in Marc Lapprand, ed., *Vian. Trois fous. Queneau. Du langage. Prévert* (Nancy: Presses Universitaires de Nancy, 1993), pp.45-53

Lee, Yoon Kyung, "Une lecture de *L'Écume des jours* de Boris Vian", in George Cesbron, ed., *Mythe-rite-symbole: vingt essais littéraires sur des textes du romantisme angevin au XIXe siècle* (Angers: Université d'Angers, U.E.R. des Lettres et Sciences humaines, 1986), pp.186-192

Leegaint, Jean-Pierre, "Un cadavre", in Jacques Duchateau, ed., *Boris Vian* (Le Revest-Saint-Martin: Le Jas, 1984), pp.89-91

Lope, Hans-Joachim, "Pia Birgander: *Boris Vian romancier: Étude des techniques narratives*", in *Romanistisches Jahrbuch XXXIII* (Berlin; New York: de Gruyter, 1983), pp.260-262

Maillard, Michel, "Colin et Chick ou la quête impossible: Lecture sémio-critique de *L'Écume des jours*", in Alain Costes, ed., *Lecture plurielle de 'L'Écume des jours'* (Paris: U.G.E., 1979), pp.194-286

Maillard, Michel, "Histoire du texte de Michel Maillard: De la réaction subjective à l'analyse sémio-critique", in Alain Costes, ed., *Lecture plurielle de 'L'Écume des jours'* (Paris: U.G.E., 1979), pp.444-448

Medici-Skobwell, Henri, "Un Vian(taire!)", in Jacques Duchateau, ed., *Boris Vian* (Le Revest-Saint-Martin: Le Jas, 1984), pp.33-34

Nicod-Saraiva, Marguerite, "Histoire du texte de Marguerite Nicod-Saraiva", in Alain Costes, ed., *Lecture plurielle de 'L'Écume des jours'* (Paris: U.G.E., 1979), pp.435-438

Nicod-Saraiva, Marguerite, "L'univers de *L'Écume des jours*", in Alain Costes, ed., *Lecture plurielle de 'L'Écume des jours'* (Paris: U.G.E., 1979), pp.67-69

Older, Julia, "Introducing Boris Vian", in Boris Vian, *Blues for a Black Cat and Other Stories*, ed. and trans. by Julia Older (London: The University of Nebraska Press, 1992), pp.ix-xxiv

Oriol-Boyer, Claudette, "L'Écho-nomie dans *L'Écume des jours*: Pour une lecture socio-critique", in Alain Costes, ed., *Lecture plurielle de 'L'Écume des jours'* (Paris: U.G.E., 1979), pp.287-354

Oriol-Boyer, Claudette, "(Une) histoire du texte de Claudette Oriol-Boyer", in Alain Costes, ed., *Lecture plurielle de 'L'Écume des jours'* (Paris: U.G.E., 1979), pp.448-454

Ory, Pascal, "Tentative d'explication d'une légende", in Jacques Duchateau, ed., *Boris Vian* (Le Revest-Saint-Martin: Le Jas, 1984), pp.85-88

Pautrot, Jean-Louis, "Boris Vian et la musique", in *Bulletin 1988-1989. Société des Professeurs Français en Amérique* (New York: Société des Professeurs Français en Amérique, 1989), pp.141-159

Pautrot, Jean-Louis, "Vian et la Musique mystification", in Jean-Louis Pautrot, *La musique oubliée: La Nausée, L'Écume des jours, A la recherche du temps perdu, Moderato cantabile* (Geneva: Libr. Droz, 1994), pp.79-128

Pestureau, Gilbert, "Boris Vian, un enfant - irrespectueux - du capitaine Verne?", in *Cahiers du Centre d'Études Verniennes et du Musée Jules Verne. No.6* (Nantes: Cahiers du Centre d'Études Verniennes et du Musée Jules Verne, 1986), pp.3-9

Poehr, Véronique, "*L'Arrache-cœur* de Boris Vian", in *Mythe-rite-symbole: 22 essais littéraires. Recherches sur l'imaginaire. Cahier XIII* (Anger: Université d'Angers, U.E.R. des Lettres et des Sciences humaines, 1985), pp.225-244

Poirot-Delpech, Bertrand, "*Les Bâtisseurs d'empire* de Boris Vian", in Bertrand Poirot-Delpech, *Au soir le soir: Théâtre 1960-1970* (Paris: Mercure de France, 1969), pp.33-35

Revol Cappelletti, Mireille, "Titoli e paratitoli nei romanzi di Boris Vian", in *Il titolo: Atti del Convegno di Acquaspanta (22-24 Settembre 1988)* (Rome: Bulzoni Editore, 1989), pp.141-150

Reybaz, André, "Boris Vian", in André Reybaz, *Têtes d'affiche* (Paris: La Table Ronde, 1975), pp.83-96

Richard, Lionel, "Vian était-il Kafkaïen?", in Jacques Duchateau, ed., *Boris Vian* (Le Revest-Saint-Martin: Le Jas, 1984), pp.26-28

Rivoire Zappalà, Marguerite, "Les Romans noirs de Vian/Sullivan, de l'imitation à la parodie", in *Il roman noir: Forme e significato, antecedenti e posterità* (Geneva: Slatkine, 1993), pp.479-503

Rosine, Josiane, "Ecumes du refoulé", in Jacques Duchateau, ed., *Boris Vian* (Le Revest-Saint-Martin: Le Jas, 1984), pp.35-38

Rudelic, Zvjezdana, "Boris Vian (1920-1959)", in Catharine Savage Brosman, ed., *French Novelists, 1900-1930* (Detroit, Mich.: Gale Research Co., 1988), pp.384-396

Russo, Maria Teresa, "Il 'roman noir' e Boris Vian: Ambiuità e parodia", in Barbara Wojciechowska Bianco, ed., *Il roman noir: Forme e significato, antecedenti e posterità* (Geneva: Slatkine, 1993), pp.453-475

Simsolo, Noël, "Dé'polar'isation", in Jacques Duchateau, ed., *Boris Vian* (Le Revest-Saint-Martin: Le Jas, 1984), pp.52-55

Terduyn, Eric, "Een ontmoeting met Boris Vian", in Jan Van Geelen and Jan Vermeulen, eds., *Litterair Paspoort 1946-1973* (Amsterdam: Uitgeverij de Arbeiderspers, 1974), pp.212-216

Trystram, Florence, "Un Sens aigu de la liberté", in Jacques Duchateau, ed., *Boris Vian* (Le Revest-Saint-Martin: Le Jas, 1984), pp.82-84

Vaquin, Agnes, "Boris Vian et Samuel Beckett", in Jacques Duchateau, ed., *Boris Vian* (Le Revest-Saint-Martin: Le Jas, 1984), pp.18-24

Vasseur, Nadine, "Jusqu'où va la zizique à Vian", in Jacques Duchateau, ed., *Boris Vian* (Le Revest-Saint-Martin: Le Jas, 1984), pp.56-60

Vaugeois, Gérard, "La Passion du cinéma", in Jacques Duchateau, ed., *Boris Vian* (Le Revest-Saint-Martin: Le Jas, 1984), pp.47-51

Vigorelli, Giancarlo, "Da Roussel a Vian", in Giancarlo Vigorelli, *Diario eurepeo: Occasioni e testimonianze critiche sulla letteratura europea 1950/1975. Parte Secunda* (Turin: Società Editrice Internazionale, 1977), pp.271-273

Webster, Paul; Powell, Nicholas, "L'arrache-cœur", in Jacques Duchateau, ed., *Boris Vian* (Le Revest-Saint-Martin: Le Jas, 1984), pp.103-121

Yaguello, Marina, "Linguiste malgré lui?", in Jacques Duchateau, ed., *Boris Vian* (Le Revest-Saint-Martin: Le Jas, 1984), pp.29-32

INTERTEXTS

(Note that the unless the edition cited in the text is itself the original version, the publication details of the edition used will be displayed after those of the original. Note also that in the case of, for example, Hans Andersen, reference to the original text would have little meaning for the purposes of this bibliography.)

Andersen, Hans, *Grand Claus et Petit Claus*, in *Andersen: Contes* (Paris: Librairie Gründ, 1995), pp.178-187

Andersen, Hans, *La Petite Sirène*, in *Andersen: Contes* (Paris: Librairie Gründ, 1995), pp.26-51

Aragon, Louis, *Le Paysan de Paris* (Paris: Gallimard, 1926); (Paris: Gallimard, 1994)

Aymé, Marcel, *Les Jumeaux du Diable* (Paris: Éditions de la Nouvelle Revue Française, 1928)

Balzac, Honoré, de, *Le Chef-d'œuvre inconnu* in *Œuvres de H. de Balzac* (Paris: Rouff, 1899); (Paris: Gallimard, 1994)

Barrie, J.M., *Peter Pan and Wendy* (London: Hodder and Stoughton, 1901); *Peter Pan* (London: Penguin, 1976)

Bazin, Hervé, *Vipère au poing* (Paris: Grasset, 1948); (Paris: Le Livre de Poche, 1996)

Beauvoir, Simone, de, *Le Deuxième Sexe II* (Paris: Gallimard, 1949); (Paris: Gallimard, 1985)

Bradbury, Ray, *Chroniques martiennes*, trans. by Henri Robillot (Paris: Denoël, 1954); *The Martian Chronicles* (London: Flamingo Modern Classics, 1995)

Breton, André, *Nadja* (Paris: Éditions de la Nouvelle Revue Française, 1928); (Paris: Gallimard, 1945)

Breton, André, *Les Vases communicants* (Paris: Éditions des Cahiers Libres, 1932); (Paris: Gallimard, 1955)

Breton, André, *L'Amour fou* (Paris: Gallimard, 1937); (Paris: Gallimard, 1995)

Breton, André, *Manifestes du Surréalisme* (Paris: Éditions du Sagittaire, 1947); (Paris: Gallimard, 1972)

Camus, Albert, *L'Étranger* (Paris: Gallimard, 1942); (Paris: Gallimard, 1990)

Carroll, Lewis, *Alice au pays des merveilles* (Paris: 1939); Alice's *Adventures in Wonderland & Through the Looking-Glass* (New York: Airmont, 1965)

Carroll, Lewis, *The Complete Works of Lewis Carroll* (London: The Nonesuch Library, 1939)

Céline, Louis-Ferdinand, *Voyage au bout de la nuit* (Paris: Denoël et Steele, 1932); (Paris: Gallimard, 1992)

Céline, Louis-Ferdinand, *Mort à crédit* (Paris: Denoël et Steele, 1936); (Paris: Gallimard, 1992)

Cheyney, Peter, *Les Femmes s'en balancent*, trans. by Michelle and Boris Vian (Paris: Gallimard, 1949); (Paris: Gallimard, 1982)

Christie, Agatha, *The Murder of Roger Ackroyd* (London: Collins, 1926); (Glasgow: Fontana/Collins, 1981)

Christie, Agatha, *Murder in Mesopotamia* (London: Collins, 1936); (Glasgow: Fontana/Collins, 1990)

Chute, Verne, *Le Funiculaire des anges*, trans. by Jean Calmes and J.G. Marquet (Paris: Gallimard, 1946); (Paris: Gallimard, 1994)

Constant, Benjamin, *Adolphe* (Paris: 1816; Geffroy, 1893); (Paris: Le Livre de Poche, 1964)

Dabit, Eugène, *L'Hôtel du Nord* (Paris: Denoël, 1929); (Paris: Gallimard, 1994)

Dumas, Alexandre, *La Dame aux camélias* (Paris: Lévy, 1872); (Paris: Gallimard, 1994)

Du Maurier, George, *Peter Ibbetson* (London: James R. Osgood, McIlvaine & Co., 1896)

Farrère, Claude, *L'Autre Côté* (Paris: Flammarion, 1928)

Flaubert, Gustave, *Œuvres complètes* (Paris: Conard, 1910); *Trois Contes* (Paris: Garnier Frères, 1961)

Freud, Sigmund, (case of the Wolf Man first published in 1918) *Case Histories II* (London: Penguin Freud Library Volume 9, 1991)

Gide, André, *La Séquestrée de Poitiers* (Paris: Gallimard, 1930)

Gracq, Julien, *Au château d'Argol* (Paris: José Corti, 1938); (Paris: José Corti, 1996)

Gravier, J.-F., *Paris et le désert français* (Paris: Portulan, 1947); *Paris et le désert français en 1972* (Paris: Flammarion, 1972)

Hammett, Dashiell, *La Clé de verre*, trans. by P.-J. Herr, Renée Vavasseur et Marcel Duhamel (Paris: Gallimard, 1949); The *Glass Key*, in *Dashiell Hammett: The Four Great Novels* (London: Picador, 1982), pp.575-784

Hesse, Hermann, *Le Loup des steppes* (Paris: Calmann-Lévy, 1947); *Steppenwolf*, trans. by Basil Creighton (London: Penguin, 1965)

Hughes, Richard, *A High Wind in Jamaica* (London: Chatto and Windus, 1934); (London: Harvill, 1994)

Huysmans, Joris-Karl, *A Rebours* (Paris: Charpentier, 1884); (Paris: Garnier-Flammarion, 1978)

Kafka, Franz, *Le Procès,* trans. by Alexandre Vialatte (Paris: Gallimard, 1946); *The Trial*, trans. by Max Brod (London: Penguin, 1953)

Kafka, Franz, *La Colonie pénitentiaire et autres récits,* trans. by Alexandre Vialatte (Paris: Gallimard, 1948); *In the Penal Colony*, trans. by Willa and Edwin Muir, in *Kafka: The Complete Short Stories*, ed. by Nahum N. Glatzer (London: Minerva, 1995), pp.140-67

Kafka, Franz, *A Little Fable*, in *Franz Kafka. The Penal Colony, Stories and Short Pieces*, trans. by Willa and Edwin Muir (New York: Schocken books, 1949); trans. by Willa & Edwin Muir, in *Kafka: The Complete Short Stories*, ed. by Nahum N. Glatzer (London: Minerva, 1995) ,p.445

Ledoux, *L'Architecture considérée sous le rapport de l'art, des mœurs et de la législation* (Paris: l'auteur, 1804); Ohayon, Jacques, ed., *L'œuvre et les rêves de Claude-Nicolas Ledoux* (Paris: Sté Nle des Éditions du Chêne, 1971)

Longus, *Daphnis et Chloé,* (Paris: Flammarion, 1892); *Daphnis and Chloe*, trans. by Paul Turner (London: Penguin Classics, 1989)

Lönnrot, Elias, *Le Kalevala, épopée finnoise* (Paris: 1876); *The Kalevala*, trans. by Keith Bosley (Oxford: Oxford University Press, 1989)

Mac Orlan, Pierre, *La Maison du retour écœurant* (Paris: Bibliothèque Humoristique, 1912); (Paris: Collection Littéraire de la Renaissance du Livre, 1924)

Mac Orlan, Pierre, *Le Quai des brumes* (Paris: Éditions de la Nouvelle Revue Française, 1927); (Paris: Gallimard, 1972)

Mac Orlan, Pierre, *Quartier réservé* (Paris: Gallimard, 1932); (Paris: Gallimard, 1994)

Miller, Henry, *Tropic of Cancer* (Paris: Obelisk Press, 1934); (London: Flamingo, 1993)

Orczy, Baroness, *The Scarlet Pimpernel* (London: Greening, 1908); (London: Hodder and Stoughton, 1980)

Queneau, Raymond, *Le Chiendent* (Paris: Gallimard, 1933); (Paris: Gallimard, 1993)

Queneau, Raymond, *Pierrot mon ami* (Paris: Gallimard, 1942); (Paris: Gallimard, 1992)

Queneau, Raymond, *Saint Glinglin* (Paris: Gallimard, 1948); (Paris: Gallimard, 1992)

Queneau, Raymond, *Les Fleurs bleues* (Paris: Gallimard, 1959); (Paris: Gallimard, 1994)

Radiguet, Raymond, *Le Bal du Comte d'Orgel* (Paris: les Exemplaires, 1926)

Sartre, Jean-Paul, *La Nausée* (Paris: Gallimard, 1938); (Paris: Gallimard, 1988)

Sartre, Jean-Paul, "Érostrate", in *Le Mur* (Paris: Gallimard, 1939); (Paris: Gallimard, 1992), pp.79-99

Sartre, Jean-Paul, "L'Enfance d'un chef", in *Le Mur* (Paris: Gallimard, 1939); (Paris: Gallimard, 1992), pp.151-245

Sartre, Jean-Paul, "L'Intimité", in *Le Mur* (Paris: Gallimard, 1939); (Paris: Gallimard, 1992), pp.103-48

Sartre, Jean-Paul, *Les Mouches* (Paris: Gallimard, 1947); (Paris: Gallimard, 1989)

Villiers de l'Isle-Adam, *L'Ève future* (Paris: Brunhoff, 1886); (Paris: Gallimard, 1993)

Wells, H.G., *The Time Machine*, in *The Works of H.G. Wells. Atlantic Edition* (London: T. Fisher Unwin, 1924-1927); in *Selected Short Stories* (London: Penguin, 1958), pp.7-83

Wells, H.G., *The War of the Worlds* in *The Works of H.G. Wells. Atlantic Edition* (London: T. Fisher Unwin, 1924-1927); (London: J.M. Dent, 1993)

Wells, H.G., *The Wonderful Visit* (London: C. Arthur Pearson, 1902)

Wolfe, Thomas, *Look Homeward, Angel* (U.S.A., 1929; London: Heinemann, 1930); (London: Penguin, 1984)

OTHER MATERIAL CONSULTED

Benjamin, Walter, *Charles Baudelaire: A Lyric Poet in the Era of High Capitalism*, trans. by Harry Zohn (London: Verso, 1992)

Benjamin, Walter, *Illuminationen* (Frankfurt: Suhtkamp Verlag, 1961); *Illuminations*, trans. by Harry Zohn (London: Fontana, 1973)

Bongie, Chris, "Fathers and Sons: The Self-Revelation of Flaubert and Céline", *Romanic Review*, 77 (1986), 428-447

Brassaï, *Paris after Dark* (London: Thames and Hudson, 1987)

Calame, Alain, "Échange de fleurs", *Europe: Revue littéraire mensuelle*, 650 (1983), 29-38

Costaz, Gilles, "Mac Orlan, poète mal entendu", *Tendances*, 68 (1970), 729-743

Goimard, Jacques, "Chronologie générale de la S.F.", *Europe: Revue littéraire mensuelle*, 580-581 (1977), 156-169

Gruber, L. Fritz, *Man Ray* (Köln: Benedikt Taschen, 1992)

Handy, W.C., ed., *A Treasury of the Blues* (New York: Charles Boni, 1925)

Hewitt, Nicholas, "'Looking for Annie': Sartre's *La Nausée* and the Inter-War Years", *Journal of European Studies*, 12 (1982), 96-112

Howatson, M.C. and Chilvers, Ian, eds, *The Concise Companion to Classical Literature* (Oxford: Oxford University Press, 1993)

Naudin, François, "Un Théorème botanique", *Europe: Revue littéraire mensuelle*, 650 (1983), 103-109

Orr, Mary, *Claude Simon: The Intertextual Dimension* (Glasgow: University of Glasgow French and German Publications, 1993)

Ory, Pascal, "The Introduction of Science Fiction into France", in *France and the Mass Media*, ed. by Brian Rigby and Nicholas Hewitt (London: Macmillan Academic and Professional Ltd., 1991), pp.98-110

Riffaterre, Michael, "Compulsory Reader Response: The Intertextual Drive", in *Intertextuality: Theories and Practices*, ed. by Michael Worton and Judith Still (Manchester: Manchester University Press, 1990), pp.56-78

Riffaterre, Michael, "L'Intertexte inconnu", *Littérature*, 41 (1981), 4-7

Riffaterre, Michael, "Interview", *Diacritics*, 11 [4] (1981), 12-16

Riffaterre, Michael, "La Trace de l'intertexte", *Pensée française*, 215 (1980), 4-18

Rifkin, Adrian, *Street Noises: Parisian pleasures 1900-40* (Manchester: Manchester University Press, 1993)

Scipion, Robert, *Prête-moi ta plume* (Paris: Gallimard, 1946)

Shattuck, Roger, "Love and Laughter: Surrealism Reappraised", in Maurice Nadeau, *The History of Surrealism*, trans. by Richard Howard (New York: Macmillan, 1968), pp.11-34

Swift, Graham, "I never pretended my novel owed no debt to Faulkner", *The Times*, 10 March 1997, p.3

Worton, Michael and Still, Judith, eds, *Intertextuality: Theories and Practices* (Manchester: Manchester University Press, 1990)

INDEX

A

Aboucaya, Jacques 169, 170, 172, 177, 178, 185, 186, 193, 204, 317
Andersen, Hans C. 93, 96, 97, 98, 263, 264, 302, 304, 317, 348, 349
Aragon, Louis 52, 105, 106, 108, 109, 111, 114, 115, 116, 117, 118, 119,
120, 124, 128, 152, 167, 202, 349
Arnaud, Noël 6, 18, 29, 100, 149, 178, 234, 235, 237, 238, 283, 308, 312,
313, 315, 317, 318, 319, 320
Asso, Raymond 153
Aymé, Marcel 297, 298, 299, 300, 301, 349

B

Balzac, Honoré de 65, 66, 349
Barrie, J.M. 162, 349
Baude, Jeanne-Marie 28, 60, 302, 342
Baudelaire, Charles 12, 17, 64, 107, 108, 110, 120, 121, 122, 127, 131, 136,
139, 157, 162, 353
Baudin, Henri 9, 312, 313, 320, 337
Bazin, Hervé 238, 239, 240, 241, 242, 243, 244, 245, 246, 349
Beauvoir, Simone de 78, 221, 236, 247, 248, 249, 250, 251, 258, 259, 260,
261, 279, 349
Benjamin, Walter 76, 107, 108, 110, 120, 127, 131, 135, 149, 350, 353
Bens, Jacques 18, 20, 24, 25, 26, 27, 28, 177, 178, 313, 320, 321
Bertold, Nicole 30, 171
Birgander, Pia 106, 313, 321, 325, 331, 338, 345
Boggio, Philippe 7, 8, 313
Bongie, Chris 122, 354
Bradbury, Ray 170, 186, 194, 349
Brassaï 193, 354
Breton, André 50, 51, 52, 53, 54, 56, 58, 59, 62, 66, 80, 87, 101, 102, 105, 123,
193, 198, 199, 200, 201, 202, 205, 206, 207, 208, 213, 216, 227, 349

C

Calame, Alain 170, 227, 228, 354
Camus, Albert 82, 121, 133, 134, 135, 141, 186, 219, 350
Caradec, François 103, 306, 308, 313, 322
Carroll, Lewis 17, 34, 50, 83, 127, 129, 130, 184, 207, 210, 212, 218, 23 275,
286, 310, 340, 350
Cavanna 4, 5
Céline, Louis-Ferdinand 17, 18, 25, 69, 80, 81, 82, 83, 92, 120, 121, 122, 129,
151, 270, 350, 354

Chapman, Stanley 50, 63, 174, 310
Cheyney, Peter 221, 350
Christie, Agatha 157, 158, 159, 160, 161, 350
Chute, Verne 161, 162, 165, 166, 167, 350
Clouzet, Jean 53, 178, 313, 324, 337
Constant, Benjamin 103, 125, 143, 149, 150, 151, 156, 350
Costaz, Gilles 283, 354
Costes, Alain 9, 19, 28, 58, 59, 60, 62, 72, 313, 324, 325, 341, 342, 343, 344
345, 346

D

Dabit, Eugène 109, 110, 111, 274, 350
Du Maurier, George 227, 228, 229, 295, 350
Duchateau, Jacques 31, 313, 325, 342, 343, 344, 345, 346, 347, 348
Dumas, Alexandre 28, 43, 90, 92, 350

E

Ellington, Duke 33, 52, 54, 60, 61, 62, 67, 76, 77, 168
Enard, Jean-Pierre 19, 326

F

Farrère, Claude 193, 195, 196, 197, 198, 201, 224, 350
Faulkner, William 16, 22, 28, 29, 32, 33, 34, 48, 83, 355
Fauré, Michel 171, 314, 326
Flaubert, Gustave 25, 43, 44, 45, 46, 49, 83, 122, 351, 354
Freud, Sigmund 56, 202, 203, 204, 213, 216, 267, 351

G

Gauthier, Michel 8, 21, 44, 49, 51, 52, 54, 80, 82, 263, 314, 326
Gide, André 221, 271, 279, 280, 351
Goimard, Jacques 170, 328, 354
Gracq, Julien 236, 265, 351
Gravier, J.F. 104, 351
Gruber, L. Fritz 112, 354

H

Hammett, Dashiel 221, 222, 351
Handy, W.C. 61, 62, 63, 354
Hesse, Hermann 186, 187, 188, 189, 190, 191, 351
Hewitt, Nicholas 2, 84, 171, 354
Howard, Richard 55, 355
Hughes, Richard 138, 140, 236, 288, 351
Hugo, Victor 20, 214, 225

Huxley, Aldous 4
Huysmans, J.-K. 53, 60, 61, 65, 180, 351

I

Ionesco, Eugène 55, 322

J

Jacob, Max 70, 287

K

Kafka, Franz 17, 18, 26, 27, 29, 73, 74, 164, 177, 178, 179, 180, 181, 351
Kessel, Joseph 180
Kristeva, Julia 9

L

Lapprand, Marc 7, 20, 39, 40, 41, 42, 306, 314, 322, 329, 331, 341, 343, 344, 345
Ledoux, C.-N. 217, 352
Longus 46, 47, 352

M

Mac Orlan, Pierre 1, 69, 70, 71, 75, 78, 109, 111, 115, 152, 153, 155, 283, 284,
286, 297, 333, 352, 354
Maillard, Michel 303, 346
Maillé, Bruno 100, 101, 102, 105, 333
Man Ray 112, 168, 192, 354
Maynial, Édouard 44, 45
Miller, Henry 103, 143, 144, 145, 146, 148, 152, 153, 167, 352
Monot, Marguerite 153

N

Niles, Abbe 63

O

Older, Julia 237, 238, 310, 346
Orczy, Emmuska 180, 181, 182, 352
Orr, Mary 17, 354
Ory, Pascal 171, 334, 346, 354

P

Pauvert, Jean-Jacques 4, 235, 308, 310, 315
Pestureau, Gilbert 2, 3, 5, 6, 7, 21, 22, 23, 28, 29, 30, 31, 32, 33, 34, 46, 48, 59,
61, 62, 63, 64, 69, 78, 79, 83, 104, 129, 130, 143, 144, 157, 164,
171, 176, 177, 180, 193, 195, 210, 214, 216, 236, 238, 252, 259,

265, 268, 269, 270, 278, 288, 306, 314, 323, 325, 334, 347
Prévert, Jacques 18, 314, 317, 322, 336, 341, 343, 344, 345

Q

Queneau, Raymond.......... 1, 18, 19, 26, 49, 69, 78, 79, 83, 90, 91, 95, 114, 115, 129, 175, 180, 183, 184, 185, 193, 201, 227, 236, 262, 270, 271, 275, 277, 280, 286, 311, 314, 322, 336, 341, 343, 344, 345, 352

R

Radiguet, Raymond 125, 352
Redonnet, Marie 47, 82
Riffaterre, Michael............................ 10, 11, 12, 13, 14, 15, 17, 22, 23, 33, 354, 355
Rifkin, Adrian 122, 123, 153, 154, 355
Rimbaud, Jean-Arthur.. 64, 225
Rybalka, Michel......... 2, 3, 6, 8, 20, 24, 29, 35, 36, 306, 314, 320, 332, 335, 337, 338

S

Sartre, Jean-Paul......29, 30, 43, 69, 74, 75, 77, 78, 79, 80, 81, 82, 84, 86, 89, 91, 93, 123, 125, 131, 132, 134, 135, 136, 139, 148, 215, 216, 220, 236, 262, 268, 269, 270, 322, 324, 353, 354
Scipion, Robert.. 77, 78, 80, 355
Shattuck, Roger.. 55, 57, 355
Simon, Claude.. 17, 354
Simsolo, Noël 18, 19, 338, 348
Still, Judith 9, 10, 11, 65, 354, 355
Sturrock, John... 63, 310
Sucarrat, F. 243, 246, 247, 249, 250, 251, 260, 339
Swift, Graham 16, 17, 355

V

Verne, Jules 130, 161, 347, 350
Villiers de l'Isle-Adam 29, 236, 252, 253, 254, 255, 256, 257, 284, 353
Vree, Freddy de 8, 37, 100, 313, 315, 340

W

Wells.., H.G. 29, 32, 163, 164, 165, 168, 170, 171, 172, 173, 175, 176, 179, 180, 181, 185, 204, 211, 287, 289, 290, 353
Wolfe, Thomas 290, 291, 292, 293, 294, 295, 353
Worton, Michael 9, 10, 11, 354, 355